The Theory and Practice of Microcredit

The remarkable speed at which microcredit has expanded around the world in the last three decades has piqued the curiosity of practitioners and theorists alike. By developing innovative ways of making credit available to the poor, the idea of microcredit has challenged many traditional assumptions about both poverty-reduction strategies and financial markets. While this has encouraged new theorising about how microcredit works, the practice of microcredit has itself evolved, often in unpredictable ways, outpacing the development of theory.

The Theory and Practice of Microcredit aims to remedy this imbalance, arguing that a proper understanding of the evolution of practice is essential both for developing theories that are relevant for the real world, and for adopting policies that can better realise the full potential of microcredit. By drawing upon their first-hand knowledge of the nature of this evolution in Bangladesh, the birthplace of microcredit, the authors have pushed the frontiers of current knowledge through a rich blend of theoretical and empirical analysis. The book breaks new ground on a wide range of topics, including the habit-forming nature of credit repayment, the institutional strength and community-based role of microfinance institutions, the relationships between microcredit and informal credit markets, the pattern of long-term participation in microcredit programmes and the variety of loan use, the scaling up of microenterprises beyond subsistence, the 'missing middle' in the credit market, and the prospects of linking micro-entrepreneurship with economic development.

The book will be of interest to researchers, development practitioners and university students of Development Economics, Rural Development, or Rural Finance, as well as to public intellectuals.

Wahiduddin Mahmud was, until recently, Professor of Economics at the University of Dhaka and is currently Chairman, Economic Research Group, Dhaka, Bangladesh. He is a founder and former chairman of *Palli-Karma Sahayak Foundation* (PKSF), the apex wholesale microcredit lending institution in Bangladesh. He is also a Senior Country Advisor of International Growth Centre, the Chairman of the South Asia Network of Economic Research Institutes, and is on the Governing Board of the Global Development Network. He served as a member of the UN Committee for Development Policy and has held visiting positions at the World Bank, UN Development Programme (UNDP), International Food Policy Research Institute (IFPRI) and Institute of Development Studies (IDS) at Sussex University.

S. R. Osmani is Professor of Development Economics at Ulster University, UK. He obtained a PhD in economics from the London School of Economics and worked at the Bangladesh Institute of Development Studies, Dhaka, and at the World Institute for Development Economics Research, Helsinki, before joining Ulster University. He has published widely on issues related to employment and poverty, inequality, hunger, famine, nutrition, rights-based approaches to development, and development problems in general.

Routledge Studies in Development Economics

For a complete list of titles in this series, please visit www.routledge.com/series/SE0266

122 **China's War against the Many Faces of Poverty**
Towards a new long march
Jing Yang and Pundarik Mukhopadhaya

123 **Exploring Civic Innovation for Social and Economic Transformation**
Edited by Kees Biekart, Wendy Harcourt and Peter Knorringa

124 **Trade, Investment and Economic Development in Asia**
Empirical and policy issues
Edited by Debashis Chakraborty and Jaydeep Mukherjee

125 **The Financialisation of Power**
How financiers rule Africa
Sarah Bracking

126 **Primary Commodities and Economic Development**
Stephan Pfaffenzeller

127 **Structural Transformation and Agrarian Change in India**
Göran Djurfeldt with Srilata Sircar

128 **Development Management**
Theory and practice
Edited by Justice Nyigmah Bawole, Farhad Hossain, Asad K. Ghalib, Christopher J. Rees and Aminu Mamman

129 **Structural Transformation and Economic Development**
Cross regional analysis of industrialization and urbanization
Banji Oyelaran-Oyeyinka and Kaushalesh Lal

130 **The Theory and Practice of Microcredit**
Wahiduddin Mahmud and S. R. Osmani

The Theory and Practice of Microcredit

Wahiduddin Mahmud
and S. R. Osmani

LONDON AND NEW YORK

First published 2017
by Routledge
2 Park Square, Milton Park, Abingdon, Oxon OX14 4RN

and by Routledge
711 Third Avenue, New York, NY 10017

Routledge is an imprint of the Taylor & Francis Group, an informa business

© 2017 Wahiduddin Mahmud and S. R. Osmani

The right of Wahiduddin Mahmud and S. R. Osmani to be identified as authors of this work has been asserted by them in accordance with sections 77 and 78 of the Copyright, Designs and Patents Act 1988.

All rights reserved. No part of this book may be reprinted or reproduced or utilised in any form or by any electronic, mechanical, or other means, now known or hereafter invented, including photocopying and recording, or in any information storage or retrieval system, without permission in writing from the publishers.

Trademark notice: Product or corporate names may be trademarks or registered trademarks, and are used only for identification and explanation without intent to infringe.

British Library Cataloguing in Publication Data
A catalogue record for this book is available from the British Library

Library of Congress Cataloging-in-Publication Data
Names: Mahmud, Wahiduddin, author. | Osmani, Siddiqur Rahman, author.
Title: The theory and practice of microcredit / Wahiduddin Mahmud and S. R. Osmani.
Description: New York : Routledge, 2017. | Includes bibliographical references and index.
Identifiers: LCCN 2016022169 | ISBN 9780415686808 (hardback) | ISBN 9781315413174 (ebook)
Subjects: LCSH: Microfinance—Bangladesh. | Rural credit—Bangladesh. | Poverty—Bangladesh.
Classification: LCC HG178.33.B3 M347 2017 | DDC 332.7—dc23
LC record available at https://lccn.loc.gov/2016022169

ISBN: 978-0-415-68680-8 (hbk)
ISBN: 978-1-315-41317-4 (ebk)

Typeset in Times New Roman
by Apex CoVantage, LLC

We dedicate this book to Simeen and Lata
for their love and inspiration,
without which this book would never have seen the light
of day.

Contents

List of figures	viii
List of tables	ix
Preface	xi
1 Introduction	1
2 Microcredit in Bangladesh: how the credit markets work	15
3 Microcredit in Bangladesh: how the microcredit model works	39
4 Theories of microcredit: group lending and moral hazard	59
5 Theories of microcredit: adverse selection and repayment enforcement	89
6 When theory meets reality: testing the theories of microcredit	131
7 Economic impact of microcredit: the experience of Bangladesh	174
8 The patterns of loan use	211
9 The economics of microenterprise	224
10 Micro-entrepreneurship and economic development	239
References	249
Index	267

Figures

3.1	Loan repayment by habit formation and cultural norms	48
4.1	Credit market equilibrium with moral hazard under individual liability	67
4.2	Credit market equilibrium with moral hazard under joint liability with cooperative behaviour	72
4.3	Credit market equilibrium with moral hazard under joint liability with non-cooperative behaviour	75
5.1	Adverse selection in the credit market: the Stiglitz-Weiss (S-W) scenario	94
5.2	Adverse selection in the credit market: the de Meza-Webb (M-W) scenario	95
5.3	Credit market equilibrium with *ex post* moral hazard	108
9.1a	Scaling up of income-generating activities: the missing middle	227
9.1b	Scaling up of income-generating activities: bridging the missing middle	228

Tables

2.1	Growth of microcredit in Bangladesh: 1996–2014	17
2.2	Distribution of households with access to credit by source of credit, poverty status and residence in Bangladesh: 2009–2010	21
2.3	The structure of the rural credit market in Bangladesh: 2010	22
2.4	Trends in the access to different sources of credit by rural households in Bangladesh by category of land ownership: 1988–2010	23
3.1	Distribution of borrowers by their perception of application of joint-liability pressure, before and now	41
3.2	Social interaction among members of group/*samity*	44
3.3	Borrowers' perception of intensity of use of coercive methods for loan recovery	46
7.1	Comparison of some characteristics of microcredit borrowers and non-borrowers in rural Bangladesh: 2010	199
7.2	Marginal effect of microcredit on asset transition by user category	200
7.3	Marginal impact of microcredit on the propensity to adopt erosive coping by user category	201
7.4	Coefficient of microcredit in regressions on household income	202
7.5	Marginal effects of microcredit and remittance income on the probability of being poor and extremely poor in rural Bangladesh: 2010	203
8.1	Declared and actual uses of microcredit loans in rural Bangladesh: 2010	213
8.2	Pattern of use of microcredit loans by poverty status in rural Bangladesh: 2010	214
8.3	Change in the pattern of use of microcredit loans by long-term borrowers in rural Bangladesh	214
8.4	Distribution of loans, including overlapped current loans, by main use	216

8.5	Distribution of microcredit borrowers using loans other than for income-generating activities (IGAs) and their distribution according to what they would have done without the loans	217
8.6	Distribution of borrowers using microcredit on non-IGA items according to how they would have raised the money for the spending without microcredit	218
9.1	Rates of return to capital by size of capital outlay in IGAs financed by microcredit in rural Bangladesh: 2010	231
9.2	Value of fixed and working capital in microcredit-financed IGAs for three poverty categories of borrowers in rural Bangladesh: 1996	233
9.3	Number of current borrowers taking microenterprise loans and size of microenterprise loan portfolios of MFIs in Bangladesh: 2012	234
10.1	Trends in the distribution of sources of revolving loan funds of MFIs (excluding Grameen Bank): 1996–2012	245

Preface

The idea for this book originated from years of our close observation of how, beginning from the classic Grameen Bank model, microcredit programmes have grown and evolved in Bangladesh. With the outpouring of vast amounts of academic literature on microcredit over the years, we have often wondered whether this extremely rich literature has missed anything of the ground-level reality or whether the microcredit practitioners have had to learn the hard way lessons that could have been predicted from theory. At the same time, we have waited a long time to write this book in order to make sure that we could distance ourselves enough from the actual happenings, at least in terms of formal involvement, in order to be able to have a dispassionate and objective view on the subject.

We also took our time in materialising the idea of the book because of what appeared to us formidable problems. The book is meant for a wide range of audience, including researchers, practitioners, university students and interested public intellectuals, and it is not easy to package materials in a way that can be accessible as well as of interest to each of these potential segments of readers. Reviewing the theoretical literature on microcredit proved difficult because there is no single theory. What we have instead is a bewildering variety of theories; the only common thread binding most of them is the idea that the way microcredit is delivered in practice helps overcome certain market imperfections – in particular, imperfections in information and in the enforcement of contract. The empirical test of microcredit theories, currently a lively area of research with already many useful insights, has equally bewildering varieties of methodologies and conceptual approaches. But perhaps the part of the microcredit literature that was most difficult to tackle had to do with the assessment of the poverty impact of microcredit, not just because of its inherent complexity, but also because of the extent of controversies, debates and emotions that it has stirred.

The book is premised on our belief that, given the maturity and spread of the microcredit system in Bangladesh, a proper understanding of the process of its growth and evolution can provide useful insights on a range of issues: how the introduction of microcredit interacts with the informal credit markets, whether credit effects are declining over time, whether market saturation and village diseconomies are taking place, whether repeated loans along with multiple programme membership result in a debt trap – as is often alleged – or helps the poor to better manage their livelihoods, or what prospects are there for scaling up income-generating activities beyond a subsistence scale of operation to more productive and sustainable enterprises. We also think that Bangladesh has now got a long enough history of experimentation with microcredit programmes to allow a Darwinian approach to analysing how the system has evolved through numerous innovations, mutations and adaptations. In particular, we look at the plausible hypothesis that loan repayment can be habit-forming and can become ingrained in the social psyche, making the system driven more by social behavioural norms rather than by the threat of coercion, and how this can have profound implications for both theory and practice. We also take note of what is happening at the microcredit frontiers as the microfinance institutions in Bangladesh are rethinking the boundaries of their legitimate activities, such as in trying to bridge the so-called 'missing middle' in the credit market in between mainstream microcredit and commercial banking.

The book project was initiated and supported by the Institute of Microfinance (InM) in Dhaka. The project was part of InM's activities under the programme called Promoting Financial Services for Poverty Reduction (PROSPER), which was supported by UKaid from the Department of International Development (DFID). The book draws from the findings of several studies and household surveys undertaken by InM, including those undertaken by one of the authors, S. R. Osmani. Preliminary drafts based on the ongoing work of the book were circulated by InM to get suggestions and feedback. We are, however, solely responsible for the views or errors and omissions contained in the book, for which none of the concerned institutions are responsible.

In the course of working on this book, we have received enormous support from the InM staff, particularly Professor Baqui Khalily, the former Executive Director of InM. We have extensively drawn upon our interactions with the microcredit practitioners in Bangladesh, who are too numerous to name here. We must specially thank Dr. Jashim Uddin and Mr. Fazlul Kader, both currently Deputy Managing Directors of PKSF (Bangladesh's wholesale microcredit lending institution), for helping us understand the modalities of microcredit programmes and interpret data.

We are greatly indebted to Nobel Peace Laureate Professor Muhammad Yunus for sharing with us his ideas and insights on the subject over long years of our association.

Last but not the least, we have received useful feedback and suggestions from our wives, Simeen and Lata, respectively, who have themselves researched and published on microcredit. They have been a source of inspiration for us in completing this arduous book project, and to them we lovingly dedicate this book.

1 Introduction

> Money, says the proverb, makes money. When you have got a little, it is often easy to get more. The great difficulty is to get that little.
>
> Adam Smith, *The Wealth of Nations*[1]

> Lawmakers and judges at all ages were tormented on the issue of recovery of unsecured loans that represent contracts freely arrived at and yet cannot be enforced without 'oppression'.
>
> John Hicks, *The Theory of Economic History*[2]

Microcredit has emerged as a hugely popular tool all over the developing world for helping poor people to help themselves by engaging in self-employed, income-generating activities. Very few poverty intervention programmes have ever managed to attain a similar scale of operation. Although one may debate the extent to which microcredit can transform the livelihoods of the poor, the simple fact that it has managed to reach credit to millions of poor people hitherto bypassed by the traditional banking system is a remarkable achievement. By developing innovative ways of making the poor creditworthy, the 'microcredit revolution', as it has come to be called, has seriously challenged many traditional assumptions about poverty reduction strategies on the one hand and financial markets on the other. While this has encouraged new theorising about how microcredit works, the practice of microcredit has itself evolved, often in unpredictable ways, outpacing the development of theory. The idea of this book is based on the premise that a proper understanding of this evolution in practice of microcredit is essential for both developing theories that are relevant for the real world and adopting policies that can better realise the full potential of microcredit. Studying the growth and evolution of microcredit in Bangladesh is of particular interest since no other country can match its experience regarding the maturity and the extent of outreach of the microcredit programmes.

1.1 How microcredit works: the theories and their empirical tests

The remarkable speed at which the reach of microcredit has expanded around the world in the last three decades has piqued the curiosity of practitioners and theorists alike. Development practitioners want to know what that something special is about microcredit so that they, too, can practise it in their own environment, with necessary adaptations. Theorists want to know why it is that the special features of microcredit seem to work, at least in terms of embracing those who were previously excluded from the formal credit network, without compromising the financial viability of the lenders. This has led to an enormous outpouring of theoretical speculations, often drawing upon the latest theoretical advances in economics and finance. The ideas and tools developed in the economic theories of imperfect information, and the related theories of screening, incentives and mechanism design – which are themselves of fairly recent origin – as well as the tools of game theory have been enthusiastically applied by a new generation of economists to unearth the secrets of microcredit.[3] At the same time, testing these theories with field-level data and experiments regarding how the microcredit model actually works has led to a new area of academic research, even though such empirical tests have not quite kept pace with new theorising.

The main features of the classic microcredit model pioneered by Grameen Bank in Bangladesh and replicated worldwide are well-known from the literature. It is a system of group-lending under which clients from poor families, predominantly women, form groups to receive collateral-free small loans that are repaid in regular weekly or frequent instalments, usually within a one-year loan cycle and for which the group bears joint responsibility. While, in theory, the model can be shown to solve a number of problems that historically plagued government efforts of providing credit to the poor, the relative importance of the various features of the model remains largely conjectural.

The problem is that there is no single theory of how microcredit works; what we have instead is a bewildering variety of theories, and the only common thread binding most of them is the idea that the way microcredit is delivered in practice helps overcome certain market imperfections – in particular, imperfections in information and in the enforcement of contract. But they differ greatly in their understanding of exactly which imperfections are being addressed and precisely how they are being overcome. Most of these theories have some *a priori* plausibility. Therefore, the only way to discriminate among them is to check empirically which theories seem to fit the reality better than others. Accordingly, researchers have increasingly turned their attention towards testing microcredit theories against empirical data. (The major theories of microcredit are discussed in Chapters 4 and 5, and empirical tests of theories are reviewed in Chapter 6.) The problem here faced by the researchers is that there may not be enough variations in the basic features of the existing lending modalities among the microfinance institutions (MFIs) in a country so as to provide data for econometric tests of the efficacy of particular lending mechanisms (Morduch, 1999, p.1586). Nevertheless, researchers are trying to get around the problem by using proxy information lying behind the actual working of the mechanisms and applying sophisticated econometric techniques, and also by drawing upon the tools of experimental behavioural economics. While this is currently a lively area of research already providing many valuable insights, this literature should not be confused with the more familiar and increasingly large body of studies aimed at empirically measuring the impact of microcredit on poverty.

Besides the econometric approach to analysing how microcredit works, another possible way is to look at the process of evolution of the system as the practitioners tried to overcome the limitations of the model and responded to the changing and varied needs of the borrowers. Bangladesh has now got a long enough history of experimentation with microcredit programmes for allowing such a Darwinian approach to analysing how the system has evolved through numerous innovations, mutations and adaptations. The classic Grameen model, which has been replicated worldwide, has evolved considerably in Bangladesh since its inception in the late 1970s. Other than Grameen Bank, the microcredit industry in Bangladesh is driven by numerous non-governmental institutions (NGOs) which were initially established for 'social mobilisation' of the rural communities along with service delivery, but later on they shifted their emphasis to the provision of microcredit to the poor – hence now commonly known as NGO-MFIs. While some of the defining features of the original Grameen model still remain widely prevalent, there now exists a wide range of variations in the lending practices, particularly among the relatively larger MFIs, with varying degrees of resemblance to the original model. More importantly, Grameen Bank itself overhauled its own lending system in 2001 with the introduction of what it calls Grameen II, allowing far more flexibility for its clients in accessing and repaying loans. An important feature of this evolutionary process is the gradual dilution of the rigorous discipline that the MFIs used to impose on borrowers through the rigid lending modalities, particularly through the system of joint liability of the group. But despite this dilution, the high loan recovery rates of MFIs do not seem to have suffered, while the credit needs of their clients are also now better served. How has this been possible?

Besides reviewing the limited amount of available literature specifically focusing on this topic, in this book we try to answer this question by drawing upon the insights of the microcredit practitioners who know from their experience how these adaptations, mutations and modifications of the original model have actually come about. (The place of microcredit in the overall rural credit market is discussed in Chapter 2 and the evolution of the microcredit model as practised in Bangladesh is analysed in Chapter 3.) In addition, we look at some recent survey findings focusing on the experience and opinion of the borrowers themselves about the evolving microcredit delivery system in Bangladesh. These findings come from two rounds of nationwide surveys of rural households: the *Poverty Dynamics Survey* carried out by the Institute of Microfinance (InM) in Dhaka in 2010 and 2013. A part of the later round of the survey, based on a sub-sample of households, was specifically designed to focus on the working of the microcredit system.

While group liability is the kingpin of how microcredit works in theory, there has been a gradual decline in the enforcement of group liability in all its usual forms: putting pressure on peers to obtain the weekly instalments one way or the other, or threatening to withhold loans to peers unless default was prevented, or actually cutting off loans to peers in case of actual default. Most MFIs in Bangladesh now follow a flexible interpretation of joint liability, namely, to expect the group members to help assess the defaulting member's actual capacity to repay and to apply pressure to recover as much loan as is possible before letting her go. Another deviation from theory is that the system of group lending, to the extent that it works in Bangladesh, is based on mutual help and trust among group members rather than the threat of applying social sanctions on the defaulting group member by her peers. In this latter respect, the microcredit movement in Bangladesh seems to have benefited from a kinship-based rural social structure in dense settlements that has helped in forming the microcredit groups from the existing networks of relatives, friends and neighbours.

Many authors have pointed out that the role of group lending contracts in ensuring high repayment rates is overplayed in the theoretical models; instead, they point to other important features that explain the successful performance of the microcredit programmes, such as the proactive role played by the loan officers of MFIs, the 'dynamic incentive' created by threat of cutting off future loans, the open public meetings, and the predominance of female clients who are particularly susceptible to public shaming (Jain and Moore, 2003; Armendáriz and Morduch, 2010, pp.137–62). In the case of Bangladesh, there have been two other reinforcing factors, namely, the socially embedded role of NGO-MFIs, who deliver a variety of non-credit services and have been able to assume a 'social guardian' role within the communities they serve; and the long experience of the MFI clients helping them to realise that it is worthwhile to invest in a long-term relationship with MFIs.

But the most unique feature of Bangladesh's experience is the evidence that loan repayment can be habit-forming and that high repayment rates maintained over a long period can lead to a social norm and culture of repayment, thus creating a social stigma attached to loan default (Mahmud, 2003; Osmani, 2015b). In the theoretical models, and also in the actual practice of repayment enforcement in some contexts, the determining factors are said to be peer pressure or sanctions along with a permissible degree of coercion. The situation is quite reversed when the repayment can be explained by the cost of non-repayment from the point of view of the borrower; the cost would include, besides the foregone benefits of future loans, the psychological cost of the social stigma and the sense of guilt from breaking a trust-based relationship. This has several implications, both for theory and practice. For the practitioners, it implies that there will be less need for coercion for repayment enforcement and for monitoring of the loan use to prevent imprudent loan use. It also makes it easier to relax the repayment modalities, like weekly instalment payments, which are major constraints in the choice of loan-financed projects and for poor households to participate in the microcredit programmes. From the point of view of theory, the implications are even deeper and more nuanced.

There is an obvious problem of moral hazard arising from the risk that the borrowers will use the loans 'imprudently' for non-productive purposes under social or economic pressures, leading to problems of loan recovery. However, most of the theoretical constructs are based on another, more subtle and nuanced kind of *ex ante* moral hazard, which arises from the so-called 'limited liability' of the borrower while using collateral-free loans for a production project, and which can lead to a systematic divergence between the objectives of the borrower and the lender regarding the use of the loan. In theory, the 'limited liability' assumption is taken to imply that the borrower has to repay the loan only if the project is successful, but not if the project fails. This can lead to the borrower's deliberate *ex ante* strategy of undertaking too-risky projects, since she is cushioned against the underside of her risky behaviour, which can be passed off to the lender. The result can be an inefficient choice of projects or too little effort expended on the project and a higher risk of repayment default. However, these sources of perverse incentives for preferring too-risky projects or putting in too little effort will disappear as soon as the 'limited liability' assumption is replaced by that of 'full liability' – that is, if the borrower could somehow be made to repay the loan under every contingency regardless of the success or failure of projects (or, as if the borrower is investing out of her own funds).

The applicability of these theoretical results, however, will depend on how the borrower actually perceives her liability for the loan, which in turn will depend on her assessment of the repayment enforcement mechanisms employed by the MFIs and(or) her own mental calculation regarding the cost of non-repayment. It is true that a collateral-free loan cannot be recovered if the borrower household does not possess the wherewithal or the necessary cash flows to repay the loan; but the question is whether a borrower interprets this as her own limited liability for the loan while making decisions about the use of the loan. It is easy to see how the nuanced form of moral hazard disappears if the cost of non-repayment is high enough to ensure repayment.[4] Even if a coercion-based repayment system works as well as the one based on inducement and moral obligation in addressing the problem of moral hazard, the latter is obviously far superior in promoting the social mission of MFIs and in strengthening the resilience of the system.

The issues regarding loan recovery by 'moral rather than material sanctions' as well as those involving limited or unlimited liability of loans are reminiscent of a debate around the lending modalities of rural co-operative societies in the colonial Bengal (Islam, 1978, p.175). According to the so-called Maclagan Committee, which was appointed to examine these issues, the principle of unlimited liability for the loans given to poor farmers could be meaningful only if 'honesty and moral obligations' could be a substitute for material assets. The failure of the co-operatives, according to the Committee, was because of the failure in materialising what it called a 'romantic' approach of unlimited liability. The success of microcredit in Bangladesh lies in no small way in finding ways of converting what was once considered a romantic approach into a realistic one. This success is also remarkable given the age-old problem of how to recover, without coercion, loans given to the poor, as mentioned in the quote from John Hicks with which we began this chapter and the book.

Overall, the microcredit system in Bangladesh has come a long way from its reliance on group liability and rigid repayment modalities to a much more flexible system that can better meet the needs of the clients, such as by making repayment schedules match with income flows from projects, or helping clients to manage livelihood vulnerabilities, or by providing larger-sized loans to progressive borrowers. The extent of these developments is often underestimated by academics – for example, when they think that the improvements to the original Grameen model 'will not happen on its own' and will need 'tweaking, tinkering and testing' until the lending system can serve various needs of financial services of the poor without, say, 'forcing one to pay for the other' (Karlan and Appel, 2011, p.113).

1.2 Measuring the poverty impact of microcredit

The part of the microcredit literature that has stirred the most controversies, debates and emotions has to do with the assessment of the poverty impact of microcredit. The early studies on the impact of microcredit almost invariably found that microcredit made a positive contribution not only in reducing poverty, but also in a host of other economic and social dimensions. These studies soon came to be questioned, however, on the grounds of econometric methodology. Doubts were raised about whether the methodologies employed in them were able to correctly identify the causal effect of credit on economic outcomes because of what is known in the econometric literature as the 'identification problem'. It was argued, in particular, that various kinds of 'selection bias' vitiate the findings of the studies and lend an 'upward bias' to the estimates of the impact of microcredit. The bias may arise from programme placement when MFIs deliberately go for areas known as less 'risky' or when individuals with better entrepreneurial ability may 'self-select' themselves into the MFI's programme.

A number of subsequent studies have tried to address this problem by using appropriate econometric techniques, and in general they confirm the existence of the beneficial impact found by the early studies – although the magnitudes of benefit may differ. These studies have been much more conscious of the likely biases in impact estimation, and the search for an appropriate identification strategy has been at the heart of their research methodology. However, questions were raised about the findings of these second-generation studies as well, resulting in a prolonged and sometimes obscure debate on econometric methodology. Indeed, one sometimes gets the feeling that the methodological concern with identification has been all-consuming, often superseding the concern with substance. An extreme version of the critique has recently emerged, however, which holds that the kind of observational data on which these studies are based are fundamentally incapable of allowing a satisfactory solution of the identification problem. According to this view, what is needed are experimental data generated by randomised controlled trials (RCTs). Such experimental data have indeed been generated over the last decade to assess the impact of microfinance in a number of developing countries, and they generally fail to find any significant developmental impact.

Although Bangladesh is not included in these countries, the negative findings of these studies – pertaining to a wide variety of contexts – have cast serious doubt on the validity of the findings of beneficial impact of microcredit.

Randomised experiments with microcredit face a dilemma. If the objective is to test hypotheses about microcredit's presumed ability to transform the lives of borrowers, one cannot rely on experiments carried out over a short time span; but then experiments carried out over longer time spans are difficult to implement due to practical reasons. The short-run impact is not only likely to be small, but it also will be heterogeneous depending on the use of the loan. Setting up a controlled experiment for measuring the long-run impact is difficult because of keeping the comparator group of non-participant households from joining a microcredit programme or other competing programmes of poverty alleviation. It is not easy to see how this dilemma can be resolved.[5] Under the circumstances, the best the researchers can do is to work with observational data, recognise that there are inherent problems with such data arising, in particular, from the existence of selection bias of the kind discussed earlier, and to do their best to tease out the causal connections by using appropriate econometric methodologies. It is true that identification of causal connections in this manner would never be as precise as would be the case with an 'ideal' randomised experiment, but we may have to settle for the second best since an 'ideal' microcredit experiment for capturing the poverty impact of microcredit in its entirety seems hardly possible. It is in this spirit that we review in this book the major attempts that have been made so far to evaluate the poverty impact of microcredit in Bangladesh based on observational data. (Chapter 7 reviews the major studies on the poverty impact of microcredit in Bangladesh, including an assessment of the randomised controlled trials that have been undertaken in other parts of the developing world.)

There is also a popular negative perception of microcredit arising from the view that the interest rates charged by MFIs are too high, particularly in relation to the rates charged by government-owned agricultural and rural banks. However, neither the findings of experimental studies nor the negative perception about interest rates that prevails in some quarters can detract from the value of the cumulative evidence presented in this book, which shows that microcredit has helped the rural poor of Bangladesh in a significant way. At the same time, we should caution that there is no justification for making sky-high claims about the potency of microcredit. Microcredit is but one of many ingredients that must come together to enable poor people to transform their lives – microcredit alone cannot bring about this transformation on a grand scale. The discourse should move on. Instead of taking rigid positions on the efficacy of microcredit in general, the protagonists should focus attention on the details of how microcredit can be made more useful for the poor – for example, by experimenting with more flexible terms and conditions of loans and larger-sized loans, by improving the efficiency of MFIs, and by exploring the means of complementing credit with other microfinance services, such as savings and insurance, as well as non-credit services. The dividends from such a shift in discourse should be highly rewarding – not least by shifting the focus of RCTs to these topics, some of which are more amenable to controlled experiments compared to the measurement of the overall poverty impact of microcredit.

1.3 Loan use, micro-entrepreneurship and microcredit frontiers

Given the difficulties of directly measuring the impact of microcredit on poverty, it is useful to look at the actual use of the loans. After all, the impact on poverty arises from the way loans are used, so that any evidence on the use of loans can provide useful insights regarding the extent and the ways the borrowers may be expected to benefit from access to microcredit. It is not easy, however, to determine from the survey responses of borrowers the actual use of loans because of the well-known problem of the 'fungible' nature of funds in household cash-flow management. One way to resolve this problem is to ask probing questions so as to engage the survey respondents in a mental exercise about the counterfactual – as we shall see in some of the evidence discussed in this book. Fortunately, the data from a number of recent surveys conducted by the InM are available to analyse various aspects of borrowers' use of microcredit loans.

The starting point in analysing these survey findings on loan use is to recognise the large deviations in the actual and the declared use of loans. The declared or officially recorded use represents a continuing anomaly arising from a misplaced initial expectation of the pioneers of microcredit that the poor would use loans only for income-generating activities (IGAs). By contrast, the MFI clients used their newfound access to credit as a means of managing their financial portfolios in the way that suits them best, including, of course, using loans for investing in IGAs. Many studies on microcredit, especially of the ethnographic variety, have focused on how the use of loans by the borrowers deviated from the expectation of the microcredit leaders – either in the context of critiquing microcredit (e.g., Karim, 2008) or for appreciating the benefit of using the loans for a variety of purposes (Todd, 1996). While the diversion of loans to non-IGA uses is now informally recognised and accepted by microcredit practitioners, the original stipulation on loan use is still retained, perhaps as a psychological barrier for the borrowers against genuinely adverse loan usage. It is thus no longer a problem, in carefully designed surveys, to elicit information from the respondents about the actual use of loans, although this might have been a problem in the early days of microcredit (Roodman, 2012, pp. 24–9).

A review of the survey findings shows that investment in IGAs is indeed the single most important broad category of the use of microcredit loans, accounting for about 40 to 60 percent of the loans. (Chapter 8 provides an extensive analysis of the evidence on the use of microcredit.) Besides investment in IGA, another important category of loan use may be defined as investment in physical and human capital; this includes both additions to physical assets (mainly the construction or repair of dwelling houses, but also purchases of land, household vehicles and equipment) and augmentation of human capital (mainly by spending on education, healthcare, and sending household members abroad as wage earners).

By combining investment in IGAs with non-IGA investment in physical assets and human capital into a broader category of 'productive use', it is found that this category accounts for the major share of loans – about 60 to 80 percent. The rest of the loans are mainly used for household consumption, which may include both meeting recurrent living expenses and the acquisition of consumer durables. Even if the use of loans to meet household consumption needs may appear wasteful, those who use loans for these purposes may do so because it helps their financial portfolio management, such as smoothing their consumption in the face of income fluctuations or supporting their livelihood strategies in other ways.

The counterfactuals of what the borrowers would have done without microcredit can provide insights on how microcredit programmes have been able to both expand the credit market for the poor as well as replace parts of the informal credit market. In the InM survey on *Impact of Microcredit on Gender Norms and Behaviour*, the respondent female borrowers were asked probing questions about whether they would have spent the same amount out of the loans (or less, or not all) on various categories of spending in the absence of microcredit and, if so, how they would have raised the money. As expected, the dependence on microcredit as the main source of borrowing for investing in IGAs was evident from these survey responses. Among the borrowers who spent the loan amounts mainly on non-productive items, about one-fourth of them would not have purchased those items at all without access to microcredit – thus indicating the role of microcredit in creating an entirely new credit market – while the rest would have purchased the items fully or partly by raising the money from other sources, including mostly from informal sources of credit, thus indicating the role of microcredit in replacing informal credit. The creation of additional credit demand was particularly evident when the microcredit loans were used for such purposes as house construction, the purchase of consumer durables or spending on health and education. But when the loans were used for meeting marriage expenses or the repayment of old loans or some type of crisis management, the alternative to microcredit would have been borrowing from informal sources – and also, in some cases, by resorting to such desperate measures as the sale or mortgage of assets. Thus, to the extent that microcredit was used for the latter purposes, it either replaced higher-cost, informal sources of credit or helped avoid even more corrosive crisis-coping mechanisms. Microcredit thus appears to have replaced a part of the traditional moneylending practices for the benefit of poor borrowers, and like any other technological or institutional innovations, it also created markets where there were none.

Apart from the findings from cross-sectional surveys regarding the way households use microcredit loans, Bangladesh's experience allows an analysis of long-term household behaviour in accessing microcredit and the long-term impact of the introduction of microcredit on the rural credit markets. The microcredit movement was initiated with two avowed goals, as expounded by its pioneers: the first was to promote income-earning opportunities for the poor through self-employment, and the second was to free the poor from the 'clutches' of moneylenders, as Muhammad Yunus, the founder of Grameen Bank, puts it (Yunus, 2004a). The ways the introduction of microcredit has interacted with the traditional informal credit markets have turned out to be much more complex and nuanced than would appear at first glance. There is, however, little systematic evidence or academic research on this topic. This is surprising, since concerns about usurious moneylending have been at the core of policy discussions on rural financial sector reform. As we shall discuss in various contexts in this book, microcredit has turned out to be useful in satisfying various kinds of credit needs beyond its initially envisaged goal of promoting self-employment through IGAs – ranging from the acquisition of consumer durables to coping with livelihood vulnerabilities. But microcredit is not suitable for meeting all kinds of credit needs of the poor – the reason why informal moneylending persists.

One apprehension about microcredit is that poor people may be tempted to make imprudent use of credit, leading to over-indebtedness, which will largely depend on the way the MFIs operate. There is not much evidence of such 'temptation borrowing' among MFI clients in Bangladesh. The MFIs with a social mission, as those in Bangladesh, have to be wary about lending practices that may need excessive coercive measures for repayment enforcement or may adversely impact the well-being outcome of their clients; thus, they have at least a triggering red signal by having to enforce repayment by coercion. However, the risk is much higher for the alternative profit-oriented model of microcredit as practiced by many MFIs worldwide. For example, the evidence from Bolivia in the 1990s, and more recently from Andhra Pradesh in India, shows how the reckless lending of some commercially motivated MFIs can have disastrous consequences (Sriram, 2010). Clearly, a standardised model that can be run in a commercially efficient manner is liable to be misused at the hands of profit-motivated MFIs in the absence of the safeguards that apply in the case of socially oriented MFIs.

This presents a dilemma for the MFIs with a social mission. In the absence of an adequate social safety net, accessing microcredit may be better than other available options for households facing livelihood shocks or other emergencies. But the MFIs are averse to such lending because of the likely problem of repayment enforcement, and also because such borrowing may lead to future impoverishment of the borrowers, which is contrary to their declared social mission of getting people out of poverty. However, the available evidence suggests that the effectiveness of microcredit in reducing livelihood vulnerabilities, particularly with some flexibility in repayment schedules, is perhaps underestimated. Even when borrowers divert credit to unintended uses, like meeting an unexpected shock, they could end up with a far more sustainable economic condition than what would otherwise be the case.

Although MFIs in Bangladesh initially emphasised credit disbursements as their primary activity and their programmes still continue to be primarily credit-led, there has been a rapid and unabated growth of members' savings kept with the MFIs; by 2014, members' savings had grown to represent well above half the outstanding loans of MFIs. Grameen Bank has been particularly successful in deposit mobilisation, with the net accumulated savings of its borrowers currently surpassing the size of its total outstanding loans to borrowers. Furthermore, the pattern of change in the deposits and withdrawals suggests that the MFI clients are increasingly using their deposits for both immediate and long-term needs.

While appropriate savings instruments can help the poor to better realise an inter-temporally optimal saving plan, it can hardly be a substitute for meeting the credit needs of the poor. Microcredit loans are typically used as business working capital which can provide additional household income, but they may not contribute much to capital accumulation; in other words, extra income can be generated without any saving on the part of the borrowing household. Even more important is the fact that, compared to any innovative saving scheme, the lending modalities of MFIs can perhaps better exploit the 'commitment factor' related to the self-discipline issue in helping their clients to save. When MFI clients use the loans, say, for house construction or their children's education or the purchase of a consumer durable, it is a way of committing to save in the form of weekly instalments out of regular household income. The findings from recent experimental research in behavioural economics, as well as some survey findings discussed in this book, suggest that the attractiveness of microcredit programmes lies at least partly in their lending modalities, which require them to repay the loans in regular small amounts, thus resembling more of a saving scheme than the repayment of a business loan (Bauer *et al.*, 2012).

The impact of the microcredit programmes in raising the incomes of participant households depends mainly on the profitability of microcredit-financed IGAs, their sustainability, and their prospects for scaling up. The estimates of profitability show that the typical microcredit borrower enjoys a rate of return well above the rates of interest charged by MFIs in Bangladesh, which in effective terms vary from 20 to less than 30 percent annually. Since the rate of return is netted from the imputed cost of family labour, the commonly held perception that IGAs are profitable only by exploiting underutilised family labour does not have much support. The profitability estimates also thus imply that the IGAs can provide employment to family labourers at the prevailing wage rate in alternative employment and also yield an additional income netted from interest payments.

A question commonly asked is this: in spite of high rates of return to capital, why do only a few microcredit-financed businesses grow beyond subsistence entrepreneurship? The problems of providing large-sized loans can explain this only partly, since capital can be accumulated from repeated loans over a long time. The answer seems to be that while returns to capital in subsistence-type businesses can be quite high, the potential tapers off quite fast with an increase in the scale of operation. There still remains the question regarding why microcredit borrowers find it difficult to expand their businesses by shifting to production and marketing technologies that are economically viable at a higher scale of operation. We try to answer this question by invoking the idea of a 'technology gap' or a 'missing middle' that prevents a process of gradual scaling up through incremental changes in the size of businesses, but requires a quantum shift in scale and technology. (These and other issues related to graduation are discussed in Chapter 9.) The challenge for the MFIs and their 'entrepreneurial' clients is to find ways of bridging this technology gap or missing middle in innovative ways by supporting and adopting appropriate production and marketing strategies (the term 'missing middle' comes from the discussions on the credit market in Bangladesh).

There are, of course, other important constraints to business expansion, such as entrepreneurial skill, motivation and business practices as has been found in many studies, including those based on randomised control trials (de Mel *et al.*, 2010). By focusing on the technology gap, we have only highlighted a relatively overlooked aspect of the problem. The view from the practitioners is that the microcredit system has created a very large pool of capable entrepreneurs eager to venture into scaled-up enterprises; but the scaling up of microenterprises beyond the subsistence level is often found to be difficult, short of embarking on a full-scale commercial venture. It is true that MFIs avoid financing start-ups and tend to be conservative in financing profitable but risky projects. But there also seems to be a threshold level of enterprise size below which economies of scale in production and marketing cannot be reaped, while the informal personalised marketing of IGA products is not suitable for scaling up beyond a very small scale of operation. However, there perhaps exists considerable unexploited potential for supporting microenterprise development through innovative schemes of marketing and product design that can help the scaling up of subsistence-type enterprises.

One of the sources of misunderstanding about the role of microcredit in poverty alleviation and economic development seems to arise from an assumption that the success of microcredit depends on the proportion of borrowers who can come out of poverty through repeated loans and the scaling up of their enterprises (Khandker, 1998). The expectation may have arisen from the pioneers' early hope of poverty alleviation through graduating borrowers and scaling up of IGAs beyond subsistence. What may not have been fully anticipated is the speed at which the outreach of microcredit has expanded far beyond the so-called 'entrepreneurial poor' to meet the various other needs of poor people's financial management, such as investing in non-IGA physical and human assets, managing livelihood vulnerabilities, and addressing self-discipline issues of saving difficulties. It became obvious that while some of the entrepreneurial poor may indeed grow out of poverty through the scaling up of their microenterprises, all clients cannot do so because of their sheer number, if not for anything else. Even if they cannot expand their businesses, that does not mean they are 'trapped' in poverty; they can still benefit from microcredit to ease their livelihood and financial management needs until graduating out of poverty by other pathways.

The fact still remains that microcredit expansion through only the replication of low-productivity, subsistence-type activities will ultimately be limited by one way or another, which led Baumol *et al.* (2007) to conclude that microenterprises backed by microcredit are unlikely to be major engines of economic growth. This may seem to have some relevance so far as the regular microcredit programmes in Bangladesh are concerned, with some symptoms of market saturation already being visible. But the frontiers of microcredit are also shifting in new directions.

Beyond supporting rural non-farm enterprises, the microcredit programmes are making inroads into the market for agricultural and crop loans through the introduction of 'seasonal loans' that have flexible repayment schedules. In recent years we have also witnessed the growth of so-called 'microenterprise loans', which are larger-sized and usually dispensed under a variety of lending modalities different from those that apply to regular microcredit loans. Already by 2014, the microenterprise loans had increased in coverage and fund allocations to account for 10 percent of the outstanding number of MFI loans and nearly 30 percent of the total amount of loans disbursed in that year.

The MFIs are increasingly inclined to play a developmental role in trying to bridge the so-called 'missing middle' in the credit market in between mainstream microcredit and commercial banking. As they are rethinking the boundaries of their legitimate activities and have become more financially self-reliant, the MFIs' social mission is extending beyond poverty alleviation *per se* to economic development. The MFIs have a potentially crucial role to play in supporting the scaling up of microenterprises, such as by providing training for the adoption of appropriate production technologies (where there is a need for scale economies in production) or by helping to access markets (where there is scale economies in marketing, including product design and quality assurance, but home-based production on a small scale can be profitable). (The links between microcredit and broader economic development are discussed in Chapter 10.)

Indeed, the growth of these NGO-MFIs in Bangladesh represents a process of institution-building that has served the poor in various ways – by providing a whole range of services besides microcredit. They now face the challenge of realising the untapped potential of the microcredit programmes by using and further consolidating their institutional strength. The MFI leaders, for example, have been advocating the case for converting some of the large MFIs into rural banks, which will ease their fund constraint in undertaking more innovative lending programmes while also exploiting the largely untapped potential of mobilising rural saving (Yunus, 2004a). The question of what kind of regulatory framework will be needed to allow the MFIs to play such bigger roles raises issues not only regarding financial regulation but also those involving the relationship between NGO-MFIs and the government, which has been aptly characterised by Sanyal (1991) as one of 'antagonistic cooperation'. But this question brings us to the political economy domain of MFIs and microcredit, which is not the subject matter of this book.

Notes

1 Smith (1776, p.93), cited from the Random House edition of 1937.
2 Hicks (1969, pp.76–77).
3 Beyond the theories of microcredit, several strands of mainstream economic theory have also been deeply influenced by the insights gleaned from the practice of microcredit, and of Grameen Bank in particular. For example, one of the earliest theoretical papers dealing with the interface between economic theory and microcredit was motivated not

so much by the desire to unearth the secret of microcredit as to learn how to enrich the mainstream theories of monitoring, incentive and screening by using the principles of group lending innovated by the Grameen Bank (Varian, 1990).
4 The logic of this *ex ante* mental calculation of the borrower applies even if she eventually decides to default because of the project's failure, resulting in bankruptcy.
5 This is likely to be a generic problem associated with experiments with social interventions of most kinds.

2 Microcredit in Bangladesh
How the credit markets work

Studying the growth and evolution of microcredit in Bangladesh can be important for several reasons. Although the microcredit model of Grameen Bank has been replicated worldwide, no other country can match Bangladesh in its experience regarding the maturity and the extent of outreach of the microcredit programmes. Bangladesh's experience thus allows an analysis of long-term household behaviour in accessing microcredit and its impact on household welfare. It is also possible to examine how the introduction of microcredit affects the rural credit markets over a long period of time, particularly in terms of the interaction of microcredit with various traditional and informal sources of credit. Another issue that has not yet been studied enough in the academic literature is whether multiple programme membership, which has increased as a consequence of the rapid expansion of microcredit, is harming or benefitting the borrowers. Other issues amenable to analysis may include the extent of resilience and long-run sustainability of the microcredit programmes, and the new challenges and possibilities emerging from a situation when the replication of the original model may near a point of market saturation. Bangladesh's experience is worth studying for another reason, namely, the lessons learned from the numerous innovations, mutations and adaptations through which the classic Grameen model has been transformed over the years. In this chapter, however, we focus mainly on the growth of microcredit in Bangladesh in relation to the rural credit markets and the credit needs of the poor.

2.1 The outreach of microcredit

The microfinance initiatives in Bangladesh formally started with the government's sponsorship of an action research programme of Muhammad Yunus in the district of Tangail to lend money to the poor without collateral. The basic premise was that credit could be used to alleviate poverty and that the poor were creditworthy, the lack of collateral notwithstanding. The initiatives gained momentum with the establishment of Grameen Bank under a government ordinance in 1983. Other than Grameen Bank, the microcredit industry is driven by numerous non-governmental institutions (NGOs) which were initially established for 'social mobilisation' of the rural communities along with service delivery, but later on shifted their emphasis to the provision of microcredit to the poor – hence now commonly known as NGO-MFIs. Among the three largest MFIs, the share of Grameen Bank in the microcredit market in terms of annual loan disbursements in 2014 was 21 percent (reduced from a much higher level in earlier years) compared to 23 percent of Bangladesh Rural Advancement Committee (BRAC)[1] and 18 percent of Association for Social Advancement (ASA).

A turning point in the NGO-led expansion of the microcredit sector was the establishment of *Palli-Karma Sahayak Foundation* or PKSF (translates into Rural Employment Support Foundation), which is an apex institution set up in 1990 to provide wholesale funding for microcredit programmes at a subsidised rate of interest to its partner NGO-MFIs. PKSF helped to expand and consolidate the sector by channelling government and donor funds to its partner NGO-MFIs, which initially included even the large ones like BRAC and ASA besides numerous smaller ones;[2] in addition, it supports institutional development and innovations, and has helped to set uniform standards of self-regulation across the industry. Indeed, PKSF is recognised as a role model of an institution to facilitate wholesaling of subsidised resources to small and localised NGO-MFIs, thus reducing the transaction costs for such transfers for both the donors and the recipient MFIs. Several of these local and regional MFIs have now grown into national-level organisations. It is through its relationship with numerous partner MFIs that PKSF has been able to support experimentation and innovations, thus pushing the microcredit frontiers in several directions, as will be discussed later in several contexts.

2.1.1 Has microcredit reached market saturation?

The phenomenal growth of microcredit in Bangladesh since the 1990s can be seen from the various indicators shown in Table 2.1, with a more than five-fold increase in the number of active borrowers.[3] These numbers of members and borrowers, however, greatly exaggerate the actual headcounts of MFI clients, because of the increasingly widespread phenomenon of individuals borrowing from multiple MFIs.[4] Moreover, the numbers of both active members and borrowers, having peaked in 2008 at 35.9 million and 29.8 million, respectively, have shown a declining trend since then. Given the evidence on the sharp increase in the incidence of borrowing from multiple MFIs in recent years (Osmani, Khalily and Hasan, 2015), the decline seems to have started even earlier, and to a larger extent than indicated by the number of loans. Whether this reflects a situation of market saturation for the outreach of regular microcredit programmes is far from clear, since there are likely to be still more potential borrowers out there who may be discouraged by the lack of suitable microloan products. For example, the newly introduced 'agricultural and seasonal loans' with somewhat relaxed criteria of eligibility and more flexibility in repayment have emerged as a fast-growing category of loans disbursed by PKSF's partner MFIs. It may also be noted that the number of loans disbursed annually by the industry as a whole has continued to rise steadily, mainly because of the increasing coverage of larger-sized loans called 'microenterprise loans'. The stagnation or decline in the coverage of regular microcredit

Table 2.1 Growth of microcredit in Bangladesh: 1996–2014 (selected years)

Indicators	1996	2000	2005	2010	2014
Number of active members (million)	8.1	13.4	24.4	35.0	34.0
Number of outstanding borrowers (million)	4.7	9.8	18.1	27.1	27.2
Annual loan disbursement (million US$)	542	827	1,889	5,014	8,340
Outstanding loan (million US$)	357	567	1,192	3,199	5,283
Members' outstanding net savings (million US$)	141	248	581	1,542	2,927

Source: Estimated from *Bangladesh Microfinance Statistics* published annually by Credit and Development Forum (CDF), Dhaka, and Grameen Bank's Annual Report.

Notes: Values in US dollars (US$) are derived at the official taka-dollar exchange rates of the relevant years. Estimates include the data of Grameen Bank and the data of NGO-MFIs reported by the Credit and Development Forum (CDF). The reporting numbers of NGO-MFIs were 351 in 1996, 585 in 2000, 690 in 2005 and 511 in 2014, which, along with those of Grameen Bank, are believed to capture most of the microcredit lending operations.

programmes may therefore reflect as much a situation of market saturation as a diversion of funds to larger-sized loans within the overall fund constraints.

In fact, contrary to the hypothesis of market saturation, one of the criticisms of microcredit as a poverty intervention tool is its inability to meet the credit needs of the extremely poor households while including the non-poor – sometimes called the 'mission drift'.[5] The MFIs regard the poorest households as credit risks since they may be less capable of engaging in IGAs. They may also lack predictable and alternative sources of income to service weekly instalment payments in case of any diversion of loans to unproductive uses or failure of their enterprises; and they are also more likely to default because of their vulnerability to external livelihood shocks. Even if the MFIs have a policy to include the poorest, such a policy is difficult to implement because field-level officers lack the motivation to put forth the extra effort needed.[6] From the demand side, the poorest households often lack resource endowments for pursuing the self-employment or multiple occupations that are often facilitated by microcredit. For example, they may lack enough space within the homestead area and the dwelling house to install a handloom or build a cowshed or run a grocery store, or to dry and process paddy, or to securely keep a rickshaw van – all of which represent some typical IGAs supported by microcredit. Moreover, the working-age members of the poorest households, both male and female, often work as day labourers, and therefore they may not have much spare time to pursue a subsidiary self-employment occupation.

There have been some special efforts in expanding microcredit coverage among the ultra-poor, though often met with only limited success. One such example is Grameen Bank's credit programme for the homeless and beggars. Recent experience with specially targeted microcredit programmes for the ultra-poor in some economically depressed areas in northwest Bangladesh shows that the coverage among these households could be increased substantially, but only with a combination of other interventions like linking with social safety net programmes and provisions of specially subsidised funding such as from PKSF, and possibly with some cross-subsidisation from the profits generated in the MFI's regular credit programmes (Khandker and Mahmud, 2012, pp.151–76). Through the *Targeting of the Ultra Poor* (TUP) programme, BRAC has combined safety net and microcredit to provide sustainable livelihoods for extremely poor women with the expectation that they will eventually qualify for regular microcredit (Matin and Hulme, 2003).

There is, however, evidence of considerable latent credit demand among targeted households, including the poorest, that could be met by the MFIs but for the rigid lending modalities. Survey results show that although the majority of the eligible households not joining microcredit programmes are found to self-select themselves out of the programmes, a main reason for this is the likely mismatch between income flows and the weekly repayment schedule (Hashemi, 1997; Osmani et al., 2015, p.164). The cash flow problems of the rural poor households arising from the seasonality and fluctuations in their incomes, along with the difficulty they face in keeping cash at hand due to pressure for immediate spending, are well-documented (e.g. Collins et al., 2009). Not surprisingly, the burden of weekly payment is cited as the major reason by prospective borrowers for not joining microcredit programmes or for dropping out (Hashemi and Schuler, 1997; Rahman, 2000, p.58; InM, 2013, pp.99–101). The risk to livelihood shocks, along with the limited flexibility in the lending modalities in helping borrowers to cope with such shocks, is also found to be a major factor behind the reluctance of poor households to join microcredit programmes (Khalily, 2013). Thus, had it not been for the rigid credit repayment modalities, the market would have been larger; and this poses a challenge as well as holds promise for further expansion of microcredit by making it more responsive to the financial needs of the poor.

The prospects of further expansion of microcredit also depend on how the MFIs redefine their targeting criteria. It is well-known that the eligibility criteria of owning less than 0.5 acre of land, first formally introduced by Grameen Bank, was meant to be only a rough screening device to identify poor households.[7] The risk of targeting error is minimised anyway by the onerous lending modalities that would hardly appear attractive to non-poor families – the requirement of attending the weekly meetings and the relatively high interest rates compared to those charged by the formal banks. Besides the flexibility in applying the targeting criteria, the MFIs are increasingly also redefining their scope of operation in order to go into credit markets that are underserved by commercial banks but are nevertheless important for promoting agricultural and small enterprise development. For example, ASA formally started in the late 1990s lending to households owning more than 0.5 acres through its Small Enterprise Development Programme. More recently, PKSF has been promoting, through its partner MFIs, agricultural loans to small farmers by formally relaxing the 0.5-acre landowning criterion. Increasingly, the MFIs consider it a legitimate extension of their developmental and poverty-alleviating role to provide credit to farmers and small entrepreneurs who are not so poor themselves, but who can generate employment for the poorest.

The aim is to ultimately address the problem of the so-called 'missing middle' in the credit market, representing potential borrowers who are not considered creditworthy enough by formal banks but not so poor as to fit the traditional MFI targeting criteria. This is a reflection of a rethinking by the MFIs about the boundaries of their legitimate activities, given their increased financial self-sufficiency. How much risk there is of a 'mission drift' in such a redefining of the role of MFIs is a topic to which we shall come back later in this book.

2.1.2 Saving mobilisation

In spite of the recent stagnation or decline in membership, a striking phenomenon is the rapid and unabated growth of members' savings kept with the MFIs (see Table 2.1). Although the programmes are primarily credit-led with savings being largely compulsory as a prerequisite to apply for credit, savings services such as open-access savings accounts and time deposits started gathering momentum in the late 1990s. The members' net savings have steadily increased to more than half of the total outstanding loans in 2014. However, Grameen Bank is much more successful in deposit mobilisation; the net accumulated savings of its borrowers, amounting to US$ 983 million in 2014, almost matched the size of its outstanding loans to borrowers in that year. In addition, Grameen Bank mobilises substantial amounts of savings from non-members as well, with an outstanding net amount of US$ 1.37 billion in 2014, which was larger than the amount of its outstanding loans to borrowers (US$ 1.13 billion). Grameen Bank also mobilises substantial deposits from non-members as well, with an outstanding net amount of US$ 825 million in 2014, while the NGO-MFIs are not legally permitted to mobilise non-member savings.

The estimates of net savings of members hide considerable activities in terms of annual deposits and withdrawals. In 2012, for example, savings deposited and withdrawn represented 62 percent and 47 percent, respectively, of the end-year net savings of that year.[8] These proportions were even much higher in the earlier years, with lower levels of net savings. It is well-known that despite limited access to most savings accounts, MFI clients access these accounts from time to time to cope with fluctuations in income or other unpredictable livelihood adversities. In fact, Meyer (2002) cites studies carried out in the 1990s that found clients of MFIs, including Grameen Bank and BRAC, resentful about compulsory saving deposits and restrictions on withdrawals from savings.

However, the observed patterns of deposits and withdrawals over time and the resulting rapid build-up of net savings suggest a preference for longer-term savings as well, such as for old age security and for meeting children's educational and marriage expenses. This shift in attitudes towards savings is also reflected in the increasing demand for various deposit schemes introduced by the MFIs. Overall, the MFI clients are increasingly using their membership in a way people use banking services – to access credit as well as to keep deposits and use such deposits for both immediate and long-term needs. This blunts, to an extent, one of the common criticisms of the microcredit system – that it emphasises credit to the neglect of saving mobilisation. We shall come back to this topic in Chapter 8.

2.2 Interactions with informal credit markets

2.2.1 Expanding access to credit or replacing traditional moneylending?

The microcredit movement was initiated with two avowed goals as expounded by its pioneers: the first is to promote income-earning opportunities for the poor through self-employment, and the second is to free the poor from the 'clutches' of moneylenders, as Muhammad Yunus, the founder of Grameen Bank, puts it (Yunus, 2004a). MFIs target land-poor households who are bypassed by the formal banks and who also constitute the bulk of the clientele for the moneylenders. It can thus be expected that the availability of microcredit at relatively lower interest rates without collateral will allow poor households to substitute microcredit for high-interest loans from traditional moneylenders and landlords. At the same time, microcredit can also be expected to expand the rural credit markets by enabling client households to undertake or expand economic activities that were not previously profitable at the high interest rates charged by moneylenders.

The way the introduction of microcredit has interacted with the traditional informal credit markets has turned out to be much more complex and nuanced than would appear at a first glance. There is, however, little systematic evidence or research on this topic. This is surprising since concerns about usurious money-lending have been at the core of policy discussions on rural financial sector reforms. As we shall discuss later in various contexts, microcredit is not designed to meet all the credit needs of the poor and cannot therefore be expected to replace the entire informal credit market. It has been mentioned already that some of the poorest households either may not be considered by MFIs as creditworthy or may themselves self-select out of microcredit programmes because of the inflexibility in lending modalities. In spite of much higher interest rates, informal money-lending has advantages in terms of flexibility in timing, loan size and repayment modes. Socially motivated MFIs are also wary of meeting the kinds of credit needs that may lead to future impoverishment of the borrowers and will require harsh means for loan recovery – an issue to be discussed in more detail in Chapter 3. On the other hand, microcredit has turned out to be useful in satisfying various kinds of credit needs beyond its initially envisaged goal of promoting self-employment through IGAs – ranging from acquisition of consumer durables to coping with livelihood vulnerabilities. Again, while replacing demand for higher-cost credit from informal sources, microcredit itself may have led to an increase in certain kinds of informal credit transactions, such as in the form of mutual help among group members in paying weekly instalments or for meeting additional working capital needs of microenterprises set up by microcredit.

Some idea about the extent and nature of inroads made by microcredit into the rural credit markets can be formed from a number of recent studies, most of which are based on nationwide surveys carried out by the InM, a sister organization of PKSF. Of these, the survey that specifically addressed the issue, *Access to Financial Services in Bangladesh 2009–10*, came up with the pattern of access to different sources of credit shown in Table 2.2 (Khalily, 2011). A few aspects of these estimates may be noted. In terms of the number of households served, microcredit is now the predominant source of credit, formal and informal combined, and not only in the rural areas but also for the country as a whole. The divide between poor and non-poor regarding access to microcredit hides the fact that the extremely poor remain largely excluded, while access among the non-poor is largely concentrated among those who are closest to the poverty line from above. Further, while microcredit has made significant inroads into urban areas, the estimates shown in the table largely depict its spread into small towns and semi-urban areas. These estimates of microcredit coverage are comparable to another recent InM survey called *Impact of Microcredit on Gender Norms and Behaviour*, which provides information on the proportion of microcredit borrowers among ever-married women aged 50 or under; this proportion is found to be 41 percent in rural areas, 50 percent in municipal wards and 14 percent in metropolitan areas (Amin and Mahmud, 2012).[9]

More insights about how rural households combine credit from different sources are provided by the findings of yet another recent nationwide rural household survey, namely, *InM Poverty Dynamics Survey 2010* (Osmani et al., 2015). The estimates of proportions of rural households taking loans from different sources, either singly or in combination, are found to be generally much higher compared to the findings of the other surveys (Table 2.3). The most likely reason is that the estimates relate to loans taken in the three years preceding the survey, and the households taking these loans, which are mostly of a short-term nature, vary from one year to another. In the case of microcredit, which is typically of one-year duration with loans that are usually repeated, not all active members borrow every year. Nevertheless, it is significant that nearly half the households have taken microcredit, with or without other types of loans, and a similar number have

Table 2.2 Distribution of households with access to credit by source of credit, poverty status and residence in Bangladesh: 2009–2010 (percent of households)

Source of credit	Poor	Non-poor	Rural	Urban	National
Formal credit	5.4	9.0	7.6	10.0	8.0
Quasi-formal (microcredit)	45.4	32.9	39.1	27.0	36.6
Informal	20.6	22.4	23.1	16.8	21.8
Total (any credit)	59.0	52.1	56.1	46.1	54.1

Notes and source: InM survey on *Access to Financial Services in Bangladesh, 2009–10*; adapted from Khalily (2011); figures do not add up to the total because of credit from multiple sources; the quasi-formal category includes, besides microcredit, some minor sources like cooperatives; poor households are defined according to the official poverty line.

Table 2.3 The structure of the rural credit market in Bangladesh: 2010 (percent of households)

Breakdown of type of loan taken in the last 3 years	% of all rural households
Any credit taken in last 3 years	69.5
Microcredit	46.4
Informal credit	45.4
Formal credit	6.4
Borrowers from single source	
Microcredit	21.1
Informal credit	19.4
Formal credit	1.9
Borrowers from multiple sources	
Microcredit and informal credit	22.6
Microcredit and formal credit	1.0
Formal credit and informal credit	1.8
All three sources	1.7

Source: In*M Poverty Dynamics Survey 2010*; estimated from Osmani *et al.* (2015, p.159).

Note: Total sample size is 6300 households, of which the number of households taking loans from any source in the last three years is 4375; data relate to 3 years preceding the survey.

borrowed from informal sources, including friends, relatives, moneylenders and landlords.[10] Another significant aspect is the overlap of microcredit with credit from informal sources, with about half of the microcredit borrowers also accessing credit from informal sources. Clearly, the MFIs do not satisfy all the credit needs of their clients who take recourse to informal sources as well.

This feature of simultaneous borrowing from MFIs and informal lenders raises important questions about the relationship between these two sources of credit. 'Informal sector' is a catch-all term for loans of various kinds which differ from each other in significant ways. Professional moneylenders, including traders and landlords who engage in moneylending besides pure professional moneylenders, are the ones who are alleged to charge very high interest rates or exploit the borrowers through interlinking markets for credit, labour and commodity trade. According to the survey results discussed above, about two-thirds of the loan amounts were from friends and relatives, and only about a fourth was from professional moneylenders (Osmani *et al.*, 2015, pp.157–200). Again, loans from friends and relatives can either be in the nature of interest-bearing business transactions or represent a benign form of mutual help and insurance. The latter type of lending, which is common in rural societies, is assumed to flourish further with the strengthening of group solidarity and social capital promoted by microcredit.[11] A commonly observed practice among microcredit group members is to help one another in meeting the weekly repayment schedules by extending short-term informal loans. But even beyond paying each other's loan instalments, microcredit may have led to more mutual financial support by fostering group cohesion and also by establishing a culture of loan repayment in the rural credit markets generally, the evidence of which will be discussed in Chapter 3. The informal loan transactions within microcredit groups are likely to have made this category of small loans from friends and relatives even more frequent.

The trends in the pattern of access to credit for rural households since the introduction of microcredit in the late 1980s can be seen from the household panel data gathered from several rounds of a nationwide survey conducted in 62 villages (Hossain and Bayes, 2009; Hossain, 2012).[12] The estimates of access to credit presented in Table 2.4 differ from the other estimates discussed above in one important respect: they refer to the main source of loans and thus do not show any overlap, so as to add up to the total proportion of households having credit access. The estimates show the role of microcredit in both increasing substantially the overall access to credit and replacing informal sources of credit. There are some differences, though, between landless and landowning households. As expected, the increased access to microcredit and overall credit is more pronounced for landless households compared to landowning ones. But for the landless households, the dependence on professional moneylenders (excluding traders and landlords) has declined very little for the period as a whole. It suggests that, for the poorer households, microcredit has not done much to substitute borrowing from one type of moneylender – the purely professional ones. It may have something to do with the kind of credit demand of the poorest households that is met by these moneylenders.

Another notable aspect of the estimates in Table 2.4 is the sharp decline in loans from 'friends and relatives', which is in contrast to the still dominant role of this category of loans as found in the *InM Poverty Dynamics Survey* discussed above. One likely reason is that short-term loans of small amounts were excluded in the panel household survey, the findings of which are reported in Table 2.4. Most

Table 2.4 Trends in the access to different sources of credit by rural households in Bangladesh by category of land ownership: 1988–2010 (percent of households)

Sources of credit	Landless households			Landowning households		
	1988	2000	2010	1988	2000	2010
Commercial/specialised banks	7.6	8.7	9.5	10.1	10.9	13.9
NGO-MFIs	2.9	19.4	33.6	3.1	10.9	20.1
Traders/landowners	6.5	6.4	1.9	5.5	3.1	1.3
Moneylenders	6.0	2.1	5.4	17.1	1.6	4.0
Friends/relatives	14.1	4.9	2.8	12.6	4.5	2.3
Total (any source)	37.5	41.5	53.2	36.5	31.0	41.7

Source: Estimated from Hossain (2012).

Notes: Landless households are those owning up to 0.5 acre of land and constituting 50 percent, 51 percent and 54 percent of all sample households in 1988, 2000 and 2010, respectively; this proportion does not reflect the extent of increasing landlessness since new households in the later rounds of the surveys were selected, so as to keep the balance between the two groups of households mostly unchanged.

loan transactions representing mutual support, including those among microcredit group members, are of this type. Even when reported, these loans are unlikely to be recorded as the main source of loans for those who access other kinds of loans. Not surprisingly, this category of loans as reported in Table 2.4 were found to be considerably costly, at an average annual rate of above 50 percent (higher than the 20 percent to 30 percent effective annual interest rate charged by the MFIs, though lower than the nearly 100 percent often charged by moneylenders), indicating that these loans represented the commercial variety of loans in the so-called category of 'friends and relatives' (Hossain and Bayes, 2009, p.285, Table 11.9).

The household panel data discussed by Hossain and Bayes (2009, pp.262–87) also show that while the incidences of borrowing from informal sources (as the main source) has sharply declined, the average loan size from these sources has increased over the three decades: from US$ 155 to US$ 537 in the case of moneylenders, and from US$ 115 to US$ 920 for friends and relatives. Thus, excepting small loans in the nature of mutual help, the informal credit market that continues to operate despite the rapid rise of microcredit seems to satisfy demand for larger lump-sum amounts. This conforms to the findings of the *InM Poverty Dynamics Survey 2010*, which show the relatively larger size of loans in the case of moneylenders and also in the case of at least a part of the 'friends and relatives' loans compared to the loans from MFIs.[13] These findings thus point to the limitation of microcredit in providing large loans, which may be one reason why recourse to informal sources of borrowing is necessary even when microcredit is available. Based on findings from household financial diaries, Collins et al. (2009, p.106) cite examples of how poor households in rural Bangladesh have to sometimes raise funds for large lump-sum expenses from a variety of sources, in addition to borrowing from the microcredit lender, such as from their own savings, gifts and interest-free loans from friends and relatives, short-term loans from local moneylenders and even the sale of household assets. Even among the relatively small proportion of rural households who can access credit from formal banks, most of them are found to borrow from MFIs or informal sources, or both (Table 2.3).

It may be noted in this context that, unlike MFIs, informal moneylenders have many enforcement mechanisms that allow them to provide relatively large-sized loans. For example, in one form of usufruct loan prevalent in rural Bangladesh, a landlord-lender uses the borrower's land until the principal is repaid; the profits from harvest provide the interest on the lender's loan. Credit repayment is also sometimes enforced by requiring the borrower household to provide free labour to work for the landlord-lender. Similarly, a trader-lender can enforce his or her claim on a borrower-farmer by deducting the interest from the market value of the crops or other agricultural products sold to, or through, the trader-lender. In the coastal areas of Bangladesh, fishermen depend on moneylenders to buy boats and fishing equipment, and in return they have to sell the catch to the trader-lenders at prices much below the market prices, which implies a very high hidden cost of credit and results in continued indebtedness. PKSF's attempt through its partner MFIs to help coastal fishermen to come out of this exploitative system of lending, locally known as *dadan* business, failed because of the required large size of loans and the clout of moneylenders in local politics.

The duality and complementarities between microcredit and the informal credit markets need to be understood in light of the nature of the credit needs of poor households. The poor need credit for a variety of reasons beyond the self-declared role of the MFIs to provide them capital for setting up small businesses. In the absence of adequate public social safety net programmes or access to any insurance mechanisms except mutual help, they need credit to cope with various emergencies and livelihood shocks to which they are particularly vulnerable, such as those caused by illness, theft, eviction from their property or natural disasters. But the credit needs of poor households also arise because of an important behavioural characteristic of their financial management, namely, that they find it more difficult to save than to borrow and pay back later. Thus, they are found to depend on credit rather than save even for the expenses that can generally be predicted or planned in advance, such as for house construction or social ceremonies like marriages (Collins *et al.*, 2009, pp.106–7). Poor households in rural areas may even lack the capacity to self-insure themselves against the regular phenomenon of income seasonality related to the annual agricultural crop cycle, let alone being able to cope with seasonal stresses of exceptional intensity in years of poor harvests (Khandker and Mahmud, 2012, pp.70–75).

It is easy to see, therefore, why poor households have traditionally relied on informal credit sources for meeting various needs – ranging from coping with unforeseen emergencies and livelihood shocks, to lump-sum spending for social ceremonies, to consumption-smoothing in the face of intermittent short-term income shortfalls. Until microcredit appeared in the picture, business capital used to constitute a relatively small proportion of the credit portfolios of these households. The land-poor households were specially disadvantaged in getting affordable business loans compared to relatively better-off farm households, which could get loans on easier terms by offering land as security.[14] Access to microcredit has thus helped the MFI clients to use credit for IGAs which were not previously profitable at the high interest rates charged by moneylenders or for which enough credit was not available from other lower-cost informal sources. However, it is now increasingly recognised that loans from microcredit programmes are used in various ways other than as business loans. Recent survey findings show that substantial portions of these loans are used for various non-business purposes such as the purchase of consumer durables, the construction or improvement of dwelling houses, spending on health and education and repayment of old loans (see Chapter 8 for detailed discussions on this). Contrary to the declared social mission of the MFIs, the loans are found to be used sometimes even to meet the wedding expenses of daughters, including the payment of dowry, even though one of the 16 vows that the Grameen Bank borrowers have to make is not to pay or demand dowry.

The use of microcredit for non-business purposes is considered by the MFIs as a deviation from their primary social mission, and also a likely source for repayment difficulties. If so, the original twin missions of the microcredit movement – to primarily provide capital for IGAs of the poor households and at the same time to free them from the clutches of moneylenders – were somewhat misconceived. However, after decades of experience, the MFIs have now begun to realise that poor people can benefit from loans beyond running IGAs. Though not yet reflected formally in the loan contracts, there is a rethinking about the legitimate boundaries of microfinance services for the poor – an issue which we shall discuss later in several contexts. This issue is reminiscent of the debate surrounding the enactment of the Co-operative Societies Act of 1904 in colonial India, when it was argued that the proposed provision of restricting loans for productive purposes alone was not only difficult to enforce, but also would be unwise if the potential borrowers had to depend on usurious moneylenders for other loans (Islam, 1978, p.179). Beyond the stipulations of the MFIs regarding loan use, the lending modalities of microcredit also make it difficult to use the loans for certain non-business credit needs. For example, microcredit loans are not suitable for meeting seasonal food stress if the current living expenses saved are not at least sufficient to pay the weekly instalments. Again, because of the timing of the loan cycle, microcredit cannot directly meet emergency needs; it can do so only indirectly when an MFI client is able to secure a loan from a moneylender with the assurance that the client will repay that loan out of her next microcredit loan. This creates yet another link, perhaps one with growing importance, between microcredit and informal moneylending.[15]

A beneficial role of microcredit in creating new demand for credit, which is not often fully appreciated, has a behavioural foundation related to the saving difficulties of the poor mentioned earlier. It is well-known that poor households face saving difficulties because of the pressure of immediate spending needs that lead to present-biased preference with a high time discount, or they may simply lack the ability to save or plan for the future in the face of uncertain livelihoods. While these explanations alone could explain the credit dependence of the poor, there is more to it. Recent studies in behavioural economics have focused on what is termed as 'time-inconsistent preference', or, simply put, a lack of self-control that can create a gap between a saving plan and its actual execution (Ashraf et al., 2006; Banerjee and Mullainathan, 2010). The poor may thus need an external 'commitment factor' to realise their saving plan. Microcredit contracts in effect provide a saving device when the loans are used for some lump-sum spending, such as for acquiring consumer durables or house construction, and repaid in regular small instalments out of household income. This is also true when the loans are used for fixed investment in income-generating projects for which the payoff period extends beyond the one-year loan cycle, so that the loans are repaid at least partly from savings out of regular household income. Recent experimental studies have shown that the attractiveness of microcredit programmes lies at least partly in their lending modalities that require, in effect, a commitment to saving in regular small amounts (Bauer et al., 2012; for more evidence on this, see Chapter 8).

Further insights on how microcredit programmes have been able to both expand the credit market for the poor as well as replace parts of the informal credit market can be gained from the findings of the InM survey on *Impact of Microcredit* on *Gender Norms and Behaviour* mentioned earlier (to be discussed in detail in Chapter 8). The respondent borrowers were asked whether they would have spent the same amount out of the loans (or less or not all) on various categories of spending in the absence of microcredit and, if so, how they would have raised the money. As expected, the dependence on microcredit as the main source of borrowing for investing in IGAs was evident from these survey responses. Among the borrowers who spent the loan amounts mainly on non-productive items, about one-fourth of them would not have purchased those items at all without access to microcredit – thus indicating the role of microcredit in creating an entirely new credit market – while the rest would have purchased the items fully or partly by raising the money from other sources, including mostly from informal sources of credit, thus indicating the role of microcredit in replacing informal credit (see Tables 8.5 and 8.6 in Chapter 8). The creation of credit demand was particularly evident when the microcredit loans were used for such purposes as house construction, the purchase of consumer durables or spending on health and education. But when the loans were used for meeting marriage expenses or the repayment of old loans or some type of crisis management, the alternative to microcredit would have been borrowing from informal sources – and also, in some cases, by resorting to such desperate measures as the sale or mortgage of assets. Thus, to the extent that microcredit was used for the latter purposes, it either replaced higher-cost, informal sources of credit, or helped avoid even more corrosive crisis-coping mechanisms. Overall, microcredit appears to have replaced a part of the traditional money-lending practices for the benefit of poor borrowers, and like any other technological or institutional innovations, it also created markets where there were none.

2.2.2 Interest rates

The likely impact on the interest rates is another aspect of the interactions between microcredit and informal credit markets. Since the spread of microcredit can undercut the monopoly power of informal moneylenders, it might be expected that the interest rates charged by them would also be reduced. But the reverse may also happen. Although moneylenders may now serve a smaller number of clients than they used to before the advent of microcredit, the cost of moneylending may have gone up due to cream skimming of borrowers by MFIs, resulting in higher risks and transaction costs for moneylenders in dealing with less creditworthy borrowers. A smaller number of clients may also lead to higher fixed costs per borrower. There is not, however, much evidence from research findings to go by.

A recent study based on survey data from 106 villages in Bangladesh came up with the expected result that MFI competition does reduce moneylenders' interest rates (Mallick, 2012). The household panel data of Hossain and Bayes (2009) show that the spread of microcredit has driven down the moneylenders' rate of interest only to a modest extent, from an average annual rate of 120 percent in 1988 to 100 percent in 2008, and even to a lesser extent in the case of loans from friends and relatives (from 53 percent in 2008 to 51 percent in 1988).

However, another recent study by Berg *et al.* (2015), which uses data from a cross-sectional household survey and takes advantage of a recently developed econometric approach for non-experimental data in the impact evaluation literature, comes up with somewhat contrary findings. The results of their study suggest that the penetration of microcredit in a village, after reaching high enough membership coverage, actually increases the moneylenders' interest rate, although there is no such effect at low levels of microcredit coverage. The authors provide a plausible explanation in terms of the higher lending costs for moneylenders with fewer and less creditworthy clients. The nature of the local economy may also be a factor in this respect. The cross-sectional data in this study come from an InM survey which was carried out in an economically depressed region of the country known for its vulnerability to extreme seasonal hunger (Khandker and Mahmud, 2012). Faced with dire situations, those who are left out of microcredit may be willing to pay high interest rates, while they may also represent high credit risks from the moneylender's point of view. These findings reflect the fact that, in spite of considerable overlaps in the markets for microcredit and traditional moneylending, the segmentation in the rural credit markets may have become even more complex, with the traditional duality between formal and informal markets being replaced by the more dominant duality between informal markets and microcredit.

The above discussion raises the question of how the interest rate of microcredit itself is determined and to what extent the demand for microcredit is responsive to the interest rate. The interest rates charged by the MFIs, which in terms of effective annual rate currently vary in the range of 20 to 27 percent, reflect a balance of their social mission of poverty alleviation and their goal of achieving financial sustainability.[16] This range of interest rates has evolved through a combination of factors: the interest rate initially set by Grameen Bank setting an industry standard or norm, a degree of self-regulation imposed by PKSF through its partner MFIs, and a cost-plus approach in which the minimum floor is determined by adding to the operating cost an 'imputed' interest rate representing the cost of fund (the actual cost of fund may not be very meaningful if the funds come as grants or concessional loans, which was the case in the early years; see Table 10.1 in Chapter 10). If the cost of fund were to be determined by the deposit rate of interest offered by the commercial banks or by the bank rate (the interest rate charged by the central bank for its refinancing facility), most MFIs would be financially self-sufficient at the interest rates they charge. However, except for Grameen Bank, MFIs are not allowed to collect deposits other than from the members of their microcredit programmes. While the MFIs were initially funded by grants and concessional loans from external donors and the government (partly channelled through PKSF), those sources have gradually dried up; but the MFIs have been able to continue to build up their revolving loan funds from operating surpluses and increasing amounts of members' savings.

There is a debate about whether the MFIs' interest rates should be capped by self-regulation, as was previously practiced, or by statutory regulation, as has been recently introduced with the establishment of the Microcredit Regulatory Authority.[17] The main argument against the capping of interest rate is that the MFIs can generate larger surpluses by charging a higher interest rate so that they can expand the size of their revolving fund and programme coverage. Accessing funds from commercial banks is, however, not an option, given the large differences between the deposit and lending rates of interest of these banks – reflecting an extremely inefficient banking sector with high costs of financial intermediation.

The case for regulating the interest rate of MFIs, on the other hand, is partly to do with public aversion against charging high interest from the poor, but mainly based on economic logic. The resentment against high interest rates has historical and religious roots and is associated in public perception with the exploitative practices of traditional moneylenders. Concerns about exploitative moneylenders and usurious interest rates motivated governments for centuries in many countries to enact anti-usury laws, which however could hardly be implemented nor drive out the moneylenders. It is because of moneylenders' high interest rates that the official view of the informal credit market has been that it served no useful purpose, until microcredit arrived on the scene and converted at least a part of the credit market for public benefit (Reddy, 2002, pp.65–82). The economic logic of controlling the interest rate, on the other hand, arises from the observation of the nature of the credit demand of the poor that allows moneylenders to continue to operate and charge very high interest rates. A deviant MFI can thus charge high interest rates by being indiscriminate about the use of loans and choice of borrowers, particularly if it is willing to use coercive measures of loan recovery; such reckless lending behaviour would not only be of obvious distress for the borrowers but also could damage the public image of the entire microcredit industry. Moreover, it is also argued that the benefit from the increased operational efficiency of the MFIs taking place over the years should go to the poor clients in the form of affordable interest rates rather than accruing to MFIs as their operational surplus.

The question still remains regarding whether and to what extent demand for credit among potential borrowers will vary with variations in the interest rate – even if within an acceptable range – which has to do with the interest-elasticity of demand for microcredit. The interest-elasticity of credit demand has policy implications regarding whether withdrawing subsidised funding of microcredit programmes and letting MFIs increase the interest rate will adversely affect their programme coverage. While the MFIs do compete, to an extent, with each other for expanding the membership of their programmes, the interest rate is only one of many features of the relative attractiveness of the loan products they offer. This makes it difficult to separately estimate the impact of the interest rate on credit demand. One rare study on this subject came up with an econometrically estimated negative interest-elasticity of credit demand among slum dwellers in Dhaka; in other words, the interest rate does matter in determining demand (Dehejia et al., 2012).

2.3 Nature of participation: long-term benefits or a debt trap?

Participation in microcredit programmes is characterised by repeated borrowings, often with increasing sizes of loans. The fact that customers continue borrowing from year to year, rejoin after a temporary exit, and maintain a high rate of repayment, can be taken as a sign that they value the microfinance services offered. But repeated borrowing from year to year is also consistent with being trapped in debt due to over-indebtedness, the anecdotal evidence of which is often cited by critics. Over-indebtedness, however, can be looked at in different ways. If we are to measure it by the size of the outstanding debt burden as a proportion of household net asset, the microcredit participants are in fact expected to be found more indebted than non-participants, at least to start with, since the very purpose of microcredit is to give loans to asset-poor households. The important indicator to look for is whether the increased debt burden leads to an accumulation or depletion of assets, which will be reflected in a change of net worth (the value of physical and financial assets netted out of the outstanding debt), or whether the debt-income ratio or the debt-asset ratio eventually increases to an unsustainable level.

2.3.1 The time-profile of participation

An opportunity to observe the long-term pattern of participation in microcredit programmes is provided by a set of household panel survey data from rural areas spread over a 20-year period. This survey was with respect to a nationally representative sample of rural households conducted by the World Bank jointly with the Bangladesh Institute of Development Studies (BIDS) in 1991/92 and 1998/99 and with the Institute of Microfinance in 2010/11. Based on information on the households which were common in all three surveys, it is possible to find the long-term pattern of programme participation, including entry, exit and re-entry in the intervening periods of the survey years.[18] The proportion of households participating in the microcredit programmes increased from 26 percent of the sample households to 68 percent during the 20-year period; another 8 percent were found to be dropouts in 2010/11, while the rest of the 24 percent never participated.[19] Remarkably, about 90 percent of the original participants in 1991/92 were found to remain with the programmes in 2010/11. Although about 10 percent of these original participants had exited by 1998/99, most of them re-entered during the later period, so that the exits of the original participants by 2010 had taken place mostly during the later period. The dropout rate is, however, somewhat higher though still low among the newer participants; about 17 percent of the entrants in the first period were found to have exited by the end of the second period (Khandker and Samad, 2014, p.142).

A trend is clear from these observed participation patterns – households that once participated in microcredit programmes mostly remained with the programmes over time, while new entries to the programmes resulted in substantial growth in membership.[20] However, one problem with these estimates based on panel household data is that the split households are merged with the original households for the purpose of analysis, which could have biased the estimates of both retention and dropout rates. For example, the programme participation rate of 68 percent among the sample households in 2010/11 seems to be too high compared to the other survey findings discussed earlier, even if we take into account that about 20 percent of the participant households were not current borrowers.[21] Nevertheless, these findings point to an important aspect of the microcredit programmes, namely, MFIs have a long-term relationship with their clients that even transcends through generations as households split. This, however, ignores switching from one MFI to another – a phenomenon that has been increasing with more competition among MFIs to attract clients.

Another notable aspect of the membership pattern discussed above is the re-entry of exiting participants. This phenomenon is captured only partly in the survey findings discussed above, which are based on only three snapshots over two decades and thus miss the phenomenon of intermittent exit and re-entry. As such, the estimates of re-entry can be made only for those who were original participants two decades ago and had exited sometime during the first decade, and then re-entered during the second decade; these households constituted only about 5 percent of the current participants in 2010/11, the final year of the survey. This proportion is much too low compared to the findings of cross-sectional surveys. For example, in the InM survey on *Impact of Microcredit on Gender Norms and Behaviour*, nearly a fifth of the currently participating microcredit members were found to have rejoined after dropping out. This proportion is also found to be nearly the same in the *InM Poverty Survey*, suggesting a good deal of churning in and out of microcredit programmes as a whole (Osmani et al., 2015).[22] Altogether, the findings from cross-sectional and panel data suggest that, although long-term membership is the norm, this can be of both regular and intermittent types.

The above evidence on the pattern of participation in the microcredit programmes does not give a picture of poor women burning their fingers once and quit, as suggested by some critiques. On the contrary, even among those who exit the programmes, a large proportion is found to be willing to re-enter, particularly if the repayment modalities are made more flexible. For example, when Grameen Bank introduced a second track of 'flexible loan' for borrowers in temporary difficulty, not only was there an improvement in the loan repayment rates, but also many former borrowers rejoined the Bank, even by repaying their previous unpaid loans (Dowla and Barua, 2006, p.248).[23] In the case of SHARE Microfin Limited, an Indian MFI which follows the Grameen model, 30 percent of its former clients were found willing to return without any conditions and another 40 percent were willing to do so if some changes were made in lending policies, while many among the rest might have naturally been weaned off of microcredit (Kabeer, 2005). Apparently, these households perceived certain benefits from long-term microcredit participation.

The concerns about the phenomenon of repeated loan cycles over a long period of time may arise from a misconception that such loan dependence can result in only two possible outcomes: either a debt trap leading to eventual impoverishment, or a gradual scaling up of micro-entrepreneurship that provides the only route for the borrowers out of poverty. Evidence suggests that in most cases, it may be neither. As already discussed, dependence on loans was a regular feature of the day-to-day financial management of poor households even before microcredit created new opportunities for using loans for IGAs. Survey findings on the use of microcredit loans show that an individual borrower may use the loans over repeated loan cycles for a variety of purposes other than investing in businesses.[24] As regards IGAs, borrowers often use the loans as business working capital that may get depleted through loan repayment; in such a case, while some household income is generated from the business, there may not be much saving in the form of asset accumulation at the end of the loan cycle. Besides the small size of the microcredit loans, the expansion of IGAs may face the problem of a possible 'technology gap' that makes it difficult to scale up the businesses beyond subsistence to a larger, commercially viable scale (see Figure 9.1 in Chapter 9). Instead, as will be discussed in the later chapters, access to microcredit is found to have helped poor rural households to diversify their means of livelihoods beyond the primary farming occupation. Some of them, the so-called 'entrepreneurial poor', may eventually graduate to more enriching non-farm self-employment by successfully scaling up their businesses, but the majority may continue to use access to microcredit as a means of pursuing a subsistence-type or subsidiary occupation until they can move out of poverty through other routes, such as finding salaried jobs in the formal sector (Osmani *et al.*, 2004).

The issue of over-indebtedness was examined by Khandker and Samad (2013) based on their set of household panel data for a 20-year period mentioned earlier. They found that for each of the survey years, indebtedness as measured by the outstanding debt as a ratio of non-land asset was, on average, higher among microcredit borrowers than among the comparator group of non-microcredit borrowers. They then applied econometric procedures to the panel data to examine the impact of microcredit participation on the households' asset accumulation and other well-being indicators. These findings are important for assessing the long-run poverty impact of microcredit, as we shall discuss in Chapter 7. In the present context, it is worth noting from these findings that microcredit participation, especially for women, yields many positive outcomes, including an increase over time in households' net worth and a decline in the debt-asset ratio.[25]

2.3.2 Multiple borrowing or overlapping

Another related source of concern regarding the possibility of over-indebtedness or a debt trap arises from the increasing incidence of simultaneous borrowing from multiple microloan providers, or 'overlapping' as it is called by practitioners. The negative perception about overlapping arises from a tendency to equate the phenomenon with over-indebtedness and a situation of hidden insolvency that can be characterised as borrowing from Paul to pay Peter. The culprit, in this view, is the increasing competition among the MFIs, which induces them to 'oversell' loans to those who are already clients of other MFIs. Such a view, however, ignores the demand side, namely, the possibility that borrowing from more than one MFI may be a benign or useful way for poor households to manage their finances in response to the problem of unmet credit demand. Unfortunately, there are very few studies that have tried to resolve these issues with any rigour and in-depth analysis.

An early study on repayment problems arising from multiple borrowing was by Chaudhury and Matin (2002); they looked at the regularity of payment of instalments by BRAC members who borrowed only from BRAC compared to those who had multiple NGO-MFI memberships. They found that borrowers with multiple memberships, and especially those belonging to chronic food-deficit households, were less likely to make regular payments of instalments (defined as being able to repay timely no less than 90 percent of their instalments). Moreover, the chronic deficit households were found to be more likely to adopt 'hard options' like reducing food consumption or engaging in further borrowing to manage the payment of instalments of multiple loans. It should be noted, however, that the repayment problem in this study is about a lapse in instalment payments and not about eventual default of loans. Moreover, the study relates to a time when new NGO-MFIs were entering the market in large numbers, and it was conducted in an area called Tangail, which is the birthplace of the Grameen Bank project and has perhaps the highest density of NGO-MFIs in the country.

A much more benign picture of multiple borrowing emerges from some recent studies undertaken by the InM to specifically focus on this issue (Osmani, Khalily and Hasan, 2015). In one of these studies, based on a household survey conducted in the Tangail district in 2007, overlapping was found to be quite rampant, with about 40 percent of the borrowers taking a second loan within one year (Faruqee and Khalily, 2011). However, the probability of overlapping resulting from the previous year's loan default was found to be low, which makes it unlikely that a defaulting borrower of an MFI got her next loan by paying off the instalment arrears from a second overlapping loan taken from another MFI. Overlapping was found to be caused by higher demand for loans for similar purposes, as in the case of loans without overlapping – that is, mostly for productive purposes and also for other lumpy expenditures such as for house construction or the acquisition of consumer durables. Another study on overlapping, based on a nationwide household survey carried out by InM in 2009, also arrived at similar findings, namely, no significant difference regarding the use of multiple loans compared to single loans, with enterprise financing being the major category of loan use in both cases (Khalily, 2013). Instead of growing indebtedness, both of the studies found positive incremental change in net assets and savings in the case of households with multiple borrowing.[26]

Osmani, Khalily and Hasan (2015) provide an in-depth analysis of the phenomenon of overlapping by combining the data from the InM's *Access to Financial Services* survey of 2009/10 mentioned earlier and a repeat survey of the same nationwide sample households carried out in 2015. The data from these surveys provide detailed credit histories of individual borrowers over the five-year periods preceding each round of the survey, and thus allow a dynamic analysis even to the extent of tracing the pattern of use of any repeated overlapped loans. The extent of overlapping at the household level (defined as a microcredit loan taken by a household before another one is repaid, irrespective of whichever household member is involved) increased slowly to 16 percent of all microcredit loans in 2010, but then increased quite sharply to 41 percent by 2015. However, this acceleration in the extent of overlapping was due much more to the increase in the proportion of borrower households taking overlapping loans rather than the households beginning to take an increasing number of overlapped loans. Further analysis of these credit histories shows that the borrower households took overlapping loans only after they had gained some experience in dealing with microcredit (as reflected in the duration of their MFI membership), and even then they did so only intermittently, suggesting that a certain degree of caution was usually applied while engaging in overlapping loans. Therefore, the recent spurt in the growth of overlapping loans should not be taken as a *prima facie* indication of irresponsible borrowing.

The study also did not find any significant difference in the patterns of loan use, irrespective of whether the comparison was between the households with or without overlapping loans or between overlapped and other loans.[27] In these comparisons, enterprise financing was found to be consistently the dominant use of loans, while overlapping did not seem to affect the relatively small proportion of loans used for the repayment of previous loans.[28] However, when the use of the repeated overlapping loans of an individual household over a five-year period (in this case, 2010 to 2015) was considered, contrasting patterns of the dynamic use of overlapping loans emerged. Those who used their first overlapping loan mainly for enterprise financing continued to do so for subsequent overlapping loans, although to a somewhat lesser extent; and these households accounted for nearly a half of the households who engaged in such overlapping. By contrast, for the other half of these households who used the major portion of their first overlapping loan for any other purpose (defined in terms of broad categories), the importance of that initial purpose sharply declined during the use of the subsequent overlapping loans, while there was an increase in the use of loans for enterprise financing.[29] Most of them managed to keep the extent of loan diversion for the purpose of repayment of old loans out of the overlapped loans to manageable proportions of 5 to12 percent. There is a question mark, however, about the group who took the overlapping loan in the first instance for repaying old loans. This group, accounting for some 13 percent of all households engaging in overlapping, was also able to use an increasing proportion of loans for enterprise financing, but they still had to devote a sizeable proportion of repeated overlapping loans (about a quarter) towards servicing old loans.

The econometric estimates show further contrasts regarding the impact of overlapping in terms of raising household income and in accumulating net assets (defined as all physical and financial assets, excluding land and housing). When the households were distinguished by their main use of overlapping loans, those who used these loans mainly for enterprise financing outperformed on both of these indicators over the other groups of borrower households, including those who did not engage in overlapping. As for the households using the overlapping loans mainly for other categories of non-productive purposes, their ability to raise income and to maintain net worth was either worse or no better than that of households who did not engage in overlapping. This, therefore, raises some concern about the economic viability of using overlapping loans for non-productive purposes, at least for the medium-term period considered in the study.

Since there is no strong evidence of increased loan default or irresponsible use of loans resulting from multiple borrowing, it seems to arise mainly from information asymmetry regarding the credit-worthiness of borrowers and the resulting credit rationing by MFIs. This hypothesis is supported by the survey finding that the average total size of, say, two overlapping loans of a borrower falls significantly short of twice the average size of loans of borrowers who do not engage in overlapping loans; this suggests that borrowers who get less than an average-sized loan from one MFI go for multiple loans (Khalily, 2013, p.95, Table 8). From the demand side, the rigidity of microcredit lending modalities sometimes forces clients to manage their finances by working with several MFIs (Meyer, 2002). Moreover, if credit ceilings are the same for all group members, which is usually the case, an entrepreneurial borrower may need to borrow from more than one MFI to obtain the total amount desired.

There remains one other alleged route through which microcredit can create a debt trap, namely, when a microcredit loan is repaid by other loans, including another microcredit loan (Sinha and Matin, 1998). However, the risk of such a debt trap is minimised by the system of regular weekly payment of instalments over the entire loan cycle, which makes it difficult to repay one microcredit loan with another (unless the borrower chooses to pay the defaulted instalment arrears in one lump-sum payment and risks being declared as a defaulter). As for paying weekly instalments by borrowing from informal sources, only small occasional loans from friends and relatives, rather than lump-sum commercial loans, would make sense for the purpose. According to the findings of the *InM Poverty Survey2010*, only about 2 percent of all loans taken during the previous three years were repaid mainly out of other MFI loans, while another 5 percent was repaid by borrowing from informal sources, mainly from friends and relatives (Osmani et al., 2015, p.188, Table 8.22). Again, according to the findings of the InM survey on *Impact of Microcredit on Gender Norms and Behaviour* mentioned earlier, the instalments of microcredit loans are rarely (in 0.2 percent of cases) paid from the borrower's other microcredit loan, and this is so irrespective of whether the repayment is for the first loan or for an overlapping second or third loan.

2.3.3 Why do the poor over-borrow?

Much of the apprehension about why microcredit may lead to over-indebtedness arises from the fact that poor people are susceptible to over-borrowing, which may lead to their eventual impoverishment. The problem of lack of self-control and time-inconsistent preferences that makes it difficult for poor people to save may also be the reason why their dependence on credit can have a potentially addictive character and why they are tempted to make imprudent use of credit, leading to over-indebtedness (Banerjee and Mullainathan, 2010; Roodman, 2012, p.290). Whether the MFI clients are thus tempted by the availability of credit to over-borrow would largely depend on the way the MFIs operate. As will be discussed in Chapter 8, there is hardly any evidence of such 'temptation borrowing' among MFI clients in Bangladesh.[30] The MFIs with a social mission, as those in Bangladesh, need to be wary about lending practices that may need excessive coercive measures for repayment enforcement or may adversely impact the well-being outcome of their clients; thus, they have at least a triggering red signal by having to enforce repayment by coercion. However, the risk is much higher for the alternative profit-oriented model of microcredit as practiced by many MFIs worldwide. For example, the evidence from Bolivia in the 1990s, and more recently from Andhra Pradesh in India, shows how the reckless lending of some commercially motivated MFIs can have disastrous consequences (Sriram, 2010). Clearly, a standardised model that can be run in a commercially efficient manner is liable to be misused at the hands of profit-motivated MFIs in the absence of the safeguards that apply in the case of the socially oriented MFIs.

A far more common explanation of why the poor may borrow beyond their means is the absence of any better option when faced with some livelihood shocks. The possibility that such borrowing might eventually lead to adverse outcomes does not necessarily make such a decision any less rational. The age-old problem of a debt trap – arising from traditional moneylending practices like tied-credit, bonded labour, and debt burden running through generations – is a real one. Perhaps this was the background in which an Indian committee on rural indebtedness famously remarked: 'the Indian farmer is born in debt, lives in debt and dies in debt' (Reddy, 2002, p.68). This presents a dilemma for the MFIs with a social mission. In the absence of an adequate social safety net, accessing microcredit may be better than other available options for households facing livelihood shocks or other emergencies. But the MFIs are averse to such lending because of the likely problem of repayment enforcement and also because such borrowing may lead to future impoverishment, which is contrary to their declared social mission of getting people out of poverty. However, the effectiveness of microcredit in reducing livelihood vulnerabilities is perhaps underestimated. Even when borrowers divert credit to unintended uses like meeting an unexpected shock, they could end up with a far more sustainable economic condition than what would otherwise be the case.

Notes

1 BRAC is recognised to be the largest development NGO in the world.
2 BRAC and ASA subsequently opted out of partnership with PKSF.
3 In addition, the Credit and Development Forum (CDF) reported an additional 1.4 million outstanding microcredit borrowers as of the end of 2012 belonging to *Palli Daridra Bimochon Foundation* (PDBF), a government rural development agency, and Islami Bank Bangladesh Ltd. (IBBL), a commercial bank having a microcredit programme.
4 The number of beneficiary households is even smaller than that of borrowers, since each household may have more than one borrower.
5 See, for example, Amin *et al.* (2003) and Hashemi (1997).
6 A survey of the central office staff of ASA conducted in 1997 found that the overwhelming proportion of them thought that certain attitudes of the field staff impeded the inclusion of the poorest, namely, lack of motivation, aversion to dealing with

troublesome cases and reluctance to work in remote areas (cited by Rahman, 2000, p.67, Table 4.5).
7 The Grameen Bank ordinance contains the stipulation of lending to households in rural areas owning less than 0.5 acre of land or owning assets worth that amount of land.
8 These figures are taken from *Bangladesh Microfinance Statistics*, annual volumes published by the CDF.
9 The estimates apply to household proportions as well, since the survey included one woman per household, but the proportions of borrower households will be underestimated because of excluding households with male borrowers only.
10 This account leaves out very short-term loans that people often take from friends, relatives and shopkeepers to be repaid within a few days.
11 It may be noted from the survey findings that, pre-dating the spread of microcredit, friends and relatives were the predominant source of small loans which were used mainly for consumption needs (Murshid and Rahman, 1990).
12 The initial household survey was based on a nationally representative sample drawn through stratified random sampling from 64 villages, and the households were resurveyed in 1994, 2000, 2004, 2008 and 2010. Additional households were included in the later surveys to compensate for attritions.
13 In the survey results reported by Osmani *et al.* (2015), the average loan size for the category of "friends and relatives" is higher than that of microcredit, which suggests that the large commercial-type loans, presumably far fewer in number, outweigh the numerous small loans that are in the nature of mutual help.
14 See, for example, the findings on credit use reported by Murshid and Rahman (1990) based on a survey on rural informal credit markets conducted by the Bangladesh Institute of Development Studies in the late 1980s. For a review of evidence on the rural credit markets in colonial Bengal, see Islam (1978, pp.157–184).
15 Todd (1996) provides rich narratives of complex financial management practices of women borrowers of Grameen Bank, who often access lump-sum money quickly from moneylenders in advance of their next Grameen loan while also borrowing small sums informally from friends and relatives to meet Grameen loan instalments. See also Collins *et al.* (2009, p.107).
16 There is now a statutory upper limit of 27 percent for the effective annual interest rate to be charged by MFIs; the effective rate is largely double the nominal rate because of the weekly repayment during the one-year loan period. For a discussion on the prevailing interest rates charged by MFIs in Bangladesh, see Faruqee and Khalily (2011).
17 For various issues regarding the market orientation of microcredit programmes and interest rate regulation, see Cull *et al.* (2009, 2011).
18 See Khandker and Samad (2014), Figure 5, p.142.
19 The information on any previous record of dropout of the initial sample was not collected.
20 Further evidence on long-term membership patterns is provided by Islam (2011).
21 Because of the household splits, the number of panel households increased from the original 1,509 to 1,758 in 1998/99 and 2,322 in 2010/11 (Khandker and Samad, 2014).
22 The rates of dropouts, permanent or transient, may be higher in economically depressed regions, such as the Rangpur region in northeast Bangladesh, which is particularly prone to seasonal hunger. The panel household data in an InM survey carried out in that region show that more than one-third of the households which joined microcredit programmes in 2008 and 2009 dropped out at the end of the second year, although the dropout rate declined subsequently (InM, 2013, p.100). Significantly, the partner MFIs of PKSF initiated a new membership drive in that region during those years to address the endemic problem of seasonal hunger.
23 These reforms in the lending modalities of Grameen Bank, known as Grameen II, were introduced when the Bank was experiencing a repayment crisis in the late 1990s.

38 *How the credit markets work*

24 For example, see Zaman (1999, Table 7), who tracks the use of successive loans from the loan history of a sample of BRAC borrowers in two areas in the 1990s.
25 Land is not included in the estimation of total assets because of abnormal increases in land prices. Household assets includes savings. The comparison is with non-participant households who were eligible for participation in the initial year according to land-holding criteria.
26 The impact on change in net assets and savings was estimated by applying econometric procedures to household panel-like data obtained from the memory recall method.
27 The comparisons were both according to the main use of the loan or in terms of the amounts of the loans, taking into account multiple uses of the same loan.
28 Enterprise financing was found to account for about half of the total amount of all overlapping loans for the five-year period of 2010–2014, while repayment of previous loans accounted for about 12 percent.
29 These estimates are with respect to the amount of the loan used, taking into account possible multiple uses of a single overlapping loan; see Osmani, Khalily and Hasan. (2015, Tables 8 through 12).
30 This is also found to be true of socially oriented MFIs in India; see Banerjee and Duflo (2011, p.171).

3 Microcredit in Bangladesh
How the microcredit model works

The main features of the classic microcredit model pioneered by Grameen Bank in Bangladesh and replicated worldwide are well-known from the literature. It is a system of group-lending under which clients from poor families, predominantly women, form groups to receive collateral-free small loans that are repaid in regular weekly or frequent instalments, usually within a one-year loan cycle, and for which the group bears joint responsibility. While, in theory, the model can be shown to solve a number of problems that historically plagued government efforts of providing credit to the poor, the relative importance of the various features of the model remains largely conjectural. The empirical studies on this subject based on worldwide experience, which will be discussed in Chapter 6, often suffer from the limitation that there may not be enough variations in the basic features of the existing lending modalities among the MFIs in a country so as to provide data for econometric tests (Morduch, 1999, p.1586). The other possibility is to undertake randomised controlled trials (RCTs) regarding the effectiveness of various features of the lending modalities, but such experimental studies are liable to be limited in scope for practical reasons. Yet another possible way is to look at the process of evolution of the system as the practitioners tried to overcome the limitations of the model and responded to the changing and varied needs of the borrowers. Bangladesh has now got a long enough history of experimentation with microcredit programmes for allowing such a Darwinian approach to analysing how the system has evolved through numerous innovations, mutations and adaptations. In this chapter, we shall look at the various aspects of this evolutionary process in the Bangladesh context before proceeding on to reviewing the theories of microcredit and their empirical tests based on worldwide experience – the subject matter of the next three chapters.

The logic of why the group-based model of collateral-free credit delivery – the so-called Grameen model – should work better than the normal lending operations of banks is that the functions of screening prospective borrowers, monitoring the use of loans and enforcement of repayment are, to a large extent, transferred to the group, which acts as the lender's agent. The incentives for this arise from the joint liability of the group for loan repayment and potential loss of access to future loans. The cost-effectiveness of this arrangement arises from the fact that, compared to socially and physically distant bank agents, group members can obtain information more easily on reputation, indebtedness, wealth and effort of fellow members. Compared to bank agents, group members also have a comparative advantage to compel repayment from delinquent borrowers by employing social sanctions; and they are also better able to assess the reason for default and to offer insurance services to those experiencing shocks beyond their control, while imposing sanctions on wilful defaulters.

The model, however, has evolved considerably in Bangladesh since its inception in the late 1970s. While some of its defining features still remain widely prevalent, there now exists a wide range of variations in the lending practices, particularly among the relatively larger MFIs, with varying degrees of resemblance to the original Grameen model. More importantly, Grameen Bank itself overhauled its own lending system in 2001 with the introduction of what it calls Grameen II, allowing far more flexibility for its clients in accessing and repaying loans. An important feature of this evolutionary process is the gradual dilution of the rigorous discipline that the MFIs used to impose on borrowers through the rigid lending modalities. But despite this dilution, the high loan recovery rates of MFIs do not seem to have suffered, while the credit needs of their clients are also now better served.

How has this been possible? Besides reviewing the limited amount of available literature specifically focusing on this topic, we shall try to answer this question by drawing upon the insights of the microcredit practitioners who know from their experience how these adaptations, mutations and modifications of the original model have actually come about. In addition, we look at some recent survey findings focusing on the experience and opinion of the borrowers themselves about the evolving microcredit delivery system in Bangladesh. These findings come from the second round of the InM's *Poverty Dynamics Survey* carried out in 2013 covering a nationally representative sample of 6,300 rural households and a further in-depth survey of a sub-sample of 900 households carried out in 2015.[1]

3.1 Group lending and repayment enforcement

In the standard arrangement of the classic Grameen model, borrowers are required in the first instance to form small groups (typically of five people), and although loans are given to individual members, the group as a whole would be responsible for each member's loan repayment under a system of 'joint liability'. Another condition is that borrowers must attend weekly meetings in which loan officers disburse and collect loans with the endorsement of the group and in a publicly transparent manner. Furthermore, the Grameen model follows a two-tier system of group formation: the five-member group is meant to be the main sphere of interaction among the borrowers and the application of joint liability, and in a second tier, these groups are coalesced into a larger body (variously called as *Kendra* or *Samity*, etc.) which provides the scope for another layer of interaction among a larger number of members. However, for some MFIs – most notably, BRAC – the larger body of *Samity* is all there is, often consisting of 20 to 40 borrowers.

3.1.1 The decline of joint liability

In practice, joint liability in the form of strict contractual obligation has rarely existed in Bangladesh and has been invoked by MFIs only in varying degrees. Peers were never formally obliged to pay up on behalf of the defaulters, although MFIs might have put informal pressure on the peers to collect money from the prospective defaulter, and in the extreme case, to pay the weekly payment on behalf of the defaulting member as a loan to her. A more common practice was that the MFIs would deny, or threaten to deny, loans to other members if one of the members were to default. Even this is changing; and increasingly joint liability takes a much looser form in which the MFIs either cajole or coerce the peers to bring the defaulting member into line instead of denying loans to the group. Grameen Bank itself, which first implemented the idea of joint liability in a systematic manner, has now formally abandoned it with the introduction of what it calls Grameen II (Dowla and Barua, 2006). However, nearly all MFIs, including BRAC, still retain it in some form or the other.

The decline and the changing character of the joint-liability system observed from the field are also evident from the findings of the sub-sample part of the *InM Poverty Survey* mentioned earlier. The group/*Samity* borrowers were asked about their perception of how frequently the MFIs invoked joint liability when one of their peers either defaulted or were about to default – both now and before (that is, at the time they first entered the microcredit market). Three types of actions by the MFIs are interpreted as enforcing joint liability: (a) putting pressure on the peers to obtain the instalment one way or the other, (2) threatening to withhold loans to peers unless default was prevented, and (3) actually cutting off loans to peers in case a default happened. The distribution of the respondent borrowers in answering this question, shown in Table 3.1, indicates that joint liability used to be regularly enforced in the past through all such MFI actions, but there has been a sharp decline in the incidence of each of such actions over the years. However, in

Table 3.1 Distribution of borrowers by their perception of application of joint-liability pressure, before and now (percent of borrowers)

MFI action	Before	Now
MFI pressures peers for instalment payment		
Frequently or fairly regularly	71.8	31.4
Seldom or never	28.2	68.6
MFI threatens group members to cut off loans		
Frequently or fairly regularly	82.0	37.6
Seldom or never	18.0	72.4
MFI cuts off loans to group members		
Frequently or fairly regularly	69.2	11.3
Seldom or never	30.8	88.7

Source: *InM Poverty Survey* (sub-sample) of 2015; adapted from Osmani (2015b).

Note: 'Before' refers to the time when the respondents joined the microcredit programmes.

the experience of a sizeable proportion of the borrowers, MFIs still frequently put some kind of pressure on the peers for preventing default in the instalment payment of a fellow group member or threaten to cut off loans to the entire group in the case of default of a member (31 and 38 percent of the borrowers, respectively, think so), even though only a small proportion (11 percent) now finds that the actual cutting off of loans for the entire group is a regular practice.

The weakening of the enforcement of joint liability was dictated mainly by the need for making membership more attractive as MFIs' competition and coverage increased, and also because the MFIs gradually found other effective mechanisms to supplement, if not entirely substitute, the functions performed by the system of joint liability. Group members understandably resent being coerced by loan officials into being made liable for a member's missed payment. It was for preventing such coercion that the original Grameen model, while allowing other members of a group to pay for a member's missed payments, imposed a limit of four weeks for doing so (Dowla and Barua, 2006, p.77). Group members also resent waiting for the next loan because of a fellow member's default, particularly when the progressive ones among them begin to access larger-sized loans. Increasing differentiation among group members in their capability to use loans may thus give rise to tension and conflict among the group members (Dowla and Barua, 2006, p.82). There is also a reluctance on the part of the MFI staff to punish everyone in the group for the problem of a single member. Instead, they find it more convenient to exclude the defaulting member and then reconstitute the group with new members after renegotiating with the compliant members (Hashemi and Schuler, 1997; Matin, 1997; Zeller et al., 2001, p.37). A flexible interpretation of joint liability in such a situation would be to expect the group members to help assess the defaulting member's actual capacity to repay and to apply pressure to recover as much loan as is possible before letting her go.[2] Another feature of the classic Grameen model that was meant to make the system of joint liability work better, namely, the sequenced loan disbursement – with two members receiving the loan first, then another two, and finally the group leader – has also thus lost much of its original logic, and its practice has been on the decline. Increased competition among MFIs has also led to much shorter 'waiting times' than before for new members to get their first loan. The remarkable aspect of all these developments is that the dilution of the original rigid lending modalities to such an extent does not appear to have adversely affected the loan repayment discipline.

Even if the enforcement of joint liability has weakened considerably, most MFIs find it useful to maintain the discipline of weekly meetings.[3] When Grameen Bank dropped joint-liability contracts under its Grameen II reformulation, it nevertheless kept its emphasis on group meetings. Group meetings have the advantage of reducing transaction costs for loan officers by gathering group members in one place at one time to quickly complete business (provided the weekly repayment system has to be retained in any case). The requirement of attending the group meetings is also a device for targeting the poor through self-selection, since women from better-off families would be reluctant to undergo the ignominy of doing so.[4] But there are also other important social dimensions. The requirement that transactions are made in public, in contrast to the privacy of a bank-client relationship in the case of the formal banking system, is in fact an integral part of the microcredit innovation. It is a cost-effective way of reducing malfeasant transactions that undermine the credit delivery systems of the government-owned agricultural and rural banks. More importantly, transactions in public view are an important way of repayment enforcement through 'shaming' in public. There is anecdotal evidence of how frantically a borrower and her husband sometimes try to raise the funds for the weekly instalment to avoid the dreaded 'red ink mark' against her name in the credit ledger book.

There are also other reasons why both borrowers and MFIs with a social mission may value the system of group lending with weekly meetings. To understand this, we need to look at how group lending with joint liability proved effective in the first place in Bangladesh. In theory, the joint-liability system, to be effective, needs mutual trust among the group members and/or their capacity to sanction one another for deviant behaviour so as to avoid the so-called 'coordination problem'. Each group member needs to believe that her fellow members will not use the loans imprudently or default wilfully since she knows that she will have to face the consequence of such deviant behaviour of the other members, and that will affect her own incentive not to behave in such deviant ways. Ideally, there needs to be an appropriate balance between such mutual trust and the threat of sanctions, since excessive sanctions against fellow members may undermine the social capital of group cohesion and mutual trust. Tilting the balance towards group cohesion has the added advantage that it encourages mutual support to cope with livelihood vulnerabilities and occasional difficulties in loan repayment. In this latter respect, the microcredit movement in Bangladesh seems to have benefited from a kinship-based rural social structure in dense settlements that has helped in forming the microcredit groups from the existing networks of relatives, friends and neighbours.[5] Survey findings show that this is indeed the case, particularly for the small five-member groups and that the groups, thus formed, worked more on the basis of mutual trust than on applying sanctions against one another (Zeller *et al.*, 2001, p.27; Kabeer, 2005; Kabeer and Matin, 2005; Osmani, 2015b).

The findings from the *InM Poverty Survey* of 2013 (main sample) show that, in the experience of the respondent group members, peer pressure or sanctions was never a major factor in repayment enforcement, *albeit* the fact that it is difficult to distinguish in such survey responses the effectiveness of threats from that of the actual occurrence of peer sanctions (Osmani, 2015b). The findings of the survey also suggest that, while mutual support among group members increased over time through group activities, this was achieved more due to the fostering of group cohesion rather than through the leverage of joint liability, the enforcement of which had been weakening anyway. Table 3.2 shows the extent of social interaction and mutual help, financial and otherwise, existing initially during group formation and fostered over time. That the microcredit borrowers value the weekly group meetings as a platform for social interactions is also supported by other studies (Kabeer, 1998; Mahmud, 2002). Clearly, the group cohesion

Table 3.2 Social interaction among members of group/*samity* (percent of respondent group members)

Type of Interaction	Group Before	Group Now	Samity (larger group) Before	Samity (larger group) Now
Mingling socially				
Yes	68.6	79.6	48.5	60.9
No	31.4	20.4	51.5	39.1
Helping each other financially				
Yes	59.2	71.5	35.0	50.9
No	40.8	28.5	65.0	49.1
Helping each other in other ways				
Yes	68.0	75.3	46.9	61.8
No	32.0	24.7	53.1	38.3

Source: *InM Poverty Survey* (main sample) of 2013; adapted from Osmani (2015b).

Note: 'Before' refers to the time when the respondent joined the microcredit group of which she is currently a member.

fostered by microcredit has proved to be far more useful beyond merely making the system of joint liability work.[6]

3.1.2 Repayment enforcement: coercion, inducement or moral pressure?

While the discipline of group lending weakened over time, other mechanisms of loan recovery seem to have gained in importance. Some observers, notably Jain and Moore (2003), have emphasised the proactive role of the MFI field staff, rather than the logic of group liability, as a more potent factor underlying the effectiveness of the microcredit delivery system in Bangladesh. Loan officers typically spend a great deal of time in the initial formation of groups, monitoring the use of loans and in 'managing' problem cases of defaulting borrowers by seeking information from fellow group members and neighbours (a loose form of what is called 'cross-reporting' in the microcredit literature). Their tasks may have been made easier by the experience gained by the MFIs over the years. For example, they know from experience that, instead of searching for the positive attributes of trustworthiness or entrepreneurial abilities of the prospective borrowers, they could use some negative screening criteria based on local knowledge (such as about potential cheats or habitual defaulters, the probability of migration or drug addiction of the husband). They also benefit from the experience of other MFIs so as to avoid particular localities unsuitable for microcredit operations, such as those that lack social cohesion, have a high rate of out-migration, or whose local economy has an extremely undiversified nature.[7] MFIs are also putting more emphasis on home visits by loan officers to gather information (as part of KYC, or 'know your customer better' in the banking vocabulary).

The evidence on the nature of long-term participation in microcredit programmes discussed in Chapter 2 is another factor explaining why credit repayment rates can be maintained even with the dilution of joint liability. Under joint liability, the threat of being cut off from future loans for the entire group creates incentive for the members to put pressure on one another for loan repayment, and joint liability ensures that this incentive works even if some individual members' own perceived benefit of access to future loans is not high enough. This 'dynamic incentive' for loan repayment seems to be sufficiently widespread among borrowers now so as to work at the individual level as well.[8] The long experience of microcredit clients in Bangladesh has helped them to realise that their relationship with the MFIs is not a transitory phenomenon, and that it is worthwhile for them to invest in a long-term relationship. This is similar to how traditional moneylenders elicit loan repayment from their clients by relying principally on developing repeated relationships with borrowers and using the threat to cut them off from future loans (Aleem, 1990; Armendáriz and Morduch, 2010, pp.140–44).[9] The relaxation of the lending modalities of MFIs has strengthened this dynamic incentive by increasing the perceived benefits of future loans. Some MFIs, Grameen Bank in particular, have further strengthened this incentive by tying an individual borrower's loan ceiling to her repayment and saving performance. There is, however, a risk that increasing competition among MFIs can erode the dynamic incentive for repayment by creating the option of switching from one programme to another, which is one reason why MFIs are putting increased emphasis on collecting information on the credit history of prospective borrowers.

The MFIs have successfully used female agency as a vehicle for both repayment enforcement and for achieving their social mission. Female borrowers, compared to their male counterparts, are found to be culturally more sensitive to social shaming and peer pressure when repayment difficulties arise, and they are also likely to use loans more prudently and commit to savings through imposed self-discipline (Morduch, 1999, p.1784; Rahman, 1999). Moreover, women members' group meetings can be a platform for disseminating social development ideas. Grameen Bank led the way to take advantage of using female agency, with the percentage of their female membership increasing from 20 to 40 percent in the early years of its establishment to 65 percent in 1985, to 91 percent in 1990 and to 97 percent currently. Another large MFI, ASA, experimented in the late 1990s to dispense with the group-liability system by leaning on the husbands or close male relatives of the female members and inducting them as associate members of the extended female groups. The experiment did poorly, even compared to male-only groups, and the system was subsequently dispensed with. The female-only groups are now the overwhelmingly dominant form of group lending across all MFIs.

Another important factor is the role of NGO-MFIs in Bangladesh, particularly the larger ones among them, as community-based organisations offering a range of non-credit services to their clients and other poor people in the community. These non-credit services encompass virtually every area of community development – relief and rehabilitation, health, education, human rights, and social and environmental protection, to name a few. This role has given the MFIs a kind of moral authority over their clients, which has been described by some authors as a new kind of patron-client relationship alongside the one already existing in the traditional structure of rural society in Bangladesh (Khan, 1996; Kamal, 2000). While such a relationship has helped loan recovery, it also puts a limit on the extent of coercion that could be applied without tarnishing the 'social guardian' image of the MFIs. Not surprisingly, it is the smaller MFIs, having less clout in the community, which pursue more rigidly the original credit delivery model. Again, among the large MFIs, only ASA does not have any community involvement other than delivering financial services; and perhaps not coincidentally, it is also unique in having to use elite pressure, mostly through the involvement of members of local government bodies, as one of its loan-recovery mechanisms.

The extent of coercion applied by MFIs for loan recovery, beyond the framework of peer pressure under group lending, remains one of the most debated aspects of the microcredit programmes in Bangladesh and elsewhere. The coercive methods used by loan officers may vary from harassment and mistreatment of clients by using threatening language and public humiliation, to seizing household assets of clients or even compelling them to take children out of school in order to repay on time. Loan officers allegedly resort to such coercive measures under pressure to achieve financial targets and maintain high repayment rates, although the official policies of MFIs do not approve of such measures (Copestake, 2007; Cons and Paprocki, 2010). In the opinion of field observers, there was much substance to such allegations so far as the period of rapid expansion of microcredit coverage in the 1990s is concerned, but the prevalence of such practices has declined since then. This view is also supported by the findings of the *InM Poverty Survey* (sub-sample) of 2015 regarding the perceptions of the respondent borrowers in this respect (Table 3.3). The MFIs in Bangladesh, unlike the profit-oriented ones, seem to have a self-correcting mechanism in response to allegations of coercive practices that tarnish their public image and are contrary to

Table 3.3 Borrowers' perceptions of intensity of use of coercive methods for loan recovery (percent of borrowers)

Method of coercion	Before	Now
Confiscation of Assets		
Frequently or fairly regularly	69.4	11.7
Seldom or never	30.7	83.3
Misbehaviour by MFI staff		
Frequently or fairly regularly	86.4	39.7
Seldom or never	13.6	60.3

Source: *InM Poverty Survey* (sub-sample) of 2015; adapted from Osmani (2015b).

Note: 'Before' refers to the time when the respondents joined the microcredit programmes.

their social mission. For example, the extent of coercion is now reportedly limited to the loan officers visiting the house of the defaulting borrower and making some nuisance in front of the neighbours.[10] Seizing of assets is not socially acceptable anymore, and there are reportedly instances of group members refusing to pay their instalments if a fellow member is seen to be unfairly mistreated – a reversal of the logic of group responsibility.

Overall, the currently prevailing view of field observers and microcredit practitioners is that a 'stick and carrot' policy of using some degree of 'public shaming' and making credit and other financial services more attractive to the clients is all that is needed for maintaining high loan repayment rates. But that does not seem to entirely explain how it has been possible to move away from the original rigid model of credit delivery while also softening the coercive measures of loan recovery. One plausible hypothesis is that loan repayment, even if enforced initially by coercive measures, is habit-forming – leading to a culture of loan repayment as a social behavioural norm (Mahmud, 2003; Banerjee and Duflo, 2011, pp.174–5).[11] Feedback from the fieldwork of researchers also indicates the rising importance of social stigma attached to loan default (Osmani, 2015b). Apart from the established norm of repayment of microcredit loans, the spread of education and increasing school enrolment also seems to have had a role. As children are going to school in increasingly large numbers, parents feel that their loss of face to their own children (as they in turn lose face to other children in the school) would be a heavy price to pay in case they were stigmatised as loan defaulters.

The above observations are supported by the findings of the *InM Poverty Survey* (sub-sample) of 2015. The overwhelming majority of the respondents (78 percent) thought that the practice of microcredit had contributed to bringing about a culture of non-default that was increasingly ingrained in the social psyche and extended even beyond the realm of microcredit to other credit transactions. When asked about precisely how microcredit had contributed to this change, the main reasons cited were habit formation (58 percent), accentuation of social sigma from default (22 percent) and increased incentive for future loans (20 percent). The strengthening of the loan-repayment culture in this way can be illustrated by the so-called Schelling diagram (Figure 3.1) used for explaining behavioural norms in terms of frequency-dependent equilibrium (Andvig, 1991; Bardhan and Udry, 1999, pp.231–2).

In Figure 3.1, the x-axis shows the percentage of borrowers repaying and the y-axis shows the benefit and cost of non-repayment for an individual borrower. The benefit, represented by the B-curve, is the monetary gain of not repaying, which is $L(1+r)$, where L is the principal loan amount and r is the interest rate. The C-curve shows the monetary equivalent of the cost arising from the sense of guilt for breaking the social norm of repayment and from the social stigma of being labeled as a defaulter; the cost depends on how many other borrowers are repaying and for how long. The initial cost curve is the lower one (C_1), which obtains after universal repayment is enforced, say, by coercive measures. This will remain as a stable equilibrium unless some shock (flood, political backlash) makes the repayment rate fall below the threshold level at point M, thus setting off a domino effect of

48 *How the microcredit model works*

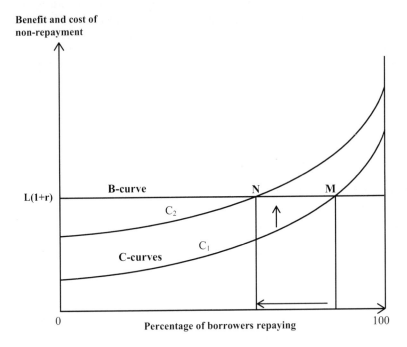

Figure 3.1 Loan repayment by habit formation and cultural norms

further decline in the repayment rate, leading to a collapse of the system.[12] Over time, the cost curve moves upward (C_2) as the repayment culture gets more firmly established, so that the tipping point for setting off a domino effect shifts to a lower level of repayment rate at point N. While a near full repayment rate is maintained in most microfinance systems to avoid a domino effect, what makes Bangladesh different is that such a state has prevailed for a long time, along with a shift in the social attitude to loan default so as to raise an individual's cost of non-repayment. That has made the microcredit system in Bangladesh resilient to shocks while also making it less necessary for MFIs to resort to coercive methods of loan recovery.

3.2 Repayment modalities and the loan size

An essential element of the classic Grameen model is the requirement of loan repayment in equal weekly instalments over a one-year loan cycle. This aspect of the loan contracts, which is in sharp contrast to the periodic lump-sum repayment schedules of commercial lending, has in fact proved to be much more enduring than the much discussed stipulation of group liability. The logic of loan repayment in fixed regular instalments, therefore, requires careful scrutiny, particularly since this requirement has proved to be a major constraint for prospective poor clients in accessing microcredit.

3.2.1 Weekly instalments

The weekly payments are, most of all, a device to ensure that the borrower has the capacity to repay her loan out of her regular household income, irrespective of the way the loan is used. The requirement to start repayment within a few weeks (along with depositing savings) is a way of testing that the household has an alternative and predictable source of income from which the weekly instalments can be paid, which is a recognition of the fact that the loans may not always be used for IGAs.[13] The structure of repayment in small frequent instalments also serves several other purposes: to address the difficulty of poor households to keep cash in hand; to detect early signs of repayment difficulties and prevent the borrower from hiding insolvency by repaying one loan with another; and to provide, in effect, a useful device for 'committed savings', such as when the loan is used for house construction or for acquiring consumer durables. As Bauer et al. (2012) observe, the repayment process looks and feels much like saving in frequent small increments from regular income rather than that of a typical business loan.

The one-year loan cycle reflects the reluctance of MFIs to risk lending, long-term and without collaterals, to poor families lacking secure legal identities. They need to reassess at the end of each loan cycle the circumstances of the borrowers (e.g. debt liabilities incurred otherwise, ties with outside family members and chances of a change of residence, and the effect of any external shocks to livelihoods). In this respect, MFIs seem to have similar concerns as in the case of informal lenders who limit their loans to sums that they can be reasonably sure to recover within a predictable time span, and during which they expect to be able to keep tabs on the borrower. The lure of another loan far off may also reduce the repayment incentive. The duration of the loan cycle, in turn, dictates the small size of the loan in relation to the household income so as to make the weekly instalments affordable for poor clients. The microcredit model is also thus designed in a way so that loans can be invested in businesses with loan values calibrated to the capacity of the business to repay the loan from its revenues within the one-year loan period, at the end of which new capital can be pumped in via a new loan (Collins et al., 2009, pp.128–9).

The constraints on poor borrowers imposed by these repayment modalities are obvious. For example, forcing weekly repayment apparently defies the logic of agrarian cash flows, given the seasonality of rural incomes with annual cycles of periods of stress (Khandker and Mahmud, 2012). Even when the loans are used as business investments, the revenue flows in most cases may not match the weekly repayment schedule. Thus, the selection of borrowers has to be, in effect, based on an assessment of each borrower's ability to repay in her worst week, which dictates that the loan size be even smaller. Not surprisingly, the burden of weekly payment is cited as the major reason by prospective borrowers for not joining microcredit programmes or for dropping out (Hashemi, 1997; Hashemi and Schuler, 1997; Rahman, 2000, p.58; InM, 2013, pp.99–101).

If the weekly repayments are to be made out of the IGA revenues rather than from household savings, it severely restricts the types of IGAs that can be financed by microcredit. Because of the one-year loan cycle, an investment in fixed capital will need a similarly short payoff period, with the fixed capital representing the net asset accumulation at the end of the period. The loans are therefore used more frequently as business working capital, which then gets depleted as the loan is repaid; this can thus create disruptive cycles of expansion and contraction of the business. The weekly repayment schedule puts further restrictions on the choice of IGAs, since most agricultural activities have distinct production cycles, resulting in a mismatch of revenue flows with the weekly payments. There are, however, some arguments in favour of the system of regular payments in small amounts, such as the attractiveness of the system in solving the self-discipline issues of the poor discussed in Chapter 2 (Bauer *et al.*, 2012). It has also been argued that the system of weekly instalments may have induced rural households to look for IGAs that yield returns on a regular basis, thus helping to diversify the rural economy.

The MFIs are aware of these problems in their lending modalities, and they have to balance the credit needs of their clients with the requirements of maintaining credit recovery discipline. Although they put much emphasis on the weekly repayment schedule, some degree of flexibility has always been allowed by loan officials for practical reasons. However, the practice of allowing potential defaulters to make deferred payments seems to have now become more frequent. Increasingly, MFIs are also finding innovative ways of rescheduling loans when there are good reasons to believe that a repayment problem has arisen due to genuine distress beyond the control of the borrowers. In the *InM Poverty Survey* (subsample) of 2015, nearly two-thirds of the respondent borrowers said that MFIs allowed them deferred payments to an extent. About a fifth of them thought that the practice of loan rescheduling due to deferred payments used to be frequent or fairly regular at the time when they joined microcredit programmes, while nearly half of them thought that this was the case at the present time.

Besides the deferred payments allowed informally by loan officers, MFIs are now introducing mechanisms to address the problems of individual borrowers who face temporary difficulties. For example, in the reformulated Grameen II, a borrower with repayment difficulty may switch to a 'flexible loan' that allows an easier repayment schedule spread over a longer period, thus providing a safety valve to avoid expulsion.[14] Even for the regular loan, called the 'basic loan', the loan period may be allowed to vary from three months to three years and weekly instalments to vary according to the seasons, provided the schedule is agreed upon in advance; however, this provision may still exist more on paper than in practice. Another deviation allowed under certain conditions by Grameen Bank and some other MFIs is to allow a borrower to borrow the amount repaid halfway through the loan cycle in order to replenish the working capital in the business in which the loan was invested in the first place. Other MFIs allow the payment of the last few instalments at a time in advance to access the next loan. One MFI, BURO Tangail, experimented on a small scale in the mid-1990s with a 'line of credit' system similar to that of commercial banks, allowing the borrower to repay only the amount of interest while retaining the principal amount of the loan for working capital; but this system did not work well and was not replicated (Alamgir, 1999a, p.42). Increasingly, MFIs are also promoting saving schemes that can help borrowers maintain their repayment schedule at difficult times (Osmani, 2015b).

The recent introduction of 'seasonal loans' and 'agricultural loans' by PKSF through its partner MFIs represents an attempt to align the repayment schedules with the timing of flows of returns from agricultural activities with production cycles, such as crop production, cow fattening or vegetable gardening. BRAC has also recently introduced a microcredit programme to provide crop loans for tenant farmers. The repayment schedules for these loans vary from the amount of the instalments increasing towards the end of the production cycle, to a one-time full repayment, say, after a six-month loan period. While earlier attempts by Grameen Bank to introduce such loans did not succeed much, PKSF's portfolios of these loans have been the fastest growing ones since their introduction (Faruqee, 2010). Grameen Bank's other experiment that did not work well was to lease capital equipment and extend the loan period up to three years; either the equipment was taken back after one year, or the borrower had the option of owning the equipment by repaying the interest and principal over the extended period. This was designed so as to address the problem of investing in a fixed investment with a payoff period extending beyond one year. The experiment met with only limited success and has not been replicated, which only goes to vindicate the logic of MFIs' loan repayment schedule and the constraints it creates on the choice of IGAs.[15]

3.2.2 Larger-sized loans for scaled-up enterprises

The microcredit programmes in Bangladesh have recently witnessed the growth of so-called 'microenterprise loans', which are larger sized and usually dispensed under a variety of lending modalities different from those that apply to regular microcredit loans. In terms of the loan size, the dividing line between regular and microenterprise loans has been in the range of equivalent to US$ 500 to US$ 650, and the shares of these loans in the number of all microcredit loans and in the annual total loan disbursements have, in recent years, risen to about 8 percent and 30 percent, respectively (see Table 9.2 in Chapter 9). Studying these loan modalities can give further insight into the constraints and untapped potential of the microcredit programmes, as we shall discuss in more detail in Chapter 9.

There are two different entry routes for accessing microenterprise loans: through graduation from regular microcredit programmes and through lateral entry. Grameen Bank's 'microenterprise' loan represents the first group and is accommodated within its regular programme under the same lending modalities with only an increase in the loan ceiling; its introduction was facilitated by the abandonment of the joint-liability system. The average size of these loans (estimated at equivalent to US$ 420 in 2013) is near the cut-off point for such loans. At the other end is BRAC's separate programme called Microenterprise Lending and Assistance (MELA), which is designed to cater to a very different group of clients with lateral entry, individual liability and significantly larger loan sizes. The loans are managed by separately trained staff and require some minimum equity participation in an existing business along with other forms of semi-legal guarantee. Other MFIs which have microenterprise loan programmes usually practice a varying mix of these two extreme models, but unlike Grameen Bank, nearly all of them treat these loans separately from regular microcredit programmes with various mechanisms of guarantee, including equity participation. Moreover, the requirement of repayment in regular instalments is common to all these lending programmes, although some programmes allow monthly instalments and a repayment period beyond one year. Most of these programmes have group lending, but with relatively more male groups, such as ASA's groups of businessmen based in local bazaars.

Perhaps the most significant aspect of the microenterprise loans is that the MFIs do not consider sufficient for these loans the system of repayment enforcement that is in place for regular microcredit loans. These larger-sized loans can be accessed mostly by relatively better-off clients who have visible business enterprises beyond the subsistence-type IGAs typically financed by regular microcredit programmes; and except in the case of Grameen Bank, the loans require some kind of informal or semi-legal security (such as third-party guarantee or agreement signed on what are called non-judicial stamps).[16] These semi-legal instruments are reminiscent of the early stage of the history of the modern banking system – as, for example, discussed by Hicks (1969, p.77). This illustrates a fundamental constraint in providing collateral-free loans to the poor or the moderately non-poor: the size of loan depends ultimately on the risk-bearing capacity of the borrowing households. Moreover, the kind of guardianship role played by the loan officials in the case of mainstream borrowers, which works as a monitoring and enforcement device, does not seem to work as well in the case of lateral entrants to the microenterprise loan programmes, which cater to clients belonging to at least a slightly higher social class. This explains why MFIs employ in these programmes loan officers who are smarter and better educated, apart from being better trained for overseeing larger-sized loans used in scaled-up businesses.

Overall, the microcredit programmes have come a long way in responding to the evolving needs of their clients and to make the system less burdensome to their clients.[17] Even then, there seem to be some basic limitations regarding the extent to which MFI's lending modalities can be made flexible without undermining credit repayment discipline, or to what extent the loan size can be increased, particularly for the relatively poorer clients. MFIs need to maintain a balance between being cautious and taking risks (Roodman, 2012, p.325). The widespread prevalence of 'overlapping', for example, indicates that they remain on the conservative side in estimating their clients' capacity to use larger-sized loans. In spite of the introduction of some flexibility in the repayment schedules, more than 92 percent of the microcredit borrowers in the *InM Poverty Survey 2010* were found to belong to programmes with weekly repayments. Again, while Grameen Bank made its lending modalities generally much more flexible through the introduction of Grameen II, the only aspect in which the rules were in fact made more restrictive was in the definition of a defaulter; namely, a borrower becomes a defaulter if the full payment due is not fully paid in the first six months, instead of the previous period of 52 weeks. This indicates the importance MFIs give to the system of regular payment of instalments, even though the practice of informally allowing default for a few weeks has increased over the years.

A basic limitation of the microcredit programmes in making the lending modalities more flexible to respond to the needs of individual borrowers arises from the very banking technology they innovated. Looked at from the perspective of traditional commercial banks, microcredit programmes involve a very high number of transactions with small loan sizes; as such, MFIs have had to innovative cost-efficient lending methodologies. The distinctive aspect of this technology is to keep the loan modalities simple, transparent and pre-fixed to avoid decisions at the level of individual borrowers. Besides economising on time and effort spent on loan decisions, lack of discretion at the level of field-level loan officers may also keep them from deviating from the loan modalities that are carefully adopted after lots of screening and field-testing. MFIs are also concerned about any lack of internal control regarding reporting by the field staff (e.g. hiding repayment problems). They are also apprehensive of the possibility that in applying any discretion, the freshly recruited loan officers may be outwitted by experienced borrower groups with a hidden agenda.

3.3 Bangladesh's experience from a theoretical standpoint

It may be useful to look at the microcredit model as it has evolved in Bangladesh from the perspective of theory, since almost the entire theoretical literature on microcredit has been inspired by the original Grameen model (Varian, 1990; Stiglitz, 1990; Besley and Coate, 1995). While we shall review this theoretical literature in the next two chapters, here we try to create a broad-brush picture of how far the theoretical rendering of the original Grameen model and its subsequent elaboration match with the evolution of the actual practice of microcredit in Bangladesh. What are the implications for theory, for example, arising from some of the emerging features of the microcredit system in Bangladesh, such as the dynamic incentives created by a long-standing relationship between borrowers and MFIs or the strengthening of a loan repayment culture based on social norms? How can theory, in turn, help us to better understand these emerging issues?

3.3.1 The problem of moral hazard revisited

The theories of microcredit put unique emphasis on the incentives created by the system of joint liability under group lending to address three apparently separate problems: (a) screening prospective group members for their creditworthiness (related to the problem of 'adverse selection'), (b) monitoring the use of a loan so as to ensure that the borrower can repay the loan (related to the problem of '*ex ante* moral hazard') and (c) enforcing repayment in the case of a potential wilful or 'strategic' default (related to the problem of '*ex post* moral hazard'). There is an obvious problem of moral hazard when a loan is used 'imprudently' for non-productive purposes under social or economic pressures so that it cannot be recovered. However, most of the theoretical constructs are based on another, more subtle and nuanced kind of *ex ante* moral hazard which arises from the so-called "limited liability" of the borrower while using collateral-free loans for a production project – and which can lead to a systematic divergence between the objectives of the borrower and the lender regarding the use of the loan.[18]

In theory, the 'limited liability' assumption is taken to imply that the borrower has to repay the loan only if the project is successful, but not if the project fails. This can lead to the borrower's deliberate *ex ante* strategy of undertaking a too-risky project, since she is cushioned against the underside of her risky behaviour, which can be passed off to the lender. The result can be an inefficient choice of projects from the point of view of the lender (as well as in purely economic terms) and a higher risk of repayment default. The same logic also explains why the borrower will put in less than optimal effort for the success of the project. However, these sources of perverse incentives for preferring a too-risky project or putting in less than the desired level of effort will disappear as soon as the 'limited liability' assumption is replaced by that of 'full liability' – that is, if the borrower could somehow be made to repay the loan under every contingency, regardless of the success or failure of the project.[19]

The above nuanced version of the *ex ante* moral hazard has important practical implications, since it will make the task of monitoring the use of a loan even more difficult than it would be otherwise. However, the applicability of these theoretical results will depend on how the borrower actually perceives her liability for the loan, which in turn will depend on her assessment of the repayment enforcement mechanisms employed by the MFIs and/or her own mental calculation regarding the cost of non-repayment. It is true that a collateral-free loan cannot be recovered if the borrower household does not possess the wherewithal or the necessary cash flows to repay the loan; but the question is whether a microcredit borrower interprets this as her own limited liability for the loan while making decisions about the use of the loan. The theory's assumption regarding the project-only use of a loan – which is far from reality, but nevertheless facilitates neat theorising – is not of much importance for this discussion, since 'limited liability' as conceptualised in theory may lead to a pre-meditated 'risky' use of the loan for non-productive purposes as well.

The way limited liability is conceptualised in theory is more akin to the system of repayment enforcement by coercion (whether in the form of peer pressure and social sanctions or directly applied by an MFI official) than repayment through inducement and moral obligation. In the former case, the implicit assumption is that the borrower would naturally tend to use the loan in 'unintended' ways and also default wilfully unless she is prevented from doing so through such coercion. In the other case of repayment through inducement and moral obligation, it is the borrower's mental calculation of the cost of non-repayment that will determine how she will use the loan and whether she will eventually repay it or not. If that cost in monetary terms is higher than the loan amount to be repaid (e.g. $L(1+r)$ as shown in Figure 3.1), it in fact represents a situation of full liability with respect to her decision regarding the use of the loan. The logic applies even if she eventually decides to default in the case of project failure leading to bankruptcy. There is an important practical implication of this: not only is there no need for coercion to prevent wilful default (*ex post* moral hazard), but also no separate monitoring mechanisms are needed to address the problem of the borrower's deliberate strategy of taking on a too-risky project (the nuanced version of an *ex ante* moral hazard). It would appear from our earlier discussion that this may well be the representative case for the contemporary practice of microcredit in Bangladesh. Notice, however, that the borrower's cost of non-repayment in Figure 3.1 includes only the frequency-dependent cost arising from the social norm and moral obligation of loan repayment. In practice, this cost will include other elements representing the forgone benefits of future loans, the loss of the savings kept with the MFI, and the discomfort from milder forms of coercion, like 'public shaming'.

Even barring the case of repayment enforcement based mainly on inducement and moral obligation, the microcredit system in practice is designed to make the borrower feel like bearing the full liability of the loan, thus weakening the theoretical, nuanced version of an *ex ante* moral hazard. Even if not guaranteed by collateral, the microcredit borrower undertakes to repay the entire amount according to the typical loan contract (called '*chukti rin*') without any mention of the means of repayment.[20] Survey findings from the responses of left-outs and dropouts of the microcredit programmes suggest that non-repayment is hardly considered an option, which is an indication of the full liability in the respondents' perception (Hashemi, 1997). Full liability is also implied in the screening process for membership, where the criterion is often based on the ability to repay out of regular household income irrespective of the outcome from the use of the loan. As regards the extremely coercive methods of loan recovery, like the confiscation of items that are valued by the borrower household but can hardly compensate the MFI for the defaulted amount, it is also a mechanism for making borrowers feel the full liability of microcredit loan.

Whether or not the coercion-based repayment system works as well as the one based on inducement and moral obligation in addressing the problem of an *ex ante* moral hazard, the latter system is obviously far superior in promoting the social mission of MFIs and in strengthening the resilience of the system (as discussed in the context of Figure 3.1). Moreover, the idea of *ex ante* moral hazard, along with the consequent need for monitoring the loan use, remains valid in either system in the obvious case of an 'imprudent' use of a loan arising from the various self-discipline issues of the poor discussed in the previous chapter. For example, the loan may be used unwisely due to immediate social and economic pressures, lack of foresight, or even because of the capture of the loan by the non-cooperative husband. The evidence in Bangladesh suggests that the microcredit system has coped well with this kind of moral hazard, possibly because of the strengthening of the repayment culture based on inducement and social norms. But the repayment problems that remain intractable are the ones arising from circumstances beyond the control of the borrowers, such as various livelihood shocks, which is an issue that can hardly be solved within the incentive structure of the basic microcredit model.

3.3.2 Issues beyond the basic microcredit model

The pioneering work on the theory of microcredit, such as by Varian (1990) or Stiglitz (1990), rightly captured the logic of the classic Grameen model. The subsequent elaboration of this theoretical literature helped to understand the various mechanisms by which some of the problems inherent in the logic of this model could be solved, and whether and how the system of group lending thereby proved more efficient than the usual lending under individual contract. One of the most important aspects of Bangladesh's experience is that some of the weaknesses of the model could be addressed not just by tinkering within the self-enforcing loan contract itself, but by incorporating other external features. For example, while the theoretical models implied that the MFIs could afford a hands-off policy, in practice there was a mix of both peer pressure from group members and direct monitoring of individual borrowers by loan officers. This was facilitated by the socially embedded organisational character of the MFIs, so that the loan officers could directly cultivate a kind of social contact with borrowers that the traditional moneylenders could do only on a limited scale.

The theorisation of microcredit has also missed some social dimensions of group lending, perhaps because of their specificity to the Bangladesh context. For example, the solution to the problem of wilful default (*ex post* moral hazard) or to the 'coordination' problem in group lending was sought in social sanctions imposed by peers, *albeit* within the limits of a 'moral society' (Besley and Coate, 1995; Conning, 2005); in contrast, the microcredit programmes in Bangladesh benefited from the kinship-based social network that led to group activities based on mutual trust and support. The usefulness of open group meetings, as distinct from that of group liability, has featured only rarely in the theoretical literature, such as by Rai and Sjöström (2013), in the context of 'cross-reporting' of information, although MFIs in Bangladesh continue to put much emphasis on such meetings for a number of reasons, not least as a platform for social 'shaming'.

It is, however, some of the unforeseen – and still not fully appreciated – developments in the actual practice of microcredit in Bangladesh that have perhaps led to the most significant deviations between theory and practice. We have already discussed the theoretical implications of the shift from a coercion-based system of repayment enforcement to one based on incentives and social norms. Similarly, while the 'dynamic incentive' arising from the long-run relationship between the MFIs and their clients has emerged as a major factor in repayment enforcement, it has been given only cursory attention from the theorists, such as by Aniket (2011a) in the context of sequenced lending among group members or by Tedeschi (2006) in the context of the possibility of microcredit lending without group liability.

We mentioned earlier the problem of repayment arising from unforeseen livelihood shocks to which the poor are particularly vulnerable and which the microcredit programmes can address only in a limited way. The theoretical literature has even much less to say on this issue, since the problem will arise even if the model works exactly as it is supposed to in theory. While such cases can be resolved sometimes by loan rescheduling or some insurance mechanisms, the MFIs have currently no clear policy guidelines for detecting the genuine problem cases and dealing with such cases. Given the likely proportion of households facing severe livelihood shocks in a year in rural Bangladesh – estimated at 5 percent by a longitudinal household survey conducted by the World Bank (Narayan and Zaman, 2008) – MFIs should be able to absorb the consequent loan defaults and allow the borrowers facing such shocks to leave the programmes. But how can they do it in a way that neither creates a moral hazard in repayment nor unduly 'shames' and stigmatises the borrower? Although the current practices of MFIs do not allow coercion such as the confiscation of assets, the stigma and shame attached to default can lead to no less painful consequences for the defaulting borrowers, and this can both tarnish the image of the MFIs and adversely affect the incentive for joining microcredit programmes.[21] Survey findings show that, besides the burden of weekly payments, the risk to livelihood shocks is a major factor behind the reluctance of poor households to join microcredit programmes (Khalily, 2013). A desirable policy option is to deal leniently with a borrower in genuine difficulty and to let her go without being branded as a defaulter (under the current policy, MFIs do not forgive a loan – a severe punishment in a society where it is considered sinful to die with debt obligation). There is a dilemma here. If the loan officers are to go by the visible signs of a livelihood shock, the other borrowers in difficulty, such as those rendered insolvent by some 'imprudent' use of the loan, will not be spared. If, on the other hand, the loan officers look for the telltale signs of genuine bankruptcy as against willful default, as they often do, it may create a moral hazard with respect to using loans in ways that lead to such bankruptcy.

Notes

1 Both the full sample and its sub-sample of households were drawn from all over rural Bangladesh through a stratified random sampling procedure; see Osmani (2015b).
2 A less generous interpretation of the use of joint liability in such a case is that any coercion on the defaulting member can be seen to be applied by fellow group members, not by the MFI itself.
3 In relatively economically prosperous areas, particularly those in semi-urban settings, even group meetings are reported to be on the decline; groups are maintained, but transactions are often made through family members at the MFI office.
4 Unfortunately, this may also keep the women from the poorest households from joining the programmes, since they may not be able to spare the time for attending the meetings regularly; see Rahman (2000), Table 4.2, p. 58.
5 Village studies in Bangladesh conducted in the early 1990s show that MFIs both benefited from and reinforced the existing kinship-based social structure; see Kamal (2000) and Khan (1996). According to these authors, kinship ties acted as the central insurance, protection and enforcement mechanisms of rural societies.
6 According to Muhammad Yunus, the original idea of group-based lending was to let the group members help each other in usefully utilising the loans, given their inexperience in handling cash (Yunus, 2004b).
7 This is based on information gathered from microcredit practitioners, field reports of PKSF officials and village notes prepared by field investigators of some recent InM surveys.

58 *How the microcredit model works*

8. In the reformulated Grameen II model, some degree of dynamic incentive for repayment at the group level is retained by tying an individual borrower's loan ceiling not only to her own repayment records, but also to the performance of the group as a whole; see Dowla and Barua (2006, pp.248–253).
9. One problem with the logic of enforcing loan repayment through the threat of future credit denial is that the borrower will start to default when the usefulness of a loan declines at some stage. Evidence in Bangladesh does not support the hypothesis, given the frequent exit and re-entry without default, which is perhaps because there are also other mechanisms for repayment enforcement at work. The loan officers, however, usually keep an eye on borrowers who are facing difficulties in loan repayment, so that these borrowers repay as much as possible in case they have to drop out of the programme.
10. In the case of the large MFIs, a recently devised practice is that the loan officers of the local branch assemble in one place at the end of a loan collection day, and if there is a reported default, swoop on the defaulter's house, to her great embarrassment.
11. Muhammad Yunus emphasises a trust-based relationship of MFIs with their clients as the main factor behind repayment; see Yunus (2004a), p.4078.
12. The risk of a "domino effect" and the consequent need for maintaining a near 100 percent repayment rate may be there even in a microcredit system where repayment is enforced entirely through coercion without any societal moral pressure, since it is not practically feasible to apply such coercive methods once borrowers start to default on a large scale.
13. Wright (2000, p.74) observes the extremely common pattern of repaying instalments from normal household income rather than from income arising from the loan.
14. Dowla and Barua (2006, pp.248–253) provide a detailed account of the transition of the Grameen Bank's lending modalities to what it calls Grameen II.
15. In most cases, the borrowers could not make full repayment according to the schedule over the extended period, and Grameen Bank faced problems about recycling the equipment recovered from them.
16. Interestingly, Grameen Bank's loans, although collateral-free, are legally secured by the government act by which it was set up; however, this legal provision was never invoked by Grameen Bank for loan recovery.
17. The extent of these innovations at the field level is often underestimated. For example, academic commentators seem to be unaware about the decline of the joint-liability system in Bangladesh while pointing out the need for "tweaking, tinkering" of the Grameen Bank's basic model so that it can better serve the poor clients – without, for example, "forcing one to pay for the other" (Karlan and Appel, 2011, p.140).
18. The idea of limited liability originated in the mercantile phase of economic development in the West in the invention of the Limited Liability Company, which gave a legal protection to an investor willing to join in partnership businesses; because this liability is limited, the investor cannot lose more from the failure of a particular business than the investor has invested in that business by acquiring equity shares (Hicks, 1969, p. 80).
19. See Ray (1998, pp.532–4) for numerical examples of such choices of projects.
20. There is sometimes even an extra guarantee for recovery, such as the clause in Grameen Bank's contract for a flexible loan: "the ownership of all businesses and assets funded by the loan belongs to the bank until the loan is repaid in full" (Dowla and Barua, 2006, p.163).
21. The public shame of being branded a defaulter may be strong enough to compel the borrower to sell assets or even withdraw children from school in order to repay the loan (Dowla and Barua, 2006, p.253).

4 Theories of microcredit
Group lending and moral hazard

Rapid expansion of microcredit around the world has been matched by an expanding body of theoretical literature on the subject. The main objective of these theories is to explain how microcredit institutions have successfully made credit accessible to the poor without compromising the commercial viability of lenders, a feat that seemed impossible to achieve in the light of past experience. In the present chapter and the next, we try to outline the main contours of this theoretical journey in a relatively accessible manner.[1] Since these theories seek to explain how microcredit has succeeded in overcoming many of the failures and limitations of the rural credit market in developing countries, a good starting point is a brief theoretical overview of the nature of the rural credit market on which microcredit has been superimposed.

4.1 Early theories of the rural credit market

A few stylised facts about the nature of the rural credit market have become part of folklore. It is commonly believed, for example, that (a) rural people have very little access to the formal banking system, (b) they try to meet their credit needs mainly by taking recourse to the informal credit market, (c) the informal credit market has two main strands: a network of friends and families which works as a mutual support system based on reciprocity, and a group of moneylenders and other professionals who lend money for profit, and (d) those who lend for profit usually charge exorbitantly high rates of interest, often exceeding 100 percent per annum. Anecdotal evidence in support of these propositions has existed for centuries; systematic empirical research is of relatively recent origin, but it by and large validates the earlier perceptions.

However, explanations of some of the observed phenomena have remained shrouded in controversy. The most contentious issue has been the explanation of very high rates of interest charged by moneylenders. The folklore has it that unscrupulous moneylenders charge exploitative interest rates by exercising monopoly power over the rural poor, who are often in desperate need of credit but are bereft of any power to bargain for a better deal. A dissident view has claimed that high interest rates actually reflect the high level of risk the moneylenders have to take while offering unsecured loans to poor people, many of whom are likely to default. At the theoretical level, the greedy monopolist view has been formalised most elegantly by Bhaduri (1973, 1977) and the risk-of-default view by Bottomley (1975).[2]

Bhaduri's (1973) moneylender is a manipulative villain whose real objective is not to earn interest income that accrues from lending, but to grab whatever assets (in particular, land) poor people happen to hold. He showed that so long as the asset is valued more highly by the lender than by the borrower, the lender would be able to use his monopoly power to set the interest rate at such a high level that the borrower would be obliged to default and the asset would pass over to the lender. Bhaduri used this idea of a 'debt trap' as part of a general theoretical framework to offer an elegant neo-Marxist explanation of how rural backwardness is perpetuated in a semi-feudal environment (Bhaduri, 1983).

Bottomely (1975), by contrast, demonstrated that monopoly and greed need not be invoked to explain high interest rates. Even in a competitive market, a high risk of default may provide an adequate explanation. For example, if it is assumed that the moneylender's opportunity cost of capital is 10 percent per annum (which, say, obtains in the formal credit market) and that about half of his potential borrowers are likely to default, his break-even rate of interest turns out to be as high as 120 percent per annum – a common enough informal interest rate observed around the developing world (Ray, 1998, p.345).

Despite their elegance and early appeal, both of these lines of theorizing have come under increasing criticism, on both theoretical and empirical grounds. Bhaduri's model, for example, turns out to be characterised by a rather unstable equilibrium, as even a small effort by the borrower to save out of current income can enable her to escape the debt trap (Srinivasan, 1979).[3] At the empirical level, Bardhan and Rudra (1978) have shown, from a careful study of rural credit markets in West Bengal, India, that the premises and the conclusions of Bhaduri's model do not, on the whole, fit the facts. The problem with Bottomley's model is primarily empirical. Most fundamentally, there is no convincing evidence of high default rates in rural credit markets. On the contrary, Timberg and Aiyar (1984) found in India that, for the cases they studied, the average default losses for the moneylenders ranged between 0.5 percent and 1.5 percent of working funds. Similarly, in a much-quoted study from Pakistan, Aleem (1990) found the default rate to be less than 5 percent in most cases he studied. An additional problem with Bottomley is that his assumption of competitive market does not fit the facts either. Almost all the evidence shows the existence of highly segmented rural credit markets in which individual moneylenders do enjoy at least a local monopoly power.[4]

A new view of rural credit market is now emerging which sees both monopolistic elements and risk of default as important features of the market, but not as simple determinants of interest rates as envisaged by earlier theorists. This new view starts from the premise that informal lenders face the same problems of asymmetric information and imperfect enforcement as do the formal lenders, but what they try to do in order to overcome these problems is very different from the response of formal lenders. Problems of information and enforcement do entail a serious risk of default, but unlike formal lenders, who tend to wash their hands off poor rural borrowers, informal lenders actually try to devise ways and means of lending that minimise this risk. Thus, it is not the high actual rate of default, as such, but the mechanisms that are devised to minimise default that can explain high interest rates. More generally, according to this new view, the clue to explaining the observed features of rural credit markets lies in understanding the manner in which informal lenders try to deal with the problems of information and enforcement, and the consequences that arise from their actions.[5]

One set of actions moneylenders take is to screen out the risky borrowers by trying to acquire as much personal information about the potential clients as they can, and then confining lending to a selected few. Quite often, they further minimise the risk of default by keeping an eye on how the borrowers utilise the loan, and by threatening them with various kinds of unpleasant consequences if they try to default on the loan. The actual rate of default is thus minimised, but the whole process may still culminate in a high rate of interest – partly because of the local monopoly power the lender comes to acquire over the clients about whom the lender has superior personal knowledge compared to other lenders, partly because of the limited amount of loanable funds available to the lender, and partly because of the transaction costs incurred in the process of screening, monitoring, etc.[6]

A somewhat different set of actions may be undertaken by those lenders who also happen to interact with their clients in other capacities, such as landlords, employers or traders. For them, linking the terms of contract in the credit market with the terms of contract in other markets (e.g., land, labour, or commodities, as the case may be) may provide a way of minimising the problems of imperfect information and enforcement that may otherwise make a credit transaction unviable. For example, a landlord-cum-moneylender can threaten a tenant-cum-borrower with eviction from tenancy as an enforcement mechanism for preventing loan default. Or, a trader-cum-lender may offer a farmer-cum-borrower lower prices on agricultural inputs in order to encourage the latter to use more of these inputs so that the borrower is not compelled to default on the loan owing to poor yield.[7]

It is also interesting to observe that, faced with the pervasive problems of imperfect information and enforcement, it is not just the lenders who try to devise mechanisms for overcoming them; the borrowers, too, can take remedial actions. Examples of institutions devised for this purpose are borrowers' self-help groups, such as credit co-operatives and Rotating Savings and Credit Associations (ROSCA), which have existed in various forms all over the world for a very long time.[8]

An important lesson that emerges from this new way of looking at the rural credit market is that any intervention designed to improve upon the workings of the existing market must be able to improve upon, or at least substitute for, the actions the market has already undertaken – from the sides of both lenders and borrowers – in response to the underlying problems of information and enforcement. As mentioned in Chapter 1, this lesson has mostly been lost on the interventions in the rural credit market made by the governments of many developing countries. Launched with the best of intentions – namely, to improve the rural poor's access to credit and to break the moneylenders' stranglehold on them – most of these interventions have failed to deliver the goods. These interventions have usually taken the form of compelling state-run institutions to enter the rural credit market, often combined with the directive of reserving a minimum proportion of advances for the so-called 'priority sectors' and offering loans at heavily subsidised interest rates. A series of systematic assessments of the impact of these interventions has come to the uncomfortable conclusion that, on the whole, they did more harm than good.[9] On the one hand, they caused financial repression by discouraging savings and led to an inefficient use of credit owing to an administratively guided, as opposed to market-determined, allocation of credit across sectors. On the other hand, cheap credit did not actually help the poor borrowers, as the benefits were cornered by the wealthy borrowers.[10] Finally, since such interventions directly undermined the financial viability of the lending institutions, they resulted in either widespread bankruptcies or an open-ended drain on the government budget.

It should be emphasised that not all the interventions failed totally. For instance, there is substantial evidence of important positive impacts on agricultural output and farmer welfare in rural Thailand following the Bank of Thailand's decision to set targets for commercial banks to lend to the agricultural sector (Fitchett, 1999). Similarly, in their careful analysis of directed credit in India, Burgess and Pande (2005) conclude that the policy had the intended effect of expanding rural bank branching, and that this succeeded in lowering poverty and expanding non-agricultural rural output. However, the general point – that government interventions in the rural credit market in the developing world have, on the whole, failed to achieve their objectives – remains valid.

The fundamental reason for this failure lies in not realising that moneylenders' power and the rural poor's lack of access to affordable credit stem from some basic problems of the rural credit market involving imperfect information and enforcement. No intervention will work without first addressing those underlying problems. As Hoff and Stiglitz (1990, p.238) observe: '. . . the moneylenders' power is unlikely to be broken by the entry of institutional credit, unless the new institutions themselves find substitutes for the direct mechanisms used by moneylenders to overcome the problems of screening, incentives, and enforcement.'

When microcredit entered the scene as an alternative institutional mechanism of delivering affordable credit to the poor, it did so by using certain methods that, knowingly or otherwise, did address precisely those problems of 'screening, incentives and enforcement'. And, according to the theories of microcredit, that is where the secret of its success lies. Within this common theme, there exists a multiplicity of theories, partly because imperfect information can pose several different types of problems for the lender, and different theories are needed to explain how various features of microcredit deal with those different problems. These problems can be classified into three broad categories: moral hazard (related to incentives), adverse selection (related to screening) and enforcement. This categorisation of the problems also provides a convenient organising framework for grouping the various theories of microcredit.[11] The problem of *ex ante* moral hazard is taken up in this chapter, leaving the discussion of adverse selection and enforcement problems for Chapter 5.

4.2 Theories of microcredit with *ex ante* moral hazard

In the general literature on the principal-agent problem, as well as in the specific literature on credit markets, including the literature on microcredit, the story of *ex ante* moral hazard is told in two slightly different ways. The difference lies in the decision variable that is supposed to be subject to moral hazard. One strand of the literature takes the level of effort expended by the agent as the relevant decision variable. The issue at stake in this case is the problem the principal faces in extracting the desired level of effort from the agent. Moral hazard consists in the fact that the agent is able to get away with putting in less effort than what is in the best interest of the principal. The other strand of the literature focuses on the choice of the project to be undertaken by the agent as the relevant decision variable. Moral hazard, in this case, consists in the propensity of the agent to adopt a riskier project than is ideal from the point of view of the principal. Both strands can be found in the moral hazard theories of microcredit. Fortunately, whether it is the level of effort or the choice of project that is taken as the object of moral hazard, it makes little difference to the main insights offered by these theories. There is, however, quite a difference in the narratives of the two ways of telling the story. In order to offer as unified an exposition as possible, we shall mainly adopt the narrative of effort, but occasionally we shall deviate from it when we find that the central message is much easier to get across through the alternative narrative of project choice.

4.2.1 The problem of moral hazard in the credit market

In order to explain how moral hazard distorts the credit market, we shall build on an approach due to Ghosh *et al.* (2001), which shows how moral hazard in effort can lead to credit rationing. Consider a project that requires a fixed investment L and has an uncertain return: Y if it succeeds, 0 if it fails. The probability of success (p) is related to the level of effort (e) through the increasing and concave function $p(e)$, such that $p'(e)>0$ and $p''(e)<0$; thus, the probability of success increases with the level of effort, but at a diminishing rate. Effort has a cost; for simplicity, the cost of effort is normalised at e, implying that cost rises proportionately to the level of effort. For the society as a whole, the expected net return from the project is given by

$$p(e).Y - e - L \qquad (4.1)$$

A higher level of effort would tend to raise the value of net return by raising the probability of success p, but it will also tend to reduce net return by entailing an additional cost of effort. The optimal (or efficient) level of effort (e^*) is the one that maximises (4.1), considering both the gain through $p(e)$ and the loss through e.[12] This is given by the first-order condition:

$$p'(e^*) = \frac{1}{Y} \qquad (4.2)$$

64 Group lending and moral hazard

Now consider the case where an entrepreneur has no money of her own and borrows the amount L at an interest rate r. She would pay back $R = (1+r)L$ if the project succeeds (we are assuming that $Y > R$), but nothing at all if the project fails, because in that case, the return from the project is zero and she has no transferable wealth to offer as collateral. The recognition that she does not and cannot pay back anything at all in the event of failure is an extreme case of 'limited liability constraint'. Given these conditions, the borrower's choice of effort level can be derived from the following optimization exercise:

$$\max_e \; p(e).(Y-R) - e \qquad (4.3)$$

$$\text{s.t.} \quad p(e).(Y-R) - e \geq 0 \qquad (4.4)$$

Equation (4.4) is known as the borrower's 'participation constraint'. It states that unless the borrower can earn a non-negative expected return, she will not borrow at all. In other words, the maximisation exercise is relevant only when the participation constraint is satisfied.

Assuming that the participation constraint is satisfied, the optimum level of effort ($\hat{e}$) is given by the first-order condition:

$$p'(\hat{e})(Y-R) = 1 \qquad (4.5)$$

$$\text{or,} \quad p'(\hat{e}) = \frac{1}{Y-R} \qquad (4.6)$$

By comparing (4.6) with (4.2), we may note that the value of $p'(e)$ implied by (4.6) is greater than that implied by (4.2), i.e. $p'(\hat{e}) > p'(e^*)$. Since the assumption of diminishing return ($p''(e) < 0$) implies that the value of $p'(e)$ falls at higher levels of effort, we can infer that $\hat{e} < e^*$. Thus, the borrower is going to expend a socially sub-optimal level of effort.

A couple of factors combine to create this inefficiency. Partly, the problem lies in the existence of the limited liability constraint. To see why, suppose the borrower was required to pay back R regardless of whether the project succeeded or failed. In that case, she would have maximised the following expected return function:

$$p(e).(Y-R) + \{1-p(e)\}(-R) - e \qquad (4.7)$$

On simplification, expression (4.7) becomes $p(e).Y - R - e$. It is evident that the first-order condition of maximisation in this case is exactly identical to (4.2), and hence the chosen level of effort would also be the same (e^*). In other words, in the absence of limited liability, the borrower would have expended the socially optimal level of effort.

One way of explaining why the borrower would put in less effort is to note an analogy with taxes. In the presence of limited liability, the repayment burden acts like a tax on success – she has to repay only if the project succeeds, not if the project fails. Roughly speaking, the point is that she is not very keen to raise the level of effort because she knows that a part of the fruit of her extra effort will be taken away by the lender. Of course, by expending less effort, she also raises the probability of failure; but that does not worry her too much, because the borrower knows that she won't have to pay anything in the event of failure. If limited liability did not exist, i.e. if she were required to pay back the loan even in the case of failure, she would have been much more careful to prevent failure by expending more effort. If the borrower knew that she would have to repay the loan in any case, she would try her best to ensure that the project didn't fail so that repayment could be made from the project's return rather than from her own purse. With limited liability, however, the borrower is not equally keen to ensure success because she knows that the cost of failure would be borne by the lender – it's somebody else's problem. It is thus the protection on the downside afforded by limited liability that induces the borrower to expend a socially inefficient level of effort.

But there is another side to the story. The problem of lax effort could have been overcome if the lender could observe and control the level of effort expended by the borrower. In that case, the lender could have made it a part of the contractual requirement that the borrower must expend the socially optimal level of effort, or else she would face unpleasant consequences like being hassled, or being cut off from future loans, or being shamed in public, and so on. It would be rational for the lender to take this course, because if social surplus is maximised, the lender's own profit could be increased too. The lender, however, faces the problem that he cannot directly observe the level of effort. He might, of course, be able to observe the outcome of effort as revealed by the output of the project; and if effort and outcome were directly related to each other, he could have deduced the level of effort indirectly by observing the outcome. But even this indirect route is denied to him by the fact that no one-to-one relationship between effort and outcome can be established because of the inherent riskiness of the project. A higher level of effort can only increase the probability of success, but it cannot necessarily ensure a better outcome, because there is always a chance that the project would fail despite the borrower's best efforts. So when the project actually fails, the lender can never be sure whether this was because the borrower was lax in her effort or because of sheer bad luck. The borrower would, of course, know the truth, but the lender won't – that's the essence of asymmetric information.

Given the existence of asymmetric information, the lender would find it pointless to try to stipulate the level of effort in the loan contract. He has, then, no option but to leave it to the borrower to decide how much effort she would expend – and we have seen that with limited liability, the borrower would expend less than the socially optimal level of effort. It is thus the combination of asymmetric information and limited liability that together leads to inefficiency in the credit market.

This inefficiency has important implications for practical questions, such as what would happen to the interest rate, and whether people's demand for credit will be met fully or not, and so on. In order to answer these questions, it is necessary to examine the nature of the market equilibrium that is likely to obtain when asymmetric information is combined with limited liability. The precise nature of the market equilibrium will depend on the market structure – in particular, on the degree of competition among the lenders, and on whether the lenders are driven purely by the profit motive or mainly by the spirit of what is coming to be known as 'social business'. But it is possible to identify some general characteristics of the credit market that are likely to prevail regardless of the market structure, and these are the ones that are of interest in the present context.

Of the two sides of the market, borrowers and lenders, we have already identified the objective function of the borrowers. Given any repayment schedule R, the borrowers would maximise expression (4.3) and choose their effort level as dictated by condition (4.6). The lenders, on their part, would try to maximise the following expected profit function:

$$\pi = p(e).R - L \qquad (4.8)$$

They will choose a level of interest r and hence a repayment schedule R that will maximise profit. They will be aware, however, that any choice about R will affect profit through two different routes – one direct and the other indirect – and the two routes will work in opposite directions. The direct route is through the presence of R in equation (4.8), whereby a higher R will entail higher profits, provided other things remain the same. The indirect route operates through $p(e)$; if R is raised, the lender will have to bear in mind that borrowers will adjust their effort level in accordance with condition (4.6), which will have consequences for the probability of success $p(e)$, and hence for their profit. To see the direction of this effect, note that according to condition (4.6), a higher R will entail a lower effort e, which in turn will induce a lower $p(e)$ and hence reduced profit.[13]

The existence of the indirect route implies that, while choosing the level of repayment burden (R), the lender must take condition (4.6) into cognizance as a constraint. It's called the 'incentive compatibility constraint' (or, simply, the incentive constraint), as it shows the values of e that the borrower will have the incentive to expend at given values of R. We have just noted that this constraint suggests a negative relationship between R and e, as shown by the IC curve in Figure 4.1. As R gets smaller, e gets bigger; and in the limit as R approaches zero, e approaches the socially optimal level of effort e^* (as condition (4.5) tends to condition (4.2)). The IC curve will thus meet the e-axis at e^*.

In order to find the market equilibrium, we now introduce the lender's iso-profit (IP) curve, which shows the combinations of R and e that will keep the lender's profit constant at any given level. It is easy to see from the profit function (4.8) that R and e will bear a negative relationship on the IP curve; for example, if R goes up, the positive effect on profit must be offset by an equal and opposite effect through lower $p(e)$, and thus lower e, in order to keep profit constant. Accordingly, the IP curve has been drawn with a negative slope in Figure 4.1. Also note that a higher IP curve indicates a higher level of profit, because for any given level of e, a higher value of R entails more profit.

The equilibrium levels of R and e will be established at the point where the lender's IP curve meets the borrower's IC curve, because it is only at this point

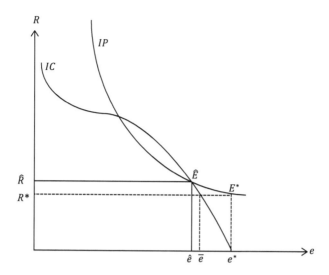

Figure 4.1 Credit market equilibrium with moral hazard under individual liability

that the pair of R and e will be consistent with the borrower's incentive while keeping the lender's profit at the target level. The target level of profit – i.e., the exact position of the *IP* curve – will depend on the market structure. If the lender is a monopolist, he will try to maximise his profit, given the incentive constraint, i.e. he will try to reach as high an *IP* curve as possible that has some point in common with the *IC* curve. If an interior solution exists, this will lead to a point of tangency between the two curves. If, however, perfect competition prevails, or the lender is a not-for-profit entity who simply wishes to break even, then the relevant *IP* curve is the zero-profit curve:

$$\pi = p(e).R - L = 0 \qquad (4.9)$$

In this case, the more likely equilibrium is at a point of intersection between the two curves, as at point $\hat{E}$ in Figure 4.1.[14] For simplicity, we shall make the latter assumption regarding market structure, and thus work with the zero-profit curve; but it is important to point out that the main qualitative conclusions drawn from the ensuing analysis would remain valid under alternative assumptions as well.

The equilibrium point $\hat{E}$ in Figure 4.1 can be characterised as 'constrained Pareto efficient', because given the existence of incentive compatibility constraint *IC*, no other pair of R and e will improve the welfare of one party without reducing the other party's welfare. However, $\hat{E}$ does not represent the unconstrained Pareto efficient outcome or the social optimum. As we have seen before, the socially optimal level of effort (e^*) lies above the level ($\hat{e}$) that would obtain under moral hazard. At e^*, however, the (unconstrained) $\hat{R}$ cannot be the equilibrium repayment, because the pair ($\hat{R}$, e^*) takes the lender above the zero-profit curve. In order to maintain the zero-profit condition, the lender would have to reduce the repayment charge to R^*; the point E^* thus represents the unconstrained equilibrium.

Comparing the unconstrained equilibrium E^* with the constrained equilibrium $\hat{E}$, we can see that the equilibrium value of R, and therefore the equilibrium interest rate, is higher for the constrained equilibrium. This is one of the important consequences of moral hazard for the credit market – namely, that the interest rate will be higher with moral hazard than without it. If repayment were to be lowered to R^* in the presence of moral hazard, the IC constraint would dictate that the borrowers choose an effort level $\bar{e}$ that is above $\hat{e}$ but still below e^*. But at this level of effort, the lender would end up below the zero-profit curve, earning negative profit. That's why the lower interest rate R^* associated with E^* will not be offered under moral hazard.

An intuitive explanation of why the interest rate happens to be higher under moral hazard – one that will prove helpful for subsequent analysis – can be given by comparing the implications of the borrower's incentive compatibility constraint and her participation constraint. At the equilibrium effort level ($\hat{e}$), the expected payoff for the borrower is $p(\hat{e})(Y-R)-\hat{e}$. According to the incentive compatibility constraint, this is the maximum possible payoff consistent with $\hat{e}$. In other words, this is the payoff the borrower must earn in order to have the incentive to offer the effort level $\hat{e}$. However, the participation constraint (4.3) suggests that if the incentive problem didn't stand in the way and the lender could somehow make $\hat{e}$ a necessary condition for borrowing, the borrower would be willing to expend $\hat{e}$ at a much lower payoff so long as it did not become negative. In fact, the pay-off could have been reduced arbitrarily close to zero, and the borrower would still expend $\hat{e}$. Thus, in a sense, the payoff $p(\hat{e})(Y-R)-\hat{e}$ is an excess or a rent that the borrower is able to extract from the market by taking advantage of the scope for moral hazard created by the combination of asymmetric information and limited liability. In the general literature on moral hazard, this is called the 'incentive rent'; and in the specific context of the credit market, it is also called the 'limited liability rent' (Laffont and Martimort, 2001).

The existence of the incentive rent entails a cost in terms of high interest rate. If the borrower didn't have to be paid this rent, the lender's profit would have been increased; but as this would violate the zero-profit condition, the market would have brought down the rate of interest so as to restore the zero-profit condition. Thus, the equilibrium interest rate would have been lower in the absence of the incentive rent. This explains why the interest rate is higher with moral hazard than without it.

This line of argument suggests that anything that lowers the incentive rent would lead to a lower equilibrium interest rate. This would be so, for example, if the borrower had some transferable wealth that could be used as collateral. The presence of collateral would mean that, in the event of project failure, the cost will no longer be borne entirely by the lender – a part of it will be borne by the borrower as well. This transfer of wealth from the borrower to the lender in the event of failure would reduce the expected payoff for the borrower, i.e. the incentive rent would fall and the lender's expected profit would rise at any given rate of interest. The necessity to restore the zero-profit condition would then set off market adjustments, leading towards a lower equilibrium interest rate.

The analogy of carrot and stick is quite useful in this context. When the presence of collateral softens the bite of limited liability, the lender can use the threat of seizing the collateral as the stick with which to induce the borrower to expend a high level of effort. But if collateral doesn't exist and limited liability binds, the lender cannot use the stick any longer; instead, he has to offer a carrot to induce effort. The 'incentive rent' is that carrot. There is a trade-off between the carrot and the stick. To the extent the stick can be used, the size of the carrot can be reduced – leading, as we have seen, to a lower equilibrium rate of interest.

Most theorists of microcredit have found it natural to assume that the stick of collateral does not exist in poor rural societies, i.e. limited liability binds. In this setting, the formal credit market, if it tried to reach out to the rural poor at all, would have to offer the carrot of high incentive rent. But this would result in a high interest rate and a correspondingly low reach of credit. The genius of microcredit, from this perspective, is that its innovative lending mechanisms have created alternative sticks – in lieu of collateral – that can be used to reduce the incentive rent and thus bring down the interest rate within the reach of the poor, and thereby extend their access to credit.

4.2.2 Solving moral hazard through group lending with joint liability

One of the most widely noted features of the way microcredit is delivered in practice is group lending with joint liability. The nature of group lending has evolved significantly over the years, in many cases giving way to individual lending; and even where group lending persists, the nature of joint liability has also evolved. Much of the theorising has, however, been based on the early practice, what is now called the classical Grameen model. In this model, those who wish to take microcredit are required to form groups, and while loans are given to individuals and not to the group, each member of the group is partially responsible for repayment by the others. The latter feature is called joint liability. We shall argue later that the way most of the theorists have modelled joint liability may have little resemblance to the way joint liability is applied in practice; but for the moment, we shall go along with the traditional formulation.

We shall use the basic model of individual lending introduced in the previous section but modify it to introduce the new element of joint liability. For simplicity, we shall assume that there are only two-member groups, and that both members of a group are exactly identical in all relevant respects – that is, they have the same function $p(e)$ relating probability of success to effort as well as the same cost of effort, and that neither has any collateral to offer, so that limited liability protects both of them equally. Joint liability demands that when one partner's project fails, and therefore she cannot repay her loan, the other partner must pay at least partially on behalf of the failed partner, provided she herself succeeds. If neither partner succeeds, then of course neither pays anything; and if both partners succeed, they pay only for themselves. The joint liability payment is denoted here by c. Using the subscripts *1* and *2* to denote the two partners, their expected payoff is given by:

$$p(e_i)(Y-R) + p(e_i)\left[1 - p(e_j)\right]c - e_i; \quad i, j \in \{1,2\}; i \neq j \tag{4.10}$$

By comparing this payoff function with the individual loan payoff function (4.2), it can be seen that the presence of joint liability acts like an additional tax on success because the fruit of success will be reduced not only by one's own repayment burden R, but also by an additional amount c in case the partner fails in her project. Unlike R, however, c is not an unavoidable tax on success. It can be avoided if the partner too succeeds. It is, therefore, in the interest of each partner that the other one succeeds. Both partners will then have the incentive to encourage, and if necessary pressurise, each other to raise the level of effort so that the probability of success increases. Joint liability will thus induce peer monitoring and peer pressure, which has the potential to mitigate the moral hazard stemming from asymmetric information and limited liability.

As we shall see below, however, it is not guaranteed that this potential will always be realised. One case where it will definitely be realised is when the group members can costlessly observe each other's effort and decide to choose their effort levels in a cooperative manner. The objective of cooperation is to choose effort levels in such a way that will maximise the payoff for the group as a whole.[15] Since the partners have been assumed to be identical in all relevant respects (including their cost of effort), the level of effort that is optimal for one will also be optimal for the other. Thus, they will solve the following common maximization problem:

$$\max_e \; p(e)(Y-R) - p(e)\left[1 - p(e)\right]c - e \tag{4.11}$$

The first-order condition gives the following incentive compatibility constraint:

$$p'(e)\left[(Y-R) - c + 2p(e)c\right] = 1 \tag{4.12}$$

The lender's zero-profit condition is given by:

$$\pi = p(e)R + p(e)\left[1 - p(e)\right]c - L = 0 \tag{4.13}$$

By substituting the equilibrium value of R $(= L/p(e) - [1 - p(e)]c)$ from (4.13) into (4.12), and upon simplification, we get the cooperative level of effort under joint liability $(\hat{e}_{jc})$ from the equation

$$p'(\hat{e}_{jc}) = \frac{1}{Y - \dfrac{L}{p(\hat{e}_{jc})} + p(\hat{e}_{jc})c} \tag{4.14}$$

In order to see the impact of joint liability on the level of effort, we would like to compare the value of $\hat{e}_{jc}$ given by (4.14) with the optimal level of effort under individual liability. We know that under individual liability, the incentive compatibility condition is given by (4.6) and the zero-profit condition by (4.9). By combining the two, we can derive the optimal level of effort under individual liability ($\hat{e}_{il}$) from the following equation:

$$p'(\hat{e}_{il}) = \frac{1}{Y - \dfrac{L}{p(\hat{e}_{il})}} \tag{4.15}$$

It can now be shown that $\hat{e}_{jc} > \hat{e}_{il}$ \hfill (4.16)

i.e., cooperative behaviour under joint liability induces a greater level of effort than what would obtain under individual liability.

We offer a simple diagrammatic proof of this proposition with the help of Figure 4.2 by adapting the IC-IP diagram introduced in Figure 4.1.[16] The proof hinges on the fact that when joint liability is introduced, both the IC and the IP curves fall compared to the individual liability case, but the IC curve falls relatively less if the borrowers behave in a cooperative manner. Comparing the zero-profit conditions (4.9) and (4.13), it may be seen that the zero-profit condition under joint liability contains an additional term $p(e)[1 - p(e)]c$, which stands for the joint liability payment the lender expects to receive from the borrowers. In order to maintain the zero-profit condition, the lender must reduce R to offset this gain. For any given level of $p(e)$, and hence for any given level of e, R must be reduced by $[1 - p(e)]c$. Therefore, if joint liability is introduced, the IP curve must fall by the amount $[1 - p(e)]c$.

Now, comparing the IC conditions (4.5) and (4.12), we can see that the IC condition under joint liability (4.12) contains an additional term $-p'(e)[(1 - 2p(e)]c$, representing the burden of joint liability payment. In order to keep the left-hand side of the equation equal to 1, the repayment burden R must fall. For any given level of $p'(e)$, and hence for any given level of $p(e)$, i.e. for any given level of e, R must fall by the amount $[1 - 2p(e)]c$. As a result, the IC curve must fall by the amount $[1 - 2p(e)]c$. This is smaller than $[1 - p(e)]c$, the amount by which the IP curve falls.[17] As can be seen from Figure 4.2, the equilibrium $\hat{E}_{jc}$ for joint liability (with cooperative behaviour) will then be established at a point where, compared to the individual liability equilibrium $\hat{E}_{il}$, the interest rate is lower and the effort level higher, as claimed in (4.16).

An intuitive explanation of this superiority of joint liability can be given in terms of what is called the 'diversification argument'.[18] Group lending with joint liability can be shown to enjoy what is called a 'diversification advantage' compared to individual liability, which enables the lender to bring down the rate of interest below what he will have to charge with individual liability. To see exactly where the advantage comes from, first consider the case of diversification with an individual loan. Suppose a borrower utilises her loan in a number

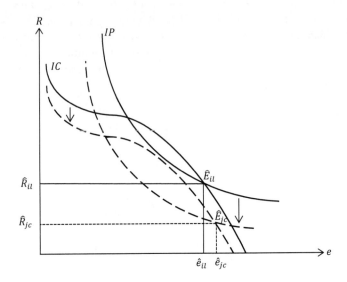

Figure 4.2 Credit market equilibrium with moral hazard under joint liability with cooperative behaviour

of imperfectly correlated projects instead of using it all on a single project, as we have assumed so far. With a single project, the borrower either repays the loan in full or she doesn't repay at all, depending on whether the project succeeds or fails. With diversified projects, however, it is likely that some projects will succeed even as others fail, so that the borrower would be able to repay, at least partially, for the failed projects out of the returns from the successful ones. Diversification thus lessens the bite of limited liability, enabling the lender to recoup more of his loan.

Something very similar happens in the case of lending with joint liability, even when every member of a group invests in a single project. With cooperative behaviour, the group as a whole acts a single entity, and the projects of all the members together can be viewed as diversified projects of that single entity.[19] Since the probability of the projects of all members failing simultaneously is less than the probability of failure of a single project, the group should be able to pay at least partially for the failed projects thanks to joint liability. Since the lender is now able to extract some penalty for failure, he can leave a smaller amount of 'incentive rent' to induce higher levels of effort.

To make the point with a more colourful analogy, we may restate the argument in terms of sticks and carrots. The lender contemplates the choice between a stick and a carrot to provide the right kind of incentive to the borrowers. Limited liability makes the stick difficult to administer, so he must offer some carrot – that's the incentive rent or the limited liability rent. When a loan is given to a group with joint liability and the group acts cooperatively, the failure by one part of the group can be punished by extracting some penalty from other parts of the group – that's the diversification advantage. In other words, joint liability provides a new stick to the lender. The emergence of this stick then allows the lender to reduce the carrot – i.e. lessen the amount of incentive rent. As more rent is transferred to the lender, his zero-profit condition ensures a reduction in interest rate and better ability to offer additional loans, which enables the lender to extend the reach of credit.[20]

This result is central to the theoretical literature on microcredit. It can explain, on the one hand, how microcredit institutions have been able to achieve exceptionally high rates of repayment despite the presence of limited liability. The explanation lies in the high level of effort induced by joint liability. With greater effort on the part of borrowers, the probability of success also increases, thereby reducing the incidence of default and improving the repayment rate. At the same time, the result on a lower interest rate explains how the microcredit sector is able to expand the access to credit for many poor borrowers. Finally, by bringing down the interest rate closer to the socially efficient level (e^*), microcredit makes it possible to finance socially valuable projects that could not otherwise be financed. Thus, in one stroke, group lending with joint liability appears to achieve the multiple goals of efficiency, equity and greater sustainability of financial institutions.

4.2.3 The importance of cooperative behaviour

Yet, the idea of joint liability as a means of overcoming moral hazard, and its role in explaining the success of microcredit, has come to be increasingly questioned on a number of different fronts. One basic difficulty is that the entire analysis behind the presumed virtues of joint liability is predicated upon the assumption of cooperative behaviour on the part of group members. If the members decide, however, to behave in a non-cooperative manner, the result turns out to be strikingly different.

Under the non-cooperative scenario, each partner decides her effort level on her own, but in doing so she must consider what level of effort the partner might choose, because her best choice of effort would depend on her partner's choice. For instance, if her partner chooses a low level of effort, thereby raising the likelihood that her project will fail, she too will choose a low level of effort so as to reduce the probability that she would be required to pay the joint liability fine for her partner's failure. Conversely, if the partner chooses a high level of effort, thereby raising the likelihood of her project's success, she too would be encouraged to put in more effort into her own project, knowing that she is now less likely to have to pay the joint liability fine. The existence of joint liability thus engenders what game theorists call 'strategic complementarity' between the two partners.

Each borrower decides her best action (i.e. choice of effort), keeping in view the possible actions by the partner; and when their actions are consistent with each other, we have the equilibrium called the Nash equilibrium. The options open to each borrower are represented by her 'best response function', which is derived by maximising the payoff function (4.8) with respect to her own effort level, given

74 Group lending and moral hazard

any effort level of the partner. These response functions are obtained by solving the first-order conditions:

$$p'(e_i)(Y-R) - p'(e_i)\left[\left(1 - p(e_j)\right)\right]c = 1 \quad i,j \in \{1,2\}; i \neq j \tag{4.17}$$

Since the partners have been assumed to be identical in all relevant respects, their response functions will also be identical, leading to a symmetric Nash equilibrium in which each partner chooses the same level of effort. In that case, expression (4.17) can be rewritten without the subscripts:

$$p'(e)(Y-R) - p'(e)\left[\left(1 - p(e)\right)\right]c = 1 \tag{4.18}$$

The lender's zero-profit function is the same as in the cooperative game given by (4.13). By substituting (4.13) into (4.18), we get the following equation that would yield the optimum effort level ($\hat{e}_{jn}$) under non-cooperative conditions:

$$p'(\hat{e}_{jn}) = \frac{1}{Y - \dfrac{L}{p(\hat{e}_{jn})}} \tag{4.19}$$

This equation is exactly identical to (4.15), which is the corresponding equation we derived earlier for the individual liability case. Therefore, the equilibrium effort levels must also be the same.

$$\hat{e}_{jn} = \hat{e}_{il} \tag{4.20}$$

We thus arrive at the somewhat surprising conclusion that joint liability will not improve upon individual liability if the borrowers behave in a non-cooperative manner. Only cooperative behaviour will ensure higher effort. One way of understanding this difference is in terms of externalities. When one partner chooses a higher level of effort, she creates an externality for the other partner because it reduces the probability that the latter would have to bear the joint liability burden. Non-cooperative behaviour, however, does not provide any mechanism for internalising this externality; therefore, the mutual benefit of higher effort cannot be captured. It is only through cooperation that the externality can be internalised, thereby ensuring that a higher level of effort will be expended by each partner.

It is instructive to go back to the *IC-IP* diagram to get a better insight into the failure of joint liability under non-cooperation. A comparison of *IC* condition (4.5) under individual liability with *IC* condition (4.18) under joint liability with non-cooperation shows that the latter has an additional term

$$-p'(e)[(1 - p(e)]c$$

which stems from the joint liability burden. In order to keep the left-hand side of the equation equal to 1, the repayment burden must fall by exactly this amount. By repeating the argument we made earlier in connection with joint liability with cooperation, this implies that the *IC* curve must fall by the amount $[1 - p(e)]c$, which turns out to be exactly the amount by which the *IP* curve will also fall. The result, as shown in Figure 4.3, is that the effort level remains the same even as the equilibrium interest falls.

What is happening here is that while the receipt of a joint liability payment enables the lender to bring down the rate of interest (so as to maintain the zero-profit condition), from the point of view of borrowers, any gain in a lower interest rate is exactly offset by the joint liability burden. As a result, they have no incentive to expend any more effort. Therefore, the probability of success will not change, and the repayment rate will not improve compared to the individual liability case. Finally, since the combined cost of the loan (including the interest rate and joint liability cost) is exactly the same as the interest rate under individual liability, the reach of credit will not expand either. Thus, all the benefits claimed for joint liability are lost if group members behave in a non-cooperative manner.

The superiority of joint liability thus hinges crucially on the assumption of cooperative behaviour. But cooperative behaviour cannot simply be assumed to emerge, especially in view of the strategic complementarity noted earlier: if a borrower is assured that her partner will exert effort, she will be encouraged to do so herself, but if she is afraid that the partner will not exert effort, she won't either. But who is to give the assurance that the partner will exert a high level of effort? We thus have a classic case of Prisoners' Dilemma, in which the absence of assurance about cooperation from the partner leads everyone to end up in the non-cooperative mode. Therefore, if joint liability is to improve upon individual liability, an incentive for cooperation must somehow be provided.

One possibility is to create the incentive internally, through the contract itself. Since the lender would prefer the borrowers to cooperate, he might try to devise

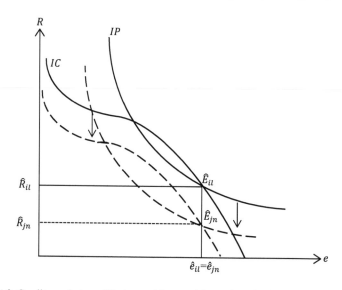

Figure 4.3 Credit market equilibrium with moral hazard under joint liability with non-cooperative behaviour

the terms of the contract in such a way that the borrowers would find it in their interest to cooperate rather than not to. This means, however, that the lender must leave a larger amount of incentive rent to the borrowers than would otherwise be needed. And, as shown by Laffont and Rey (2003), the amount of incentive rent required to induce cooperation under joint liability (and costless monitoring) is exactly the same as in the case of individual liability. There is, therefore, no hope of improving upon individual liability through this route.

An alternative is for the borrowers themselves to create the incentive externally, by devising a mechanism that would prevent deviant behaviour. In the general literature on moral hazard involving a principal and multiple agents, this kind of cooperation-inducing mechanism is called a 'side contract', a contract through which the agents bind themselves to an agreement. It is assumed that the agents will, if necessary, take the help of a third party to enforce the contract. In his classic paper on joint liability in the credit market, Stiglitz (1990) invoked precisely such a side contract.

A formal side contract enforced by a third party is, however, a rather fanciful idea in the context of rural societies in which people's behaviour is usually guided by informal codes of conduct, as encapsulated in the concept of a 'moral economy' (Scott, 1976). In this setting, a side contract must be interpreted as an informal agreement enforced by social norms. The most natural interpretation of an enforcement mechanism in this context is the use of social sanctions of the kind that is approved by the norms of a moral economy. If it can be assumed that borrowers are able and willing to impose social sanctions on each other in case anyone deviates from cooperative behaviour (and, additionally, that monitoring is costless), joint liability can indeed be shown to achieve the cooperative equilibrium, thereby ensuring its superiority over individual liability (Conning, 2005). The case for joint liability with costless monitoring, therefore, rests ultimately on the assumption that group members can threaten social sanctions to enforce contracts in ways that external lenders cannot.

4.2.4 The problem of costly monitoring

The preceding discussion was based on the premise that monitoring is costless. Further complications arise, however, when it is recognised that monitoring is not actually costless. Some of the costs of monitoring are obvious – namely, the time and effort that are needed to find out what others are doing. A second and less obvious, but perhaps more important, type of cost relates to the use of social sanctions discussed earlier. Peer monitoring would be useless without the backup of peer pressure and peer sanctions, but imposing pressure and sanctions on the peer is not a costless activity for the one who does the imposing. There is not only the psychological cost of doing unpleasant things to one's friends and relatives, there is also a probable cost of weakening the fabric of social capital in a way that might be harmful for the imposer herself.[21] This, too, must be counted as the cost of monitoring. The first type of cost will be high in societies where social capital is weak, while the second type will be high where social capital is strong; either way, there is no escape from the cost of monitoring.

One immediate consequence of recognising that monitoring can be costly is that it takes us back to the most basic question: what, after all, is the advantage of group lending over individual lending if costs of monitoring are to be incurred anyway? Of course, if one believes that peer monitoring would be less costly than lender monitoring, one can still claim the superiority of group lending (under cooperative behaviour). But this belief needs empirical support. Of the two types of monitoring costs we have distinguished, the first type (time and effort) would most likely be higher for the lender, but the second type (the psychological and social costs of imposing sanctions) would probably be less. The net effect is an empirical matter.

In any case, theoretically, the more interesting question is: if the lender and the peers had access to the same technology of monitoring, implying the same per-unit cost of monitoring, would group lending still be superior? Madajewicz (2011) argues that it would be, because even if the technology of monitoring were the same, the two types of monitoring would have very different impacts on the lender's profit and the borrowers' incentive. When the lender monitors an individual loan, he must recoup the costs of monitoring from the borrower by raising the interest rate. But, as we know, in an environment of moral hazard, a higher interest rate will only serve to distort the borrower's incentive – by inducing her to reduce her efforts, because in the presence of limited liability, the repayment burden acts like a tax on success. By contrast, when the peers monitor each other, they do so by using their labour endowments, which is not subject to limited liability and therefore does not distort incentive. In consequence, effort levels will be higher and interest rates lower under peer-monitored group lending compared to lender-monitored individual lending.

In an extension of this theme, Conning (1996, 2005) compared peer monitoring with 'monitoring by delegates', whereby the lender engages a 'delegate' or a third party to do the monitoring on his behalf. The delegate may be either a bank official or a local person who knows the borrowers well. In addition to monitoring, the delegate may also be encouraged to either lend additional funds to the borrowers or underwrite their loans so as to increase his stake in the borrowers' success.[22] Drawing upon the recent theories of financial intermediation through delegates (e.g., Holmstrom and Tirole, 1997), Conning shows that, despite many advantages of delegated monitoring, peer monitoring will still generally outperform it, because the lender will have to reimburse the delegates for their costs of monitoring, which will make a dent in his profits in a way that peer monitoring will not.

These findings would seem to suggest that the superiority of joint liability lending survives the recognition that monitoring can be costly. But there are a couple of important qualifications to this conclusion. The first relates to the case where borrowers happen to be risk-averse. The second raises a more basic question: when monitoring is costly, can we safely assume that borrowers will actually monitor each other?

The case of risk-averse borrowers has been analysed by Madajewicz (2011). Most of the theoretical literature on microcredit has assumed borrowers to be risk-neutral, as has our exposition so far. This is done mainly as an expositional simplification, although for poor borrowers, risk-aversion would be a more natural assumption. Madajewicz finds that the introduction of this plausible assumption makes a striking difference to the analysis of joint liability.[23] Essentially, the problem is that for risk-averse borrowers, joint liability induces two different kinds of incentives which pull in opposite directions. The standard, positive incentive is that it induces the borrowers to monitor each other so that they don't have to pay the joint-liability penalty for the partner's failure. This positive incentive has been widely recognised in the literature, *albeit* under the assumption of risk-neutrality. But there is also a negative incentive, which has largely been ignored in the literature as it was swept aside by the ubiquitous assumption of risk-neutrality.

In order to understand the nature of this negative incentive, it will be convenient to change our narrative slightly – from one of moral hazard in the choice of effort to that of moral hazard in the choice of projects. Each borrower is assumed to have a choice between two projects – one safe and the other risky; the projects have the same expected return, but the risky project has a higher return when it succeeds. The problem of moral hazard arises because in the presence of asymmetric information and limited liability, the borrower may be inclined to adopt the risky project (because success would give her a higher return while failure doesn't worry her owing to limited liability), even though the lender wants her to adopt the safe project. Joint liability is expected to mitigate this moral hazard by giving an incentive to the borrowers to monitor each other so that they adopt the safe project – this is the positive incentive referred to earlier.

But now compare the situations facing an individual liability borrower and a joint liability borrower when they choose the safe project. For the individual liability borrower, adoption of the safe project will yield a certain return. For the joint liability borrower, however, the return is no longer certain, because even though her own project will give a certain return, her overall return becomes uncertain as she may have to pay a joint liability fine in case the partner chooses the risky project and it fails. In other words, joint liability replaces a certain outcome with a lottery, whose outcome depends on her partner's choice and her luck. If the expected return from the lottery is the same as the certain return, this particular consequence of joint liability does not make any difference to the risk-neutral borrower, but it does to a risk-averse one – she does not like the risk associated with the lottery. In order to mitigate that risk, she may become inclined to adopt the risky project herself, in the hope that if the project succeeds, its higher return would enable her to better bear the risk emanating from the partner's end. Joint liability may thus induce a borrower to choose a risky project, even though, as an individual liability borrower, she might have chosen the safe project – that's the negative effect of joint liability under risk-aversion.

In his pioneering paper, Stiglitz (1990) did recognise this possibility, but he argued that it could be ignored because the negative effect would be of second-order importance compared to the positive effect if the joint liability fine is made arbitrarily small. Madajewicz correctly argues, however, that the idea of an arbitrarily small joint liability fine is plausible only if monitoring is costless (which Stiglitz assumed). If monitoring is appreciably costly, the joint liability fine will

Group lending and moral hazard 79

have to be large in order to give the borrowers the right amount of incentive to monitor. In that case, the negative effect will no longer be insignificant, and the net effect of joint liability would depend on the relative strengths of positive and negative incentive effects. Thus, with costly monitoring and risk-averse borrowers, the superiority of joint liability as a means of overcoming *ex ante* moral hazard cannot be taken for granted.

If we revert to the assumption of risk-neutral borrowers, the negative effect pointed out by Madajewicz would not exist. Joint liability with peer monitoring would now be superior to individual liability, even with costly monitoring. But we still need to confront the second, and more fundamental, problem with costly monitoring: will the peers actually find it worthwhile to monitor each other, when doing so involves costs?

The answer is no, if they are left to their own devices. The reason lies in the existence of a strategic complementarity in the decision to monitor, of the same kind as the one we saw in the case of the decision to exert effort: it is worthwhile for one borrower to monitor only if the partner also monitors, but not otherwise. If my partner monitors me and ensures that I exert a high level of effort and my project succeeds, I shall be keen to monitor her, too, so that her project doesn't fail, saddling me with the joint liability burden. But if she doesn't monitor me and I exert a low level of effort and my project fails, I shall be aware that I won't have to pay the joint liability fine on her behalf (owing to limited liability protection) if my partner also exerts a low level of effort and her project fails; therefore, I shall have no incentive to incur the cost of monitoring. Given this strategic complementarity in costly monitoring, self-interested borrowers acting on their own will end up in a non-cooperative equilibrium with no monitoring and low level of effort.[24] Monitoring, like effort, becomes subject to moral hazard.

Clearly, costly monitoring, like costly effort, won't just happen; it must be induced in an environment of asymmetric information and limited liability. What can be done to induce it? As in the case of effort, we can think of two broad alternatives – one external to the credit contract, and the other internal to it. The external inducement is, again, the use of social sanctions. As the fear of social sanction induces a borrower to exert a high level of effort, it also, at the same time, induces her to monitor the partner lest the liability of the latter's failure should be paid for by the fruits of her effort. If costs of monitoring are high, the severity of sanctions must also be high to induce monitoring; but with an appropriate level of sanctions, monitoring will always happen, whatever the cost.[25] Thus, as in the case of costless effort, social sanctions can come to the rescue of joint liability lending in the case of costly monitoring, ensuring that borrowers will exert a higher level of effort compared to individual lending.

There are, however, a couple of problems with this external solution. There is first a problem of conceptual inconsistency, which has largely been ignored in the literature so far. The inconsistency stems from the implicit assumption that the cost of monitoring and the cost of sanctions are independent of each other. But this assumption does not hold if, as we have argued, the psychological and social costs of imposing sanctions on a peer should be counted as part of the cost of monitoring. In that event, instead of overcoming the problem of costly monitoring, social sanctions may indeed accentuate it. If sanctions are to be used to induce monitoring, it must now be allowed that the cost of monitoring will go up; in response, sanctions will have to be made more severe to counter the heightened cost of monitoring. But then the cost of monitoring will rise even more, and in response, sanctions will have to be made even more severe, and so on, creating an upward spiral that may not have an equilibrium. In the limit, it may so happen that the very fabric of social capital, which gives legitimacy to social sanctions, will suffer such an irreparable damage that sanctions may lose their effectiveness altogether.

The second problem is of an empirical nature. Social sanctions may not work well where social capital happens to be weak. This is true of many environments, especially urban environments, in which microcredit institutions happen to work. Some alternative inducement mechanism must exist in those environments.

Mechanisms internal to the contract may offer the necessary alternative. Conscious of the existence of moral hazard in monitoring, the lender may want to provide an incentive to the borrowers so that they actually monitor each other. This incentive will have to be provided on top of the usual incentive for exerting effort. The question then arises: would joint liability lending still retain its superiority over individual lending? In the case of costless monitoring, we noted earlier that while the lender can indeed provide the necessary inducement to monitor, the amount of incentive rent required is just as high as in the case of individual lending, so that joint liability lending can claim no superiority over individual lending. In the case of costly monitoring, however, the picture is more complicated – it depends crucially on the sequence in which decisions are taken on monitoring and effort levels.

In the presence of costly monitoring, the strategic interactions among borrowers induced by joint liability can be seen as a game involving two kinds of decisions. The first decision involves whether to monitor or not, and the second decision involves whether to exert a high level of effort (or to choose the safe project) or not. These decisions may be taken either simultaneously or sequentially, and their implications for the success in inducing monitoring are radically different.

Consider first the case of simultaneous decision-making.[26] We can think of a simple game in which there are only two group members, each of whom makes a binary choice regarding both monitoring and effort. If they decide to monitor, they incur a cost m, and if they do not monitor, the cost is zero. If they choose a high level of effort, they achieve a high probability of success denoted by $\bar{\pi}$; and if a low level of effort is chosen, they achieve a low probability of success denoted by $\underline{\pi}$. The cooperative outcome will be achieved when each borrower chooses the strategy pair $(\bar{\pi}, m)$. If these strategies are chosen simultaneously, it can be easily demonstrated that $(\bar{\pi}, m)$ cannot be a Nash equilibrium.

If $(\bar{\pi}, m)$ is to be a Nash equilibrium, it must be a symmetric best response for both players. But this cannot be so, because if borrower *1* chooses $(\bar{\pi}, m)$, borrower *2* will reason that her best response is in fact $(\bar{\pi}, 0)$; given that borrower *1* will choose a high level of effort, borrower *2* has no incentive to incur the cost of monitoring m, but she will choose a high level of effort spurred by the knowledge that she was going to be monitored. Borrower *1* will then reason that her best response to borrower *2*'s ($\bar{\pi}$, *0*) is ($\underline{\pi}$, *0*), because if her partner is not going to monitor, she can get away by lowering the level of effort. Borrower *2* will then change her response to ($\underline{\pi}$, *0*), because if her partner is going to choose a low level of effort, she doesn't want to increase the likelihood of being liable to pay for her partner's failure by raising her own probability of success. Thus, the only symmetric equilibrium of the game is ($\underline{\pi}$, *0*), the non-cooperative strategy. In essence, the problem stems from the strategic complementarity that is inherent in monitoring and in effort, as discussed earlier.

The whole idea of inducing peer monitoring through joint liability thus collapses if monitoring and effort choices are made simultaneously. In recognition of this problem, Conning (2005) and Laffont and Rey (2003) assumed a sequential structure of the decision-making process, in which the borrowers first decide on their monitoring level and then decide the effort level in light of the monitoring decision made earlier. Once this sequence is allowed, it gives the lender the opportunity to commit the borrowers to monitoring by giving them an appropriate amount of incentive rent. This is what prevents peer monitoring from collapsing in this framework.

This formulation enables the authors to ensure that joint liability will lead to a cooperative outcome, *albeit* at the cost of a higher incentive rent (compared to costless monitoring); and then they go on to ask whether joint liability is still superior to individual liability. Their answer is that it depends on the extent to which monitoring is costly. The higher the costs of monitoring, the higher is the amount of incentive rent that must be left to the borrower to ensure that they do monitor each other. If the costs are very high, the incentive rent may turn out to be even higher than in the case of individual lending. Therefore, the conclusion is that joint liability lending will be superior to individual lending even without the help of social sanctions, provided the costs of monitoring are low.

One problem with this formulation is that the sequential structure that is assumed here is rather artificial. In the case of a one-period loan where all the borrowers receive loans simultaneously, there is no reason to suppose that borrowers will choose their monitoring level before choosing the level of effort. There is nothing to prevent them from making the two decisions simultaneously.

By contrast, a sequential structure emerges much more naturally if one considers the idea of a conditional loan that was a common feature of the classic Grameen model. In this model, only one member of a group was first given a loan; the second member received a loan only after some time, once the bank was reasonably confident that the first borrower would be able to repay her loan. If the first member was found to be delinquent, the second member would be denied the loan when her time came. Loans for the remaining members were similarly staggered and made conditional on good repayment history of those who had borrowed first. When a loan is offered in this conditionally sequential manner, the choice of monitoring and the choice of effort get naturally separated in time.

Roy Chowdhury (2005) and Aniket (2011a), among others, explore the implications of this temporal separation of the two choices. They both compare simultaneous lending with sequential lending but under different assumptions about the decision-making process in simultaneous lending. Roy Chowdhury assumes that borrowers not only take a loan at the same time, but they also decide on monitoring and effort decisions at the same time, i.e. simultaneous lending is combined with simultaneous decision-making. Aniket, on the other hand, assumes a sequential decision-making structure (*à la* Conning and Laffont-Rey), in which the borrowers first decide on monitoring and then on effort.

As we have seen before, if decisions on monitoring and effort are taken at the same time, joint liability fails to induce a positive level of monitoring. Therefore, under the decision-making framework assumed by Roy Chowdhury, simultaneous group lending can claim no superiority over individual lending. His concern was to investigate whether group lending can reclaim its superiority with a sequential financing scheme, given that such a scheme provides a natural mechanism for separating the monitoring choice from the choice of effort.[27] Not surprisingly, he finds that sequential financing does give an edge to group lending, because it is able to generate a positive level of monitoring.

The intuition behind this result is quite simple. Suppose, in period 1, borrower *A* receives the loan. For her, there is only one decision to make: whether to exert a high level of effort or not. Borrower *B* also has only one decision to make: whether to monitor borrower *A* or not. In making this decision, borrower *B* will be aware that if she does not do the monitoring in the current period, borrower *A* will exert a low level of effort, which will raise the probability of her failure; and this in turn will jeopardise borrower *B*'s prospect of receiving a loan in the second period. By monitoring, she may be able to ensure that borrower *A* chooses a high level of effort, so that the loan gets repaid and she herself receives a loan in the second period. Therefore, regardless of whether borrower *A* monitors borrower *B* in the second period or not, it is in the interest of borrower *B* to monitor borrower *A* in the first period. The temporal separation of monitoring and effort thus dissolves the strategic complementarity that induces non-monitoring in a simultaneous loan contract.

It may be noted that the preceding argument did not invoke any joint liability payment at all. What induces monitoring here is not the desire to avoid the repayment burden on behalf of a failed partner, but rather the desire to receive one's own loan in the future. The stick of joint liability fine is replaced by the stick of denial of a loan to the peers as the means of achieving the desired level of monitoring and effort. This change of stick makes a big difference to the relative strengths of alternative credit contracts. With sequential financing, group lending is able to induce a positive level of monitoring and can thus claim superiority over individual lending, even without the help of a joint liability fine,[28] while it cannot do so with simultaneous financing relying on joint liability alone.

For Aniket (2011a), the issue was slightly different. The question was not whether simultaneous or sequential financing could give group lending an advantage over individual lending by inducing a positive level of monitoring, because under his assumed decision-making framework, simultaneous lending could also induce positive monitoring, as demonstrated by Conning and others. For him, therefore, group lending was superior to individual lending in any case (provided the costs of monitoring are not very high), no matter whether financing was simultaneous or sequential. His question was: given that both modes of financing can induce positive monitoring, which one is more efficient, in the sense of being able to finance more of socially desirable projects? The answer would depend on the amount of incentive rents that must be left to the borrowers under alternative schemes, because the lower the rent, the lower would be the rate of interest (consistent with the lender's zero-profit condition) and the greater would be the lender's ability to finance socially profitable projects. Aniket demonstrated that sequential lending was more efficient because it enabled the lender to reduce the amount of incentive rent.

The reason lies in the nature of the borrowers' incentive compatibility constraints that must be satisfied under alternative schemes. Under simultaneous lending, two different incentive compatibility constraints must be satisfied. First, there is a collective incentive constraint that is meant to ensure that all group members decide to monitor at the desired level and exert a high level of effort rather than opt for the softer option of no monitoring and low effort. And then there is an individual constraint that is meant to ensure that, given the commitment on monitoring already made by the group, each individual has the incentive to expend the desired amount of effort. Since the first constraint incentivises two tasks – namely, monitoring and effort – simultaneously, the rent associated with the first constraint is larger compared to the individual constraint, where only one task (namely, effort) is incentivised. In the case of sequential lending, however, the group's collective incentive compatibility condition does not need to be satisfied, as the two tasks do not need to be incentivised simultaneously. By separating the monitoring and effort decisions temporally, sequential financing enables the lender to offer only a single-task incentive in each period – namely, the incentive to monitor to one borrower and the incentive for effort to her partner. It is this replacement of a two-task incentive by a one-task incentive that enables the lender to reduce the incentive rent under sequential lending, which in turn makes sequential lending more efficient than simultaneous lending.

4.3 Concluding observations

Moral hazard is endemic in credit markets as a consequence of asymmetric information between borrowers and lenders. When this is combined with limited liability of borrowers, owing to their inability to offer collateral, borrowers would tend to behave in ways that are neither socially optimal nor privately profitable for the lenders. For instance, they would tend to exert less effort on their projects or take up projects that are too risky. In either case, the probability of default would rise and the lenders would suffer, which is an important reason why poor borrowers (with limited liability) are usually not entertained by the formal banking system, and why moneylenders charge exorbitant interest rates.

As a consequence, poor people find themselves severely credit-constrained everywhere in the world. The microcredit revolution has helped overcome this problem by devising ways that minimise borrowers' incentive to indulge in a moral hazard type of behaviour.

According to the theorists of microcredit, the principal aspect of microcredit delivery models that serves this purpose is the presence of joint liability – the stipulation that if one member of a group happens to default, other members are to be penalised by the lender one way or the other. Faced with the prospect of this penalty, each member of a group would find it in her interest to ensure that other members succeed so that they don't have to default. Group members will then have the incentive to encourage, and if necessary pressurise, each other to behave in a way that raises the probability of success. Joint liability thus creates the potential to mitigate the moral hazard type of behaviour that stems from the combination of asymmetric information and limited liability.

It is important to recognise, however, that this potential may not always be realised. The most clear-cut case where the potential will certainly be realised is when the following conditions are met: (a) the group members behave in a cooperative manner, (b) monitoring is costless, and (c) the borrowers are risk-neutral.

One way to understand the importance of cooperative behaviour is to think in terms of externalities. When one partner decides to exert a higher level of effort (or to choose a less risky project), she creates an externality for her partners because it reduces the probability that the latter would have to bear the joint liability burden. Unless a mechanism can be found to internalise this externality, borrowers would not actually exert a sufficiently high level of effort (or choose a sufficiently safe project). Non-cooperative behaviour does not provide any mechanism for internalising the externality. On the contrary, borrowers may be tempted to hitch a free ride on each other, knowing that the burden of failure would be shared by the peers. Cooperative behaviour is needed to avoid this kind of free riding and to internalise the externality.

But it cannot simply be presumed that cooperative behaviour will happen just because it is in the best interest of borrowers; the Prisoners' Dilemma type of reasoning may end up in non-cooperative behaviour. Co-operation must, therefore, be induced. One possibility is for the lender to provide an additional incentive for cooperation, but theory shows that in this case joint liability lending is no better than individual lending. An alternative is for the borrowers themselves to take actions so as to promote cooperation – for instance, by applying social sanctions on deviant behaviour. The presumption here is that faced with the prospect of a joint liability fine, group members will monitor each other and threaten to impose social sanctions on those who tend to behave in a non-cooperative manner, thus ensuring that cooperative behaviour is indeed achieved.

But the invocation of social sanctions becomes problematic once it is recognised that monitoring involves costs. If monitoring were costless, it would be sensible to infer that borrowers would engage in as much monitoring as necessary to induce their partners to desist from a moral hazard type of behaviour. With costly monitoring, this inference is no longer valid. One problem arises if borrowers happen to be risk-averse rather than risk-neutral, as is typically assumed in the theories of microcredit. When risk-aversion is combined with costly monitoring, joint liability actually increases the incentive to take up risky projects, thereby increasing the probability of default. If this negative effect of joint liability is sufficiently strong, even cooperative behaviour may not suffice to overcome the moral hazard problem.

Even in the standard case of risk-neutrality, costly monitoring creates a problem. The recognition that monitoring involves costs induces a strategic complementarity in the decision-making of group members – in the sense that a borrower would find it worthwhile to monitor only if the partners also monitor, not otherwise. Monitoring then itself becomes subject to moral hazard. The right amount of monitoring won't simply happen just because it would be good for everybody – the free-rider problem will once again stand in the way. The question then arises as to what can be done to induce the right amount of monitoring.

There are two possible answers to this question. One possibility is to invoke, once again, the use of social sanctions. The threat of sanctions imposed by the peers may induce borrowers to engage in the level of monitoring required to avoid moral hazard, even though such monitoring would involve costs. The other possibility is for the lenders to engage in conditional sequential lending so as to offer a dynamic incentive to borrowers to avoid moral hazard. In this case, only one member of a group is first given a loan, with the condition that other members would be offered loans later only if the first member were to repay her loan on time. When a loan is offered in this conditionally sequential manner, the choice of monitoring and the choice of effort get separated in time. And this temporal separation of the decisions involving monitoring and effort dissolves the strategic complementarity that induces non-monitoring in a simultaneous loan contract when monitoring is costly.

The upshot of this discussion is that, if people are assumed to be completely self-interested rather than altruistic, the system of joint liability cannot, by itself, solve the problem of moral hazard that is endemic in the credit market. Joint liability must be combined with either the mutual imposition of social sanctions by the borrowers, or the provision of dynamic incentive by the lenders through conditional sequential lending. Some such combination would work if borrowers are risk-neutral. If, instead, the borrowers happen to be risk-averse, even this is no longer guaranteed; the superiority of joint liability over individual liability then becomes an empirical matter.

Notes

1 The present chapter deals with theories that view microcredit as a means of tackling the problem of moral hazard in credit markets; the next chapter reviews the theories that view microcredit as an institutional device to overcome two other problems of credit markets – namely, adverse selection and repayment enforcement. Given the generally high level of mathematical rigour of most of these theories, it would be impossible to give a real flavour of their insights without occasionally allowing some technical details to creep in; but in all such cases, we have tried to keep the algebra to the

minimum and to rely more on the use of diagrams and, even more so, on verbal explanations of the underlying intuition.
2. Ray (1998, Chapter 14) provides simple expositions of these models, as well as a very good overview of the empirical features of and theoretical explorations into the rural credit market.
3. For more on this theoretical debate, see Bandopadhyay and Ghatak (1982).
4. See the evidence provided, for example, by the papers in a special issue of the *World Bank Economic Review*, 1990, edited by K. Hoff and J. Stiglitz. Neat summaries of these and other evidence can also be found, *inter alia*, in Ray (1998), Banerjee (2004), and Conning and Udry (2007).
5. For forceful exposition of this view, see Hoff and Stiglitz (1990), Besley (1994), Ray (1998) and Banerjee (2004).
6. In what can be seen as a precursor of the modern view, a perceptive British colonial officer made the following observation about the rural moneylender of Punjab in the early 20th century: "He is always accessible, even at night; dispenses with troublesome formalities, asks no inconvenient questions, advances promptly, and if interest is paid, does not press for repayment of principal. He keeps in close personal touch with his clients, and in many villages shares their occasions of weal or woe. With his intimate knowledge of those around him he is able, *without serious risk*, to finance those who would otherwise get no loan at all" (Darling, 1925; emphasis added).
7. Illuminating analyses of such interlinked transactions can be found, *inter alia*, in Bardhan (1984), Basu (1987), Braverman and Srinivasan (1981), Braverman and Stiglitz (1982, 1986) and Mitra (1983). A simple intuitive analysis of the underlying logic of inter-linkage is offered by Ray (1998), Chapter 14.
8. For modern theoretical treatments of these institutions from the perspectives of information and enforcement, see Banerjee *et al.* (1994) on credit cooperatives and Besley *et al.* (1993) on ROSCAs.
9. The intellectual leadership of this research programme was given by the "rural finance group" of the Ohio State University in the 1980s. The main findings of their research are presented in Adams *et al.* (1984) and von Pischke *et al.* (1983). Concise statements of the main arguments can be found in Adams and Graham (1981), and Schaefer-Kehert and von Pischke (1986).
10. Interest rates held below the market equilibrium level necessarily led to rationing of credit, and the rationing process typically favoured the wealthy borrowers for a number of reasons. First, as the transaction costs of dealing with small loans demanded by poorer borrowers were found to be high relative to the interest rate that the banks were allowed to charge, the banks preferred to deal with the larger loans demanded by wealthier borrowers. Second, since low interest rates implied that rents were transferred from the lender to the borrower, it led naturally to a competition for cornering those rents, and it is the wealthy borrowers who had the social and political clout to win this battle. As a result, interest rate restrictions almost everywhere led to the exclusion of poorer borrowers from subsidised credit; and it happened with such regularity that it came to be described as the "iron law of interest rate restriction" (Gonzalez-Vega, 1984).
11. There are, of course, theories that deal with multiple problems at the same time; we have grouped them according to what is taken to be the major problem in the models concerned.
12. We are assuming risk-neutrality on the part of both borrowers and lenders. Introducing risk-aversion will complicate the exposition, but it will not alter most of the conclusions. We shall, however, take up an important implication of risk-aversion later in the analysis.
13. Applying the implicit function theorem to equation (4.6), it is easy to show that $d\hat{e}/dR < 0$. Intuitively, condition (4.6) shows that a higher R will lead to a higher value of $p'(e)$, and, with diminishing returns, this can only happen at a lower value of e.

Group lending and moral hazard 87

14 Given the assumptions made, it can be shown that if the two curves intersect at more than one point, the borrower would choose the lowest point, and also that, at the chosen point of intersection, the *IC* curve would be steeper than the *IP* curve, as in Figure 4.1. For details, see Ghosh *et al.* (2001).
15 This is indeed the assumption made by Stiglitz in his classic paper that first systematically analysed the role of joint liability and peer monitoring in mitigating moral hazard in the credit market (Stiglitz 1990). His analysis drew upon a principal-agent analysis of how peer monitoring can improve incentive-monitoring in the presence of costly information on the part of the principal in the insurance market (Arnott and Stiglitz, 1991), and applied the idea to a credit market in which moral hazard leads to credit rationing á la Stiglitz and Weiss (1981, 1987).
16 A more rigorous proof would involve solving the complicated differential equations (4.14) and (4.15), which, however, may not have closed-form solutions. An alternative is to assume specific functional forms of the probability function and the cost of effort function, which makes it easier to arrive at closed-form solutions; see, for example, Ghatak and Guinnane (1999). Yet another approach is to simplify the whole problem by assuming that there are only two levels of effort, and thus only two probabilities of success, high and low, which again makes it easier to obtain closed-form solutions; see, for example, Laffont and Rey (2003). But these alternative approaches involve a loss of generality; by contrast, our diagrammatic approach retains a high level of generality, *albeit* at the cost of a little bit of rigour.
17 This is true for any value of $p \in [0,0.5)$. If $p > 0.5$, the *IC* curve will actually rise rather than fall, but this will only reinforce the conclusion that follows.
18 This explanation is offered most clearly by Conning (1996, 2005) and is also referred to by Laffont and Rey (2003). The basic argument was first applied to the credit literature, though in a slightly different context, by Diamond (1984).
19 This way of reformulating the joint liability problem renders the analysis structurally similar to one particular strand in the general literature on moral hazard, which studies the principal agent problem with a single agent in a multi-task setting but facing limited liability (Holmstrom and Milgrom, 1991; Itoh, 1993), or where a single agent manages a multiple-outcome, single-task project under limited liability, as in Innes (1990).
20 It should be pointed out that while we have identified a reduction in interest rate as the vehicle through which the efficiency of a credit contract translates in the marketplace, this is not the only possible way of presenting the argument. Several other vehicles could be chosen – e.g., the size of loan, the size of collateral, and the size of project return. We have assumed a given loan size; but if loan size were allowed to vary, efficiency would be expressed as the lender's ability to offer a larger loan. Similarly, we have assumed that the borrower has no collateral at all; but if instead we had assumed that different borrowers had different amounts of collateral (*albeit* less than the repayment burden so that limited liability still applied to some extent), the same efficiency would have found expression in smaller collateral requirement. Finally, we have assumed just one project with a given return, when it succeeds; but if different borrowers were assumed to have different returns, efficiency would be measured by the extent to which a lender was able to finance projects with lower returns (but still higher than the socially optimal return). Narratives involving all these vehicles are found in the literature – for example, the interest rate narrative is found in Ghatak and Guinnane (1999) and Laffont and Rey (2003); the loan size narrative is found in Stiglitz (1990) and Madajewicz (2004, 2011); the collateral narrative is found in Conning (1996, 2005); and the project return narrative is found in Aniket (2011a). For the sake of uniformity of exposition, we have chosen, by and large, to tell the story in terms of interest rates (with some exceptions), but the diversity of channels through which the efficiency of a loan contract might be expressed in the marketplace must be recognised.

88 Group lending and moral hazard

21 The edifice of a moral economy is based on the foundation of reciprocities – i.e. people belonging to the same social network helping each other out at times of crisis. If members of a network gang up on their peers to impose sanctions on each other, these reciprocities may not survive, which will eventually harm not only those on whom sanctions are imposed, but also those who impose them.
22 Banerjee *et al.* (1994) had earlier investigated the role of such delegates in the context of German cooperatives of the 19th century.
23 The classic paper by Stiglitz (1990) did assume risk-aversion on the part of borrowers, but most of the subsequent contributions were based on the assumption of risk-neutrality.
24 See Roy Chowdhury (2005) for a formal demonstration of this proposition.
25 A formal proof can be found in Ghatak and Guinnane (1999).
26 The argument in this paragraph and the next draws upon Conning (2005).
27 Roy Chowdhury (2005) analysed the problem in the context of moral hazard in project choice arising from asymmetric information on the verifiability of project outcome – known as the problem of audit – rather than moral hazard in the choice of effort. However, the basic argument can be easily recast in terms of choice of effort.
28 Roy Chowdhury shows, however, that the efficiency of loan use and repayment performance can be improved further by adding a joint liability fine to the conditional sequential loan.

5 Theories of microcredit
Adverse selection and repayment enforcement

Ever since the classic work of Arrow (1963) and Akerlof (1970), it has become well-known that when informational asymmetries exist, the market can behave in strange ways. In particular, bad products and bad clients may drive good products and good clients out of the market – a kind of market failure that has come to be known as adverse selection.[1] In a couple of pioneering papers, Jaffe and Russell (1976) and Stiglitz and Weiss (1981) applied this idea to the credit market and showed that when lenders cannot distinguish between 'good' and 'bad' borrowers, the market-clearing interest rate might allow too many 'bad' borrowers and too few 'good' borrowers than is desirable from the lender's point of view. In consequence, the lender might resort to credit rationing, leaving a part of the demand for credit unsatisfied.[2] This would be socially inefficient, although it would be a rational response for the lender – a classic case of market failure.[3]

Another endemic problem of the credit market is that even when the borrower may have earned enough return to be able to repay the lender, she may not want to do so, and the lender may not be able to do anything to enforce repayment. The lender's inability to enforce repayment may stem from various sources, including the limited liability constraint associated with the absence of collateral. If the borrower does not have a tangible collateral that can be lawfully seized by the lender without incurring too high a transaction cost, the only conceivable option left to the lender is either to do something unlawful (such as threatening violence or seizing household assets that were not pledged as collateral), or to apply some kind of social pressure. The problem, however, is that while these options may be available, to some extent, to local moneylenders, neither option is really open to a formal lender who has his reputation to protect and the long arm of the law to contend with. Aware of this limitation, dishonest borrowers may choose to default even when they are able to repay. This is the problem of *ex post* moral hazard, also known as the problem of strategic default.[4]

An emerging body of microcredit theories claims that microcredit institutions contain a number of features (especially the joint-liability mechanism) that can help avoid, or at least minimise, both the adverse selection problem and the enforcement problem, and thereby improve the performance of the credit market. This chapter provides an analytical review of these theories.

5.1 Adverse selection in the credit market with individual lending

Before proceeding to the theories of microcredit that address the issue of adverse selection, we will first set the stage by explaining how asymmetric information tends to create adverse selection in the standard credit market with individual lending. Following Stiglitz and Weiss (1981), we take as the starting point that there are borrowers with different degrees of riskiness; borrowers themselves know how risky they are, but the lender does not. While in real life one would expect to find a continuum of borrowers with different levels of 'risk', for simplicity we shall assume that there are just two types of borrowers, called 'risky' and 'safe'. The probability of success of their respective project is denoted by p_s for safe borrowers and p_r for risky borrowers, where $0 < p_r < p_s < 1$. The lender is unable to distinguish between safe and risky borrowers; however, he is assumed to know that safe and risky types exist in the population in the proportions θ and $(1-\theta)$, respectively.

Both types of borrowers are assumed to have an outside option of value v that they can earn with certainty if they do not invest; v thus constitutes the opportunity cost of the project from the point of view of the borrowers. Neither type of borrower has any collateral to offer, nor do they have any liquid assets of their own, which means that they must borrow if they are to invest at all. Each project has two possible outcomes: success or failure. When the project succeeds, it yields the return R_s per dollar of investment to the safe borrowers and R_r to the risky ones, and if it fails, it yields zero to both types of borrowers. The outcomes of the projects are assumed to be independently distributed.

As in Chapter 4, the lender is assumed to operate on a zero-profit basis. His cost of fund is denoted by ρ, which also stands for the social cost of funds, so that the overall social cost of investment in a project is given by $(\rho + v)$. The lender's task is to choose a rate of repayment r (principal plus interest) per dollar of loan, which will maximise the borrower's utility while satisfying the lender's own zero-profit condition.

If the lender knew the borrower's risk attribute, he could have charged two different rates of interest to the two types of borrowers, commensurate with their levels of risk, and consistent with his own zero-profit condition:

$$r_i p_i - \rho = 0; \quad i = s, r \qquad (5.1)$$

In equilibrium, we shall have

$$r_i^* = \frac{\rho}{p_i}; \quad i = s, r \qquad (5.2)$$

Since $p_r < p_s$, equation (5.2) would entail $r_s^* > r_r^*$. This would be an efficient outcome, as riskier borrowers would be required to pay a higher interest rate.

Adverse selection, repayment enforcement 91

However, this solution does not work in a situation of asymmetric information where the lender cannot distinguish between the two types of borrowers, because the risky borrowers would pretend to be safe so as to pay the lower interest rate meant for the safe borrowers; the lender's zero-profit condition would not be satisfied in that event – he will go bankrupt. In technical jargon, we say that a 'separating contract' (or a 'separating equilibrium') does not exist in this situation.

The question then arises whether there exists a 'pooling contract' or a 'pooling equilibrium' where the same contract is offered to both types of borrowers without violating the zero-profit condition. Furthermore, if such equilibrium does exist, what are its characteristics – in particular, will it attract both types of borrowers or only one, and will it be efficient? It turns out that a pooling equilibrium does indeed exist, but its characteristics depend critically on the nature of risks and returns faced by the borrowers.

In their classic paper on asymmetric information in the credit market, Stiglitz and Weiss (1981) assumed that both safe and risky borrowers had the same expected return but the risky borrowers had a greater spread around the mean – known as the assumption of mean-preserving spread. In the present context, this assumption implies the following relationships:

$$p_s R_s = p_r R_r; \ R_r > R_s; p_r < p_s \tag{5.3}$$

In this formulation, when a project succeeds the risky borrower gets a higher return compared to the safe borrower, but her project succeeds less often, yielding the same expected return. An alternative formulation was proposed by de Meza and Webb (1987), in which the two types of borrowers get the same return when the project succeeds, but the risky borrower has a lower expected return because of her lower probability of success:

$$p_s R_s > p_r R_r; \ R_r = R_s; p_r < p_s \tag{5.4}$$

Theories of microcredit have been developed under both sets of assumptions. Since the implications of these assumptions for the nature of equilibrium in the credit market are very different, we need to understand their implications for individual contracts first before embarking on an elucidation of the theories of microcredit. To this end, we shall analyse the consequences of offering a pooling contract to individual borrowers first under the Stiglitz-Weiss (S-W) scenario and then under the de Meza-Webb (M-W) scenario.[5]

5.1.1 *Pooling equilibrium with individual contracts under the Stiglitz-Weiss (S-W) scenario*

Let the common expected return (per dollar of investment) to the two types of borrowers be denoted by $\bar{R}$ and the common interest rate charged by the lender by r[6].

92 Adverse selection, repayment enforcement

Let us also assume that the project is socially productive, whichever type of borrower undertakes it. We then have the following relationships:

$$\bar{R} = p_s R_s = p_r R_r \tag{5.5}$$

$$\bar{R} - p_s r < \bar{R} - p_r r \tag{5.6}$$

$$\bar{R} > \rho + v \tag{5.7}$$

The participation constraints of the two groups of borrowers are

$$\bar{R} - p_s r \geq v, \text{ and} < \bar{R} - p_r r \geq v \tag{5.8}$$

The critical rates of interest at which the two groups will participate are then given by

$$\hat{r}_s = \frac{\bar{R} - v}{p_s} \text{ and } \hat{r}_r = \frac{\bar{R} - v}{p_r} \tag{5.9}$$

Since $p_s > p_r$, we must have $\hat{r}_s < \hat{r}_r$. The equilibrium interest rate must be no greater than these critical values for the respective borrower group for the borrowers to participate in the credit market. Defining the average probability of success as $\bar{p} = \theta p_s + (1-\theta) p_r$, the equilibrium interest rate under a pooling contract can be derived from the lender's zero-profit condition as follows:

$$r^* \bar{p} = \rho, \text{ or, } r^* = \frac{\rho}{\bar{p}} \tag{5.10}$$

Whether a particular type of borrower will participate in the credit market or not will depend on where r^* happens to lie in relation to the critical values ($\hat{r}_s$, $\hat{r}_r$). By comparing the equations for $\hat{r}_r$ and r^*, it may be noted that r^* must always be less than $\hat{r}_r$.[7] This leaves us with two possibilities: either ($r^* < \hat{r}_s < \hat{r}_r$) or ($\hat{r}_s < r^* < \hat{r}_r$). In the first case, both groups will participate, but in the second case, only the risky group will participate and the safe group will stay away.[8]

The second possibility gives rise to adverse selection in the credit market under asymmetric information. The absence of safe borrowers also means that the credit market is inefficient, because by assumption, all borrowers have socially productive projects. If safe borrowers cannot participate in the credit market, some of the socially productive projects do not get undertaken. Thus, under the S-W scenario, the credit market may suffer from underinvestment.[9]

5.1.2 Pooling equilibrium with individual contracts under the de Meza-Webb (M-W) scenario

The M-W scenario differs from the S-W scenario in that we now have a common return for both types of borrowers when the project succeeds rather than a common expected return. Let this common return be denoted by $\tilde{R}$. The expected net returns will now be different for the two types of borrowers, even though the pooling contract offers the same interest rate to both:

$$p_s(\tilde{R} - r) > p_r(\tilde{R} - r) \tag{5.11}$$

The fact that expected returns now differ between the two types of borrowers allows us to examine an interesting case where the safe borrowers are socially productive while the risky borrowers are not, i.e.

$$p_s\tilde{R} > \rho + v; \quad p_r\tilde{R} < \rho + v \tag{5.12}$$

The participation constraints of the two groups of borrowers are

$$p_i(\tilde{R} - r) > v \quad i = r, s \tag{5.13}$$

The critical rates of interest at which both groups participate are then given by

$$\hat{r}_s = \tilde{R} - \frac{v}{p_s} \quad \text{and} \quad \hat{r}_r = \tilde{R} - \frac{v}{p_r} \tag{5.14}$$

Since $p_s > p_r$, we must have $\hat{r}_s > \hat{r}_r$. Note that this is opposite to what we found for the S-W case. The reason is that as the risky borrowers have a lower expected return in the M-W case, the critical interest rate above which they will not participate must be lower compared to the safe borrowers. As before, whether a particular group participates in the credit market or not will depend upon the relationship of these critical values with the equilibrium interest r^* (as given in (5.10)). From (5.12), we have

$$\tilde{R} - \frac{v}{p_s} > \frac{\rho}{p_s} \quad \text{and} \quad \tilde{R} - \frac{v}{p_r} > \frac{\rho}{p_r} \tag{5.15}$$

By using (5.4) and (5.10) and noting that $p_s > \bar{p} > p_r$, we see that the inequalities in (5.15) imply that r^* can be either greater than $\hat{r}_s$ or smaller than $\hat{r}_r$ or somewhere in between. In the in-between case $\hat{r}_s > r^* > \hat{r}_r$, only the safe borrowers will participate in the credit market and the risky borrowers will stay away – the complete opposite of the result found for the S-W scenario. This will be a socially efficient outcome though, because by assumption, the risky borrowers are socially unproductive. Now consider an alternative case where $\hat{r}_s > \hat{r}_r > r^*$. In this case, both groups will participate, but this will be an inefficient outcome because socially unproductive, risky borrowers have also come to the fold. This is also a case of adverse selection, but of a different kind. Here the selection is adverse not because some good borrowers are put off by the pooling contract (as in the S-W scenario), but because some bad borrowers are attracted by it.

94 Adverse selection, repayment enforcement

And inefficiency in the credit market arises not from underinvestment but from overinvestment.[10]

In both the S-W and M-W scenarios, the possibility of adverse selection arises from the equilibrium r^* taking a value within a particular range. Since, with given ρ, the value of r^* depends on the average probability of success $\bar{p}$ (see equation (5.10)), which in turn depends on the proportions of risky and safe borrowers in the population (as measured by the parameter θ), the likelihood of adverse selection itself depends on these proportions. The following diagrammatic analysis helps to see these relationships more intuitively.

Figure 5.1 represents the S-W scenario and Figure 5.2 represents the M-W scenario. In both cases, the rays p_s and p_r going through the origin stand for the probabilities of success: the slopes of these two rays are equal, respectively, to the probability of success of safe borrowers (p_s) and of risky borrowers (p_r). Since $p_s > p_r$, the p_s ray is steeper than the p_r ray. The average probability of success ($\bar{p}$) is represented by a line lying in between these two rays. The exact location of this line will depend on the proportions of safe and risky borrowers in the population. The higher the proportion of safe borrowers (θ), the closer it will be to the p_s ray.

In Figure 5.1 (the S-W case), the returns to the project R_s and R_r for the safe and risky types, respectively, are shown on the x-axis, and the social cost of capital ρ is shown on the y-axis. We now proceed in three steps. In the first step, we locate on the y-axis the point of expected return $\bar{R}$. Given that $\bar{R} = p_s R_s = p_r R_r$, the location of $\bar{R}$ on the y-axis can be found by drawing a horizontal line that cuts the p_s and p_r rays just vertically above the points R_s and R_r, respectively. In the second step, we locate the critical interest rates $\hat{r}_s$ and $\hat{r}_r$ on the x-axis. Noting from (5.9) that $p_s \hat{r}_s = p_r \hat{r}_r = \bar{R} - v$, we first locate the point $(\bar{R} - v)$ on the y-axis and then draw a

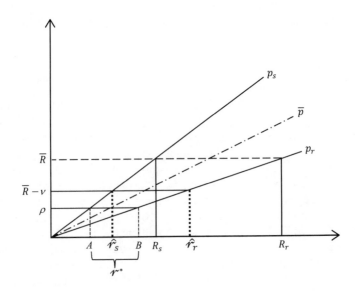

Figure 5.1 Adverse selection in the credit market: the Stiglitz-Weiss (S-W) scenario

Adverse selection, repayment enforcement 95

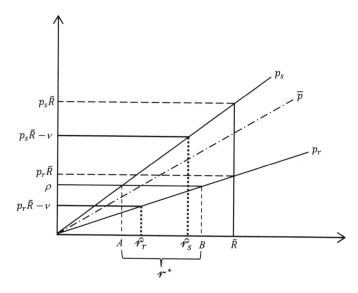

Figure 5.2 Adverse selection in the credit market: the de Meza-Webb (M-W) scenario

horizontal line from that point. From the points at which this line intersects the p_s and p_r rays, we then draw vertical lines on the x-axis, which will give us the critical values $\hat{r}_s$ and $\hat{r}_r$.

Finally, we locate the equilibrium interest rate r^* on the x-axis. Noting from (5.10) that $\bar{p}r^* = \rho$, we see that this can be done by first locating the point ρ on the y-axis and then following a procedure similar to the one used in the second step: draw a horizontal line from ρ, locate the point of intersection with the $\bar{p}$ ray, and then locate the point vertically below on the x-axis – this will represent r^*. As θ varies from 0 to 1, the $\bar{p}$ ray will span between the rays p_r (when $\theta = 0$) and p_s (when $\theta = 1$). Accordingly, the equilibrium r^* will lie within the range represented by the line segment AB on the x-axis.

Clearly, depending on the value of θ, which determines the location of $\bar{p}$ ray, r^* can lie either to the right or to the left of $\hat{r}_s$. There is a critical value of θ, which underlies the $\bar{p}$ ray as drawn in Figure 5.1, at which r^* will be equal to $\hat{r}_s$. For any lower value of θ, the $\bar{p}$ ray will be flatter than what has been shown in the diagram, and the corresponding r^* will lie to the right of $\hat{r}_s$. In that case, safe borrowers will not participate in the credit market. This is where adverse selection comes in.

Intuitively, the problem arises from the fact that the lower the value of θ, i.e. the higher the proportion of risky borrowers in the population, the higher the pooling interest rate will have to be in order to allow for an increased risk of default. But as the interest rate goes up, the contract becomes less and less attractive to safe borrowers who have a lower return (when the project succeeds), while the risky borrowers may still be interested as they enjoy a higher return when the project succeeds.[11] That is why, when the value of θ falls below a critical level, adverse selection sets in.

For a diagrammatic treatment of the M-W scenario (in Figure 5.2), we follow the same three steps as in Figure 5.1. The main difference is that in the first step, we now have only one return R on the x-axis but two different points of expected returns on the y-axis. Accordingly, in the second step, we locate two points on the y-axis instead of one, representing $(p_s \tilde{R} - v)$ and $(p_r \tilde{R} - v)$, respectively. In the third step, we again draw a horizontal line from ρ on the y-axis, but we deliberately place ρ above the point representing $(p_r \tilde{R} - v)$ to reflect the assumption that risky borrowers are socially unproductive. Then, following the same logic as in Figure 5.1, we locate the critical interest rates $\hat{r}_s$ and $\hat{r}_r$ on the x-axis and the range $\overline{AB}$ within which the equilibrium interest rate r^* will lie.

As θ varies from 0 to 1, making the $\overline{p}$ ray span between the rays p_r (when $\theta = 0$) and p_s (when $\theta = 1$), there will be a critical value of θ, and hence a particular location of $\overline{p}$ (as drawn in the diagram), at which r^* will be equal to $\hat{r}_r$. For any lower value of θ, the $\overline{p}$ ray will be flatter, so that r^* will lie to the right of $\hat{r}_r$. In this situation, the risky borrowers will stay away from the credit market and only the safe borrowers will participate; this will be an efficient outcome, since only the safe borrowers are socially productive, by assumption. However, for any higher value of θ, the $\overline{p}$ ray will be steeper and r^* will lie to the left of $\hat{r}_r$. In this situation, the socially unproductive, risky borrowers will also join the credit market, leading to adverse selection.

To see the intuition behind this adverse selection, note that when the proportion of risky borrowers is high, the average risk of default is also high, so that the lender is obliged to offer a pooling contract with a high interest rate. Up to a point, safe borrowers will not be put off by high interest rate because their expected return may be high enough to satisfy their participation constraint, i.e. to enable them to recoup the opportunity cost v after repaying the loan. However, risky borrowers may want to stay away because their expected return is too low to recoup the opportunity cost. But as the proportion of safe borrowers rises, the overall risk of default declines, which allows the lender to offer a pooling contract with a lower interest rate. And if this proportion rises high enough, the interest rate may fall enough to attract the risky borrowers. To make the point differently, the existence of safe borrowers creates a pecuniary externality for risky borrowers by helping to keep the interest rate low. The more numerous the safe borrowers are, the bigger is the externality. And if they are sufficiently numerous to bring the equilibrium interest rate below the critical level consistent with the participation constraint of risky borrowers, adverse selection will occur.

5.2 Joint liability as a solution to adverse selection

One strand of microcredit theories has tried to demonstrate how the adverse selection problem discussed above is mitigated by the modalities of microcredit, in particular by the mechanism of group lending. Before discussing these theories, it might be useful to first note how the problem might be resolved in the context of individual lending. In the general literature on adverse selection (in any market), the standard approach is to look for a menu of contracts with two characteristics: first, each contract in the menu should be compatible with the participation constraint of the principal (which in the present context means that each credit contract must satisfy the lender's zero-profit condition); and second, different types of agents (which in this case means borrowers) will choose different items from the menu depending on what suits them the best, thus leading to a separating equilibrium. Since each type of agent will maximise the agent's own utility through his choice of contract while keeping the principal on his reservation utility, the outcome will be Pareto efficient. In the context of adverse selection in the credit market, a solution along this line was suggested by Bester (1985).

The menu of contracts Bester suggested consists of two instruments: the rate of interest (r) and the amount of collateral (c). The lender can offer a range of contracts (r, c) by varying the levels of the two instruments. In order to satisfy the zero-profit condition, contracts with higher interest rates must be coupled with lower values of collateral and vice versa. Faced with this choice of contracts, borrowers of different risk types will choose differently. The low-risk types will choose contracts with a low interest rate and high collateral, because they are confident about not being obliged to part with the collateral very frequently. By contrast, the high-risk types will choose contracts with a high interest rate and low collateral, because they are more likely to fail and hence more likely to lose their collateral. This is, of course, exactly what the lender wants: he wants to charge higher interest rates for the riskier borrowers. The problem is that he cannot achieve this goal when his menu of contracts consists of only one instrument – namely, the interest rate – because the high-risk types will pretend to be low-risk, choose the low interest rate contract, and thereby break the zero-profit condition of the lender. This outcome is neatly averted, however, by coupling the additional instrument of collateral with the interest rate. If, now, the high-risk borrowers try to pretend to be low-risk and choose low interest rates, they will be obliged to offer high collateral, which they do not want to do. Out of their own interest, they will then choose the 'high-interest low-collateral' option. Adverse selection is thereby avoided, and efficiency is achieved.

While theoretically elegant, the problem with this solution is that there might be a limit to what the borrowers can put up as collateral owing to the wealth constraint. In particular, if the 'low-interest high-collateral' contracts require levels of collateral that are higher than what the low-risk borrowers can afford to offer, then many low-risk types will be forced to stay out of the market, thus allowing adverse selection to creep back in. A possible way out was suggested by Besanko and Thakor (1987), who showed that low-risk borrowers may be able to offer supplementary collateral by way of a guarantee from co-signees. This mechanism is expected to work because the co-signees, who are assumed to belong to the same community as the borrowers and are therefore likely to be able to distinguish between different risk-types, should be willing to co-sign the loan application of low-risk borrowers but not that of high-risk borrowers.

It is this idea – that local knowledge can be harnessed as a substitute for hard collateral –that was exploited by the theorists of microcredit working with models of adverse selection. With group-based lending, the instrument of collateral is replaced by joint-liability payment. If the lender now offers a menu of contracts (r, c) in which low rates of interest (r) are coupled with a high joint-liability payment (c) and vice versa, it can be argued, following Bester's logic, that safer borrowers would opt for the 'low-interest high-joint-liability' option while risky borrowers will choose the opposite combination. Once again, a separating equilibrium should emerge and adverse selection be avoided.

It turns out, however, that when collateral is replaced by joint-liability payment, the application of Bester's logic is not straightforward. Since the choice of contracts is now made by groups rather than individuals, the most we can argue, based on Bester's logic, is that groups of safe borrowers would opt for the 'low-interest high-joint-liability' option while groups of risky borrowers will choose the opposite combination. In other words, for Bester's logic to apply to group lending, the groups must be homogeneous in nature, consisting of members of the same risk-type. But this begs the question: who is going to ensure that groups will be homogenous? What is to prevent formation of heterogeneous groups containing members of different risk types? This is where the importance of local information comes in. The lender may not know who are low-risk and who are high-risk borrowers, but in a closely knit society, the borrowers themselves are likely to know each other's type. What is needed, therefore, is an incentive mechanism that will induce the borrowers to form only homogeneous groups.

One possibility is to follow a strategy suggested by Varian (1990). He proposed a screening mechanism in which borrowers themselves form groups amongst themselves but the lender ensures that only safe borrowers will form groups, leaving out the risky borrowers. The lender does so by interviewing at random any one member of a group and trying to assess whether that particular member is a good type or a bad type. If the interviewee is assessed to be a bad type, the whole group will be rejected. This will give incentive to the safe borrowers to form groups only with other safe borrowers.

A practical problem with this procedure is that the lender's assessment process may not be entirely reliable, in which case the whole practice of group-based lending will be rendered inefficient. More fundamentally, direct intervention by the lender is not really necessary to ensure the formation of homogeneous groups. In a couple of influential papers, Ghatak (1999, 2000) has shown that if a lender offers joint-liability contracts, homogeneous groups will be formed in an endogenous manner. The very logic of joint liability will lead to 'assortative matching', whereby safe borrowers form groups only with safe borrowers and risky borrowers form groups only with risky borrowers.

Consider the logic that drives the process of group formation. Every borrower, regardless of her risk type, would want to form a group with a safe partner because this will minimise the prospect of joint-liability payment, and thereby maximise her own expected payoff. But not every borrower will attach the same value to having a safe partner. A safe borrower would value a safe partner more than

Adverse selection, repayment enforcement 99

would a risky borrower. This is because, being a safe borrower, she is more likely to succeed and therefore more likely to have to pay the joint-liability penalty if she joins with a risky partner.[12] In other words, the expected joint-liability cost of being associated with a risky partner is higher for a safe borrower than for a risky borrower. Correspondingly, the benefit of being associated with a safe partner is higher for a safe borrower than for a risky borrower. Therefore, a safe borrower values a safe partner more than does a risky borrower. Given this difference in valuation, safe borrowers will be driven towards other safe borrowers, leaving risky borrowers to form groups amongst themselves.

A little bit of formal logic may help clarify the point better. Consider the simplest case of two-person groups, in which the first person is designated by i and her partner by j, where both i and j can be of either the safe type (s) or the risky type (r). The probabilities of success are denoted by p_s and p_r for the safe and risky types, respectively. In keeping with the Stiglitz-Weiss assumptions, $p_s > p_r$, but the safe type has a lower return ($R_s < R_r$) when the project succeeds (and both have zero return when the project fails) so that both types have the same expected return: $p_s R_s = p_r R_r$. Take any joint-liability contract, denoted by (r, c), where, as before, r stands for the (gross) rate of interest and c for the joint-liability penalty. The expected payoff (U) of borrower i with a partner j is given by

$$EU_{ij}(r, c) = p_i p_j (R_i - r) + p_i (1 - p_j)(R_i - r - c) \tag{5.16}$$

The first part of the right-hand side of (5.16) stands for the payoff when both i and j succeed, and the second part stands for the payoff when i succeeds but j fails.[13] The payoff function can be rewritten as

$$EU_{ij}(r, c) = p_i (R_i - r - c) + p_i p_j c \tag{5.17}$$

It can now be easily worked out that $EU_{ss} - EU_{sr} = p_s(p_s - p_r)$. This is the gain, from the point of view of a safe borrower, of having a safe partner compared to having a risky partner. From the point of view of a risky borrower, the corresponding gain is given by $EU_{rs} - EU_{rr} = p_r(p_s - p_r)$. Since $p_s > p_r$, the gain from having a safe partner is clearly greater for a safe borrower than for a risky borrower. A safe borrower will, therefore, value a safe partner more than will a risky borrower.

It is this difference in valuation that guides the nature of group formation. If the process of group formation is completely voluntary, the groups will be formed in a way that satisfies a principle known as the 'optimal sorting property'.[14] This principle says that groups are formed optimally when members not in the same group could not form another group without making at least one of them worse off. Given the difference in valuation noted above, it is easy to see that only assortative matching, leading to homogenous groups, satisfies this property. Clearly, if a safe borrower were to find herself in a heterogeneous group, she would be worse off compared to being in a homogenous group of safe borrowers, because a risky partner is less valuable to her than a safe partner.

One further issue needs to be addressed, however, before the optimality of assortative matching can be firmly established. If side payments were allowed among the borrowers, one would have to ask: can the risky borrowers entice the safe borrowers to form heterogeneous groups with them by offering a bribe? The answer is 'no', and the reason again lies in the difference in valuation noted above. The risky borrower may well try to bribe the safe borrower, because after all, she too prefers a safe partner to a risky one, but she would fail to do so because the maximum value she attaches to having a safe partner is less than the maximum value the safe borrower herself attaches to having a safe partner. In other words, the maximum amount a risky borrower would be willing to offer as a bribe is less than what the safe borrower would demand as compensation for giving up a safe partner. Side payments can thus never be large enough to induce safe borrowers to form groups with risky borrowers. Therefore, only assortative matching can occur.

Once it is established that only homogenous groups are formed comprised of borrowers of similar risk types, it is easy to demonstrate how lenders can induce a separating equilibrium by offering a menu of contracts with varying combinations of (r, c). The crucial point here is that borrowers of different risk types will have different trade-offs between r and c. To see how, first note that with assortative matching equation (5.16) transforms into

$$EU_{ii}(c, r) = p_i R_i - \{p_i r + p_i(1 - p_i)c\} \tag{5.18}$$

Noting that the expected return $p_i R_i$ is a given constant for a particular situation, we can view (5.18) as generating a set of indifference curves between r and c. The marginal rate of substitution between them is given by

$$\frac{dc}{dr} = \frac{1}{1 - p_i}$$

Since $p_s > p_r$, it follows that the indifference curve is steeper for the safe borrowers.[15]

This implies that to receive a small reduction in the interest rate, safe borrowers would be willing to pay a higher amount of joint-liability penalty than risky borrowers. Safe borrowers are confident that, since they have safe partners, they won't have to pay the joint-liability penalty very often; they are therefore happy enough to accept a higher value of penalty for the benefit of enjoying a lower interest rate. By contrast, a risky borrower is more concerned about joint-liability payments since she has a risky partner who is very likely to fail more often than the partner of a safe borrower. That's why she is keen to keep the joint-liability penalty low, even at the cost of a higher interest rate. Taking advantage of this difference in trade-off, the lender can offer a menu of contracts with varying combinations of (r, c). Faced with this menu, safe groups will choose a contract with a low interest rate and a high joint-liability penalty, while risky groups will choose the opposite combination. The group lending mechanism thus gets rid of the adverse selection problem, because safe borrowers are no longer driven away from the credit market.[16]

Though theoretically elegant, this result has to contend with a rather serious practical problem: namely, that hardly any microcredit institution offers contracts with varying degrees of joint-liability penalty. The most common practice is to offer a single contract. The question, therefore, arises whether group lending can overcome the adverse selection problem by offering just a single contract. The answer, somewhat surprisingly, turns out to be 'yes'. The argument is slightly more subtle than in the case of a menu of contracts, but the essential point is that even with a single contract (r, c), safe borrowers may be induced to stay in the credit market because they would *effectively* pay less than risky borrowers.

Note that under joint liability, the cost of credit has two components – r and c. Both components are, of course, conditional. A borrower pays nothing if her project fails. But if it succeeds, she will pay r if the partner also succeeds, which has probability p_j, and $(r + c)$ if the partner fails, which has probability $(1-p_j)$. Thus, conditioned on the borrower's own success, the expected cost of credit for borrower i is $[p_j r + (1-p_j)(r + c)]$, which reduces to $r + (1-p_j)c$. Since, under assortative matching, a safe borrower will have a safe partner, her expected cost of credit is $r + (1-p_s)c$; by the same token, the expected cost of credit for a risky borrower is $r + (1-p_r)c$. Since $p_s > p_r$, the expected cost of credit must be lower for the safe borrower.

The underlying idea is simply that, since assortative matching ensures that the partner of a safe borrower is less likely to fail than the partner of a risky borrower, a safe borrower will have to pay the joint-liability penalty less often. Therefore, a safe borrower whose contract is conditioned on her own success will face a lower effective cost of credit than a risky borrower. In consequence, even a single contract may succeed in generating a separating equilibrium in which both types of borrowers co-exist, thereby eliminating the problem of adverse selection.[17]

The avoidance of adverse selection not only helps the safe borrowers by enabling them to get access to the credit market, it also helps the risky borrowers, as the presence of safe borrowers helps to bring the interest rate down. Group lending with joint liability thus marks a Pareto improvement over individual lending under asymmetric information. In fact, Ghatak (2000) reaches the even stronger conclusion that group lending leads to the socially efficient outcome, i.e. the first best outcome that the market would have reached with individual lending if informational asymmetries did not exist.[18] Finally, the presence of safe borrowers also helps to reduce the overall rate of default, which may explain how microcredit programmes have achieved remarkably high repayment rates around the world.

5.3 Avoiding adverse selection without assortative matching

The preceding discussion of the benefits of group lending is entirely contingent on the assumption that potential borrowers know each other well enough to be able to tell who is a safe borrower and who is not. It is this assumption that makes assortative matching possible, which in turn drives the rest of the results. But local knowledge cannot always be assumed to be so complete in all areas – for example, in urban areas or in sparsely populated rural areas. Can joint-liability contracts still avoid adverse selection in such environments? Will assortative matching still occur? More fundamentally, is assortative matching actually necessary for group-based lending to work? Attempts to answer these questions lead to some interesting insights into group lending as a means of overcoming adverse selection.

If potential borrowers do not know each other's type, there is no reason to expect assortative matching to occur. It may still happen as a matter of coincidence, but heterogeneous grouping is the more likely outcome. Armendáriz de Aghion and Gollier (2000) show, however, that even with heterogeneous grouping, joint-liability contracts may lead to a Pareto improvement over individual liability contracts under certain conditions. The secret lies in the fact that the very act of group formation, no matter what type it is, creates a 'collateral effect' through cross-subsidisation amongst borrowers, as successful members pay up for the unsuccessful ones. This collateral effect renders group formation into an effective risk-pooling mechanism, which enhances efficiency. The 'collateral effect' allows the bank to reduce the interest rate, which in turn allows some safe borrowers to participate who may have been forced out of the credit market by a high interest rate under individual lending.

Joint liability, in fact, induces two opposing effects in this case. A reduction in the interest rate through the collateral effect is the positive effect. But there is also a negative effect which stems from the obligation to pay the joint-liability penalty for a failed partner. Since mixed matching is possible, any borrower would have to reckon with the prospect that she might land with a risky partner, which would render this obligation even more onerous. This is the 'joint-responsibility effect', which acts as a disincentive to join group lending. The safe borrower will participate only if the incentive of a lower interest rate is strong enough to outweigh the disincentive of the joint-responsibility effect.

The balance of these two opposing forces depends critically on the relative returns of the safe and risky borrowers when their projects succeed. If the return for the safe borrower is not high enough to pay fully for the default of a risky partner but the return for the risky borrower is high enough, then the collateral effect will outweigh the joint-responsibility effect for the safe borrower. The reason is that, in this case, the safe borrowers bear the joint-liability burden only partially, while the risky borrower bears the burden fully (in case she succeeds). The risky borrowers thus contribute relatively more to the overall collateral effect and contribute more towards the reduction of the interest rate. In other words, the superior ability of risky borrowers to pay the 'collateral' enables the safe borrowers to enjoy some reduction in the interest rate as an externality. The higher the return of the risky borrower compared to that of the safe borrower, i.e., the greater the degree of externality, the more likely it is that the collateral effect will outweigh the joint-responsibility effect for the safe borrowers. Therefore, the likelihood is stronger that joint liability will be able to avoid adverse selection, even without assortative matching.[19]

The idea that group lending will not always lead to positive assortative matching but may still mark an improvement over individual lending has been carried forward in several directions. This new brand of theories makes an even more radical departure than Armendáriz de Aghion and Gollier by demonstrating that group lending may not induce positive assortative matching of risk, even when borrowers are aware of each other's risk types, and yet adverse selection may be avoided. What matters for the lender's success in avoiding adverse selection is that he is able to induce an equilibrium in which safe borrowers find it worthwhile to enter the credit market.[20] Whether the safe borrowers choose to team up with other safe borrowers or with risky borrowers, or some with risky and some with safe borrowers, does not really matter so long as they do enter the credit market. In this spirit, this new brand of theories seeks to identify conditions in which the equilibrium without adverse selection may not be characterised by positive assortative matching of risks. Two strands of such theories may be distinguished. One strand deals with adverse selection but by emphasising aspects of microcredit delivery other than joint liability, and the second strand deals with the problem of enforcement in the face of strategic default. The first strand is taken up below, leaving the second strand for section 5.4, which deals with the issue of enforcement in general.

In a couple of related papers, Gangopadhyay and Lensink (2009) and Katzur and Lensink (2011) examine the implications of co-signing as an alternative to joint liability as a means of avoiding adverse selection. This is still a case of group lending, but with a difference. The co-signed loan contract specifies that two individuals simultaneously apply for a loan, but only one of the borrowers is liable for the loan of the other; she is the co-signer. As such, this may be described as a case of one-sided or asymmetric joint liability, as distinct from the two-sided or symmetric joint liability assumed in the standard literature.[21] As in the symmetric case, however, the co-signer will pay joint liability only if she herself succeeds while her partner fails.

The authors assume that the borrowers operate in the Stiglitz-Weiss scenario in which the expected returns are the same for everyone. For simplicity, all safe borrowers are assumed to have the same probability of success, and likewise all risky borrowers also have the same probability of success *albeit* less than that of safe borrowers. Finally, side payments are allowed, i.e. borrowers are allowed to pay each other with the objective of forming groups with the peers they prefer.

Assuming, for simplicity, that there are only two-person groups, we have four possible ordered pairs *{s, s}, {s, r}, {r, s}* and *{r, r}*, where the first person of the pair is designated as the co-signer and the second person as the principal applicant. The authors prove that under the assumptions made the heterogeneous group *{r, s}* – the one with a risky borrower as the co-signer and a safe borrower as the principal applicant – will emerge in equilibrium. A simple intuitive proof is offered below.

Let us first compare the two heterogeneous pairs *{r, s}* and *{s, r}*. The two pairs will have exactly the same expected aggregate gross return since, by assumption, every borrower has the same expected return. They will also have the same expected aggregate repayment burden excluding joint liability (i.e., the repayment a borrower must make on her own account when she succeeds), since both groups consist of the same pair of borrowers with only their positions reversed and the position has no bearing on own-account repayment. However, they will differ in terms of the amount they are expected to pay by way of joint liability, which in turn will make a difference to the expected aggregate payoff. In this regard, the *{r, s}* pair can be seen to have two advantages over *{s, r}*. First, since the principal applicant in the first pair is less likely to fail, the need for paying joint liability will also be less. Second, since the co-signer in the first pair is more likely to fail, she will have fewer occasions to pay joint liability for any given failure of the partner. On both counts, the *{r, s}* pair will have to pay less by way of joint liability. Accordingly, this pair will have a higher expected aggregate payoff than *{s, r}*. It will also be the one preferred by both borrowers, because with side payments they can both be better off in an outcome that offers a higher expected aggregate payoff. Therefore, if a heterogeneous group is formed at all in equilibrium, it can only be of the type *{r, s}*.

Now compare *{r, s}* with *{s, s}*. Once again, the aggregate expected return will be the same in the two cases, but there will be differences on two counts. First, unlike in the previous case, there will be a difference in the amount of own-account repayment, as the composition of the two groups is not the same. Since the co-signer of the heterogeneous group is a risky borrower who fails more often, the aggregate own-account repayment will be lower for *{r, s}*. Second, since joint liability doesn't have to be paid when a co-signer herself fails, the joint-liability burden will also be lower for *{r, s}*. For both reasons, the expected aggregate payoff will be higher for *{r, s}* compared to *{s, s}*. This implies that a safe borrower will have the incentive to look for a risky borrower rather than a safe borrower as her co-signer.

But would a risky borrower agree to be the co-signer of a safe borrower? That depends on what other options are open to her. One option is to seek to reverse the role, i.e. to go for *{s, r}* instead of *{r, s}*. But this will not work since, as we have already seen, *{r, s}* dominates *{s, r}* in equilibrium. The other option is to co-sign another risky borrower, i.e. form the group *{r, r}*, but this would not be a preferred option either because the co-signer will have to pay joint liability more often with a risky partner than with a safe partner. Thus, when asked by a safe borrower to be her co-signer, the risky borrower can do no better than to agree. Therefore, the pairing *{r, s}* will dominate all other pairings; hence the emergence of negative assortative matching.

Co-signing will thus achieve the objective of avoiding adverse selection, *albeit* by matching risky borrowers with opposite-risk types rather than with similar types as in the standard symmetric joint-liability case. Moreover, as a means of avoiding adverse selection, co-signing can be shown to have a couple of advantages over symmetric joint liability.[22] First, co-signing can achieve the socially efficient outcome associated with full information in a wider set of circumstances compared to symmetric joint liability. The second advantage relates to the outreach of microcredit. Under the standard joint-liability contract, the client's project payoff necessary to induce her to enter the credit market may be prohibitively high for small entrepreneurs. By contrast, in certain settings, the co-signed contracts can significantly reduce the threshold value of the project return, thereby ensuring a wider outreach of microfinance schemes.

5.4 Theories of microcredit dealing with the enforcement problem

The enforcement problem stemming from *ex post* moral hazard poses a rather more serious problem to the lender than *ex ante* moral hazard discussed in Chapter 4. There the lenders were at least dealing with honest borrowers, in the limited sense that they would voluntarily repay if only the project return were high enough; the task facing the lender was to induce the borrower to behave in a way that would increase the project return (either by exerting more effort or by choosing a less risky project). Here, by contrast, lenders are dealing with dishonest borrowers who wouldn't repay even when the project return permits them to do so. How do you induce such borrowers to behave in a way that will not put the lenders out of business?

If all borrowers were prone to strategic default and lenders had no way to prevent it, potential borrowers without collateral would never receive a loan if the credit contract were seen as a one-time transaction. Since the lender knows that the borrower would not repay, he would not offer the loan in the first place. A possibility opens up, however, if we allow repeated transactions, in which the same pair of borrower and lender enters a credit contract over and over again. The lender can then threaten not to offer a loan in the future in case the borrower defaults. If this threat is credible and the borrower values the availability of a future loan sufficiently, it may be possible to devise a credit contract that induces the borrower not to default.

One potential problem is that the threat may not work because the borrower might have access to other lenders to fall back upon if the first lender cuts her off. While this possibility cannot be denied, access to other lenders will not necessarily render the threat from the first lender completely toothless. After all, if a borrower defaults to one lender, her reputation would be sullied, which may make her access to other lenders more difficult – in particular, she may have to accept more onerous terms and conditions compared to what she would have received from the first lender. Default may thus have a real cost for the borrower, even if she has access to other lenders.

It is this cost of default that could make the denial of a future loan a credible threat.[23] With this threat, it can be shown that the lender may be able to offer a mutually beneficial contract that allows the credit market to function, even in the absence of any collateral. We shall presently demonstrate, however, that the outcome in this case will be socially sub-optimal – this is the inefficiency of a credit market characterised by *ex post* moral hazard. We shall also see that, as in the case of *ex ante* moral hazard, the source of this inefficiency lies in the incentive rent that the lender must leave with the borrower. The point is that the mere threat of cutting off future loans is not enough to prevent strategic default. Sure, the loss of a future loan would inflict a cost on the borrower, but this loss will be weighed by the borrower against what she will gain by defaulting, and only if the loss outweighs the gain would she decide not to default. The lender must, therefore, find a way of making the gain from repaying greater than the gain from defaulting. It

106 Adverse selection, repayment enforcement

is this imperative to provide a necessary incentive to the borrower that creates the possibility of a socially sub-optimal outcome.

5.4.1 Features of a credit market in the presence of strategic default

Let us consider an individual who has the production function $Y = F(L)$, where Y is output and L is the amount of capital invested, and the technology exhibits diminishing marginal returns: $F'(L) > 0$, $F''(L) < 0$. Let the per-unit cost of capital be denoted by ρ. If the individual relies entirely on her own capital and she is risk-neutral, she would decide her optimal level of investment L^* by maximising:

$$F(L) - (1+\rho)L \tag{5.19}$$

The solution L^* given by the following first-order condition is the socially optimal level of investment in the absence of externalities:

$$F'(L^*) = 1 + \rho \tag{5.20}$$

Now consider the case where the investor has no money of her own, so that investment has to be made entirely from a loan. Also assume the ideal case where there is no *ex post* (or, for that matter, *ex ante*) moral hazard; the lender knows that the borrower will duly repay her loan, i.e. the enforcement problem does not exist. The lender then offers a loan at the interest rate r that satisfies his zero-profit condition, and the borrower maximises her net return (which also stands for her utility function if the borrower is risk-neutral):

$$F(L) - (1+r)L \tag{5.21}$$

The borrower is assumed to have an outside option of value v, which she can earn if she were not taking the loan. She will take the loan only if the net return from it is no less than v; this defines her participation constraint:

$$F(L) - (1+r)L \geq v \tag{5.22}$$

The borrower then chooses L so as to maximise the utility function (5.21) subject to the participation constraint (4.22). The first-order condition is

$$F'(L) = 1 + r \tag{5.23}$$

And the lender's zero-profit condition is

$$(1+r)L = (1+\rho)L \tag{5.24}$$

The last equation implies that $r = \rho$; using it in (5.23), we can see that the amount of capital the borrower would invest in this case is exactly the same as in the first case, where the borrower's own funds were invested. If the optimal amount of loan L^* given by (5.20) satisfies the participation constraint (5.22), that will be the equilibrium loan. This shows that, in the absence of strategic default, the credit market will achieve the social optimum.

Let us now introduce the possibility of strategic default. In the absence of the lender's ability to enforce repayment, the only way the credit market can operate in this situation is by providing the incentive to repay. And since the incentive to repay is introduced through the non-renewal threat, the behaviour of the credit market in this case is best analysed in the framework of a repeated game in which the lender and the borrower can interact with each other over and over again. For simplicity, we shall assume an infinitely repeated game in which the lender will continue to offer a loan in every period so long as the borrower repays the loan in the previous period; if the borrower defaults at any stage of the game, the lender employs the trigger strategy of not lending to her ever again. The task facing the lender is to figure out how to set the interest rate and the loan size so that the borrower will have the incentive to repay (so as not to forgo the benefits of future loans), thus obviating the need for employing any external enforcement mechanism.[24]

Recall that the borrower has an outside option of value v, i.e. if she decides to default at any stage, she is assured of earning v forever. She also has a positive time preference, i.e. she prefers her current income to a future income, and the degree of time preference is expressed by the discount factor δ (< 1). We use R to denote the repayment burden $(1+r)L$. The incentive compatibility (*IC*) constraint which will induce the borrower to repay can now be stated as follows:

$$F(L)+\frac{\delta}{1-\delta}v \le \frac{F(L)-R}{1-\delta} \qquad (5.25)$$

The left-hand side of the inequality shows the payoff to the borrower if she decides to default after taking a loan. It has two parts. The first part, $F(L)$, stands for what she gets in the first period if she defaults; obviously she gets to retain the whole output of the project without repaying anything. The second part shows what she would get in the subsequent periods once she has defaulted – it's the discounted present value of her outside option v, which she will receive forever. The right-hand side of the inequality shows the payoff if the borrower decides never to default: it's the discounted present value of the net return *[F(L) − R]* that she will receive after repaying her loan in every period forever.

Thus, inequality (5.25) says that the payoff from default must be less than the payoff from repaying. If the pair *(R, L)* satisfies this inequality for given values of v and δ, the borrower will decide to repay of her own accord, even though she could have gotten away with not repaying if she wanted to. With a little bit of algebra, the incentive constraint (5.25) can be rewritten as

$$\delta\left[F(L)-v\right] \ge R \qquad (5.26)$$

Recalling that $R = (1+r)L$, the participation constraint (5.22) and the zero-profit condition (5.24) can also be rewritten, respectively, as

$$F(L) - v \geq R \qquad (5.27)$$

$$R = (1+\rho)L \qquad (5.28)$$

If the credit market is to operate in a Pareto efficient manner while avoiding strategic default, the equilibrium pair $(\hat{R},\hat{L})$ must maximise the net returns $[F(L) - R]$ given by (5.21), as well as satisfy the incentive constraint given by (5.26), the participation constraint given by (5.27) and the zero-profit condition given by (5.28).

A diagrammatical approach to the derivation of $(\hat{R},\hat{L})$ is offered in Figure 5.3.[25] The production function is represented by the concave function $F(L)$. The lender's zero-profit line (5.28) is given by the upward-sloping straight line *IP* (standing for iso-profit line), which starts from the origin and has the slope $(1+\rho)$. For the interest rates that satisfy the zero-profit condition, the net return to the borrower $[F(L) - R]$ is shown by the vertical gap between the production function $F(L)$ and the *IP* line.

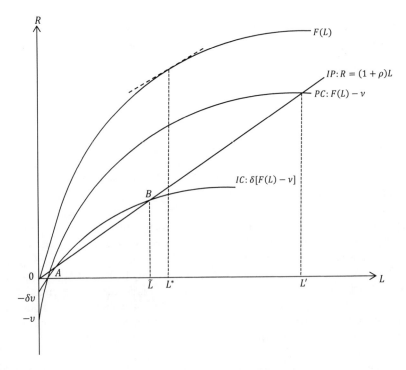

Figure 5.3 Credit market equilibrium with *ex post* moral hazard

The curve *PC* (standing for participation constraint) represents the difference $F(L) - v$. All points on or below this curve satisfy the participation constraint (5.27). However, if the zero-profit condition is also to be satisfied, only those values of L are relevant for which the *PC* curve remains above the *IP* line. This sets an upper limit to the size of the loan (L'), beyond which the borrower would not be interested because the net return falls below her outside option (thanks to diminishing returns), i.e. her participation constraint is not satisfied.

The curve *IC* represents the discounted difference $\delta[F(L) - v]$. All points on or below the *IC* curve satisfy the incentive constraint (5.26). It is clear that, since $\delta < 1$, this curve will lie below the *PC* curve (for all positive values); this means that any point that satisfies the *IC* constraint will also satisfy the *PC* constraint (5.27) (but the converse is not true). If the zero-profit condition is also to be satisfied, only those values of L are relevant for which the *IC* curve remains above the *IP* line. This sets the upper limit to the loan size (L), corresponding to the upper intersection point A of *IC* and *IP*, beyond which the *IC* condition is not satisfied. There is also a lower limit (L^0) corresponding to the lower intersection point B. Clearly, only the points *(R, L)* lying on the line segment AB, or equivalently, only the loan amounts falling within the range (L^0, L) can satisfy all three constraints (5.26), (5.27) and (5.28).

If the socially optimal value L^* (one that maximises the borrower's payoff function (5.21) subject only to the lender's zero-profit condition) falls within the range (L^0, L), it will satisfy all three constraints. That is, in spite of the threat of *ex post* moral hazard, the market will reach the social optimum; there will be no inefficiency.

The more interesting case, however, occurs when L^* lies beyond the upper limit L (this is the case depicted in Figure 5.3). Two features of this case are worth noting. First, the constrained optimal loan size is then given by $\tilde{L} < L^*$, i.e. the equilibrium loan size will be less than the socially optimum level – the credit market will be inefficient.[26] Second, if $L^* \leq L'$, the borrower's participation constraint is satisfied at L^*; she will, therefore, be willing to borrow L^* at the given interest rate, but the lender will not offer more than L in order to avoid strategic default – the borrower will be credit-constrained. Thus, the credit market will be characterised by both inefficiency and rationing. To get an insight into the reason for this inefficiency, note that the incentive constraint (5.26) can be rewritten as follows:

$$F(L) - R \geq \delta v + (1-\delta) F(L)$$

or, $$F(L) - R \geq v + (1-\delta)\left[F(L) - v\right] \qquad (5.29)$$

Now compare this with the participation constraint (5.27), which says that for the borrower to take a loan it's enough that the net return $F(L) - R$ is equal to v. But the incentive constraint (5.29) says that for the borrower not to default it's not enough that the net return equals v; it must exceed v by at least the amount $(1-\delta)[F(L) - v]$. This additional amount is the measure of the 'incentive rent' that the lender must leave with the borrower in order to give her the incentive not to default.[27] In Figure 5.3, this rent is given by the vertical difference between the PC curve and the IC curve.

It is this compulsion to provide an incentive rent that creates the possibility that the socially optimum amount of a loan may not be offered by the lender. In Figure 5.3, L^* is such that the net return $[F(L^*)-R]$ exceeds v but falls short of $v+(1-\delta)[F(L)-v]$. In other words, while the participation constraint is satisfied, the incentive rent is not enough to deter default. Knowing this, the lender will not offer the loan L^*, even though the borrower is willing to take it.

If the lender offers any loan at all, it will be different from L^*; but different in what way – more or less? Our diagrammatic analysis showed earlier that the amount of loan offered by the lender would be less than L^*. To understand the intuition behind this result, consider the implication of the incentive constraint being violated by L^*. From (5.26), the violation implies that

$$R > \delta\left[F(L^*) - v\right]$$

$$\text{or, } (1+r)L^* > \delta\left[F(L^*) - v\right] \tag{5.30}$$

This inequality can be interpreted as follows. At any point in time, the borrower thinks that she can save the repayment amount $(1+r)L^*$ by defaulting; this is her gain from the act of default. If she does decide to default, then of course in the next period she will have to forgo the surplus $[F(L^*)-v]$, and the right-hand side of (5.30) will give the present value of that loss. The inequality (5.30) thus shows that, at every point in time, the gain from defaulting today is greater than the loss tomorrow, which is why the lender is unwilling to lend the amount L^*.

Faced with this situation, the lender will want to adjust the volume of the loan so that the temptation to default falls. For this to happen, the marginal gain from defaulting must fall relative to the marginal loss as the loan size changes. From (5.30), the marginal gain from defaulting is $(1+r)$ and the marginal loss is $\delta F'(L)$. Therefore, the temptation to default will fall only if $\delta F'(L)$ becomes progressively smaller relative to $(1+r)$. But since r is fixed at ρ by the lender's zero-profit condition, the marginal gain from default $(1+r)$ remains constant in the present framework. As a result, the marginal loss from defaulting $\delta F'(L)$ must be allowed to rise in absolute terms, and given δ (and given diminishing returns), this is only possible if L is lowered.[28] That's why, when the incentive constraint binds, the lender will offer a loan that is below the socially optimal level.

To summarise, the imperative to provide the borrower with an 'incentive rent' so as to deter strategic default creates the possibility that the socially optimal level of loan will not be offered by the lender, even if the borrower was willing to take it. In this situation, the socially optimal level of loan will induce default, because the gain from defaulting would exceed the loss. The lender must then adjust the size of the loan so that the marginal gain from defaulting gets smaller relative to the marginal loss. In the present framework, this can only be achieved by offering a smaller amount of loan than is socially optimal or is desired by the

Adverse selection, repayment enforcement 111

borrowers. Strategic default thus leads to inefficiency as well as rationing in the credit market.

It follows that any mechanism that reduces the incentive rent will enable the credit market to get closer to efficiency and reduce rationing. Several features of the microcredit market have been interpreted in this light. It has been argued that these features enable the lenders to reduce the incentive rent and thereby improve the functioning of the credit market in the face of the threat of strategic default. Some of the major theoretical analyses along these lines are reviewed below.

5.4.2 *Joint liability as a mechanism to deal with strategic default*

In a classic paper, Besley and Coate (1995) examined the role of the joint-liability system in microcredit operations in mitigating the problem of strategic default. The underlying premise of their approach is that, regardless of the liability system – joint or individual – the bank tries to enforce repayment by imposing a penalty on the borrower. The penalty could take the form of denial of future credit as discussed above; but it could also include other elements such as hassling, naming and shaming, mental torture, and so on. We have seen above that when the bank lends to an individual, the penalty of denying a future loan could work in preventing strategic default, but at a cost – namely, that the amount of the loan would be socially inefficient and the borrowers would be credit-rationed. The question that Besley and Coate pose is: will the system of penalty work better if the bank were to lend with joint liability rather than individual liability?

Strictly speaking, Besley and Coate do not explicitly address the issue of social inefficiency. Instead, they focus on repayment rates, i.e. on the success in mitigating strategic default as reflected in repayment rates; and the question they ask is whether joint liability is better than individual liability in improving repayment rates. One could argue, however, that any mechanism that improves repayment rates by reducing the incentive to default would enable the bank to offer a smaller amount of incentive rent needed to resist the temptation to default; and, as we have seen, anything that reduces the incentive rent helps the credit market move closer to efficiency. In that sense, the Besley-Coate analysis could also be taken to be speaking to the broader concerns of the efficiency of the credit market, even though the immediate focus is on repayment rates.[29]

Their paper starts with the presumption that joint liability should help reduce strategic default. After all, since accepting joint liability means being liable to be punished for the partner's default as well as one's own, a borrower who considers repaying to be worthwhile on her own account will try to ensure that she is not penalised on her partner's account. To that end, the borrower will try to apply peer pressure on her partner, and if it doesn't work, she may even pay up on the partner's behalf.

A closer examination reveals, however, that this presumption is not necessarily valid. The main insight of Besley and Coate is that in the context of strategic default the logic of joint liability generates two countervailing forces – one positive and the other negative; and if the negative force dominates, joint liability may actually turn out to be worse than individual liability. The positive effect is that group members whose projects have earned high returns may have an incentive to repay the loans of members whose projects have yielded insufficient returns to make repayment worthwhile. The negative effect arises when the whole group defaults, even when some members would have repaid under individual lending. The main task of the paper is to identify the conditions under which one or the other force will dominate. It also shows how group lending may harness social collateral, which serves to mitigate the negative effect.

The effect of joint liability on the incentive to repay is shaped by the strategic interdependence that joint liability generates. In order to capture this interdependence, the formal analysis of the Besley-Coate model takes the form of a two-person, two-stage game. In the first stage, the borrowers simultaneously choose between the strategies of whether or not to contribute to the pool of repayment. If both players take the same decision in the first stage, the game stops there – either both repay or neither does. If they decide differently, the game goes to the second stage, where the player who had decided to contribute must now decide whether to repay for the partner or to default.

The decision to repay will, of course, depend on how severe the penalty of default is relative to the repayment burden (r). The group as a whole is taken to be in default, even if only one member defaults; in that event, both members will face the penalty – that's the essence of joint liability. However, the severity of penalty may not be the same for them; it would depend on the returns they respectively earn from loan-financed projects. The model stipulates that the penalty imposed by the bank is an increasing function of project return, which is *ex ante* probabilistic, but the *ex post* outcome is assumed to be observable. Thus, borrowers who are fortunate enough to earn higher returns are liable to pay a heavier penalty.

This link between penalty and project return implies that the incentive to repay (or to default) is a function of project return. At low levels of return, the penalty of default may be too low compared to the repayment burden to make repayment worthwhile, so the borrower will be inclined to default. However, since the penalty rises with return, there must be a 'critical' level of project return for any given repayment burden, denoted by $\varphi(r)$, above which the penalty is higher than repayment – so the borrower will be willing to repay. By extending the logic of this argument, there is another critical level of return $\varphi(2r)$ beyond which the penalty is higher than $2r$ – the combined repayment burden of the group (composed of two borrowers). Clearly, if a borrower receives a return above $\varphi(2r)$, she would be willing to repay $2r$ from her own purse, i.e. to repay on behalf of both herself and her partner, even if the partner decides to default, rather than incur the heavy penalty of group default. These two critical levels – $\varphi(r)$ and $\varphi(2r)$ – define three regions of project return (θ): namely, $\theta \geq \varphi(2r)$, $\varphi(2r) > \theta \geq \varphi(r)$, and $\theta < \varphi(r)$. Accordingly, we can identify six possible cases of pairs of project returns accruing to the two borrowers:

(a) For both borrowers, $\theta \geq \varphi(2r)$.
(b) For one borrower, $\theta \geq \varphi(2r)$; and for the other, $\varphi(2r) \geq \theta \geq \varphi(r)$.

(c) For one borrower, $\theta \geq \varphi(2r)$; and for the other, $\theta < \varphi(r)$.
(d) For both borrowers, $\varphi(2r) \geq \theta \geq \varphi(r)$.
(e) For one borrower, $\varphi(2r) \geq \theta \geq \varphi(r)$; and for the other, $\theta < \varphi(r)$.
(f) For both borrowers, $\theta < \varphi(r)$.

Now compare repayment under joint and individual liability in each of these cases. There will be full repayment in cases (a) and (b) regardless of the liability system, because, as noted above, any return above $\varphi(r)$ induces repayment under individual liability, while a return above $\varphi(2r)$ for at least one borrower induces full repayment under joint liability. At the other extreme is case (f), in which there will be default under both systems, because the project return, and hence the penalty, is simply too low to induce either partner to repay. Thus, in these three cases, there will be no difference in repayment under the two systems.

The difference begins to emerge when we consider the other three cases. In case (c), under individual liability, one borrower will repay (the one with $\theta \geq \varphi(2r)$) but the other will not (the one with $\theta < \varphi(r)$). Under joint liability, however, full repayment will be made because the borrower with a high return will find it worthwhile to repay on behalf of both borrowers, even though her partner is going to default. This is a clear case where joint liability succeeds in mitigating the problem of strategic default.

Case (d) is slightly tricky. Under individual liability, both borrowers will repay. However, under joint liability, an ambiguity arises because there are now two possible equilibria. Both players are aware that each has earned enough to make repayment worthwhile on one's own account, but that does not necessarily ensure that both will repay – it all depends on what each borrower believes the partner is going to do. If one borrower believes that the other will contribute, there is no problem – each will repay the amount *r*. But if one borrower is pessimistic about the other's intentions, then she won't repay either. The problem here is that although the first borrower is happy enough to repay *r* on her own account, she knows that a total repayment of *r* will not satisfy the bank. In order to avoid penalty, a total amount of *2r* must be repaid, but since she does not earn a high enough return to make repayment of *2r* worthwhile, she will decide to default. Thus, each borrower will end up defaulting and paying a penalty that is greater than the repayment burden. This is clearly a Pareto inferior outcome compared to the first equilibrium, but the players may easily end up there because of a coordination failure. If the borrowers can somehow reach the Pareto superior equilibrium, the repayment outcome under joint liability will be the same as in individual liability – full repayment will be made in both cases. But if coordination failure leads to the Pareto inferior equilibrium, joint liability will turn out to be inferior to individual liability.

Case (e) tilts the case further against joint liability. Under individual liability, the first borrower will repay and the second borrower will default. By contrast, under joint liability, both will default. The problem is similar to the case of the pessimistic equilibrium discussed above, except that default by one partner is a certainty in this case, and not just a conjecture. Knowing that the partner is going to default, the other borrower will reckon that in order to avoid a penalty, she will have to repay **2r**, which she will not find worthwhile paying given her project return. Thus, she will default under joint liability, even though she would have repaid under individual liability.

In summary, the relative performance of joint and individual liability in terms of repayment depends critically on the distribution of project returns. There are a number of cases where there is no difference in performance (namely, cases (a), (b), (f) and the Pareto superior outcome of case (d)). There is one case where joint liability clearly outperforms individual liability – that is the case of one borrower earning a very high return ($\theta \geq \varphi(2r)$) and the other borrower earning a very low return ($\theta < \varphi(r)$). On the other hand, joint liability turns out to be inferior to individual liability when either one borrower earns a moderate return ($\varphi(2r) \geq \theta \geq \varphi(r)$) and the other earns a low return ($\theta < \varphi(r)$), or both earn moderate returns but end up in a Pareto inferior outcome due to coordination failure. In the latter two cases, joint liability will aggravate the problem of strategic default instead of mitigating it.

Clearly, one way of making joint liability a more effective weapon against strategic default is to raise the level of penalty. There are, however, limits to how far a microcredit institution can go towards raising the penalty given the social mission it professes to have of serving the poor. Besley and Coate argue that this limitation can be overcome to some extent by harnessing one aspect of group lending that is absent from individual lending – namely, the potential of imposing social sanctions on deviant behaviour. Borrowers who are in a position to repay on their own account will try to ensure that the partner also repays so that they don't have to bear the full repayment burden on behalf of the group. To that end, they will be willing to threaten the potential defaulters with social sanctions, and this threat is likely to be more credible, as well as socially more acceptable, than anything the bank itself might try. If the power of sanctions is sufficiently strong, the potential negative effect of joint liability may be mitigated in full, rendering it superior to individual liability as a mechanism for preventing strategic default.

The Besley-Coate analysis was based on the assumptions of a given interest rate and a given penalty function. This raises the question: if the bank had the freedom to design a contract by choosing the right kind of penalty function and the right level of repayment burden, what kind of contracting system would it choose – individual or joint liability? Laffont and N'Guessan (2001) addressed this question by taking a mechanism design approach and by allowing for collusion among borrowers instead of assuming a non-cooperative sequential game. Despite these differences in approach, they reinforce the Besley-Coate result by demonstrating that if the bank's enforcement mechanism is weak group contracting may be worse than individual contracting because the negative effect of joint liability overwhelms the positive effect. Social sanctions then remain the only instrument available to make group lending better than individual lending.[30]

This recognition has led to further inquiries into how to make the best use of social sanctions to improve the efficacy of group lending in overcoming strategic default. Bond and Rai (2008) argue that, in the presence of unequal social power relations, symmetric group loans as practised by most microlenders are not the best way to harness the power of social sanctions. The main insight of their paper is that when people differ in their ability to impose sanctions on each other, or equivalently, in their susceptibility to sanctions from each other, the bank should be able to enhance the effectiveness of the sanctions by refining their loan contracts in such a way that makes good use of unequal power relations among the borrowers. They consider several possible ways of doing so and come up in favour of co-signed loans.

They start from the premise that the ideal solution would be for the bank to offer asymmetric loans, tailoring them to the borrowers' respective susceptibility to sanctions. In particular, the bank should provide bigger loans to weaker or less-powerful borrowers who face larger sanctions in the event of default – the reason being that, since weaker borrowers are vulnerable to tougher sanctions, they would have a higher willingness to repay. But a sense of fairness, as well as the bank's inability to observe borrowers' power relations accurately, prevents it from making such asymmetric loans in practice. In theory, both the problem of fairness and the inability to observe power relations could be overcome through a revelation mechanism, i.e. by offering a menu of contracts to choose from. The menu would be designed in such a way that the borrowers would reveal the internal power relations through their choice of contracts. In particular, less-powerful borrowers will voluntarily choose larger loans and the more powerful ones will choose smaller loans. Bond and Rai show, however, that this will work only if all the borrowers are highly productive, which would rarely be the case in reality. Thus, in practice, group loans are constrained to be symmetric, even though asymmetric loans would be more efficient.

But Bond and Rai argue that an alternative mechanism is available – namely, co-signed loans, which would yield better results than symmetric group loans when power relations are very unequal. Under both mechanisms, the prospective borrowers must form groups in order to receive loans, but the difference is that, while in symmetric loans both members of a group receive a loan and are jointly liable for each other, under the co-signing system only one person receives the loan and the other merely co-signs or guarantees the borrower.

To see how co-signing may outperform symmetric joint liability loans, assume that the bank offers loans of a standard size α (to be interpreted as the amount to be repaid, including principal and interest) and also imposes a standard penalty c for default. Social sanction s represents an additional penalty for default. The cost of this penalty would depend on the relative power of the members of a group, as measured by their relative susceptibility to sanctions, which is denoted by μ and takes the value in the range $(0, 1/2)$. When μ equals $1/2$, there is an equal power relation and both members of the group are equally susceptible to sanctions, whose cost to the borrower is given by $(1/2)s$. In the case of unequal power relations, we shall use μ to denote the susceptibility of the stronger party and $(1 - \mu)$ for the weaker party. Clearly, the lower the value of μ, the stronger is the first party.

Consider first the case where power is equal ($\mu = 1/2$) and the loan size is such that $a < c+(1/2)s$. A standard joint-liability symmetric loan will work very well in this case, because the cost of default is higher than the repayment burden for each member, which will ensure that both members will repay. But now suppose the relation becomes unequal, i.e. μ gets smaller than 1/2. As μ gets smaller, the cost of default to the stronger party, $c + \mu s$, also gets smaller, while the cost of default to the weaker party $c+(1-\mu)s$ gets bigger. For sufficiently small μ, we may end up with the following relationship: $c+\mu s < a < c+(1-\mu)s$. In this case, with a symmetric loan, the bank will receive payment only from the weaker party, while the stronger party will default. One way of avoiding default is to give the loan only to the weaker party and to make the stronger party the co-signee so that by threatening the heavy sanction $(1-\mu)s$ she can induce the weaker party to repay. Thus, under unequal power relations, co-signing is likely to ensure better repayment performance than symmetric joint-liability loans.[31]

Sinn (2013) identifies an alternative way of strengthening the enforcement power of social sanctions: it is to offer loans to group members sequentially, instead of simultaneously as in the Besley-Coate model. The argument focuses on the problem identified by Besley and Coate that when project returns fall in an intermediate range for both borrowers, each may opt for strategic default under the joint-liability system, even though both would have repaid under individual liability.

Besley and Coate showed that one possible way of avoiding such strategic default is to harness the social collateral of group members: with sufficiently strong social sanctions, it may be possible to induce the borrowers to reach the Pareto superior equilibrium in which both of them repay. Sinn argues that, for any given strength of social sanctions, their effectiveness can be improved by switching from a simultaneous to a sequential loan, provided the bank's own enforcement mechanism is not strong enough to prevent default. The advantage of a sequential loan is that, as one borrower waits her turn to be allocated her loan, she will threaten her borrowing partner with social sanctions should she strategically default so as to ensure that she will receive her own loan when her turn arrives. Similarly, once a borrower has repaid her loan, she will pressurise her peer into repaying hers so that she doesn't become liable for repaying a second loan as well. Thus, in sequential lending, both borrowers will have the incentive to apply social sanctions on each other and thereby avoid strategic default.[32, 33]

But social sanctions cannot always be relied upon to come to the rescue. Some societies may not have enough social capital to make such sanctions effective, and even where sanctions can be applied there are limits to how far they can be pushed without doing lasting damage to the social fabric.[34] This raises the question of whether alternative mechanisms can be devised to make group lending an effective strategy against strategic default. Several authors have taken up this question.

Armendáriz de Aghion (1999) identifies a couple of such design issues: namely, group size and the structure of monitoring within groups. Besley and Coate assumed two-person groups for simplicity of analysis, but in the real world groups are usually larger and Armendáriz argues that banks can improve the efficacy of joint liability by carefully choosing the group size. Large size has the advantage that it makes the joint-liability burden lighter for each successful borrower, as the burden is likely to be shared among several members. On the other hand, it also raises the possibility of free-riding by unsuccessful borrowers. A group size that optimally balances these two opposing effects would make for greater efficacy of joint liability.[35]

Armendáriz de Aghion (1999) also examines the importance of the monitoring structure. In particular, she compares the mutual monitoring structure, in which all borrowers simultaneously monitor each other, with the rotating monitoring structure, in which members take turns in monitoring each other. She finds that the relative efficacy of the two structures to improve repayment performance depends on the relative strengths of fixed versus variable costs of monitoring. If the variable cost is low and the fixed cost is high, the rotating structure (of the kind observed in the classic Grameen lending model) turns out to be better than mutual monitoring.

5.4.3 Enforcement under asymmetric information

The preceding discussion assumed that the lender knows all the relevant characteristics of the borrowers; his only problem was to devise a way of ensuring that default would be avoided. In other words, there was no informational asymmetry. But this assumption is not very realistic since, as we have noted earlier, asymmetric information is pervasive in credit markets. When the enforcement problem has to be dealt with in an environment of asymmetric information, the lender's task becomes doubly complicated.

Two types of informational asymmetry are relevant here. The first is the same as the one we discussed in the context of adverse selection – namely, the lender's inability to distinguish between safe and risky borrowers. The second type of asymmetry is specific to the problem of enforcement – it arises from the lender's inability to distinguish between strategic default and a different kind of default that might be termed as 'genuine default'. The latter refers to the case where a borrower is genuinely unable to repay because she has been subject to some negative shock, e.g. her project return may have been unexpectedly low or the loan (or the proceeds from the loan-financed project) had to be diverted to meet some unforeseen but essential family needs. The borrower will know whether her default is strategic or genuine, but the lender may not.

Devising an incentive-compatible contract for avoiding default becomes especially challenging under such asymmetric information. Some theories of microcredit have shown that the group lending system assumes an added importance in this situation. These theories emphasise an aspect of group lending that has received relatively less attention in the literature. Most theories of microcredit emphasise the role that groups play in ensuring either peer pressure (in moral hazard theories, both *ex ante* and *ex post*) or peer screening (in adverse selection models). In so doing, they depict borrower groups mainly as an adversarial institution – one whose main function is either to screen out untrustworthy members or to put pressure on those who are eventually accepted. But in reality groups also play a mutually supportive role, whereby members help each other out in hard times. It is this peer support aspect of group lending that is emphasised by most theories dealing with the enforcement problem in an environment of asymmetric information. In these theories, group lending is viewed as a mechanism for strengthening the bonds of mutual insurance among the borrowers.[36]

Informal mutual-insurance mechanisms of one kind or another have existed in traditional societies for centuries. Recently, these mechanisms have come under intense theoretical and empirical scrutiny.[37] There is, by now, quite a strong body of empirical evidence that, just like the informal credit market, the informal insurance mechanisms also do not work very well, and for much the same reasons: namely, informational asymmetries and enforcement problems.[38] In the face of systemic shocks which afflict a large swathe of the population at the same time, mutual insurance is not expected to work in any case. But the evidence suggests that, even in the case of idiosyncratic shocks, where the need and scope for mutual insurance are evidently high, the optimal amount of insurance is not generally provided. At the heart of this failure lies the scope for free-riding that is created by an asymmetry of information and the limitations of enforcement mechanisms that exist, even within traditional societies.

Group lending based on joint liability can improve upon this situation by giving borrowers an incentive to offer insurance to the peers who need it. The result would be a simultaneous improvement in the insurance market and in the credit market. Indeed, an improvement on the insurance front would be the reason for an improvement on the credit front. From this perspective, Sadoulet (2000) examined the case in which the lender resorts to conditional sequential lending, i.e. he gives a credible threat of non-renewal of future loans in case of group default. Faced with this threat, prospective borrowers will try to choose group members in such a way that by offering mutual insurance in bad times, they maximise the possibility of preventing strategic default. In this way, strategic default will be minimised through the very process of endogenous group formation.

An interesting aspect of this model is that, when the process of group formation is thus driven by the desire to prevent strategic default through the provision of mutual insurance rather than by the desire to prevent moral hazard or adverse selection, the groups may turn out to be characterised by negative assortative matching as opposed to assortative matching, as in the adverse selection models *à la* Ghatak and others. In other words, high-risk borrowers may want to form groups with low-risk borrowers, and vice versa.

The crucial point here is that faced with the non-renewal threat borrowers' incentives to default and their incentive to provide mutual insurance in order to prevent default will both vary depending on their risk types. Once the current project succeeds, a riskier borrower will have a higher incentive to default next time around compared to a safer borrower, because the former might reckon that her next project is more likely to fail, and hence future loans are not likely to be of much use to her anyway. By contrast, a safer borrower will have a higher incentive to provide insurance to the partner because she has a bigger incentive to ensure the receipt of future loans (as her project is more likely to succeed in the future). Thus, the incentive to default and the incentive to provide insurance will both vary with risk types, but in opposite directions. It is this opposite nature of variation in the two incentives that leads to the possibility of negative assortative matching by creating a complementarity between opposite risk types.

Consider the choice of a partner from the perspectives of a riskier borrower first. Since a safer borrower would be more eager to provide insurance, the riskier borrower would be better off teaming up with a safer partner because other risky borrowers like herself would not be willing to offer the same degree of insurance. But wouldn't a safer borrower want to team up with a safer partner rather than with a riskier one in order to minimise the need for providing insurance? Yes, she would, but the problem is that she won't succeed in doing so. Both safer and riskier borrowers will want to have a safer partner, but the riskier one would end up winning the contest. Since riskier borrowers need a higher degree of insurance compared to safer borrowers, they would outbid the latter in the attempt to join up with safe borrowers. A safe borrower would, therefore, always team up with someone riskier than herself. The process of group formation will thus culminate in negative assortative matching.[39] The only qualification is that the riskier borrower must not be so risky that the cost of insuring her outweighs the expected benefit of ensuring the continuity of future loans. Since the 'too risky' borrowers will not be accepted as partners by safer borrowers, they must form homogeneous groups amongst themselves. The upshot is that one should expect to find heterogeneous matching at the lower end of the risk distribution and homogeneous matching at the upper end.

The idea that group lending can be used as a means of inducing peer support has also been used by models that deal with the other type of asymmetric information – i.e. the lender's inability to distinguish between strategic and genuine default. If the group as a whole is going to default because some members cannot help defaulting for genuine reasons (i.e. bad luck), those who are able to help the unlucky members by paying up on their behalf might do so in order to avoid the penalty of group default. The greater assurance of mutual insurance, engendered by the joint-liability system, would help bring into the credit network many of those who would otherwise shun borrowing for fear of facing the unpleasant prospect of 'genuine' default.

The joint-liability system can thus improve upon the functioning of the credit market by reducing the prospects of both strategic and genuine default. Harnessing of social capital plays a crucial role in all of this, but in different ways for the two kinds of default. For strategic default, it works by activating social sanctions, and for genuine default, it works by encouraging social support. But, one way or the other, joint liability helps to mitigate the problem of default.

The only problem is that joint liability can go too far – it may overkill in its attempt to prevent default. To see how, note that, like individual default, group default too can be either strategic or genuine. The default is strategic when the lucky members are capable of paying on behalf of the group as a whole but won't (because the penalty of default is smaller than the gain from defaulting). But the default is genuine when the group can't avoid default simply because the projects of group members, taken together, have yielded an insufficient return to pay off the liabilities of all the members. Under asymmetric information, the bank is unable to distinguish between the two cases; so the joint-liability system penalises the group in both cases.

That's where the problem of overkill comes in. It is one thing to try and prevent default when the borrowers are able to repay either singly or as a group, but quite another to try and enforce repayment when group default will occur for genuine reasons. In the latter case, while the borrowers are made to suffer, the bank does not gain anything in return because repayment will never be made despite the penalty, and the penalty itself can only be non-pecuniary in nature (e.g. hassling, withholding or denying future loans, etc.). The consequence is a deadweight loss for the society as a whole.

It follows that anything that will minimise the possibility of penalty in the event of genuine difficulty, while at the same time preventing strategic default when the group as a whole is capable of repaying, will constitute an improvement. Since the bank cannot distinguish between genuine and strategic default through direct observation, such an improvement can only be brought about, if at all, by some kind of revelation mechanism, i.e. a mechanism through which the borrowers themselves are made to reveal the nature of default. Rai and Sjöström (2004) suggest that adding a kind of cross-reporting game to joint liability will achieve this goal.[40]

The cross-reporting game works as follows. If a group member defaults, then instead of penalising the group as a whole the bank will penalise a particular borrower, who may or may not be the defaulter. The rule is that borrower j receives a harsh punishment only if another borrower i reports that borrower j is withholding some output from the bank. This allows an unsuccessful borrower i to threaten her successful partner j by saying: 'You had better help me repay, or I will tell the bank that you refused to help even though you had the means to do so and they will impose a harsh punishment on you'. This threat – indeed the sheer possibility of this threat – will induce the successful borrower j to help repay i's loan if she can. On the other hand, if j is genuinely unable to help i, then i cannot gain anything by threatening j in this way.[41] Therefore, no threats are made and no harsh punishments are imposed when both borrowers fail, which eliminates the possibility of deadweight loss.

An alternative approach to reducing the deadweight loss inherent in the joint-liability system has been suggested by Tedeschi (2006). He focuses specifically on the case in which the joint-liability penalty takes the form of denial of future loans. The deadweight loss in this case arises from the fact that denying a person loan on all dates in the future is an unnecessarily harsh measure, because it entails the loss of potential surplus which the society could have enjoyed from the utilisation of future loans. While it may be necessary to accept some loss of surplus in order to deter strategic default, the aim should be to minimise this loss. Tedeschi suggests that the best strategy would be to delay rather than deny future loans and to let the length of delay vary depending on the likelihood of default.[42]

He envisages a process in which the lender and the borrower may alternate between lending and punishment phases. At the beginning of the process, the borrower and the lender engage in a lending phase during which it is only when one loan is successfully repaid that another loan is given. If, in any period, the borrower defaults, it triggers the onset of a punishment phase during which no new loans are extended to the borrower in default. The punishment phase lasts for a certain period that is sufficiently long to prevent a borrower from strategic default, but not so long as to unduly punish a borrower who defaults for genuine reasons (faced with a negative shock). After the punishment has been served, the borrower may return to the lending phase, with prior unpaid debts forgiven. The task facing the lender is to determine the optimal length of the punishment phase, given the information at his disposal.[43]

5.4.4 Enforcement without joint liability

The preceding discussion shows that two features of microcredit lending mechanisms – namely, joint liability and sequential lending – can, in principle, mitigate the enforcement problem, especially when the two features operate together, which is usually the case. But theorists' attention has recently shifted to other features of microcredit institutions which may also help tackle the problem.[44]

One such feature is the institution of public meetings that most microcredit lenders routinely hold for the purpose of disbursing loans and collecting repayments from the borrower groups. It has been argued that, whether wilfully or not, such meetings also serve to deal with the enforcement problem better by strengthening the bonds of mutual insurance, which helps improve repayment performance. In making an argument along these lines, Rai and Sjöström (2013) start from the point made in the preceding section that joint liability imposes a deadweight loss even as it promotes mutual insurance. While the strategy of cross-reporting *á la* Rai and Sjöström (2004) and the idea of delaying rather than denying a loan *á la* Tedeschi (2006) may reduce the extent of deadweight loss induced by joint liability, one may ask a more fundamental question: is it possible to improve the prospects of mutual insurance through a lending mechanism that does not rely upon the powers of joint liability and thus does not involve the deadweight loss in the first place? Rai and Sjöström (2013) argue that the regular holding of public meetings is precisely such a mechanism.

The argument turns on the inter-linkage between insurance and the credit market noted earlier. In the absence of full insurance, lending may also be inefficient because, in the face of uninsured risk, projects with high expected returns but also with high risk would not be undertaken. By contrast, if the borrowers could side contract with each other informally to fully insure themselves against all kinds of risks, lending would be efficient. The problem, however, is that individuals taking part in informal insurance arrangements face similar (*albeit* lesser) problems of enforcement and asymmetric information as do outside insurers and lenders – being unable to always distinguish between strategic and genuine default. It follows that any mechanism that improves information sharing among the borrowers would improve the performance of the credit market by making possible a greater degree of mutual insurance. Public meetings can be seen precisely as such a mechanism – they enhance the borrowers' ability to side contract by allowing the sharing of information about each other.[45]

One implication of this argument is that, so long as regular public meetings are conducted by the lenders, it does not matter whether joint or individual liability is practised; all that matters is that a group of borrowers comes together regularly and discusses their situation openly so that information is shared amongst them. The hypothesis is that, to the extent that this process helps reduce the asymmetries of information amongst borrowers, the scope for mutual insurance will improve and therefore loan repayment will also improve (insofar as potentially genuine defaulters are prevented from defaulting with the help of informal insurance).[46]

Yet another feature of microcredit that has recently come under theoretical spotlight is the system of frequent repayment in small instalments. For example, in the classical Grameen model, borrowers were required to repay in weekly instalments over a period of one year. As noted in Chapter 2, this system is actually changing in many countries, including Bangladesh, with less frequent repayment schedules becoming increasingly common. However, in most countries at most times, a frequent repayment schedule has been the norm, and theorists have argued that this institution has served to mitigate the enforcement problem.

The argument has taken several alternative forms. In one of the earliest contributions on this issue, Jain and Mansuri (2003) saw the institution of frequent repayment as a means of improving repayment performance by involving moneylenders with the microcredit market.[47] Their premise was that the obligation to make frequent repayments would force the borrowers to take temporary loans from local moneylenders since the income stream from loan-financed activities may not be continuous enough to make frequent repayment possible. And, the argument went, once the moneylenders get involved, they would use their local knowledge as well as local power to ensure, in their own interest, that borrowers used their loans well so that they would be able to repay better.

This is an interesting argument as it implies the counter-intuitive result that the expansion of microcredit would strengthen the hold of moneylenders instead of weakening it, as is commonly believed. But the empirical validity of the argument is open to doubt. There is no evidence of overall strengthening of moneylenders' hold in the rural credit market – certainly not in Bangladesh, where the rate of interest charged by them has been almost halved over the years.[48] More importantly, the premise that the mismatch between income stream and repayment schedule pushes borrowers into the arms of moneylenders is itself not convincing. Most poor households in rural areas pursue multiple occupations, so that even if the income stream from the loan-financed project is not continuous enough, they may still be able to make frequent repayments by drawing upon other sources of income, such as wage labour, which is fairly continuous.

A more convincing explanation of how the institution of frequent repayment might improve repayment performance is based on an altogether different premise – namely, that poor people find it particularly difficult to save.[49] One reason for this difficulty lies in the absence of appropriate savings instruments, which is especially true for rural areas. But there is also a more fundamental, psychological, reason. Recent advances in behavioural economics have shown that people may find it difficult to save because of present-biased preferences, which means that even though they might highly value future consumption, they may still give in to the temptation to consume more at present than what would be rational from the point of view of the value they attach to future consumption. This tension between what people would rationally like to do and what they actually end up doing is sometimes depicted as a conflict between a patient 'future self' and an impatient 'present self' (Strotz, 1955–56; Elster, 1977; Thaler and Shefrin, 1981). Laibson (1997) has captured this tension formally as a system of inter-temporal preferences that exhibits 'hyperbolic' time-discounting instead of linear discounting, as assumed in standard models of inter-temporal choice.

An implication of present-biased preferences is that people would find it hard to save unless a way was found to commit them to saving – an idea that has been christened as 'commitment savings'.[50] In reality, instruments of commitment savings are not widely available. From this perspective, microcredit can be seen as filling a gap in the financial market by providing a device for making commitment savings through the institution of frequent repayment. Having borrowed from a microcredit lender, a borrower is committed to making frequent payments in small amounts, usually every week. The commitment to repay, and the small amount borrowers are required to save at a time, together enable poor borrowers to overcome the temptation to consume more at present than they would rationally like to do.[51] The founding father of microcredit, Professor Yunus, was quite clear in his mind that this was precisely what the feature of frequent repayment was meant to achieve: 'Borrowers find this incremental process easier than having to accumulate money to pay a lump sum . . .' because it is '. . . hard to take a huge wad of bills out of one's pocket and pay the lender. There is enormous temptation from one's family to use that money to meet immediate consumption needs.' (Yunus, 2003, p.114).

Microcredit from this perspective is nothing other than a savings device; the only difference from other savings devices is that the sequence of saving and spending is reversed. In the usual case, people first save and then spend; in the case of microcredit, they first spend (through borrowing) and then save. The normal process is fraught with the trap of temptation arising from present-biased preferences; microcredit offers a way out of that trap by offering a commitment device in the form of frequent small repayments.[52]

This way of looking at things sheds useful light on a criticism sometimes made of microcredit along the line that, instead of saddling poor people with the burden of debt, microfinance institutions should enable them to save so that they can work their way of out poverty with the help of their own resources. This line of criticism misses the point that microcredit is indeed enabling poor people to save – *albeit* to save *ex post* rather than *ex ante*.[53] The implication of all this for repayment enforcement is quite straightforward. By enabling borrowers to save *ex post*, the institution of frequent repayment should reduce the probability of default and thereby improve the lender's ability to enforce repayment.[54]

5.5 Concluding observations

This chapter has reviewed recent theoretical explorations that try to explain how microcredit is able to minimise the problems of adverse selection and repayment enforcement that are endemic in the credit market. When lenders cannot distinguish between 'risky' and 'safe' borrowers, the credit market may be populated by too many 'risky' borrowers and too few 'safe' borrowers than is desirable from either the lender's or the society's point of view. In the extreme case, 'risky' borrowers might even drive out 'safe' borrowers completely. This is the classic case of adverse selection. A strand of microcredit theories has claimed that microcredit institutions have evolved a number of features that can help avoid adverse selection and thereby improve the performance of the credit market.

A standard solution to the adverse selection problem would be to offer a menu of contracts such that the two types of borrowers will self-select themselves into the type of contract that suits them the best while maximising the lender's profit at the same time. In jargon, what is needed is a separating contract that would allow both types of borrowers to stay in the market. But the microcredit institutions cannot offer separating contracts for a practical reason – namely, that they do not want to be seen as discriminating between different types of borrowers. A lender would normally offer the same contract to everyone who asks for the same type of loan.

Theorists have pointed out, however, that by adopting the group lending policy, in conjunction with joint liability, microcredit institutions have created an incentive structure that effectively turns a uniform contract into a separating one. The logic of precisely how joint liability does this trick can be seen in two steps. First, it leads to assortative matching, which leads to the formation of homogenous groups in terms of risk attributes, i.e. safe borrowers form groups amongst their own kind, as do the risky borrowers. Second, since safe borrowers have only safe partners, they are less likely to pay the joint-liability fine; and therefore the effective cost of their loans would be lower than that of risky borrowers, even though the nominal interest rate may be the same. A uniform contract in terms of interest rate thus becomes a separating contract in terms of the effective cost of the loan. This is what enables safe borrowers to stay in the market, thus overcoming the problem of adverse selection.

The underlying logic of this argument hinges crucially on an empirical assumption – namely, that borrowers know about each other's risk attributes. In other words, while asymmetric information is assumed to prevail between lenders and borrowers, no such asymmetry is allowed between the borrowers themselves. This assumption may not always be true, however, especially in sparsely populated rural societies or in urban areas where people may not be intimately familiar with each other. Will the joint-liability system still work to avoid the possibility of adverse selection? Theorists have shown that it might still do so, although in this case assortative matching may not occur.

The joint-liability condition also plays an important role in the models that theorists have used to explain how microcredit helps overcome the enforcement

Adverse selection, repayment enforcement 125

problem. Two sources of the enforcement problem need to be distinguished here – namely, strategic default (the case where a borrower might be tempted to default even though she is capable of repaying the loan) and genuine default (the case where the borrower fails to repay for genuine reasons, such as the failure of the loan-financed project). The manner in which group lending works to ensure better enforcement is different for the two types of default.

In the case of strategic default, the main theoretical finding is that joint liability alone may not be able to solve the enforcement problem; indeed, in some cases it may actually aggravate it. This is because joint liability induces two opposite incentives with regard to strategic default – a positive incentive that tends to reduce default and a negative incentive that tends to increase default. One or the other incentive would dominate, depending on the pattern of project returns. One way of mitigating the negative effect is to invoke social sanctions that borrowers might impose on one another to punish deviant behaviour. Thus, as in the case of *ex ante* moral hazard discussed in Chapter 4, joint liability needs the support of social sanctions to be effective in the case of *ex post* moral hazard as well. Furthermore, as in the case of *ex ante* moral hazard, in this case too social sanctions can be rendered more effective if the lenders provide a dynamic incentive by engaging in sequential rather than simultaneous lending to the group members.

In the case of genuine default, the joint-liability system works in a very different way to ensure better enforcement. The main insight here is that the prospect of facing the joint-liability burden induces borrowers to help each other in times of distress; thus, peer support rather than peer pressure is the key force here. In the theories dealing with genuine default, group lending is viewed as a mechanism for strengthening the bonds of mutual insurance among the borrowers, especially when used in conjunction with sequential lending. By inducing mutual insurance, the joint-liability system reduces the probability of default and thus mitigates the enforcement problem.

Joint liability is, however, not the only aspect of microcredit institutions that can contribute towards strengthening the lender's ability to overcome the enforcement problem. Other aspects, such as a frequent repayment schedule and the holding of public meetings amongst borrowers, have also been shown to have properties that can potentially improve repayment performance.

Notes

1 Akerlof (1970) analysed the second-hand car market, where sellers have private information about the condition of the car that buyers can hardly know about. He showed that, given such information asymmetry, the price mechanism would work in such a way that bad cars ('lemons' in American parlance) would tend to drive good cars out of the market. Ever since, the phrase 'the lemons problem' has become synonymous with the problem of adverse selection in general.
2 There is a difference, however, in the nature of credit rationing in the two models. In Jaffe and Russell, credit rationing takes the form of offering a smaller loan amount than what is demanded by the borrower at the market rate of interest. By contrast, in the main model developed by Stiglitz and Weiss, it takes the form of the lender randomly denying loans to some borrowers even if they were prepared to pay a slightly higher

126 *Adverse selection, repayment enforcement*

interest rate than what was prevailing in the market. For a comprehensive review of credit rationing, see Jaffe and Stiglitz (1990). An early application of the idea of credit rationing in the context of rural economies of the developing world can be found in Carter (1988).

3 The possibility or the necessity of the Stiglitz-Weiss type of credit rationing has been questioned, however. Two main conclusions emerge from this literature. First, the existence of credit rationing requires additional assumptions that may or may not hold in specific circumstances. Second, even if there is no credit rationing, the fact remains that adverse selection will render the market outcome inefficient. Thus, inefficiency rather than credit rationing *per se* remains the most robust conclusion of this literature. See, for example, Hubbard (1998), de Meza and Webb (2006), Arnold and Riley (2009) and Agur (2012).

4 There is, of course, another kind of default which we might call genuine default; it occurs when borrowers are not able to repay the loan even if they want to. When strategic default coexists with genuine default and the lender is unable to distinguish between the two, it creates a rather special problem for the credit market. We shall discuss both types of default.

5 Technically speaking, both sets of assumptions imply that the probability distribution of returns to the safe borrower stochastically dominates that of the risky borrower, but in two quite different ways: the M-W case represents first-order stochastic dominance whereas the S-W case represents second-order stochastic dominance. On the difference between the two kinds of stochastic dominance, see Rothschild and Stiglitz (1970).

6 Strictly speaking, r stands for repayment per dollar of loan, i.e. interest plus one dollar of principal. For terminological simplicity, we call it the interest rate, meaning it is to be interpreted as a gross interest rate.

7 This is so because $(\bar{R} - v) > \rho$ (from (5.7)) and $\bar{p} > p_r$ by definition.

8 It may seem odd that we are using the term 'pooling equilibrium' to describe a situation where all the safe borrowers are left out, but this is merely a consequence of our simplifying assumption of a discrete probability distribution with only two values of project return. If instead we had assumed a continuous probability distribution with many different returns and their corresponding probabilities, we would have had a truly pooling equilibrium with a mix of risk profiles, but with some borrowers at the upper end of the probability distribution being left out by adverse selection.

9 For further analysis of the underinvestment problem under asymmetric information in the credit market, see Gale (1990), Jaffe and Stiglitz (1990) and Hubbard (1998).

10 The problem of overinvestment under asymmetric information is further analysed by Bernanke and Gertler (1990).

11 Even though their projects are also more likely to fail, it does not worry them so much because the limited liability constraint protects them from repayment in case of failure. Of course, failure may still be a concern, as a very high probability of failure might make the expected return fall below the opportunity cost v, but until that point is reached, i.e. so long as the participation constraint does not bind, failure does not matter.

12 Recall that a joint-liability penalty is paid only when a borrower herself succeeds in her project while her partner fails.

13 There are actually four possibilities: (i) both i and j succeed, (ii) i succeeds and j fails, (iii) i fails and j succeeds, and (iv) both i and j fail. Since i does not receive anything nor pays anything if she fails, only the first two cases enter in her payoff function.

14 For more on this property, see the pioneering work of Becker (1993) on assortative matching in the context of the marriage market.

15 As such, the preferences of the two types of borrowers satisfy what is known as the 'single-crossing property', which is essential for the existence of a separating equilibrium under asymmetric information. See Fudenberg and Tirole (1991), Chapter 7.

16 The preceding discussion has assumed the Stiglitz-Weiss scenario. Ghatak (2000) demonstrates that if we instead assume the de Meza-Webb scenario, a similar logic will entail that the group lending mechanism can be used to drive the socially unproductive risky borrowers away from the credit market, thus avoiding adverse selection of the other type. See also Tassel (1999) for an analysis very similar to Ghatak's, and Laffont and N'Guessan (2000) and Laffont (2003) for more on the implications of group lending under the de Meza-Webb scenario.
17 This statement is valid for the S-W scenario. For the M-W scenario, the corresponding result is that even a single contract can eliminate adverse selection by driving socially unproductive risky borrowers away. See Ghatak (1999, 2000) for formal proof of both propositions.
18 The latter conclusion has been contested, however. Gangopadhyay *et al.* (2005) point out that the efficiency result is contingent on a curious feature of the optimal contract derived in Ghatak (2000) which entails that the amount of joint liability in the groups exceeds the sum of individual liabilities. The problem with this feature is that when one member of the group fails and the other succeeds, the latter may prefer to announce that both succeeded and pay the interest rate for both rather than paying each her own loan plus joint liability for her partner. If this anomaly is removed by adding the constraint that the amount of joint liability cannot exceed the amount of individual liability, the result – that joint-liability contracts mark a Pareto improvement over individual liability contracts – still goes through, but the efficiency result does not. In a recent paper, Katzur and Lensink (2012) have shown, however, that the efficiency result can be restored, even with the new constraint, if the project outcomes of members within a group are assumed to be correlated rather than statistically independent, as assumed by Ghatak.
19 Like Ghatak (1999), Armendáriz de Aghion and Gollier also maintain the Stiglitz-Weiss assumptions about risk distribution. As Laffont and N'Guessan (2000) demonstrate, however, while most of Ghatak's major findings remain valid under the alternative scenario of de Meza-Webb assumptions, the same is not true about the findings of Armendáriz de Aghion and Gollier. In particular, with heterogeneous groups, in which borrowers do not know each other's risk type, joint liability can no longer be shown to generate the 'collateral effect' that is necessary to bring the interest rate down below the level that would obtain under individual lending.
20 We are assuming here the context of the Stiglitz-Weiss information scenario.
21 This model builds upon the work on co-signing by Besanko and Thakor (1987) discussed earlier in this chapter. A major difference, however, is that in the Besanko-Thakor model the co-signer does not invest and therefore does not borrow, whereas in the present model both the co-signee and the principal applicant borrow. An important implication is that the risk profile of the co-signer does not play a role in the Besanko-Thakor model, but it does play a role in the present model.
22 For proof of these propositions, see Gangopadhyay and Lensink (2009) and Katzur and Lensink (2011).
23 There remains a deeper problem, however, which may render the threat useless even if the borrower's access to other lenders either does not exist or is compromised if it does. This has to do with a point first made by Bulow and Rogoff (1989), who were writing in the context of sovereign lending, but it has serious implications for all models involving denial of future credit. They show that' if the borrower can save at the same rate as the lender, then credit denial is useless as a means of ensuring loan repayment. The reason is simple: rather than repay one dollar today to obtain a future loan, the borrower would rather just save the dollar and effectively self-finance the promised future loan (Bond and Krishnamurthy, 2004). This argument implies that if the threat of denial of future credit has to have any deterrent power, some other conditions must be satisfied. Two such conditions may be mentioned. First, the borrower's credit needs may increase over time, in which case recycling the defaulted loan won't suffice. Second,

128 *Adverse selection, repayment enforcement*

the borrower could face impediments in trying to save; in other words, borrowing may be easier than saving, which can happen if people have time-inconsistent preferences, an issue taken up elsewhere in this book. Our discussion throughout this chapter assumes that some such condition is satisfied.

24 The exposition below builds upon the analysis of strategic default in Ghosh et al. (2001).
25 This is an adaptation of Figure 4 in Ghosh et al. (2001).
26 Since $F'(L^*) = (1+r) = (1+\rho)$, at L^* the tangent to the curve $F(L)$ must equal the slope of the *IP* line, where the gap between $F(L)$ and the *IP* line, representing the payoff of the borrower, will be maximised. It follows from the concavity of $F(L)$ that, for all $L < L^*$, the gap, and hence the payoff to the borrower, will be a rising function of L. Therefore, even though any loan size within the range (L^0, L) is feasible, the constrained optimum will occur at the highest feasible value of L, i.e. L.
27 Since $\delta < 1$ and $F(L) > v$ (so long as the participation constraint is satisfied), this additional amount must be a positive quantity. Also note that a lower δ implies higher incentive rent, i.e. the more impatient the borrower is, the greater is the incentive rent needed to deter default.
28 In a different framework where the zero-profit condition does not apply, there would be scope for adjustment through variation in the interest rate as well.
29 Other authors have taken up the issue of efficiency more explicitly. For instance, Arnold et al. (2013) show that even if group lending improves the repayment rate, the equilibrium will still be characterised by the kind of allocational distortions that are found in credit markets with an enforcement problem. Social sanctions may ameliorate the problem, but they will not remove it entirely.
30 Bhole and Ogden (2010) argue, to the contrary, that even without social sanctions, group lending will outperform individual lending provided (1) the amount that a successful borrower owes for the borrower's defaulting partner is optimally determined, and (2) the penalty is allowed to vary across group members. Although theoretically interesting, these results are not of much practical relevance since the necessary conditions are hardly likely to be satisfied by microcredit as practised in the real world.
31 One might think that this system will not work well in practice because an outside bank is unlikely to know which member of the group is stronger and should therefore be made the co-signee. But this is not really a problem because the bank doesn't need to decide who should be the co-signee. That decision can be left to the group, and the stronger party will emerge as the co-signee. This is because the weaker party will never agree to be the co-signee since she knows that she simply does not have the power to impose a high enough sanction on the stronger party to prevent her from defaulting. Only the stronger party will agree to be the co-signee because she has the power to ensure that the weaker party will repay.
32 This argument is similar to the temporal separation argument made by Aniket (2011a) in the context of *ex ante* moral hazard. See the discussion in Chapter 4.
33 Chowdhury et al. (2014) further develop the idea that sequential lending can help mitigate strategic default, even without bringing in social interactions.
34 On this, see the discussion in Chapter 4 on the role and limits of social sanctions in mitigating *ex ante* moral hazard and the evidence presented in Chapter 3 that such sanctions are rarely imposed, at least in the present-day microcredit market in rural Bangladesh.
35 The importance of choosing the group size optimally so as to enhance the efficacy of group lending is further examined – in the context of different types of market failure – by Ahlin (2015) and Bourjade and Schindele (2012), among others.
36 A pioneering analysis of the mutual insurance aspect of group lending is offered by Rashid and Townsend (1992).

37 See, *inter alia*, the collection of papers in Dercon (2005) and the works cited therein, and the excellent survey article by Fafchamps (2011).
38 See, for example, the evidence cited in Besley (1995), Townsend (1994) and Udry (1994).
39 Chatterjee and Sarangi (2005), Roy Chowdhury (2007) and Guttman (2008) provide alternative analyses of how the threat of non-renewal of loans can lead to negative assortative matching.
40 The cross-reporting strategy they recommend is similar in spirit to the one proposed by Brusco (1997), who studied moral hazard in team production and showed that workers can stop co-workers from shirking by threatening to send negative reports about effort levels. The logic underlying these reporting games is close to that of the implementation model proposed by Hurwicz *et al.* (1995) in the general literature on mechanism design.
41 Rai and Sjöström (2004) demonstrate that this cross-reporting strategy is robust to collusion, i.e. when the group as a whole is able to repay the loans, the threat of cross-reporting cannot be used by the borrowers as a means of sharing the returns amongst themselves by depriving the bank of its due share.
42 The strategy proposed by Tedeschi is an adaptation of Green and Porter's (1984) dynamic collusion game to the specific context of the credit market.
43 The extent to which this strategy will reduce the deadweight loss depends on the richness of information on the basis of which lender determines the length of the punishment phase. It can be shown that, given the information set assumed by Tedeschi, the length of the punishment phase is not the first best; a better outcome could be reached by using borrower histories, which do not belong to the information set assumed in Tedeschi's model. See, however, Sadoulet (2005) for a model that incorporates borrower histories.
44 An early recognition of the importance of other features of microfinance can be found in Armendáriz de Aghion and Morduch (2000). The authors develop the arguments further in Armendáriz and Morduch (2010).
45 Empirical support for the conjecture that the social interactions made possible by public meetings improve borrowers' collective capacity for risk-pooling is provided by a combined survey and field experiment carried out in India by Feigenberg *et al.* (2013), which shows that borrowers who meet more regularly are less likely to default, other things remaining the same.
46 Rai and Sjöström (2013) cite data from the Green Bank experiment in the Philippines (Gine and Karlan, 2014) to support the point about the irrelevance of the liability system for loan repayment when public meetings take place regularly. For more on the evidence on the relative efficacy of individual and joint liability, see the discussion in Chapter 6.
47 Jain and Mansuri made the argument in the context of *ex ante* moral hazard, but the logic of their argument applies equally to *ex post* moral hazard as well.
48 This does not rule out the possibility that moneylenders may be able to strengthen their hold in certain specific areas for specific reasons. For evidence of this kind and a possible theoretical explanation, see Berg *et al.* (2015).
49 For evidence, see, among others, Ashraf *et al.* (2006) and Collins *et al.* (2009).
50 For a wide-ranging analysis of the implications of present-biased preferences for the lives of the poor, see Banerjee and Mullainathan (2010); and, for analysis specifically on the implications for savings, see also Banerjee and Duflo (2011), Chapter 8.
51 See Fischer and Ghatak (2010) and Tsukada (2014) for formal modelling of this interpretation of the frequent-repayment aspect of microcredit. Chowdhury *et al.* (2014) extend the idea to show that frequent repayment reduces the incentive to default in the context of sequential lending.
52 This conjecture is supported by a field experiment carried out by Bauer *et al.* (2012) in India, which showed that present-biased women were more likely to borrow from a microcredit lender. See also the discussion in Chapter 8.

53 This argument does not contradict the proposition that offering a combination of savings and loan products might be even better than offering loans alone. For formal modelling along this line, see Aniket (2011b) and Basu (2015).
54 Empirical evidence on this point is not very conclusive, however. For instance, in a field experiment carried out in India, Field and Pande (2008) found no difference between weekly and monthly repayment in terms of repayment behaviour. This does not, however, necessarily negate the interpretation of frequent repayment given above, because even a monthly repayment schedule can be seen as a better commitment device than less frequent (say, six-monthly or annual) schedules and one-off repayment.

6 When theory meets reality
Testing the theories of microcredit

Visionary practitioners have created the microcredit revolution, and theorists have tried to explain exactly how they did it. But have the theorists correctly captured the essence of practitioners' innovations? This question can only be answered by confronting theory with reality. The answer is not of mere academic interest, though that is important too; it may have important practical implications as well. Since different theories emphasise different aspects of microcredit delivery and offer different hypotheses about how it works, an understanding of which theories are empirically 'relevant' and which are merely 'esoteric' may also help identify and strengthen the truly potent aspects of microcredit practice. In Chapter 2, we touched on these issues in light of the experience of the evolution of the microcredit system in Bangladesh; but it may be noted that the experience of Bangladesh is unique in some respects, such as the maturity of the system and the flagship role of Grameen Bank. Here, instead, we attempt a review of the relevant academic literature based on worldwide experience.

As we have seen in the preceding two chapters, economists have used a great deal of ingenuity to delve underneath the practice of microcredit and understand the logic that drives its success. There is no single theory, however – not even a unified theoretical framework with multiple extensions. What we find instead is a bewildering variety of theories; the only common thread binding most of them is the idea that the way microcredit is delivered in practice helps overcome certain market imperfections – in particular, imperfections in information and in the enforcement of contracts. But they differ greatly in their understanding of exactly which imperfections are being addressed and precisely how they are being overcome. Among the variety of imperfections, some pick out adverse selection for particular attention, some emphasise moral hazard, others focus on strategic default arising from imperfect enforcement, and yet others highlight the imperfections in informal insurance that lead to default even when a borrower is willing to repay. Among the mechanisms through which microcredit is presumed to overcome these problems, most theorists point to joint liability as the prime driver; others emphasise dynamic incentives, and yet others speak for some of the less discussed features, such as frequent repayment, public meetings, and so on. Many of the theories emphasise the role of social capital in sustaining the mechanisms that make microcredit work, but they differ on the relative importance they attach

132 *Testing the theories of microcredit*

to harnessing the existing social capital as opposed to creating new forms of social capital or strengthening the existing ones. They also differ in what they deem to be the most relevant aspect of social capital for the successful operation of microcredit – whether it is people's knowledge of each other, or their sympathy for each other, or their ability to impose social sanctions on their peers, and so on.

It is conceivable that there is some truth in all or most of the ideas that theorists have toyed with, but there still remains the question as to which features of microcredit are more important than others in practice. Moreover, are some features more universally potent than others, or is everything context-specific? Only a wide range of empirical studies, covering different times and places, can answer these questions satisfactorily. Such studies are already underway, but there is still a long way to go. Our current state of knowledge has not reached a stage where we can offer definitive answers to most of the questions of interest. But a few tentative answers have begun to emerge to at least some of those questions.[1] In this chapter, we shall present our understanding of the current state of knowledge with regard to the following three sets of issues:

(a) Which aspect of market failure does the group lending mechanism help overcome most commonly and most successfully, if at all – is it adverse selection, or *ex ante* moral hazard, or strategic default, or inadequate informal insurance?
(b) Does social capital really play a role in sustaining the microcredit delivery mechanisms that help overcome market failures? If so, which aspects of social capital are most relevant for this purpose?
(c) Is joint liability really the key to microcredit's success? Or, can individual liability do equally well, if not better, when supported by other features of microcredit delivery (for example, dynamic incentives, or frequent repayment, or public meetings, and so on)?

Before discussing the answers that have emerged so far, we need to address a prior question, however. While the theories of microcredit differ greatly from each other, most of them share the premise that rural credit markets are characterised by pervasive asymmetries of information that lead to pathologies such as adverse selection and moral hazard, and also by the problem of inadequate enforcement. Together, these problems can be described under the common rubric of the 'agency problem'. Before examining whether and how microcredit helps redress the pathologies created by the agency problem, we need to ask: is the premise itself valid? Is there any empirical evidence for the existence of the agency problem, or is it all a figment of the theorist's imagination?

6.1 Is there evidence for the agency problem in the rural credit market?

Economists have tried to look for the evidence, but it has not proved an easy task. The very concept of asymmetric information implies that it would be difficult to observe, for if it were not so the asymmetry would probably not have existed in the first place. The challenge is one of 'observing unobservables', as the title of a paper in this field aptly describes (Karlan and Zinman, 2009). The only feasible way of going about the task is to check if the observable predictions of a theory embodying the agency problem can be matched with evidence. For instance, the pioneering work of Stiglitz and Weiss (1981) on asymmetric information in the credit market predicts that lenders will not raise the interest rate (or, alternatively, the loan size) beyond a certain level for fear of inducing either adverse selection or moral hazard to an extent that it begins to hurt their profits. Looking at a data set on a large number of microcredit lenders from around the world, Cull *et al.* (2007) found evidence in support of this prediction.[2]

Three categories of lenders were covered in the data set – namely, those who lend mainly on an individual liability basis, those who lend with group liability (the Grameen-type lenders), and those who lend on the basis of village-level group liability (the so-called village banks). For the subset of individual liability lenders, the authors found an inverted U-shaped relationship between interest rate and profitability – as interest rate rises, profitability first rises and then falls, just as the Stiglitz-Weiss theory predicts. The turning point comes at around the 60 percent interest rate, with very few lenders being observed charging above that rate, which is again consistent with theory.

There is, however, a problem with this evidence. In order to claim that we have found evidence for a theory, it is not enough that the predictions of the theory fit the facts. What we need is a 'discriminating test', i.e. a test that will assure us that the observed facts are consistent only with the theory in question and not with any alternative explanation. This is not the case here. As the authors acknowledge, the same inverted U-shaped relationship between interest rate and profitability is also consistent with a simple theory of a downward-sloping demand curve for credit. At a high enough interest rate, the demand for credit may become so elastic that further increase in the rate will induce negative profit at the margin. In other words, the observed facts cannot discriminate between the competing hypotheses of the agency problem and elastic demand.

Cull *et al.* (2007) then proceed to offer some additional evidence that does take them closer to a 'discriminating test'. They seek to establish a relationship between interest rate and the extent of delinquency as measured by 'loan portfolio at risk'. If the lenders are confronted with the agency problem, a higher interest rate should lead to greater delinquency through either adverse selection or moral hazard, and this is also what is observed (up to a point, which is at about a 40 percent interest rate). This is more of a discriminating test because neither the theory of demand nor any other known theory predicts a positive relationship between interest rate and delinquency.[3]

Once the existence of the agency problem is accepted, there arises the even trickier problem of trying to ascertain exactly what kind of agency problem exists – in particular, is it mainly a problem of adverse selection or of moral hazard or both; and if it is both, which is more important? The kind of evidence Cull *et al.* presented on the positive relationship between interest rate and delinquency (or, alternatively between loan size and delinquency) is consistent with both an adverse selection explanation and a moral hazard explanation. The empirical task, therefore, becomes even more challenging if one tries to identify the precise nature of the agency problem, let alone ascertain the relative importance of different types of agency problem.[4]

In the jargon, this type of challenge is known as the 'identification problem' – a term we shall come across rather frequently throughout this book. In essence, it refers to the problem of isolating the causal effect of one or more factors from that of others that might work in tandem to influence a particular phenomenon (in this case, the default rate). The problem becomes especially serious when some of the causal factors cannot be easily observed or measured, as is the case with adverse selection and moral hazard. Researchers try to devise an 'identification strategy' that will credibly isolate the effects of the causal factors of interest. Quite often, however, success in finding this strategy depends on the nature of the data. Either there must be something special in the data that the researchers can 'exploit' for the purpose of identification, or the right kind of data must be constructed with the help of 'experiments'. There are examples of both these approaches in the present case.[5]

An example of the former type is the study by Klonner and Rai (2007), who tried to ascertain the existence of adverse selection in the credit market by looking at the operations of a ROSCA (Rotating Savings and Credit Association) in India. There are various types of ROSCAs, and the particular one this study considered is known as a bidding ROSCA. Every month, the members contribute to a pool of funds which goes to the highest bidder; the higher the bid, the higher is the effective rate of interest the winner has to pay. Previous winners are barred from bidding in the subsequent auctions until everybody has had a chance to win the common pot, and then the process may start all over again. The way the system works, the early winners end up paying higher effective rates of interest compared to the later winners.[6] This means that in the ideal world, the early winners would be those who have a higher willingness to pay for the privilege of using the common fund. However, in the real world, the early winners may actually be the more 'risky types', who, according to the theory of adverse selection, are more tempted by high interest rates compared to the 'safe types'. Thus, if adverse selection exists, one would expect to find a risk profile where early winners are riskier and late winners are safer.

But suppose the effective interest rate is capped at some relatively low level, which can be done by putting a ceiling on how much one can bid (recall that the effective interest rate varies positively with the amount of the winning bid). Then almost everybody will want to bid up to the highest permissible level, and the allocation will have to be done by some other mechanism – say, a lottery. In that case, the risk profile will be random; the previous pattern of early winners being characterised by more risk will disappear. Thus, a comparison of the risk profile before and after the imposition of the ceiling will give a clue to the existence of adverse selection. With adverse selection, the two risk profiles will differ systematically; without adverse selection, there will be no systematic difference between the two. This is the 'identification strategy' adopted by Klonner and Rai. For this strategy to work, of course, a ceiling on the winning bid must be imposed by some exogenous source. In this case, the imposition came from an edict of the Indian Supreme Court, which restricted the winning bid up to a maximum of 30 percent of the common pool in 1993 and then relaxed it in 2002. Both the imposition of the ceiling and its subsequent relaxation gave the authors an opportunity to apply their identification strategy (of comparing the risk profiles of early and later winners). They did find systematic differences in the risk profiles before and after these events, which attest to the existence of adverse selection.[7]

Another example of identifying the elements of asymmetric information by 'exploiting' a special feature of the data set is a recent study of payday loans in the USA by Dobbie and Skiba (2013).[8] The study 'exploits' the fact that the amounts of loan offered by the lenders are a discontinuous function of net pay. The sample firms offered loans in $50 increments, up to but not exceeding half of an individual's net pay. This practice gives rise to several loan eligibility cut-offs around which very similar borrowers are offered different-sized loans. The authors' identification strategy consists in comparing the average level of default for individuals earning just above and just below these cutoff points.[9]

Normally, the agency problem will manifest itself in higher loan sizes being associated with higher default rates. This could happen through a combination of adverse selection and moral hazard, and without further information, it will not be possible to separate the two. Fortunately, such separation becomes possible when there are discontinuities of the kind noted above. The discontinuities ensure that a borrower with income just above the cutoff point will get a much bigger loan compared to the borrower with income just below the same cutoff point. But this difference in loan size is not something that the borrowers voluntarily 'chose' to have; it was imposed on them by an exogenously imposed cutoff. As such, there is no reason to believe that a risky borrower chose a higher loan size and a safe borrower chose a smaller one, as would happen in the event of adverse selection. In other words, the possibility of adverse selection is ruled out if one compares the repayment performance of borrowers just below and just above the cutoff point. If one nonetheless finds that those who took out bigger loans have higher default rates (after controlling for observable personal characteristics), this must be due to moral hazard. This is how it becomes possible to separate out the effect of moral hazard on the default rate.

Furthermore, since the difference in the default rates of large and small loans in the overall sample (not just those around the cutoffs) reflects a possible combination of moral hazard and adverse selection, one can also obtain a separate estimate of adverse selection by subtracting the effect of moral hazard from the overall difference. By following this procedure, the authors estimated that borrowers who chose $100 larger loans were 6.0 to 7.8 percentage points more likely to default – on account of adverse selection alone – than observationally equivalent borrowers who chose smaller loans.

The existence of adverse selection in the credit market is thus credibly established by Klonner and Rai (2007) for an Indian ROSCA and by Dobbie and Skiba

(2013) for the US payday loan market. But there are not enough studies of this kind to permit a broad generalization about the existence of adverse selection (or of moral hazard, for that matter) in the credit markets around the world where microcredit has spread in recent years. The problem is mainly methodological. As we have seen, the identification of adverse selection or moral hazard requires the existence of some special features of the data set – for example, an exogenously imposed cap on the winning bid, as in the case of the Indian ROSCA, or exogenous eligibility cutoffs, as in the US payday loan market. Most real-world data on the credit market are not blessed with such special features which researchers can 'exploit' for the purpose of identification. As an alternative, some researchers have turned to generating the right kind of data with the help of experiments.

The use of experimental data has become increasingly common in the field of research on microcredit, as in economics generally, and we shall have a good deal to say on its strengths and weaknesses in Chapter 7, where the poverty impact of microcredit is evaluated. Here we shall introduce it briefly. Using a terminology due to Harrison and List (2004), we can classify experiments in economics into three categories: laboratory experiments, framed field experiments, and field experiments. In laboratory experiments, non-standard subjects are put through some tasks to simulate people's behaviour in real-world situations; in field experiments, the subjects are actual agents whose behaviour is to be analysed but their choices and options are constrained in a manner designed by the researcher to allow credible inferences about causal connections; and framed field experiments are a kind of hybrid which uses non-standard subject pools but adds a 'field context' familiar to the subjects to the task undertaken in the experiment. All three types of experiments are found in the research on microcredit, and some of these will be discussed later in this chapter. For the moment, we will look at a study by Karlan and Zinman (2009), which used a novel field experiment in South Africa to isolate the effects of adverse selection from moral hazard.

The experiment was conducted among the clients of a South African finance company that typically lends at 200 percent per annum and involved two stages. In the first stage, offers of loans were sent out through mail-order to a large number of clients who were randomly assigned three alternative interest rates. In the second stage, those who accepted the initial mail-order offer were given a contract, but at this stage an element of surprise was introduced by randomly offering to a subset of the clients a smaller interest rate (r^c) than the original offer, while the remainder was offered the original rate (r^o). Those who accepted the contract at this stage were also offered two randomly assigned interest rates on future loans (r^f) in order to test for the effect of dynamic incentive. The design thus produced a set of borrowers who selected themselves in at identical rates but then faced different repayment incentives in the future, and another set of borrowers who selected themselves in at different rates but then faced identical repayment incentives. It is this particular aspect of the experimental design that permits separation of the effects of adverse selection from that of moral hazard.

In the first stage, the individuals decided whether to take up the solicitation's offer rate (r^o), which could be 'high' or 'low'. The subset of clients who took up the offer at the high r^o then split up into two groups: those who were randomly surprised with a new lower interest rate $r^c < r^o$ (group A), and those who continued to receive the high rate $r^c = r^o$ (group B). The members of groups A and B thus self-selected at the same rate of interest, but they subsequently faced different repayment incentives. Self-selection at the same interest rate ensured that the two groups should not differ systematically in their average risk profile; therefore, any difference in their repayment performance (after controlling for the effects of observable personal characteristics) would be a consequence of moral hazard alone, i.e. the result of differential incentives for repayment stemming from two different contract rates.[10]

Having thus identified moral hazard, the researchers identified the effect of adverse selection by noting that those who received the lower contract rate (r^c) did not all receive the same initial mail offer (r^o). Some of them were randomly offered a higher rate and some were offered a lower rate. Thus, the defining characteristic of this sub-sample is that the clients self-selected at different offer rates, but subsequently they all faced the same contract rate. Since the *ex post* repayment incentive was the same for all members of this sub-sample, any difference in their default rates (after controlling for the effects of observable personal characteristics) must be due to differences in their innate riskiness – this is the measure of the adverse selection effect.[11]

The authors' empirical results indicate weak evidence of an adverse selection effect and strong evidence of a moral hazard. A rough estimate suggests that moral hazard explains perhaps 13 percent to 21 percent of default in their sample.

6.2 Identifying the pathways of joint liability

Although the evidence is limited and the findings are somewhat mixed, the preceding discussion shows that the agency problem does exist in the credit market and that the problem manifests itself in the form of both adverse selection and moral hazard. Different forms of the agency problem may not be equally strong everywhere, but they do seem to exist. This establishes at least a *prima facie* case that the theories of microcredit, which purport to show how its various features, and especially joint liability, help overcome these problems, has some broad relevance in reality. But this still leaves open the question: which kind of agency problem are microcredit practices in general, and joint liability in particular, able to overcome in practice? Are they more successful in dealing with the problem of adverse selection, or with moral hazard, or with strategic default, or the imperfections in informal insurance? In other words, what exactly are the pathways through which joint liability works in practice, if at all?

One way of addressing this question is to set up a competition among alternative theories of microcredit embodying different pathways of joint liability and check whose predictions fit the data best. If, for example, one observes the data for some microlenders who practice joint liability and finds that the predictions of Ghatak's model of adverse selection fit the observed data better than, say, the Stiglitz-Weiss model of moral hazard, one could conclude that joint liability is better at removing adverse selection than moral hazard. In a classic paper, Ahlin and Townsend (2007) adopted precisely such an approach.

They empirically compared four canonical models of microcredit against data from rural Thailand. Of these four, two were moral hazard models – namely, those of Stiglitz (1990) and Banerjee *et al.* (1994); one was a limited enforcement (or strategic default) model, due to Besley and Coate (1995); and the final one was the adverse selection model of Ghatak (1999). The authors were able to compare these models empirically by exploiting the fact that under a common set of assumptions these models yielded different predictions about the repayment rate. For this purpose, they analysed the repayment data of a large sample of borrowers served by the Bank of Agriculture and Agricultural Cooperatives (BAAC), the largest microfinance institution in Thailand. But first, to ensure comparability, they had to extend and modify the standard models so as to bring them under a common set of assumptions. Once this was done, a number of differences emerged in their testable predictions.

First, the models differed in the implications of raising the joint-liability payment. A higher joint-liability payment raised the gain from monitoring and hence raised repayment in the moral hazard model of Banarjee *et al.*, but it reduced repayment in Ghatak's model of adverse selection by screening out more of the safer borrowers (if interest rate was kept fixed).

Second, the models also differed in the consequences of the presence or absence of cooperation among group members. In Stiglitz's model of moral hazard, the absence of co-operation led to the adoption of riskier projects and thus a reduced repayment rate. By contrast, in the Besley-Coate model of strategic default, non-cooperation was consistent with carrying out the threat of penalties on a defaulting group borrower, so repayment rates were higher under non-cooperation.

Finally, the models differed in their implications of the assumption that the project returns of the borrowers were correlated with each other. Theory predicts that a positive correlation in project returns can be a negative force for repayment in the Besley-Coate model, as it increases the possibility that project returns will be low at the same time, which might induce mass default. But a positive correlation in returns is a positive force in the models of Stiglitz and Ghatak.

These differences in testable predictions about repayment rates allowed Ahlin and Townsend to test the relative validity of alternative models. Perhaps, not surprisingly, they found that no single model fitted the data best. Instead, different models seemed to work better under different physical and socio-economic environments. Thus:

- The strategic default model of Besley and Coate (1995) was found to fit best in the relatively poor and semi-arid Northeast.
- The Ghatak (1999) and Stiglitz (1990) models fitted best in the relatively well-developed central region, in predictions about screening and to a lesser extent about the covariability of returns.
- The monitoring prediction of Banerjee *et al.* (1994) fitted well in the prosperous central region.

- Finally, the predictions of Banerjee *et al.* (1994) and Besley-Coate (1995) models that cooperation would lower repayment was evident in most cases, but the positive prediction for the Stiglitz model came in quite strongly in the central region.

These findings seem to suggest the general conclusion that joint liability may be better at dealing with strategic default in low-infrastructure areas, while it tackles information problems (in particular, adverse selection) better in more developed areas. There exists, however, a subtle difficulty in drawing this conclusion too firmly. The empirical tests conducted by Ahlin and Townsend (2007) are, in the first instance, tests of the models, as modified by them. But they cannot necessarily be treated as tests of the pathways of joint liability as embodied in these models. The problem is that the models' predictions are conditioned as much by the workings of joint liability as by many other auxiliary assumptions that are also embedded in the models; and it is not easy to judge whether the differences in predictions are driven by joint liability as such, or by its interactions with the auxiliary assumptions.[12]

The only way to get around this problem is to employ model-independent tests. In other words, one could directly try to find out whether the possible pathways of joint liability lead to better repayment performance. For example, instead of asking whether a joint-liability model embodying peer monitoring yields predictions about repayment that fit data better than the predictions from alternative models, one could simply ask: is there any evidence that peer monitoring improves repayment performance among microcredit borrowers? Of course, this approach is not without its challenges either. In the first place, one would have to find credible measures of peer monitoring. Second, one would have to disentangle the effects of peer monitoring from those of other factors that may also have a bearing on repayment performance. Finally, further complications will arise if one is interested in learning not just whether peer monitoring works, but also whether it works better than other pathways, such as self-selection, peer support, etc.

Of the growing number of studies that have tried to identify the empirically relevant pathways of joint liability, some have met these challenges better than others. We shall first consider what these studies have to say about the empirical significance of self-selection in joint liability lending as emphasised in the models of Ghatak (1999, 2000) and others, and then examine what we have learnt so far about how successfully joint liability induces peer monitoring and peer pressure to avert *ex ante* moral hazard *á la* Stiglitz (1990) and *ex post* moral hazard *á la* Besley and Coate (1995).

6.2.1 The pathway of peer selection

In one of the earliest studies to undertake a systematic empirical enquiry of the pathways of joint liability, Wenner (1995) found strong support for the role of self-selection. Using a survey among joint-liability groups of a well-known microfinance institution called FINCA (*Fundacío Integral Campesina*) in Peru, he carried out an econometric analysis of the determinants of repayment performance with a special focus on the role of selection. Two explanatory variables were used for this purpose: a variable that reflected whether the borrowers were screened on the basis of reputation at the stage of group formation, and another variable to capture whether the groups had a written code of conduct that members were expected to adhere to after the group was formed. Both variables were deemed to proxy the selection effect, the latter being taken as a stronger mechanism of self-selection than the former, and both variables were found to have a negative effect on loan default after controlling for other factors.

Wenner took this as evidence in support of joint liability's success in inducing self-selection that weeds out risky borrowers and thus improves the repayment performance of the group. But the inference may not be that straightforward, because the variable representing the presence of a code of conduct can be given multiple interpretations. Wenner justifies its interpretation as a selection variable as follows:

> While informal screening according to reputation may be seen as a porous device wherein social customs, kinship, friendship ties may or may not result in group of truly creditworthy individuals, the existence of a written code can be seen as a formal device that sets a uniform minimum standard for membership selection. Thus, the written code can induce self-selection.
>
> (Wenner, 1995, p.270)

While the argument sounds plausible, it does not rule out the possibility that the code of conduct could also facilitate peer monitoring and peer pressure, leading especially to the kind of cooperative behaviour envisioned in some of the moral hazard models.[13] In that sense, Wenner is not actually able to disentangle the different pathways through which joint liability is supposed to work.

In their study of group lending in rural Bangladesh, Sharma and Zeller (1997) also carried out an econometric analysis of the determinants of repayment performance, and included an explanatory variable to indicate whether the group self-selected themselves or were formed by the lenders. The groups that formed on their own were found to have a better repayment performance after controlling for other factors. This result would seem to attest to the power of joint liability to mitigate adverse selection when the borrowers are given an opportunity to self-select, but the inference is not beyond doubt. What the results directly indicate is that self-selected groups perform better than lender-formed groups, but it does not say anything about why they do so. Avoidance of adverse selection, i.e. screening out risky borrowers, is indeed one possibility, but it's not the only one. It is also possible that self-selected groups have enough social capital amongst themselves to be able to monitor each other better so as to avoid *ex ante* moral hazard, or to be able to exert peer pressure better so as to avoid *ex post* moral hazard (strategic default), or to be able to provide peer support better so as to avoid genuine default at times of distress. Thus, once again, the mere finding that self-selection has a positive influence on repayment does not enable us to identify the empirically relevant pathways of joint liability.

For such an identification to be possible, a minimum requirement is that the effects of alternative pathways should be accounted for in the analysis so that their independent effects can be separated out. In very different ways, this was done by Gomez and Santor (2003) and Simtowe *et al.* (2006).

Gomez and Santor (2003) studied a sample of clients of the microfinance institution called Calmeadow in Canada, which offers both group and individual loans. The starting point of their analysis is a regression of default on a dummy variable representing whether a borrower belongs to a group or not, and a long list of control variables. The coefficient of the dummy variable reflects whether group lending yields superior repayment performance than individual lending. If it does, the coefficient captures the overall effect of all the pathways through which group lending helps to reduce default. In other words, the initial regression on its own could not disentangle the pathways of joint liability – in particular, it could not distinguish between the selection effect that mitigates adverse selection and the incentive effect that mitigates moral hazard. In the next step, however, the authors estimated another regression with the same explanatory variables by using a statistical technique called 'propensity score matching' (PSM) that, under certain conditions, removes the possible effect of self-selection.[14] If the two regressions yielded identical estimates of the coefficient of group lending, one would conclude that the selection effect does not exist; otherwise, it does. The authors found that the coefficient was actually reduced by some 20 percent in the second regression, which suggests that the selection effect was indeed operating to help reduce default.

A rather different approach was adopted by Simtowe *et al.* (2006) in their study of group lending in Malawi. Unlike Gomez and Santor, they only considered clients belonging to groups and tried to explain differences in moral hazard found in the groups' behaviour rather than differences in their repayment performance.[15] In the econometric analysis, the explanatory variables included separate variables for peer selection, peer monitoring and peer pressure, in addition to a number of control variables. They found that groups that were formed through peer selection suffered from less moral hazard compared to groups formed by outsiders. This result may seem similar to that found by Sharma and Zeller (1997) for Bangladesh, but there is a crucial difference. Since the present study includes separate explanatory variables to capture peer monitoring and peer pressure, one can interpret the selection effect in this study as capturing the mitigation of adverse selection with much greater confidence than in the case of the Sharma-Zeller study.

None of these studies, however, directly tested for the mitigation of adverse selection – it is, at best, an inference drawn from the observed effect of self-selection on either repayment behaviour or the borrowers' choices of the use of funds. According to theory, adverse selection is avoided through assortative matching, whereby borrowers with similar riskiness come together in a group, and in particular, safe borrowers form groups with other safe borrowers. A direct test would therefore require learning something about the 'riskiness' of the members of endogenously formed groups.

In their study of group lending in Georgia, Kritikos and Vigenina (2005) tried to extract this information by asking group members how they evaluated the riskiness of the business projects of their fellow group members on a scale ranging from 'all businesses were quite risky' to 'all businesses were quite safe'. This variable, which the authors denote as 'group quality', was found to be positively and significantly related to a respondent's own risk quality, suggesting the presence of assortative matching.

Giné et al. (2010) tried to investigate the nature of risk matching in a 'framed field experiment' in urban Peru. Working with a group of subjects drawn from actual microentrepreneurs (potential microcredit borrowers), they carried out a number of laboratory experiments to ascertain the effects of various lending mechanisms.[16] In one segment of these experiments, some subjects were randomly given the opportunity to form groups endogenously, while others were denied this opportunity. The purpose was to check whether the endogenously formed groups exhibited risk profiles consistent with the hypothesis of assortative matching. The assessment of risk profiles was made possible by the fact that background information about the subjects and a lottery game had already enabled the authors to grade the subjects on a scale of riskiness. When the subjects were given identical joint liability contracts, it turned out that the endogenously formed groups did exhibit assortative matching, i.e. safe subjects tended to associate with other safe subjects, thus validating theory.

Yet, the issue was not fully resolved. Apart from the legitimate question one may ask about whether a laboratory environment alters people's behaviour,[17] one must also take note of the fact that quite a few studies have arrived at the opposite conclusion – namely, that self-selected groups often tend to be heterogeneous in risk attributes.

One of the earliest empirical studies to find this apparent paradox is that of Zeller (1998). In an analysis of group lending in Madagascar, he came up with two rather startling conclusions. First, self-selection did not necessarily lead to homogeneous matching in terms of risk attributes, as measured by the riskiness of the projects adopted.[18] Second, risk-heterogeneous groups were actually superior in terms of repayment performance. Although all groups were endogenously formed, both heterogeneous and homogenous groups were found in practice. The superior performance of the heterogeneous groups was confirmed by an econometric analysis of determinants of repayment performance, which showed that variability in the riskiness of assets held by group members was positively associated with repayment. Zeller explained the superior performance of the heterogeneous groups in terms of the advantage of risk-pooling among members with projects of different degrees of riskiness: 'The results therefore indicate that heterogeneity of asset holdings among members, and related intra-group diversification of on- and off-farm enterprises, enables members to pool risks so as to better secure repayment of the loan' (Zeller, 1998, p.618). The underlying hypothesis is that when some borrowers face shocks, the variability in asset types within the group ensures that not everybody will be faced with the shock at the same time; so through a form of mutual insurance the 'lucky' members will be able to help out the 'unlucky' ones, thereby keeping up the repayment rate for the group as a whole.

It was precisely on the basis of this kind of argument involving risk-pooling and mutual insurance that Sadoulet (2000) built a theoretical model challenging the prediction of assortative matching *á la* Ghatak (1999, 2000) and suggesting instead that heterogeneous risk-matching would be the equilibrium outcome under plausible assumptions.[19] In a companion paper, Sadoulet and Carpenter (2001) went on to test the prediction of the theory by using data on group lending from Guatemala. Their findings were identical to those of Zeller, namely, that self-selection did not necessarily lead to homogeneous risk-matching and that joint liability induced mutual insurance within heterogeneous groups, but their empirical methodology was much more sophisticated. One difficulty with accepting the Zeller study at its face value is that the mere existence of heterogeneous groups does not invalidate the hypothesis of assortative matching. The reason is that, even when assortative matching is the equilibrium outcome, heterogeneous groups may emerge due to various kinds of matching frictions.[20]

The matching frictions theory states that homogeneous matching only holds in a frictionless world, and that all heterogeneity comes from matching frictions. Therefore, the hypothesis of assortative matching can be challenged only if the extent of heterogeneity found on the ground is deemed to be more than what can be expected on account of frictions alone. The methodological challenge is to figure out how to judge whether the observed heterogeneity is consistent with matching frictions or not. Sadoulet and Carpenter devised a novel methodology to meet this challenge. First, they demonstrated analytically that if frictions were the only reason for heterogeneity, there would exist no systematic relationship between borrowers' first best choice of risks (i.e. the amount of risk that would be taken in the frictionless word) and the observed risk pattern – i.e. any deviation from the first best would be purely random. Therefore, if the deviation was found to be systematic, it would indicate the existence of heterogeneity over and above what could be explained by frictions alone. In other words, it would indicate that borrowers actually chose heterogeneity as an equilibrium outcome.

While this argument suggests what would constitute a valid empirical test of heterogeneity, there remains the empirical challenge of finding credible measures of first best risks, which are by definition not observed. The authors devised a methodology for obtaining such measures from observed data and implemented it on data on group lending in Guatemala. They found evidence in support of their hypothesis that borrowers consciously self-selected into heterogeneous groups as an optimum choice; it was not just a matter of frictions. Following exactly the same methodology, Lensink and Mehrteab (2007) arrived at the same conclusions for group lending in Eritrea.

The logic of heterogeneous risk-matching is very different from that of assortative matching. Both are supposed to be induced by joint liability and both are expected to contribute to better repayment performance, but for very different reasons. Assortative matching is a mechanism for mitigating adverse selection, and it improves repayment performance by screening out risky borrowers. By contrast, heterogeneous matching is a mechanism for risk-pooling, and it improves repayment performance by inducing mutual insurance that prevents genuine default when borrowers face negative shocks. In other words, while both types of matching are induced by peer selection, the distinctive feature of heterogeneous matching is that peer selection is followed by peer support for mutual insurance. Therefore, one way of judging the prevalence of heterogeneous matching is to observe how widespread the phenomenon of peer support and mutual insurance is among self-selected groups.

There is indeed widespread evidence of the existence of peer support and informal insurance within self-selected groups. For example, Wenner (1995) found such evidence for Costa Rica.[21] He noted that while 75 percent of the groups got into repayment difficulties because of adversities faced by individual members, group delinquency (non-repayment or delayed repayment) was kept down to less than 50 percent through peer support. In a study of women's groups in Burkina Faso, Paxton *et al.* (2000) observed that the group was the main source of funds that the women relied on in the face of adversity. In bad times, they rarely borrowed from their husbands, families or other friends. Some indirect evidence also comes from Rai and Klonner's (2007) study of co-signed loans in India. Faced with the evidence that co-signing helps improve repayment, the authors tried to identify the pathways through which the improvement occurs. In particular, they tried to distinguish between the co-signers' role as a monitoring device and their role as an insurance device, and found evidence in support of the latter. Although this evidence relates to co-signing, which is a different mechanism from the ones employed by most group lending schemes, the authors rightly note that 'We believe our results on cosigners give some empirical support also to certain group lending theories, in particular the one of peer support, and help explain group lending's remarkable popularity over the past 30 years' (p.4).

In sum, the existing empirical studies provide support to the hypothesis that joint liability induces self-selection of a kind that improves repayment performance and thereby helps reduce the adverse effects of market imperfections. But some controversy remains as to precisely how the selection effect operates. The standard theory suggests that the main effect of self-selection is to screen out risky borrowers through assortative matching. Although there is some evidence in support of this hypothesis, there is also a great deal of evidence in support of the alternative hypothesis that the main effect of self-selection is to create opportunities for peer support and mutual insurance, often through the formation of groups that are heterogeneous in risk attributes, contrary to the predictions of standard theory.

6.2.2 The pathways of peer monitoring and peer pressure

The first systematic study to empirically estimate the impacts of peer monitoring and peer pressure on group performance was undertaken by Wydick (1999) using data from Guatemala. Performance was judged by several criteria, including repayment and incidence of moral hazard (measured by the extent to which a loan was misused, i.e. the funds were diverted from the purpose for which the loan was originally taken).[22] Econometric analysis was used to identify the determinants of each of these indicators of performance, separately for rural and urban groups and also for the combined sample.

The explanatory factors included separate variables to measure peer monitoring and peer pressure, and these were supplemented by a host of control variables. Peer monitoring was measured by the following indicators: (a) average distance between the members' businesses, (b) knowledge about other members' weekly sales, and (c) whether the members were engaged in the same line of business. The following indicators were used to measure peer pressure: (a) whether members were willing to apply pressure on others, (b) whether the member felt that applying pressure was difficult, (c) whether members stated that they had a moral obligation to repay the group loan, (d) whether the members said that they repay in order to stay on good terms with the group, and (e) group size.

The study found evidence for a statistically significant, *albeit* moderate, effect of peer monitoring on the mitigation of moral hazard and a correspondingly positive effect on repayment performance. The effect of peer pressure was also observed but it was more limited, confined only to rural areas.

Following a methodology similar to Wydick's, Hermes *et al.* (2005, 2006) also found in their study on Eritrea that peer monitoring helped to reduce moral hazard, but with the twist that only monitoring by the group leader mattered, while monitoring by other group members did not make much difference. The authors offered two possible explanations of this finding. First, other members did not try to monitor seriously because of the cost of monitoring; instead they tried to free-ride on the leader, who was the one that really had to answer to the MFI. Second, other members may have tried to monitor, but their effort was not effective because those who were monitored did not take them seriously. Group members felt pressured to behave prudently only when the group leader monitored, perhaps because only the leader was believed to have the real power to sanction moral hazard behaviour due to the leader's status as the representative of the group to the MFI.

Although rightly hailed as a path-breaking attempt to empirically identify the pathways of joint-liability lending, Wydick's methodology suffers from a number of shortcomings. First, it did not use any variables that actually captured whether peer monitoring was applied or not. Three proxy variables were used instead, each of which only stood for the ease of peer monitoring. If monitoring did occur, these variables would indicate where it was likely to be easier or more effective, but they do not themselves tell us anything about the extent to which monitoring actually occurred. Thus, the conclusion that peer monitoring is effective (*albeit* moderately) is mostly presumptive. Second, since the groups were self-selected, it is conceivable that the proxy variables used for peer monitoring and peer pressure also reflect, to some extent, the effect of peer selection. After all, if self-selection leads to the formation of groups in which members know each other well, then an indicator such as knowledge about each other's weekly sales would capture the effect of self-selection as much as it would the effect of peer monitoring. This will create an upward bias in the estimated effect of peer monitoring.

Subsequent studies have tried to deal with these problems in different ways. Simtowe *et al.* (2006), in their study on Malawi, included a separate variable indicating whether the group was formed through screening and self-selection. The idea was that if the effect of self-selection was thus controlled for, the variable indicating peer monitoring would provide an unbiased estimate of monitoring itself. They did find that monitoring reduced moral hazard, defined broadly to include both the misuse of funds and strategic default. While the methodology employed in this paper marks an improvement over Wydick's, there still remains the problem that the measures of peer monitoring did not reflect the extent to which monitoring actually occurred.[23]

Gomez and Santor (2003) followed an alternative technique in their study on Canada, which we have already discussed in the context of selection effect. While comparing the repayment performance of group and individual lending programmes, they used the technique of 'propensity score matching' (PSM) to remove the selection effect that operates before the formation of a group. Accordingly, any difference that was found in the repayment of group-based and individual borrowers could be attributed to influences such as peer monitoring and peer pressure that operate only after the group has been formed. The results showed that these post-group-formation effects contributed much more towards improving repayment performance compared to the selection effect.

While Gomez and Santor used a novel econometric technique to remove the selection effect from the survey data, Karlan (2007) exploited special features of programme design for the same purpose and arrived at similar conclusions. His analysis was based on the clients of FINCA-Peru, whose process for assigning individuals to groups creates a natural experiment with quasi-random group formation. When lending groups are formed, the initial members do not select each other. Instead, when individuals seeking a loan come to FINCA, they are put on a list. Once this list contains 30 names, a group is formed. Since no self-selection is involved, any observed difference in the repayment performance of the groups (after controlling for the effects of personal characteristics) can be attributed to *ex post* factors such as peer monitoring and peer pressure. Going beyond this indirect attribution, Karlan also presented direct evidence of monitoring and enforcement, such as knowledge of each other's default status, as well as direct evidence of punishment, such as the deterioration of relationships. To him, all this constituted 'solid evidence that peer monitoring and enforcement effectively reduce default rates' (p.F55).

Support was lent to this conclusion by an experiment carried out in Paraguay by Carpenter and Williams (2010). These researchers combined elements of laboratory and field experiments. Their subjects were actual microcredit borrowers and their performance was observed in the field, not in the laboratory; but before they were given joint-liability loans, they were subjected to laboratory experiments in order to ascertain their 'propensity to monitor'. Borrowing from the behavioural economics literature, the researchers developed an experiment to measure individual propensities to monitor one's peers in a social dilemma game with incentives similar to group lending,[24] and then tested whether the monitoring propensities of women about to enter an actual group-lending programme predicted loan performance six months later.

Their results showed a significant correlation between peer monitoring and group loan performance. Specifically, they found that individuals in groups populated by inherently 'nosy' monitors were approximately 10 percent less likely to have problems repaying their loans. The estimates were robust to differences in the formulation of the peer monitoring measure and the inclusion of a number of other important controls. In fact, when the controls were added, the point estimates increased substantially. It should be noted that the experiment measured only the propensity to monitor, not the actual extent of monitoring. Yet, the authors boldly concluded that 'These results suggest that, regardless of whether or not group lending leads to measurable reductions in poverty, it is the case that the groups' moral hazard is attenuated by peer monitoring' (Carpenter and Williams, 2010, p.4).

A startlingly contradictory piece of evidence was found, however, by Giné and Karlan (2014). They, too, isolated the selection effect from the effects of peer monitoring and peer pressure, but they did so through field experiments carried out with the help of the Green Bank in the Philippines. In one of the experiments, they started out with a set of joint-liability groups that were self-selected; but at one point in time a randomly chosen subset of these groups was dismantled and its members were converted into individual liability borrowers, while the rest of the groups continued in the joint-liability mode. Since the whole set of borrowers was self-selected in the first place, the two subsets were expected to contain borrowers with similar risk characteristics. In other words, if joint liability did confer any benefit through the avoidance of adverse selection, both subsets should have enjoyed those benefits equally. Therefore, if the performances of the two subsets were compared after the conversion occurred (after a reasonable lapse of time) and the joint-liability group was found to perform better, this would constitute evidence in support of the positive effects of peer monitoring and peer pressure, uncontaminated by the effect of peer selection.

In the event, no difference was found in the repayment performance of the two subsets of borrowers, which led the authors to conclude that monitoring and enforcement are not the pathways through which joint liability helps, if at all. In fact, direct measures of monitoring showed that, to some extent, monitoring went down after some of the joint-liability groups were converted into individual liability. This suggests that joint liability does induce stronger monitoring, as theory predicts, but the comparison of repayment performances demonstrated that whatever extra monitoring takes place, it does not translate into any tangible benefit in terms of loan repayment.

To complicate matters further, yet another experiment, carried out by Cason *et al.* (2012), seems to contradict the finding of Giné and Karlan and to restore confidence in the peer monitoring pathway of joint liability. The experiment was carried out in laboratories in India and Australia, with an experimental design that ruled out the possibility of the selection effect contaminating the incidence and impact of peer monitoring.

The experiment demonstrated that the effectiveness of peer monitoring depends critically on the cost of monitoring, something that Giné and Karlan did not consider. The researchers found that if the cost of peer monitoring was lower than the cost of lender monitoring, peer monitoring resulted in higher loan frequencies, higher monitoring and higher repayment rates compared to lender monitoring. However, in the absence of monitoring cost differences, lending, monitoring and repayment behaviour were mostly similar across group-based and individual-based lending schemes.

On the whole, the weight of evidence seems to point to the effectiveness of the pathway of peer monitoring. All the studies that have examined the impact of peer monitoring, including that of Giné and Karlan (2014), agree that joint liability induces stronger peer monitoring. And all studies, with the exception of Giné and Karlan, also agree that through enhanced monitoring, perhaps combined with enhanced peer pressure, joint liability leads to reduced moral hazard and better repayment performance. The study by Giné and Karlan has the merit that it cleverly separated out the selection effect before pronouncing on the monitoring effect, but so did some of the other studies that have found a positive contribution of peer monitoring.

6.3 Joint versus individual liability: which works better?

Of the various features of the practice of microcredit, the one that has attracted the most attention from academics is joint liability – the idea that if any member of a group fails to repay her loan the lender will penalise the whole group, not just the member who defaults.[25] It is this mutual liability for each other that is supposed to render it feasible for the microlender to deliver small loans to poor people without any collateral. And it is this aspect of group lending that has been analysed most extensively in the theories of microcredit, with theorists trying to explain precisely how it contributes to the success of microcredit and exactly which imperfections of the credit market it helps address, and how.

The theoretical models based on the concept of joint liability have generally viewed it as the single most important feature responsible for the widespread success of microcredit. But there has always been an undercurrent, even in mainstream theory, that there are some potential problems with joint liability – problems of such magnitude that they could even call into question the presumed superiority of joint liability over individual liability. It has been long recognised, for example, that the demonstration in Stiglitz's (1990) classic paper that joint liability helps improve loan repayment by overcoming moral hazard is a 'local first-order result' in the sense that it applies only to a very small amount of joint-liability penalty. A very high joint-liability penalty can be counter-productive, putting too much risk on risk-averse borrowing partners. The implication, as Townsend (2003, p.474) observes, is that ' . . . if the interest rate, loan size and degree of joint liability are exogenous controls implemented by a formulaic lender, there would be no presumption that groups dominate individual loans, were borrowers allowed to choose.'

Giné and Karlan (2014) provided a neat summary of some of the other concerns with joint liability. First, clients dislike the tension caused by the threat of punishment that group liability inevitably entails. Such tension among members could not only result in voluntary dropouts, it could also harm social capital among members, with far-reaching consequences. Second, bad clients can free-ride over good clients, causing default rates to rise: some borrowers may not repay loans because they believe that their peers will pay off the loans for them. As the model of strategic default developed by Besley and Coate (1995) shows, under certain conditions, even the threat of social sanctions may not be able to prevent such behaviour. If the peers indeed pay up for the defaulter, repayment will not suffer in the short term, but repeated episodes of this kind will erode the whole foundation of group liability by creating mistrust and resentment. Third, group liability is inherently discriminatory against safer borrowers, as they are required to repay the loans of their peers more often than the risky borrowers. This may eventually lead to the disillusionment of safe borrowers and a breakup of the group. Fourth, as a group matures, tensions emerge over time due to a divergence in the terms of credit demanded by the members – some need bigger loans than others, some prefer a longer repayment period than others, and so on. Such heterogeneity in credit demand may erode the basis of cooperative behaviour; for example, clients with smaller loans may be reluctant to serve as a guarantor for those with larger loans.

The notion that joint liability may not be the 'miracle cure' it was hyped up to be has received a significant boost in recent years by an important shift that has been taking place in the practice of microcredit itself. More and more lenders are moving away from group lending towards an individual-lending mode, the most dramatic example being the pioneer Grameen Bank itself, with its new style of microcredit delivery being dubbed as Grameen II. In view of all this, it has become more important than ever, especially from a policy perspective, to ask which mode of liability works better in practice, or to be more nuanced, which mode works better under which conditions?

A growing body of empirical studies has begun to address these questions. We shall try to distil some lessons from these studies in this section. For this purpose, we shall classify the studies into two groups – those that purport to give a black-and-white answer to the question 'which mode is better', and the more nuanced ones that allow for the possibility that different modes may work better under different circumstances.

Among the former group of studies, we find all three possible answers – good, bad and indifferent. For instance, in his study of Malawi, Diagne (2000) gives his verdict against joint liability. He reports that groups that expected joint liability not to be fully enforced performed much better in terms of repayment than groups in which it was expected to be fully enforced. Furthermore, the majority of the partially paid delinquent loans consisted of good borrowers who defaulted because of the joint-liability nature of the contracts. There are, however, reasons to take these findings with a grain of salt. Diagne tells us that for the microcredit groups he studied, the features of peer selection, peer monitoring and peer pressure, etc., did not typically exist, because the selection and monitoring activities were performed mainly by the lender. This suggests the possibility that joint liability may not have worked well in this case simply because the social capital that is necessary for joint liability to function well did not exist. It is pertinent to note here that the impact of joint liability on enforcement was found to worsen when some members had doubts about the repayment intentions of other members – a situation that occurred in 62 percent of credit groups. Obviously, trust, an essential foundation of group lending, was singularly lacking in this case.[26]

A contrasting finding is presented by Gomez and Santor (2003) in their study on microcredit in Canada. The microfinance institution they studied (Calmeadow) offered both group and individual loans to clients in the same locality, with the borrowers themselves deciding which mode of lending to accept. The MFI maintained detailed records on various social, economic and demographic characteristics of the borrowers, which were supplemented by a survey carried out by the authors to elicit information on the borrowers' attitudes and their social capital attributes. The data set thus provided a unique opportunity to compare the performance of the two modes of lending after controlling for other relevant factors. The authors found a lower propensity to default among group-based borrowers compared to the individual borrowers. Just as the absence of social capital was presumably the reason for group lending's failure in Diagne's sample in Malawi, so it is the presence of social capital that seems to make the difference here. This is evident from the observations that

> Individuals who have known their fellow members before forming the peer group are less likely to default. Likewise, default is less likely if a great deal of trust exists in the group or if group members feel a moral obligation to their peers. Lastly, individuals who have "social capital" are less likely to default, since individuals who belong to an association, club, or sports team report higher repayment rates.
>
> (Gomez and Santor, 2003, pp.7–8)

One potential ambiguity regarding the Gomez-Santor finding is that one cannot be sure whether the superior repayment performance of group borrowers is due to some unobserved differences between group and individual borrowers or due to the innate logic of joint liability itself. If the answer points to the former, it would not nullify the value of group lending as such; it would simply mean that joint liability may be the right mode of lending for some but not for others.[27] In any case, it would be useful to know which of the two interpretations is valid, and in order to find an answer, Gomez and Santor employed the methodology of PSM to create a counterfactual of individual borrowers who are 'like' the group borrowers in all relevant senses. If the counterfactual is accepted as reasonably valid, the observed superiority of group repayment can be interpreted as the innate superiority of joint liability itself. Gomez and Santor recognise, however, that there are well-known limitations to the PSM methodology, and that the best way to go about the task is to randomise, i.e. to randomly assign prospective borrowers to group and individual lending modes, so that the comparison of repayment performance can reveal the innate differences between the two modes of lending rather than the unobserved differences between the two groups of borrowers. The problem for them was that the MFI was not willing to go along with a randomised controlled trial (RCT).

Giné and Karlan (2014) were more fortunate; they were able to persuade the Green Bank in the Philippines to conduct a rich randomised experiment. We introduced this experiment earlier in the context of pathways of joint liability. As noted there, initially the MFI used to lend only to group borrowers. For the purposes of comparison, the researchers conducted two separate experiments to create random sets of individual borrowers. The first experiment was carried out in areas in which Green Bank had pre-existing group lending operations, and the second experiment took place in new areas where the Bank had not operated before. In the pre-existing areas, the Bank randomly converted some centres from group-lending mode into individual-lending mode, but the borrowers were required to continue the practice of attending regular group meetings for repayment. A comparison of the performance of converted individual borrowers with that of continuing group borrowers provided an opportunity for judging the relative merits of the two modes of lending. Yet another opportunity came from the second experiment, which was carried out in new areas. There the Bank randomly picked some centres for group lending, some for individual lending, and yet others for phased individual lending (group lending for the first loan cycle, converted into individual lending thereafter if the first loan was successfully repaid). A comparison of the new group-based borrowers with the new individual borrowers provided a second opportunity to judge the relative merits of group and individual lending. There was an essential difference between the two comparisons, however. In the pre-existing areas, both sets of borrowers were self-selected as group members before the experiment began. Therefore, one should not expect to find any difference between their performances on account of the selection effect of joint liability that operates before a loan is taken (the inclusion of only safe borrowers, for example). Any difference between them would reflect only the incentive effects (against moral hazard) that operate after a loan is taken. By contrast, the second comparison is more comprehensive, encompassing both incentive and selection effects (since, in this case, only the group borrowers were self-selected).

The conclusion from both experiments was that the two modes of lending did not differ significantly in terms of loan repayment performance, thus casting doubt on the presumed superiority of joint-liability lending. This finding has caused a lot of stir in the literature on microfinance, and understandably so because of the careful manner in which the study was carried out, with two different types of randomization providing highly credible identification strategies. One may still raise some queries about the interpretation, though.

Take first the result of the first comparison – the one between continuing group borrowers and converted individual borrowers in the pre-existing areas. The authors interpret this result as indicating that peer monitoring induced by joint liability is not really effective in solving moral hazard any more than individual liability. In order to explain this counter-intuitive result, they speculate that peer monitoring may have been replaced by lender monitoring, but they admit to having no evidence to support it.[28] A number of alternative explanations were also suggested. First, if self-selected borrowers were inherently trustworthy, the likelihood of which was demonstrated by another experiment by Karlan (2005), they would repay, whatever the lending mode. Second, if the selection effect allowed the inclusion of only borrowers with strong social networks, it is conceivable that they would continue to repay the loan even without joint liability in order to protect their networks. Third, since the borrowers continued to repay as a group in public meetings, they had their reputation at stake if they were to default.

All these speculations are intended to support the conclusion that peer monitoring did not have any tangible effect. Yet, the result also admits to an alternative interpretation that is consistent with the effectiveness of peer monitoring; it is based on the idea of habit formation. If joint liability indeed induces the kind of behaviour that prevents moral hazard (of both *ex ante* and *ex post* types) by encouraging peer monitoring, it is conceivable that, once such behaviour has become widespread and ingrained in the psyche of borrowers, it would become a habit and its effect would persist, even after joint liability had been dispensed with. It is instructive to note that the extent of peer monitoring was found to have declined after the conversion of groups into individual borrowers, and yet repayment did not suffer. This is entirely consistent with the habit-formation hypothesis.[29]

The second comparison – the one between group borrowers and individual borrowers in the new areas – would seem to offer much stronger support to the conclusion of the non-superiority of joint liability, because the individual borrowers in this case were fresh clients, not having gone through the experience of working under joint liability. But even here, the relevance of habit formation cannot be ruled out. Although the geographical areas in which the second experiment was conducted were new for the Green Bank, it is still possible that, if those areas were previously served by other microcredit lenders, a culture of regular repayment may have already been created in the society at large, which could have had a spillover effect on the Green Bank borrowers as well. The possibility of such a spillover effect is actually evident from the first experiment in the pre-existing areas. The experiment allowed new members to join the bank over time, and they were found to maintain as good a repayment record as the converted individual borrowers and the continuing group borrowers. This is consistent with the existence of the spillover effect of habit formation. In so far as this effect worked, even the second experiment cannot claim to have demonstrated the ineffectiveness of joint liability. The only problem is that we cannot be sure whether the spillover effect actually worked, because the authors did not provide any information about the prevalence of microcredit in the new areas before the entry of Green Bank, in contrast to the pre-existing areas – where, we are told, the bank had competition in 72 percent of the communities at the time the first experiment started.

There is another feature of the new areas that is worth mentioning. The authors found that in these areas '... credit officers were less likely to create groups under individual liability, and qualitatively this was reported to us as caused by unwillingness of the credit officer to extend credit without guarantors in particular barangays' (Giné and Karlan, 2014, p.69). One must wonder why credit officers would be reluctant to offer individual liability contracts if, as the study claims, the mode of liability does not affect repayment. Do the credit officers know something that the researchers don't? It must be remembered that offering a particular form of contract was not a matter of choice for the bank officers; who will offer what was determined by a random assignment process. Thus, credit officers in charge of centres which were assigned the individual liability mode had to offer this contract no matter what they thought of it. The fact that they did not think of it very favourably probably implies the existence of some difficulty in implementing individual liability. One possibility is the increased cost of lender monitoring that individual liability could entail; the credit officers could be worried that if the cost of monitoring became too high, they wouldn't be able to maintain the repayment rate in the future.

The cost of monitoring is indeed one of the fundamental issues in any comparison of alternative modes of liability. Much of the theorising on microcredit is, in fact, based on the presumption of the lower cost of monitoring under joint liability. The importance of this presumption has recently been demonstrated empirically by Cason *et al.* (2012). They compared the relative efficacy of peer versus lender monitoring under laboratory conditions and found that the assumption about the cost of monitoring was crucial to the result. If the cost of monitoring under an individual liability programme was no different from that under a joint liability programme, then the two modes provided almost equivalent performance. If, however, the cost of peer monitoring was lower compared to the cost of lender monitoring, joint liability dominated. The relative effectiveness of the two modes of liability was thus seen to be critically dependent on the relative costs of monitoring.

The study by Casan *et al.* belongs to an emerging group of empirical works that, instead of giving a black-and-white answer to the question of which mode of liability is better, take a more nuanced approach and try to establish the conditions under which one or the other mode can be expected to dominate. The other studies in this group can be classified into three categories: those that examine the possibility that different modes of liability may be appropriate for different types of clients, those that try to elucidate the trade-offs inherent in joint liability, and those that examine the viability of joint liability under 'crisis' situations.

One of the earliest studies in the first category is by Madajewicz (2003) on Bangladesh. In a companion theoretical paper, she had established that, among the credit-constrained borrowers, joint liability may be preferable for the poorer borrowers, but individual liability may be preferable for the less poor (Madajewicz, 2004, 2011). The reasons for the negative effect of joint liability on the wealthier borrowers were two-fold. First, they received a smaller loan under joint liability compared to individual lending. Second, they chose less productive (also less risky) projects under joint liability than under individual lending. These findings were based on the assumption that larger investments allow the adoption of more profitable but also more risky projects. Since joint liability discourages risk-taking (via the elimination of moral hazard), wealthier borrowers who can otherwise afford to take the risk in search of profitability are prevented from undertaking large investments. For them, individual liability is the better option. Evidence from Bangladesh confirmed this prediction; beyond a point, the wealthier among the credit-constrained borrowers were found to earn lower profits from joint-liability lending compared to individual lending. While interesting, this finding is compromised by an identification problem. As the author herself acknowledges, lower profits at higher wealth levels under joint liability could be due to diminishing returns rather than to the negative effect of joint liability as such.[30]

Vigenina and Kritikos (2004) also found that the relative merit of the two modes of liability depended on the nature of the clients, but the relevant characteristic here was not just the level of wealth but also the nature of the enterprise. They started from the premise that anyone who has sizeable collateral to offer would normally opt for individual lending because of the costs involved in joint-liability lending. On the other hand, only those with no or little collateral to offer would opt for joint liability. But by studying the clients of two microlenders in Georgia, one of whom offered individual loans and the other joint-liability loans, they noticed that joint-liability clients included many borrowers who did have sizeable assets to offer as collateral. This suggests that there are other determinants of the choice between the two modes of borrowing besides collateralizable wealth.

The authors postulated that an important consideration was the nature of the enterprise. If the enterprise held the promise of expansion, the borrower would like to have an increasing loan size over time, but this was only available for individual lending, because under joint liability, the loan size would be restricted in order to avoid moral hazard. By contrast, if the enterprise was essentially static in nature so that the repetition of small loans was all that was needed, joint liability may be chosen. In short, the hypothesis is that

> If an individual and a group lending organization operate in the same market niche, there will be a self-selection process not only with respect to the wealth status but also with respect to the financial needs which are determined by the expected dynamics of the borrower's business.
>
> (Vigenina and Kritikos, 2005, p.14)

Empirical tests supported this hypothesis: the borrowers with less dynamic businesses were shown to have a higher probability of choosing the joint-liability mode after controlling for other possible determinants of choice, such as interest rate and level of education.[31]

In the second category, there are several studies that suggest that there are inherent trade-offs in joint liability; and whether joint liability will outperform individual liability or not depends on where the balance of the trade-off lies in particular circumstances. Giné et al. (2010) and Fischer (2013) used experimental methods to examine the trade-off between risk-taking and risk-sharing induced by joint liability. Giné *et al.* focused on *ex ante* moral hazard in project choice (i.e., excessive risk-taking) and abstracted from *ex post* moral hazard and strategic default considerations. The question they asked is: which mode of liability is better able to extract the benefits of dynamic incentives (i.e. the practice of giving future loans with favourable terms contingent on timely repayment of current loan) by preventing *ex ante* moral hazard? It was acknowledged that adding dynamic incentives to a loan contract would reduce moral hazard and improve repayment performance regardless of the liability mode used. The issue is, under which mode the benefit would be larger.

For this purpose, they first modified the existing moral hazard models of microcredit by changing a crucial assumption. Following the footsteps of Stiglitz (1990), most of the models assume that safer projects have either the same or a higher expected return than riskier projects. Giné *et al.* (as well as Fischer) replaced this assumption with the more plausible assumption that riskier projects have a higher expected return (since investors must be compensated for higher risks). Armed with this assumption, they were able to show theoretically that joint liability under dynamic incentives induced two opposite forces. On the one hand, it encouraged more risk-taking than under individual liability. The reason is that risk-averse borrowers, who would normally choose low-risk, low-return investments under individual liability, will switch to the risky investment under joint liability whenever they are matched with a less risk-averse joint-liability partner.[32] On the other hand, under dynamic incentives, joint liability induced more risk-sharing and mutual insurance compared to individual liability. The first effect worked towards worsening the relative repayment performance of joint liability, while the second effect tended to improve it. The net effect would depend on the balance of the two effects.

The experimental results of Giné *et al.* demonstrate that joint liability increases risk-taking under dynamic incentives, as expected, but it also simultaneously improves the repayment rate. Repayments rise due to the insurance effect: joint liability forces the borrowers to insure each other more – passing the cost of limited liability back to the clients. An econometric estimate suggests that including a joint-liability clause increases loan repayment by about 20 percent via the insurance effect.

Fischer (2013) conducted a similar exercise but allowed for more variations in the type of contracts offered to the experimental subjects. Five contractual terms were allowed: autarky, individual lending (with the possibility of voluntary transfer), joint liability, joint liability with explicit peer approval of project, and an equity-like contract. Two levels of monitoring were allowed – perfect and imperfect. As in the case of Giné *et al.*, the difference in repayment performance across the contract types arose from the opposite effects of risk-taking and risk-sharing. According to the experimental results, the net effect was that adding informal transfers (moving from autarky to the individual liability treatment) reduced default rates by two percentage points from the autarkic level. Moving from individual to joint liability further reduced default rates by about 0.2 percentage points when approval rights were explicit. Finally, equity generated no defaults, as increased risk was almost always hedged across borrowers with the worst possible joint outcome still sufficient for loan repayment. Each of the differences in default rates was significant at the 5 percent level. Thus, Fischer's results lend support to the finding of Giné et al. that repayment does improve with joint liability, and the reason lies in higher levels of mutual insurance.[33]

A slightly different kind of trade-off was examined by Abbink et al. (2006) and Kono (2006). Instead of *ex ante* moral hazard, they looked at *ex post* moral hazard (strategic default) and explored the trade-off between free-riding and risk-sharing. The first study was conducted as a laboratory experiment, while the second was carried out as a framed field experiment in Vietnam. Joint liability encourages free-riding, as some group members feel tempted to default strategically in the hope that her peers will pay up so as not to incur joint liability fine.[34] At the same time, joint liability also encourages risk-sharing and mutual insurance, especially with dynamic incentives.[35] In order to assess the net effect of these two opposite forces, Abbink et al. first established a best-case scenario of repayment under individual lending (though there was no individual lending in the experiment) and compared it with repayment under group lending. The game was set up in such a way that free-riding would lead to no repayment in a single-round game. Although there were dynamic incentives in the experiment, the game was to end after a finite number of rounds, and the terminal point was known to all in advance. In this setting, the logic of backward induction suggests that there should be no repayment even in a repeated game. However, the experiment showed that group members actually repaid well, and with a repeated game they repaid even more frequently than in the best-case individual lending scenario. This was made possible by the fact that dynamic incentives under joint liability created a high level of risk-sharing and mutual insurance, which was large enough to outweigh the free-riding effect.[36]

The same trade-off – between free-riding and risk-sharing – was also investigated by Kono (2006), but this time through a framed field experiment in Vietnam rather than a laboratory experiment, and the results turned out to be different. Joint liability was again found to instigate free-riding and promote risk-sharing at the same time, but on this occasion the balance of forces was in the wrong direction. The negative effect of free-riding overwhelmed the positive effect of risk-sharing, leading to a lower rate of repayment under joint liability. Even after introducing a cross-reporting system or punitive measures among borrowers, joint liability could not outperform individual lending.

These studies on trade-offs bring an important lesson to the fore. The choice between joint and individual liability cannot be posed as an absolute. Their relative merit will depend critically on joint liability's power to prevent moral hazard and promote risk-sharing in any given context. This power, in turn, will depend greatly on the social capital that either pre-exists among group borrowers or develops over time as they interact with each other repeatedly. If social capital is of the kind and magnitude that permits on the one hand adequate peer monitoring and peer pressure to eliminate moral hazard, and creates on the other enough peer support to promote a high degree of risk-sharing and mutual insurance, the balance of the trade-off will lie in favour of joint liability; otherwise, individual liability will prevail. Much will also depend on what other measures, apart from joint liability, the MFIs add to their practice of group lending for the prevention of moral hazard and the promotion of mutual insurance.

Let us turn finally to the category of studies that examine the viability of joint-liability lending at times of crisis. In what is perhaps the first published paper to provide empirical evidence on the relative merits of joint and individual liability, Bratton (1986) compared the performances of three types of agricultural lending in Zimbabwe. Two of them were offered by the Agricultural Finance Corporation (AFC); they gave both individual loans and mandatory group loans (the term 'mandatory' implies that the farmers were required to sell their crops collectively to the official marketing board). In contrast, an NGO named Silveira House (SH) offered voluntary group loans based on joint liability typical of most MFIs. Bratton compared the repayment performance, along with several other performance indicators, of the three modes of lending in three consecutive years, two of which were normal weather-wise but the third was afflicted by a severe drought. His results showed that groups performed better in normal years but did very poorly, compared to individual borrowers, in the drought year. He explains the findings thus:

> Group lending ... appears viable under 'normal' conditions, but counterproductive when farmers are exposed to extreme environmental stress. The logic of collective action in different organizational settings supports this view. Individuals will struggle to repay even when they are stringently deprived in order to maintain eligibility for credit. By contrast, farmers with joint liability loans have little incentive to pay their share unless they expect other group members to do the same.
>
> (Bratton, 1986, p.126)

The final sentence in this quotation holds the key. Joint liability induces an inter-dependence among group members. Under normal circumstances, such inter-dependence may stand them in good stead by raising a protective shield against moral hazard and boosting the practice of mutual insurance, but at times of crisis the same inter-dependence may cause the whole system to unravel through a 'domino effect' – as one person defaults under genuine pressure, it encourages others to do so even if they could have repaid, simply because they want to avoid the burden of join liability.

A couple of recent episodes of this kind of unravelling of joint liability under crisis situations have been analysed insightfully by Giné et al. (2011) and Breza (2012). The crisis in both cases was caused by human action rather than natural causes. Giné et al. examined a case in the south Indian state of Karnataka where a Muslim religious body called the Anjuman Committee of the town of Kolar issued a *fatwa* (religious edict) in January 2009 banning all Muslims from repaying their microcredit loans by claiming that charging interest was *haram* (forbidden). As expected, the *fatwa* engendered a serious crisis for the MFIs, but in so doing it also provided a unique opportunity for researchers to study precisely how the domino effect operates in a crisis. In particular, it provided a natural experiment in which the domino effect on loan repayment could be isolated from other possible causes.

Giné *et al.* set out the nature of inter-dependence implicit in the idea of the domino effect in the form of the following hypothesis: members of a joint-liability group are more likely to default on their loans when the proportion of defaulting members in a group increases. The problem in testing this hypothesis is that repayment rates are also the result of selection, incentive effects, and correlated observed and unobserved shocks. An identification strategy is, therefore, needed to separate out the effects of these other factors. The authors found such a strategy by exploiting two facts of the data. First, the *fatwa* directly affected the repayment rates of the Muslim borrowers, not of the Hindus. As a result, Muslim-dominated groups faced a greater repayment crisis compared to Hindu-dominated groups. Second, many borrowers had loans from several groups, which differed in the density of the loans to Muslims. The existence of borrowers with multiple loans provided an opportunity to control for the possibility that borrowers from Muslim-dominated groups may be inherently different from those in Hindu-dominated groups. The identification strategy in this case consisted of observing the variation in the behaviour of the same individuals across multiple groups with differing densities of Muslims. The idea was that, since the initial default would be higher in the Muslim-dominated groups, the domino effect, if it exists, would be stronger in these groups compared to the Hindu-dominated ones. This can be tested by comparing the propensity to default of the borrowers who are members of both types of groups. The central finding of the study was that the same borrowers indeed had higher default rates for the loans they had taken as members of Muslim-dominated groups compared to the loans they had taken as members of Hindu-dominated groups. The implication is that once the Muslims started to default following the *fatwa*, the domino effect took hold, affecting the larger body of the clientele.

The existence of the domino effect clearly demonstrates the vulnerability of joint liability at times of crisis. Any comprehensive assessment of the relative merits of joint and individual liability lending must therefore weigh any putative benefits of joint liability in good times against its vulnerability in bad times. It should be noted, however, that even at times of crises it may not be all bad news for joint liability. While joint liability may face bigger repayment problems than individual liability during a crisis, one must also ask how the two systems would fare in the immediate post-crisis period of recovery. And if one looks at the bigger picture, embracing both crisis and recovery, which system comes out better? A recent study by Breza (2012) sheds some light on this question, *albeit* indirectly.

The context is a large-scale default episode that took place in the Krishna District of Andhra Pradesh, India, in March 2006. Prior to this incident, the microcredit movement launched by the NGOs was coming under intense criticism amid fears of over-indebtedness of poor borrowers and allegations of usurious interest rates and abusive collection practices – which, according to the detractors, even led to a spate of borrower suicides. In this backdrop, the District Collector (the government bureaucrat in charge of district administration) announced that his constituents should stop repaying their microloans' and launched his own alternative programme of financial inclusion. Within days of the announcement, all borrowers ceased repaying their loans, causing a serious crisis in the microcredit sector. A retraction was made in mid-2006, and the worst of the crisis was finally over in early 2007.[37] Soon after the defaults, the local MFIs, including *Spandana*, one of the biggest in India, began to re-establish collections in the affected villages. They also suspended the joint-liability feature of the loans and offered new loans for those who fully repaid their outstanding debts. Gradually, some borrowers began to repay the loans they had earlier defaulted on; and by November 2009, some 40 to 50 percent of borrowers had fully repaid their liabilities. The objective of Breza's study was to investigate whether repayment was helped or hindered by 'peer effects', i.e. the effect that the peers' repayment behaviour had on one's own incentive to repay.

She first established that peer effect exists, i.e. if the peers start to repay a borrower will also feel more inclined to repay.[38] She also quantified the effect: she estimated, for example, that if a borrower's peers shift from full default to full repayment, the borrower is 10 to 15 percentage points more likely to repay. The peer effect, of course, cuts both ways, for if the peers start to default a borrower might be inclined to default too. In order to capture the net effect, Breza simulated a model of a borrower's behaviour, capturing both the negative effect when the crisis unfolds and the positive effect when the process of recovery starts. She found that the peer effect was asymmetric in the sense that the positive effect during recovery was stronger than the initial negative effect. Thus, she concluded that peer effects actually improved repayment rates relative to a counterfactual without peer effects.

It should be noted that Breza's focus was not on the mode of liability as such, but on 'peer effects' on repayment. Since peer effects can operate even without joint liability – for example, if borrowers are individually liable but are required to pay together in group meetings – the study does not directly address the debate on joint versus individual liability. However, since joint liability is the prime vehicle through which inter-dependence among peers has been established by MFIs, it has lessons for the present debate as well. The main lesson is that the fact that joint liability is vulnerable to the domino effect during crises does not necessarily constitute a case against it; how it operates during the recovery phase should also be taken into account. The net effect will almost certainly be context-specific: positive in some cases, negative in others.[39]

6.4 Does social capital play a role in the success of joint liability?

Almost all theories of microcredit invoke the help of social capital in sustaining the pathways through which group lending is supposed to work. A rare exception is Armendáriz de Aghion and Gollier (2000), who built a model to show that even if complete strangers were randomly put together in a group, the very logic of joint liability would ensure that their repayment performance will be superior to that of individual borrowers in the face of asymmetric information.[40] Almost all other theories accord a central role to social capital in some form or the other. One may broadly distinguish two kinds of social capital – namely, informational social capital and relational social capital. Both of them are evident in the theories of microcredit. Informational social capital plays a role in either avoiding adverse selection through peer selection, which requires intimate knowledge of each other's risk characteristics; or in mitigating moral hazard through peer monitoring, which requires knowledge of each other's projects or effort or use of funds. Relational social capital plays a role either in preventing strategic default through peer pressure, which requires a kind of social relationship that permits some members to impose sanctions on others; or in avoiding genuine default through peer support, which requires a degree of social cohesion. In other words, social capital is ubiquitous in the theories of microcredit, and its role is almost invariably assumed to be supportive of group lending.

Yet, surprisingly, most of the early attempts to empirically assess the role of social capital in group lending found its effect to be either insignificant, or even more curiously, negative (after controlling for other factors)! For example, Sharma and Zeller (1997) found that closer 'social ties' among group members actually accentuated moral hazard and worsened repayment performance in Bangladesh. In Wydick's (1999, 2001) study of Guatemala, closer 'social ties' seemed to have had no effect on mitigating moral hazard and actually had a negative effect on the provision of mutual insurance. In Burkina Faso, Paxton *et al.* (2000) found that 'social homogeneity' accentuated the group's repayment problem. In another study on Bangladesh, Godquin (2004) observed that 'group homogeneity' had no effect on repayment performance while 'social ties' had a negative effect. Simtowe *et al.*'s (2006) study of Malawi used as many as six different indicators of 'social ties' and found a significant effect for only one of them: distance among the villages from which the group members came. In their study of rural Thailand, Ahlin and Townsend (2007) also observed a negative relationship between 'social ties' and repayment performance. The only study that came up with an unambiguously positive result is an earlier one on Malawi by Zeller (1998), who found that measures of 'social cohesion' were positively correlated with good repayment performance.

The overwhelmingly negative nature of the findings has obviously demanded some serious explanations. A couple of them have been offered. The most common explanation is that closeness of social ties actually inhibits group members from imposing social sanctions on each other. The reason is that peer pressure and the imposition of social sanctions inflicts a cost on the imposers themselves, which has implications for peer behaviour. As Sadoulet and Carpenter (2001, p.7) explain: 'If enforcement through social collateral is more expensive than direct enforcement mechanism . . ., groups having to resort to such methods will have to be faced with higher default rates.' The second explanation has to do with the failure of social ties to provide adequate mutual insurance when fellow members are faced with genuine difficulties. Wydick explains this phenomenon in the following terms:

> The best explanation for this appeared to be that if insurance between members is manifest as shock-contingent credit, groups of friends (with a high rate of time preference) seemed to prefer that the lending institution suffer the consequences of the shock instead of an unfortunate friend in the group.
> (Wydick, 1999, p.479, fn. 5)

While these explanations of the negative finding sound plausible enough, there are reasons to question the validity of the finding itself. Most of the studies discussed above suffer from one or more of the following four problems. First, the proxies used to capture the relevant variables, especially the extent of social capital, leave a lot to be desired. Second, the econometric techniques used by most of them were not refined enough to capture all the pathways through which social capital might have influenced repayment behaviour. Third, the identification of the effect of social capital remains problematic because of insufficient attention paid to an endogeneity problem. Finally, most of these studies ignore the fact that there are different types of social capital, and the analyst must be careful about which particular type to focus on, bearing in mind the purpose for which it was being used and the context in which it was being used. Subsequent studies have been much more alive to these problems, and their findings are much more supportive of the positive role of social capital.

An example of dubious proxies is Sharma and Zeller's use of the number of relatives in a group as a measure of social ties. To confine the existence of social ties only to relatives is clearly unduly restrictive and may well explain the negative result; for after all, it may be far more difficult to impose sanctions on one's own relatives than on non-relative peers. Godquin's measure of 'social ties' – the number of years for which a group has been in existence – is equally problematic. Based on this measure, the author is able to explain the negative effect of social ties on the ground that, as borrowers become more familiar with each other over time, it becomes more difficult to impose sanctions on each other. But there are other interpretations of the negative effect that render the age of the group a dubious proxy for social ties. For instance, Matin (1997) and Paxton et al. (2000) have noted that older groups may face greater difficulties in keeping up loan repayments because of a 'matching problem'.[41] To take another example of dubious proxies, Godquin measures social homogeneity by similarity in age and education, without offering any convincing explanation as to why homogeneity along these particular dimensions should be relevant for influencing the repayment behaviour of a group.

In some cases, the measurement of the dependent variable is also problematic. Many of the studies use 'the extent of misuse of funds' as the measure of moral hazard – misuse being defined as the diversion of funds from the original purpose (e.g., Wydick, 1999; Hermes et al., 2005). But fund diversion is not the only conceivable type of moral hazard; in fact, the kinds of moral hazard that the theories are mostly concerned with are the choice of risky projects and the shirking of effort. Indeed, it is conceivable that peers may not even regard fund diversion as a moral hazard if they are aware that this was being done to meet some urgent family needs, something they themselves would have done under similar circumstances. In that case, it is entirely plausible that the closeness of social ties may not result in peer pressure for preventing the diversion of funds, even though the same peers may well have tried to prevent shirking or the adoption of unduly risky projects. Therefore, the observed inability of social capital variables to influence moral hazard, as measured, does not necessarily imply that social capital is impotent in this regard.

Simtowe *et al.* (2006) use an additional indicator to capture moral hazard in the form of strategic default – by asking the chairperson of the group whether some members wilfully defaulted. But this is not a very convincing measure, because the real test of the effectiveness of social capital lies in the extent to which it is able to prevent wilful default – i.e. the number of times wilful default could have happened but did not because of peer pressure, rather than the number of times it did happen. The problem that may arise from using 'observed' default as the dependent variable is evident from the following comments:

> ... availability of information within the relatively small groups facilitated monitoring and enforcement. As a result, most of the reasons for default could be classified as "uncontrollable," and thus strict social sanctions were not imposed. Instead of pressure, the groups felt sympathy for the member with arrears and offered assistance.
>
> (Paxton *et al.*, 2000, p.651)

This statement implies that peer monitoring has already taken care of moral hazard, and peer pressure has already taken care of strategic default. Two sources of default have thus already been eliminated. Consequently, the effect of social ties on reducing default through peer monitoring and peer pressure is not captured simply because the propensity of such default is not observed.

The second problem arises from the fact that the econometric procedures used do not always allow for a comprehensive assessment of the role of social capital. For example, Wydick (1999) explicitly defines peer monitoring, peer pressure and social ties as three dimensions of a broad conception of social cohesion, but uses a methodology that fails to capture all the dimensions. He actually uses all three dimensions as explanatory variables, but the way he does so creates the problem: all three are used at the same time in the same regression on moral hazard. When the coefficient on 'social ties' turns out to be insignificant, Wydick is led to conclude that social ties have no effect on moral hazard. But this is misleading, because the other two variables had positive effects, and social ties may well have operated through them, especially in view of Wydick's recognition that peer monitoring and peer pressure are also dimensions of social cohesion, of which social ties are a component.

The point is that it may be more appropriate to treat peer monitoring and peer pressure as functions of social ties and other aspects of social cohesion. In that case, the appropriate methodology would consist of a two-stage procedure: the first step would assess the effect of peer monitoring and peer pressure on moral hazard, and the second step would assess the effect of social ties on monitoring and pressure. The danger of putting them all together in a single one-stage regression is that, if social ties work through strengthening peer monitoring and peer pressure, an insignificant coefficient of social ties may simply mean that once its effects on monitoring and pressure are controlled for, there remains no further effect of social ties. But that would not signify the impotence of social ties. The same problem exists in the work of Simtowe *et al.* (2006) on Malawi. They recognise that social ties are a potential factor in determining the quality of peer monitoring and peer selection. And yet, they use measures of social ties in the same regression on moral hazard that also includes measures of monitoring and selection.

The third problem – that of endogeneity – is neatly explained by Karlan:

> Typically, showing that higher social connections cause higher loan repayments is a difficult task due to selection and group formation issues. Using observational data, since most group lending programmes rely on peers to screen each other and form groups, fundamental endogeneity problems exist when analysing the impact of social connections on lending outcomes. For instance, if groups are formed within neighbourhoods, and neighbourhoods with stronger social network also have more economic opportunities, then empirically one should observe a correlation between the social connections of a group and its likelihood to repay.
>
> (Karlan, 2007, p.F53)

But such correlation could, in reality, be the consequence of economic opportunities rather than of social connections. Karlan further argues that if social capital is measured by activities or involvement with others in the community (as is common), then an omitted variable problem may arise, because those with stronger entrepreneurial spirits may also have stronger social connections. In that case, it would be difficult to disentangle the effect of social connections from that of entrepreneurial spirits.[42]

Researchers have resorted to a number of devices to get around this problem of identification. Karlan (2007) himself made use of the special programme design of FINCA-Peru that (as discussed earlier) eliminated the selection effect by instituting a quasi-random process of group formation. In eliminating the selection effect, the process also eliminated the possible effect of unobserved dimensions, such as economic opportunities that could be correlated with social connections through 'neighbourhood effects'. As some of the groups were randomly endowed with more social connections than others, the outcome was a natural experiment in which the 'pure' effects of social connections could be identified. Karlan found that the strong social connections of the group were indeed correlated with better loan repayment and higher savings.

164 *Testing the theories of microcredit*

A couple of caveats to this finding should be noted, however. First, while the process of quasi-random group formation successfully solved the identification problem arising from neighbourhood effects, it is not clear that the process also solved the identification problem arising from a possible correlation between social connections and innate entrepreneurial spirits. If the two are indeed correlated, as Karlan argues, then a group endowed with more social connections would also be endowed with more entrepreneurial spirits, even if the members of the group came together through a random process. Second, by eliminating the selection effect, the process of group formation also eliminated one route through which social connections may help improve repayment performance – namely, the avoidance of adverse selection. As a result, Karlan's estimates can, at best, be regarded as a lower bound of the positive effect of social connections.

Abbink *et al.* (2006) adopted the technique of a laboratory experiment in which students in the social sciences at the University of Erfurt participated in a microfinance game. The student subjects were formed into 31 borrowing groups of varying sizes. The game involved a stochastic element: each student-borrower faced a 1/6 probability of a negative shock, forcing the borrower to depend on fellow members to repay the amount due on the group loan. To isolate the effect of social ties, two separate recruitment techniques were used. Some groups were formed of students registering individually for the experiment, which minimised the degree of social ties between members. Other participants registered together in groups; in these groups, social ties were found to be stronger. Since self-selected groups were expected to select based on prior social ties, a comparison of the two group types (holding other factors constant) would indicate the impact of social ties on repayment. The experiment found that social ties had a positive effect on loan repayment, but only at the beginning. The effect faded away in the subsequent rounds.

The fading away of the effect of social ties seems puzzling. One possible clue lies in a loophole which the authors themselves recognise. The experiment allowed both types of groups the same degree of interaction after the group was formed. In the real-world setting, however, the pre-acquainted group is more likely to interact *ex post*, and that may make a difference to their repayment performance over time. Perhaps a more important reason, as observed by Armendáriz and Morduch (2010), is that the participants were required to play the game for a known fixed number of times. It is well-known from the theory of repeated games that it is difficult to sustain cooperation in a finitely repeated game. The intuition is easy to grasp through a process of backward induction. If cooperation has to be sustained either through the lure of rewards or through the fear of punishment in the subsequent rounds, there can be no incentive for cooperation in the final round. But if it is understood by all concerned that there is not going to be any cooperation (no reward and no punishment) in the final round, there will be no cooperation in the penultimate round either. Thus, through a process of backward induction, it can be established that non-cooperation will be the equilibrium outcome in every round.

Clearly, the feature of finite games must be dispensed with if the experimental method is to offer any meaningful insight into the effect of social capital on group lending. This was precisely what was done by Cassar *et al.* (2007), following a methodology commonly adopted in the literature on experimental public good games. Since an infinitely repeated game cannot possibly be played in a laboratory, the trick is to simulate it by introducing an element of uncertainty about when a particular group was going to be dissolved. Thus, after taking care of the problem of finite interactions, and also after eliminating the endogeneity problem of self-selection by using only exogenously formed groups, Cassar *et al.*(2007) found that relational social capital had a sustained positive effect on the group's repayment performance.

Feigenberg *et al.* (2013) adopted a clever experimental approach to isolate the effect of social interactions. Their study is based on a combination of field and experimental data from a West Bengal MFI (VFS), which gives loans to individuals but requires regular group meetings. The experiment consisted of varying the frequency of meetings from weekly to monthly and observing the impact on social interactions. Microfinance clients were randomly assigned to repayment groups that met either weekly or monthly during their first loan cycle, and then graduated to the same meeting frequency for their second loan. By randomizing the extent of social interactions, the study was able to establish its causal role in determining the rate of repayment (or default).

Long-run survey data and a follow-up public goods experiment revealed that clients initially assigned to weekly groups interacted more often and exhibited a higher willingness to pool their risk with group members from their first loan cycle nearly two years after the experiment. They were also three times less likely to default on their second loan. It should be noted that the study has nothing directly to say on group lending with joint liability, since the clients were all individual borrowers who were required to attend group meetings for repayment. However, since the joint-liability mode of lending typically requires regular meetings of the group members, its findings are relevant to the question of whether and how the social interactions required by group lending can promote repayment performance.

The reader would have noticed that we have been using many different terms, such as 'social ties', 'social cohesion', 'social homogeneity', 'social connections', etc. to denote social capital. This is because different studies have deployed different terms, and that is indeed one source of confusion in drawing a clear picture about the role of social capital in group lending. This is not simply a matter of terminological profligacy, for they are not different names for the same idea. Rather, they stand for different aspects of social capital, which is an inherently multi-faceted concept.[43] This raises the question: are all aspects of social capital relevant for good performance of group lending, or only some of them are, and if so, which ones? Also, one might ask: is it possible that different aspects of social capital contribute to the success of group lending in different ways, and that their relative importance may vary depending on the socio-economic environment in which group lending operates?

A number of recent studies make it clear that the forms of social capital matter, and that the context matters too. When Ahlin and Townsend (2007, p.F43) found, in rural Thailand, that social ties had a negative effect on group performance, they were quick to add that 'This idea must be qualified. Social structures that enable penalties can be helpful for repayment, while those which discourage them can lower repayment'. The reason for this qualification was their finding that, contrary to the generally negative effect of social ties, social sanctions proved to be an effective tool for reducing default in the poor northeast region of Thailand. That's why they were keen to differentiate between different aspects of social capital, arguing that the aspects of social capital that facilitate social penalties for the non-repayment of group loans can be helpful to group lending, while the aspects that inhibit social penalties can be harmful. Furthermore, the context was also important, because whatever aspects of social capital permitted the imposition of sanctions in the poorer northeast either did not exist or were not effective in the richer central region, where sanctions did not seem to have any significant impact on group behaviour.

In their framed field experiments in South Africa and Armenia, Cassar *et al.* (2007) were able to identify more clearly which aspects of social capital worked and which didn't in support of group lending. They found that relational social capital in the form of personal trust between individuals and social homogeneity within groups had a positive effect on group performance. In contrast, informational social capital, in the form of simple acquaintanceship with other individuals, or an individual's general trust in society, had no impact.

Finally, adopting a modern sociological approach to the measurement of social capital, Dufhues *et al.* (2013) confirmed the idea that different aspects of social capital were effective in different contexts. The starting point of their analysis is the observation that the literature on loan performance within credit groups concentrates on intra-group ties to the exclusion of ties to persons outside the group. An important aspect of social capital is thus left out. Furthermore, the measurement of social ties has usually been rather crude, focusing, for instance, on the role of relationships like friends, relatives or neighbours. The authors' approach to measuring social ties was more elaborate. They used a survey tool from the field of sociology that involves the use of instruments referred to as the 'name generator' and the 'position generator' to measure the respondent's personal network. These network data were then used to create measures of the 'individual social capital' of the borrowers.[44] Using these measures and building on the well-known distinction between 'bonding' and 'bridging' social capital, the authors created four categories of social capital: bonding, bridging, bonding-link and bridging-link.[45] Their econometric analysis relating the loan repayment of the groups to these measures of social capital, along with a host of controls, found that the effects of social capital varied according to the socio-cultural context. For instance, bonding social capital was found to be effective in Thailand, while bridging-link social capital was effective in Vietnam.

One final point needs to be stressed in the context of identifying the aspects of social capital that are most relevant for group lending. The aspect that has been emphasised most repeatedly in both the theories of microcredit and in empirical tests of the theories is the ability of group members to impose social sanctions on each other and to penalise a delinquent member who either can't or won't pay up to protect her fellow members from the obligations of joint liability. This emphasis on penalties and sanctions as the basis of cooperative behaviour accords well with Coleman's (1993) observation that social capital functions as a source of social control.

But it is necessary to make a distinction between 'control and sanctions' on the one hand, and 'trust and reciprocity' on the other, as the basis of social cooperation. It is not clear from the accumulated evidence that punishment is the principal mechanism through which social capital works. To cite just a couple of examples, Paxton et al. (2000, p.645) observe in their study on Burkina Faso: 'It is interesting that very little peer pressure was measured in the face of default (one on a scale to four). Most respondents valued village harmony over the continued access to these loans'. And again,

> In rural areas of Burkina Faso where most village members are related and very much interconnected in their daily lives, village social harmony is important. In addition, the existence of a hierarchical social system giving certain caste members and elders a privileged social position makes peer pressure difficult in some situations. In fact, some elderly women who had defaulted were never pressured even though the other women privately felt resentment.
>
> (Paxton et al., 2000, p.650)

Similarly, in a framed field experiment in Vietnam, Kono (2006, p.24) report that 'We introduced penalties in order to capture the effect of social sanctions on the repayment decision, however, in our experiment penalties were no longer exacted once the group ended in default'.

By contrast, a growing body of evidence is beginning to emerge, which, although still quite small, highlights the importance of trust in the context of group lending. A pioneering work in this field is by Karlan (2005). He set out to investigate whether trust played any role in influencing the repayment behaviour of microcredit borrowers. For this purpose, he selected a sample of clients of FINCA-Peru and carried out a laboratory experiment to obtain measures of trust among them.[46] He then observed their repayment performance and tried to ascertain whether any link existed between trust, as measured in the laboratory, and group repayment, as observed in the field.

He found that to understand the role of trust, it was necessary to make a distinction between 'trustworthy' and 'trusting'. His results show that persons identified as more 'trustworthy' were more likely to repay their loans one year later, but persons identified as more 'trusting' saved less and had more repayment problems. 'Trustworthiness' is thus seen to be the key to good group performance, as opposed to social connections, etc., that purport to stand for the group member's ability to impose social sanctions. Thus, in answering the question as to why some groups perform badly, Karlan proposes the simple answer: some individuals are inherently untrustworthy.

Karlan also tried to make a finer distinction between 'innate' trustworthiness and what might be called 'contingent' (not his term) trustworthiness driven by a fear of reprisal. Although he found evidence for both types in his experiment, the overwhelming evidence lent support to the view that innate trustworthiness was the main driver of good loan repayment.

The importance of trust is also evident from the study of Gomez and Santor (2003) on microcredit borrowers in Canada. They, too, measured the level of trust among potential borrowers and found that the propensity for moral hazard was reduced when 'low trust' groups were removed from the sample, leaving groups within which there existed a higher degree of trust before applying for the loan.

Finally, we can recall the findings of Cassar *et al.* (2007) that relational social capital in the form of 'personal trust' made a positive contribution to group repayment, while informational social capital in the form of mere acquaintances did not make any difference. Their interpretation of the latter finding is especially instructive:

> Since social sanctions are generally ineffectual without at least weak social ties between individuals, our study suggests that potential social sanctions may not be the most important component of relational social capital to influence group loan repayment; interpersonal trust appears to be more important.
> (Cassar *et al.*, 2007, p.F91)

The authors also note how the effectiveness of dynamic incentives depends critically on the level of trust among group members:

> Group lending is heavily dependent on dynamic incentives. Individuals have an incentive to repay group loans if they believe a critical mass of other members will do the same in order to receive future group loans. The belief that other members will contribute in the current round is partially a function of the social capital that exists within the borrowing group.
> (Cassar *et al.*, 2007, p.F90)

The belief that the authors are referring to here is nothing other than the trust the group members have of each other.

6.5 Concluding observations

It would appear that the academic literature on microcredit, at least the empirical part of it, is finally coming round to a view that the pioneers of microcredit have all along believed to be true. In a recent attempt to clarify what his original conception of microcredit really stood for, Yunus (2011) stated that 'Most distinctive feature of Grameencredit is that it is not based on any collateral, or legally enforceable contracts. It is based on "trust", not on legal procedures and system.' Although he did not state it explicitly, the exclusive reference to trust implies that his conception of microcredit does not rely on informal social systems of penalties and social sanctions either. Under group lending, members are expected to repay loans not out of fear of punishment by their peers, but out of trust that if they pay up, either for themselves or on behalf of their peers in distress, others will not try to free-ride on them.[47] The practice of microcredit would thus seem to be based on a much more elevated conception of human nature than the self-centred *homo economicus* that the theories of microcredit typically assume. Recent empirical evidence seems to suggest that the practitioners were more right than the theorists.

Notes

1 For previous surveys of the relevant literature, see especially Ghatak and Guinnane (1999), Guttman (2006), Hermes and Lensink (2007), Armendáriz and Morduch (2010), Karlan and Morduch (2010) and Fischer and Ghatak (2011).
2 The data set covers 124 MFIs in 49 developing countries and was collected by the Microfinance Information Exchange (MIX), a not-for-profit private organisation that aims to promote information exchange in the microfinance industry. These data, collected for publication in the *Micro Banking Bulletin* (MBB), were adjusted by the authors to help ensure comparability across institutions.
3 The test is not foolproof as the relationship between interest rate and delinquency turns negative beyond about a 40 percent interest rate, which is not consistent with agency theory.
4 Ausubel (1999) offers an early discussion of this challenge in the context of the credit market. Chiappori and Salanie (2003) and Finkelstein and McGarry (2006) do so for the insurance market.
5 For attempts to isolate the effects of adverse selection and moral hazard in other markets, see Chiappori and Salanie (2000) on the insurance market, Cardon and Hendel (2001) on health insurance, Edelberg (2004) on the consumer loan market and Shearer (2004) on labour contracts.
6 Klonner and Rai (2007) give a lucid explanation of why this is so, with the help of numerical examples.
7 This is a drastically simplified account of what Klonner and Rai actually did to identify the existence of adverse selection, but it gives the essence of their strategy. The actual statistical work was made complicated by the fact that they had to empirically estimate the risk profiles of the winners (since 'riskiness' is not directly observable), and the process of estimation had to ensure that the 'observed' risk profiles truly reflected the innate riskiness of winners instead of being contaminated by other factors, such as moral hazard. One implication of this procedure is that while the authors were able to identify the existence of adverse selection, after controlling for the possible effect of moral hazard, they were not able to infer anything about the existence of moral hazard itself.
8 The system of payday loans (short-term unsecured loans to be paid back on the borrower's payday) in the United States may seem far removed from the microcredit sector of the developing world, but there is actually one fundamental similarity between the two – in both cases, the borrowers have very little access to the formal banking sector due mainly to the high transaction costs of small loans and potential agency problems stemming from the absence of collateral.
9 Technically, this strategy is called the 'regression discontinuity' approach to identification; we shall come across other examples of this approach later in the book.
10 Moral hazard was further identified by comparing the repayment behaviour of borrowers who both selected in and contracted at identical rates, but faced different dynamic repayment incentives from randomly assigned future interest rates r^f that were conditional on repayment of the initial loan.

11 Karlan and Zinman note that this difference in default rates may reflect not just the differences in the hidden innate riskiness of the clients, but also their hidden differential propensity to exert effort. Accordingly, they avoid the term 'adverse selection' in this context, which strictly speaking refers to differential riskiness, and instead use the more general term 'hidden information', which is also commonly used in the literature on the economics of information. We use the term 'adverse selection' loosely here to imply the effect of hidden information, and also use the term 'selection effect' synonymously.

12 The authors themselves acknowledge as much: The evidence is not direct evidence of a given impediment to trade. Rather, it is evidence about how well a model that features a given impediment to trade does in explaining repayment data. In this context, lack of evidence for a given model may be due to its featured impediment to trade being less important *or* to its auxiliary assumptions failing to hold (Ahlin and Townsend, 2007, footnote 3, p.F13).

13 It is instructive to note that in his study of repayment performance in Malawi, Zeller (1998, p.617) also included a variable representing the presence of a code of conduct and found a positive impact on repayment, as did Wenner, but he did not interpret it as a selection variable. Instead, he expected that '. . . such rules can increase transparency and therefore reduce intragroup frictions and costs of coordination . . .', which is consistent with our alternative interpretation.

14 Essentially, this technique tries to create a counterfactual in which the two groups of borrowers are endowed with the same kind of innate attributes, including risk attributes. This ensures that if self-selected groups tend to be 'safer' than the average borrowers because of the screening-out of risky borrowers, the counterfactual group of exogenously selected borrowers will also be equally 'safer'. Therefore, there should not be any difference between the performances of the two groups on account of the selection effect. As a result, any difference found between the two groups' performance from PSM-based regressions can be attributed to factors other than self-selection.

15 Although the authors motivated their paper by referring to the preponderance of *ex post* moral hazard (strategic default) in Malawi, their analysis defined moral hazard more broadly to include aspects of *ex ante* moral hazard (choice about the use of funds) as well: 'The incidence of moral hazard in each credit group was captured by asking the chairperson of each group about whether some members had defaulted wilfully, or whether they had misused loan funds that were meant for an investment' (Gomez and Santor, 2003, p.15).

16 The experiments of Giné *et al.* had, in fact, a much larger scope, and one of their main objectives was to judge the relative merits of joint and individual liability lending. We shall discuss the findings of these experiments in greater detail below when we take up the evidence on this comparison.

17 This is an important issue in experimental economics; see, for example, the insightful discussion in Levitt and List (2007).

18 The projects undertaken were primarily agricultural. Those who had plots in the rainfed upland, where returns were highly variable depending on the vagaries of nature, were counted as having 'risky' projects, while those having plots in the irrigated low land were deemed to have 'safe' projects.

19 See our discussion in Chapter 5.

20 'These frictions include limited partner availability, informational problems that limit borrowers' monitoring ability, social codes restricting enforcement of sanctions and characteristics that impede borrowers' credibility in promising or requiring transfers' (Sadoulet and Carpenter, 2001, p.3). In the general literature on equilibrium matching, the implications of market imperfections and other matching frictions have been

examined, for example, by Kremer and Maskin (1996), Legros and Newman (2002) and Shimer and Smith (2000).

21 More evidence will be cited later in this chapter in connection with our discussion of the role of social capital in group lending.
22 A third criterion was the creation of mutual insurance; we shall discuss this aspect later in connection with the role of social capital.
23 The indictors were (a) the extent to which members had access to information about each other's business, (b) the extent to which group members were willing to engage in peer-monitoring activities to enforce proper loan use and report misuse of loans, and (c) whether they had any rules that encouraged joint ownership of enterprises.
24 The 'dilemma game' was originally devised to measure propensities to cooperate (by making financial contribution) for a common cause and to punish free-riders through social sanctions. In the present experiment, the game was slightly tweaked to permit the measurement of the propensity to monitor. After the contribution stage, but before punishment was allowed, the participants were asked if they wanted to have access to the contribution decisions of the other members of their experimental group. If the participant paid a small fee, she was shown the contribution levels of all the participants. Only those who paid the monitoring fee were eligible to socially sanction the other participants. The willingness to pay the fee for the privilege of gaining knowledge about the peer's contributions was taken as the measure of the propensity to monitor.
25 The majority of theoretical models assume a particular form of group penalty, namely, that if one member fails to repay, other members of the group must pay up (either in part or in full) on her behalf. It is arguable that this concept of joint liability may not always conform to the way group penalty has actually been practised on the ground. But we shall leave this issue aside for the moment, and treat the empirical debate about the relative merits of joint and individual liability as referring to the idea of joint liability as modelled in theories.
26 The importance of trust will be discussed further in the next section.
27 As we shall see presently, a good deal of evidence points towards this conclusion.
28 There was no evidence, for example, that credit officers were working any harder after conversion into individual liability. The authors also note that it was not part of the credit officers' training to engage in discussions with the clients about how they were investing their funds (Giné and Karlan, 2014, p.78).
29 Recall our discussion in Chapter 3 of the importance of habit formation in the microcredit sector of Bangladesh.
30 There is also the problem that while her theory requires that both wealthier and poorer borrowers are credit-constrained, the author has not established that the wealthier borrowers in her sample are really credit-constrained. She simply assumes that they are because they, too, are poor, whereas actually they own land between 1.5–2 acres, which is beyond the reach of most people commonly regarded as poor in rural Bangladesh.
31 The methodology may be questioned, however, on the ground of endogeneity. The authors use information on whether business expanded since the first loan to measure the dynamism of the enterprise, but the problem is that expansion is likely to be endogenous to the availability of credit and the size of the loan offered by the MFI.
32 This result is diametrically opposite to the predictions of most models of microcredit and is explained solely by the difference in assumption about the distribution of project return.
33 Fischer himself emphasises the finding that equity-like contracts outperform all other types. He actually argues against joint liability on the ground that it reduces efficient risk-taking. But this is slightly misleading. His results show that when joint liability is not linked with explicit peer approval of projects, risk-taking under joint liability is statistically no different from risk-taking under individual liability. It is only with

explicit project approval that risk-taking under joint liability falls below that of individual liability. But then explicit project approval by peers is hardly a common practice in the world of microcredit; it is more of an artificial construct created for the purpose of Fischer's experiments. One must acknowledge, of course, that an equity-like contract proved to be the best for both risk-taking and repayment, but one must also ask whether this type of contract is feasible in reality, especially since it involves third-party enforcement of equal income distribution in Fischer's formulation.

34 See the discussion on the Besley-Coate model in Chapter 5 for an elaboration of the free-rider effect.
35 The tension between free-riding and risk-sharing is theoretically investigated by Impavido (1998) and Armendáriz de Aghion (1999).
36 Of course, this requires deviation from individual rationality assumed in game theory, but such a deviation has been found to occur in several 'public goods' experiments, where free-riding has been curtailed for the sake of gaining 'social approval'. See, for example, Gächter and Fehr (1999).
37 However, subsequently the Krishna default crisis was repeated several times, and on a much larger scale. The biggest crisis came in October 2010, when the government of the state of Andhra Pradesh issued an emergency ordinance severely restricting the operations of all MFIs in the state.
38 The technique was to test whether a borrower's own probability to repay was correlated with the peer's probability to repay. This is a tricky exercise, however, because the two probabilities may be correlated due to many common characteristics that the borrower might share with her peers and therefore may not reflect the 'pure' inter-dependence that peer effect stands for. The author used a regression discontinuity approach to solve this problem of identification.
39 Breza's own judgement (not an empirically validated statement) is that the abandonment of joint liability in the immediate aftermath of the Krishna crisis was probably a good idea, because its presence might have hindered the emergence of early repayers whose action would trigger more widespread repayment through the peer effect. Even if she is right in this judgement, it does not necessarily detract from the possible value of joint liability in instilling a culture of peer effect in the first place.
40 As we saw in Chapter 5, however, their conclusion is critically dependent on particular assumptions about the distribution of returns to the borrowers. Under alternative but equally plausible assumptions, the conclusion no longer holds.
41 Members of a group may be more likely to repay the loan in their first credit cycle rather than in subsequent loan cycles, since in the first time period each member has explicitly sought a loan and agreed to the terms and conditions that are usually fairly similar if not identical across members. However, as loan cycles pass, some individuals may continue with the group and accept the subsequent terms and conditions even if they do not match their individual preferences and changing economic situation (Paxton et al., 2000, p.641). This may create tension within the group, resulting in a greater likelihood of default on the one hand and a lesser likelihood of peer support to prevent default on the other. von Pischke et al. (1998) offer a number of other reasons why repayment may decline over time.
42 For a fuller discussion of the problems of identification involved in estimating the effects of social capital, see, in particular, Manski (1993, 2000).
43 For a very helpful analytical survey of the literature, see Sobel (2002).
44 See Glaeser et al. (2002) for an elaboration of the concept and measurement of 'individual social capital', as distinct from 'community-level social capital' as defined in the classic works of Coleman (1988) and Putnam (1993). In the context of the credit market, and the economic arena generally, a helpful definition is provided by Karlan (2005, p.1689): 'Individual-levels social capital can be defined as the social skills and

networks that enable an individual to overcome imperfect information problems and form contracts with others'.
45 Roughly speaking, bonding refers to the strength of intra-group ties and bridging refers to the strength of external ties. Bonding-link and bridging-link refer to social distance in, as distinct from the strength of, the two types of ties.
46 The type of experiment he carried out is known as a 'trust game' in the literature on experimental economics. Examples of how this experiment works can be found in Berg *et al.* (1995), Glaeser *et al.* (2000) and Barr (2003).
47 The trust-based experiment carried out by Cassar *et al.* (2007, p.F91) indeed found evidence for reciprocity rather than free-riding: "when a member experiencing a negative shock is helped by others to repay the group loan, the benefiting member is more likely to contribute in the subsequent round."

7 Economic impact of microcredit
The experience of Bangladesh

In the early days of microcredit, it was taken as axiomatic that access to credit would bring economic benefits for the poor. This belief was based on the recognition that credit plays an important economic role by acting as a bridge between the present and the future. Costs of production are incurred in the present, but returns will accrue only in the future. If the producer doesn't have enough capital to cover the costs, access to credit becomes essential in order to ensure that profitable activities can, in fact, be undertaken. Similarly, in the face of negative shocks of various kinds, access to credit enables a household to protect its current level of consumption by borrowing against future income and thus helps avoid excessive hardship in adverse circumstances. Poorer households have traditionally been deprived of these economic benefits of credit because the formal banking system was not willing to lend to them, while village moneylenders, who might be willing to lend, charged exorbitant rates of interest. Faced with the credit constraint, poor people were thus less able to undertake potentially profitable economic activities and to avoid excessive fluctuations in consumption. It was, therefore, reasonable to expect that once they gained access to credit, they should be able to improve their economic well-being by earning more from productive activities and by being better able to smooth consumption over time.

The early studies of the impact of microcredit in Bangladesh seemed to confirm these expectations. The first systematic attempts to measure the impact of microcredit on the economic well-being of borrowers were made by Mahabub Hossain in the 1980s. Using household surveys as well as official records of the Grameen Bank, by far the largest provider of microcredit at the time, he assessed the impact of credit on the Bank's borrowers in two separate studies (Hossain, 1984, 1988). The main findings of the follow-up study, carried out in 1985 using a survey of 280 households in seven villages, of which five were programme villages and two were controls, are also presented in Hossain (2002). The economic well-being of the borrowers was compared with two control groups – eligible non-borrowers from programme villages and eligible households from non-programme villages. The borrowers were found to fare better than both types of control groups in terms of most of the economic indicators the study looked at – namely, household income, extent of poverty, level of employment, indebtedness to village moneylenders, and value of accumulated assets. The obvious implication was that by softening the credit constraint faced by the poor, Grameen Bank had enabled the borrowers to engage more fully and more gainfully in economic activities and thereby helped raise their living standard.

In yet another early study of the impact of microcredit, Rahman and Khandker (1994) evaluated the impact of three major microcredit programmes in Bangladesh on the employment and productivity of the rural poor. The study was based on a survey that subsequently became famous around the world as the basis of a large number of studies on the impact of microcredit, which, as we shall see, generated excitement and controversy in almost equal measure. The survey was carried out by the Bangladesh Institute of Development Studies (BIDS) with the help of the World Bank in 1991/92 and covered nearly 1800 rural households served by microfinance programmes of the Grameen Bank, the Bangladesh Rural Advancement Committee (BRAC), and the Bangladesh Rural Development Board (BRDB). The sample also included a control group of households in areas not served by any microfinance programmes. Following a methodology similar to Hossain's, Rahman and Khandker compared participants in programme villages with both non-participants from the same villages and eligible households from non-programme villages. The findings once again demonstrated the positive impact of microcredit. All three credit programmes were found to be successful in expanding the opportunities for productive self-employment. In particular, access to credit was found to enable the poor borrowers to switch from low-paid wage employment to more remunerative self-employment. (Most of the important early studies on the reach and impact of microcredit on various dimensions of the economy and society of rural Bangladesh can be found in Wood and Sharif [1997] and Osmani and Khalily [2011].)

These early studies soon came to be questioned, however, on methodological grounds. Doubts were raised about whether the methodologies employed in them were able to correctly identify the causal effect of credit on economic outcomes – a problem known in the econometric literature as the 'identification problem'. A number of subsequent studies have tried to address this problem by using appropriate econometric techniques, and in general they confirm the existence of the beneficial impact found by the early studies – although the magnitudes of benefit may differ. An extreme version of the critique has recently emerged, however, which holds that the kind of observational data on which these studies are based are fundamentally incapable of allowing a satisfactory solution of the identification problem. According to this view, what is needed are experimental data generated by randomised controlled trials (RCTs). Such experimental data have indeed been generated over the last decade to assess the impact of microfinance in a number of developing countries, and they generally fail to find any significant developmental impact. Although Bangladesh is not included in these countries, the negative findings of these studies – pertaining to a wide variety of contexts – have cast serious doubt on the validity of the finding of the beneficial impact of microcredit.

We review the debate on the economic impact of microfinance in this chapter and try to come to a judgement about where we currently stand on this subject. Our conclusion is that careful econometric investigations generally confirm that microcredit has had a salutary effect on the economic lives of the poor in Bangladesh, the negative findings of the RCTs notwithstanding. The discussion is structured as follows. Section 7.1 attempts to offer an intuitive explanation of what are rather complex methodological issues of identification. Section 7.2 undertakes a critical review of the RCTs in microcredit and comes to the conclusion that, despite the theoretical superiority of this approach, in practice they have not proved capable of shedding much useful light on the medium to longer-term effects of microcredit. As a result, we have no option but to try and extract whatever valid lessons we can from the studies based on observational data. We next review (in sections 7.3–7.5) most of the important studies that have examined the impact of microcredit in Bangladesh by using observational data but after taking due care of the identification problem, and draw some broad conclusions in section 7.6.

7.1 The methodological challenge

The primary methodological challenge in evaluating the impact of any intervention, including microcredit, is to identify the 'causal' effect of the intervention. In the simplest case, the causal effect can be easily 'identified' – i.e. the inference that a purportedly causal variable (in this case, credit) actually 'caused' the outcome (for example, higher economic well-being of the borrowers) can be deemed to be valid – if the causal variable has a property called 'exogeneity'. This property is said to exist, and the causal variable is defined as 'exogenous', when either (a) it has no correlation with any of the other possible explanatory variables that may also affect the relevant outcome, or (b) in case such correlated explanatory variables exist, they have all been included in the analysis so that their effects on the outcome can be separated out before estimating the impact of the variable in question. If these conditions are not met, the explanatory variable in question is deemed to be 'endogenous' as opposed to 'exogenous'. The impact assessment of such endogenous explanatory variables is fraught with a serious problem – known as the 'endogeneity' problem. In essence, the problem is that the measured impact of an endogenous variable will capture not only its own causal impact, if there is any, but also the impact of the excluded variables with which it happens to be correlated. In that case, the true causal impact will not be 'identified' – in particular, the measured impact will be a 'biased' estimate of the true impact unless measures are taken to eliminate the bias. Doubters of the methodologies used in the early studies of microcredit's impact argue that there are good reasons to suspect that the measured impacts of credit could suffer from such endogeneity bias. They further argue that there are reasons to believe that the bias is likely to be 'upward', i.e. the measured impact is likely to be greater than the true impact, if there is any. This means that we might find a positive impact even when there is none. As a result, they conclude, the inference that microcredit has led to higher living standards of the borrowers cannot be trusted.

The endogeneity bias may be of various types. The most common, in the context of microcredit, is perceived to be the problem of 'selection bias', which in turn may arise from different sources. For example, the MFIs may deliberately select the better off among the poor as their clients so as to ensure a better chance of their loans being repaid. In that case, the evidence of the higher income of the borrowers compared to non-borrowers cannot be interpreted as evidence for the beneficial effect of credit because it may simply reflect MFIs' selection policy. Alternatively, individuals with a better entrepreneurial ability may 'self-select' themselves into the MFI's programme while those with a lesser ability self-select out of it. Once again, the higher income of borrowers cannot be interpreted as being caused by credit because the real cause may lie in the unobserved differential abilities of borrowers and non-borrowers. In either case, the causal effect of credit will not be 'identified'.

Yet another type of selection bias may arise because of the preferences of the MFIs regarding programme placement. They may deliberately select villages of certain types – for example, relatively better-off villages – so that they can insure against possible loss by offering credit to 'safer' borrowers. If any such systematic difference between the programme and control villages is not properly accounted for, then a straightforward attribution of the income gap between participants and non-participants to the effect of credit will be a mistake, because at least a part of the gap may arise from the difference in the types of villages in which the two groups of people happen to live. The estimate of the effect of credit will then be subject to what is known as 'programme placement bias'. Once again, the causal effect of credit will not be 'identified'.

Moreover, in all these cases, if selection indeed occurs in the manner described, the resulting 'selection bias' will be 'upward' – i.e. the effect on income will be inflated as a result of either the MFIs selecting the better-off clients or more prosperous villages, or more able clients self-selecting themselves into the programme. In consequence, the inference that access to credit has led to higher income will not be credible.[1]

The problem here is that the effect of credit is getting mixed up with the effect of the selection process. This means that the true causal effect of credit could have been identified if somehow the selection process could be incorporated in the assessment exercise, in effect treating it as one of the explanatory variables, so that its effect could be separated out – leaving only the pure effect of credit. But the problem is that it may not always be possible to include the selection process explicitly in the analysis – for example, when the clients self-select themselves on the basis of some unobservable characteristics (such as entrepreneurial ability), because, by definition, one cannot capture what is unobservable. In that case, the credit variable will necessarily be endogenous owing to its correlation with the excluded variable, namely, the 'selection process', which too has a bearing on the observed outcome. The identification problem emanates from the fact that at least a part of the variation in credit (i.e. the fact that some individuals get credit and some don't) is correlated with the 'excluded' selection process. As a result of this correlation, when we find that a variation in an outcome (such as income) is associated with a variation in credit, we cannot be sure whether the observed variation in outcome is being caused by the observed variation in credit or by the correlated but hidden variation coming from the selection process.

This way of looking at the problem suggests a possible way out of it. The fact that the hidden selection process causes some variation in the credit variable is what makes this variable endogenous. But this does not mean that the entire variation in credit must be endogenous; there may be some part of the variation which is its 'own', so to speak, in the sense that it does not reflect a variation caused by the hidden selection process or by any other excluded variable. This 'own' part of the variation in credit can be described as an 'exogenous' variation. If somehow the extent of this exogenous variation in credit could be identified, one could try to see how much variation in the outcome variable is associated with it; this would then enable us to measure the true impact of credit – i.e. the effect of credit would be identified despite its endogeneity. This is precisely what analysts try to do when they look for an 'identification strategy' that would permit drawing a causal inference about an endogenous explanatory variable.

There are various ways of extracting this 'exogenous variation' in the endogenous variable. Correspondingly, there could be many different identification strategies, some being more effective than others depending on the nature of the data at hand.[2] As we noted, the early studies of the impact of microcredit did not, in general, address the issue of selection bias, and as such did not concern themselves with identification strategies. But subsequent studies have been much more conscious of the problem, and the search for an appropriate identification strategy has been at the heart of their enquiry. Indeed, one sometimes gets the impression that the methodological concern with identification has been all-consuming, often superseding the concern with substance.

Despite the high degree of econometric sophistication employed by many of these studies, all of them have recently come under attack from a group of researchers who argue that observational data will necessarily be an imperfect basis for causal analysis, no matter what techniques are used to overcome the identification problem. Statistical theory suggests that the best way to identify the causal effect of an intervention is to carry out an experiment in which recipients and non-recipients of the intervention are randomly chosen. Such experiments are known as randomised controlled trials (RCT) and have long been in vogue in scientific enquiries, especially in biomedical research. The randomisation of the selection process ensures that no kind of selection bias can contaminate the data, and therefore when the outcomes of the two groups are compared after a lapse of time, one should be able to identify the true causal impact of an intervention – or 'treatment', as it is commonly known in the literature, reflecting its biomedical origin. For this reason, RCTs are rightly regarded as the 'gold standard' of impact evaluation. Despite their obvious theoretical attraction, the social sciences have been slow in using RCTs. However, a spate of such studies has been carried out over the last decade to assess the impact of microcredit, and they have generally failed to find any appreciable impact on the economic upliftment of borrowers. These findings have led many commentators to reject altogether the more positive findings based on observational data, and to conclude that RCTs have conclusively demonstrated that microcredit does not have the transformative effect on the lives of the poor that the proponents of microcredit have all along claimed (e.g., Roodman, 2011a). In view of both the intrinsic importance of RCTs and the radical conclusions being drawn from them, these studies need to be examined closely. The following section undertakes this exercise.

7.2 A critical review of randomised experiments on the impact of microcredit

The most celebrated experimental study on the impact of microcredit carried out so far is a randomised controlled trial conducted in the urban slums of Hyderabad (India) between 2005 and 2010 (Banerjee *et al.*, 2015). Following essentially the same methodology of this pioneering study, several other randomised experiments have been carried out in a variety of other contexts – namely, rural Morocco (Crépon *et al.*, 2015), urban and rural Mexico (Angelucci *et al.*, 2015), rural Mongolia (Attanasio *et al.*, 2015) and rural Ethiopia (Tarozzi *et al.*, 2015). All five of these studies randomised at the level of some geographical area (slum, town or village) and introduced group lending in the treatment areas.[3] A couple of other experiments – one in Bosnia Herzegovina (Augsburg *et al.*, 2015) and another in the Philippines (Karlan and Zinman, 2010, 2011) – followed somewhat different methodologies, using individual-level rather than area-level randomisation and allowing only individual lending instead of group lending.

While trying to draw lessons from these studies, the first thing to note is that the modalities of lending adopted in some of the experiments were very different from the standard practices of microcredit lenders in Bangladesh and most other developing countries. (For a discussion of how the microcredit market works in different parts of the developing world, see the collection of papers in Hulme and Mosley [1996].) For example, the exclusive focus on individual lending makes the lessons learnt from the latter two studies less than profoundly relevant from the perspective of Bangladesh, where group lending still predominates despite some recent forays into individual lending. More importantly, both these experiments deliberately offered loans to relatively less-worthy borrowers: the Philippine experiment lent only to those who were deemed just marginally creditworthy according to a credit-scoring system developed specifically for the MFI involved, and the Bosnian experiment chose to lend only to those who were previously turned down by the participating MFI as not being creditworthy. This is in complete contrast to the practice in Bangladesh and most other countries, where the MFI officials go to great lengths to screen out doubtful cases, either through direct investigation or through peer screening (which is one of the main functions of the group lending system). There is also an oddity among the first group of studies – namely, the Mexican experiment. It involved a microlender that charged interest rates at over 100 percent per year, which is exorbitant by the standards of Bangladesh, where interest rates seldom exceeded 40 percent even before the regulatory authority imposed a ceiling of 27 percent in 2010. There should be little surprise if experiments that deliberately focussed on less-worthy borrowers or charged exorbitant rates of interest discover that microcredit did not deliver the goods it promises to do.

The Ethiopian study is also rather odd, but for a different reason. Unlike most other studies, it found very large positive impacts on many of the outcomes of interest, but they turned out to be statistically insignificant. For example, the net revenue from self-employed activities was found to be as much as 68 percent higher for the treatment group compared to the control group, and yet nothing conclusive could be inferred from this because it lacked statistical significance owing to unusually large standard errors. In trying to explain this oddity, the authors suggest that the problem may lie in the design of the experiment (Tarozzi et al., 2015). Originally designed to measure the impact of a family planning intervention – with or without concurrent intervention in microcredit – this experiment chose a sampling design that was meant to minimise the standard errors of family planning outcomes but not necessarily the standard errors of microcredit intervention outcomes. As a result, the experiment lacks the statistical power to discriminate between alternative hypotheses regarding the impact of microcredit. This implies that the failure of this study to find a statistically significant positive impact of microcredit may have more to do with its design problems than with the failure of microcredit as such.

The experiments carried out in India, Morocco and Mongolia are much more relevant for our present purpose as they do not suffer from any obvious oddities in terms of either lending modalities or sampling design. Many of their findings are, however, strikingly similar to those of the other studies whose oddities we have noted above. Some of the most interesting findings that emerge from all seven studies, with varying degrees of precision and with some exceptions, may be summarised as follows.[4]

First, microcredit has helped a sizeable segment of the treatment group to invest more in their existing business enterprises, but not so much to create new businesses. Second, microcredit has enabled another segment of the treatment group to increase their holdings of assets and durable goods. Third, both an increased level of business investment and the acquisition of durable goods have been financed mainly by cutting down on inessential consumption and partly by supplying more labour, and in some cases by drawing down savings. Fourth, neither an increased rate of investment nor a higher level of labour supply has enabled the treatment group as a whole to achieve a significantly higher level of income. Fifth, consistent with the finding of unchanged income, the majority of studies have found no significant improvement in the level of overall consumption either; there has only been a reallocation of consumption away from inessential consumption towards durable goods. As a result, there has been no discernible impact on poverty as standardly measured. Finally, in general there has been no significant improvement in other dimensions of welfare – such as health expenditure, education expenditure, women's empowerment, etc.

It is the final three findings taken together that have led to the widely held view that the presumption of microcredit's ability to alleviate poverty has been severely undermined by the recent spate of randomised experiments. There are, however, good reasons to argue that this conclusion is not based on as solid a ground as it might appear at first sight.

Leaving aside the oddities of some of the experiments mentioned earlier, a common problem with all seven of them is that whatever light they shed on the impact of microcredit relates only to the immediate aftermath of borrowing. In general, the evaluation of the treatment effect was undertaken within one to two years of intervention, with the sole exception of the Indian study, which we shall discuss more fully below. In most cases, the authors themselves acknowledge that the time span over which the impact was evaluated may not have been long enough to capture the effect on income and consumption.

One possible reason for this is that those who invested in existing businesses did not reach the optimal scale of operation. In most of the studies, increased investment in business was almost invariably found to be associated with a combination of a cut in inessential consumption, an increased labour supply and reduced savings. This suggests that the amount of credit the households received was not sufficient to reach the desired scale of business, which is why they were trying to augment their funds in various ways. It is entirely plausible that for the poorer borrowers the amount of augmentation was simply not large enough to bridge the gap. One of the findings of the Indian experiment is highly illuminating in this regard. The study found that, while for the vast majority of borrowers, increased investment in existing businesses did not yield significantly higher profit, there was an exception for the top end of the business enterprises, where profits did indeed go up. The authors do not quite explain this asymmetry and instead draw the rather misleading conclusion that '. . . contrary to most people's belief, to the extent microcredit helps businesses, it may help the larger businesses more' (Banerjee et al., 2015). This conclusion is misleading because it ignores the time dimension which may favour large businesses: the better-off households may be able to augment their funds more quickly – by drawing down their savings, for example – as compared to the poorer borrowers, and hence they may be able to reach the optimal size sooner. Given time, however, even the poorer borrowers might be able to get closer to the optimal size and thus begin to earn higher profits. There is, in fact, an indication of this happening in the Indian study itself. About 12–18 months after the intervention began, only the top 5 percent of businesses were found to earn higher profits (compared to the control group), but after three years the range of higher profit-earning businesses expanded from the top 5 percent to the top 15 percent (Banerjee et al., 2015). Corroborating evidence of the effect of time dimension can also be found in the Mongolian study, which shows that 'Enterprise profits increase over time as well, particularly for the less-educated' (Attanasio et al., 2015).[5]

The time dimension is also important for those borrowers who borrowed initially to acquire some durable goods rather than for the purpose of business investment. Since this type of borrowing does not directly lead to higher income, one should not expect to find any positive impact on income or overall consumption in the immediate aftermath of borrowing. However, after taking repeated loans over several years, they might start to invest in business enterprises once their demand for durables has been met.[6] One can find evidence in support of this hypothesis from a recent study of overlapping borrowing in the microcredit sector of Bangladesh. Using a nationally representative panel data set spanning a four-year period (2010–2014), the study found that those who took the initial loan mainly for home improvement used a large fraction of their subsequent loans for income-generating enterprises – and in the process they were eventually able to earn a significantly higher level of income (Osmani *et al.*, 2015).

The preceding discussion suggests that, in order to make credible inferences regarding the medium- to long-term impact of microcredit, the evaluation must be made over a longer time span than has been the case with most of the experimental studies. The sole exception so far is the Indian study, and as such its findings demand special attention.

Unlike the other experiments, the Indian experiment has been evaluated twice – the first time after 12–18 months from the time the intervention began, and the second time after three years. The first evaluation obviously had too short a time span, which is why the second evaluation was considered necessary. The authors of the study placed a strong emphasis on the finding that, even after the lapse of three years, the treatment group didn't seem to have any visible edge over the control group in terms of income, overall consumption and other developmental outcomes such as health, education and women's empowerment. This is the basis of their oft-repeated claim that even though microcredit seems to expand the borrowers' freedom to optimise their inter-temporal choices, it does not appear to have the kind of 'transformative power' that the practitioners of microcredit tend to claim for it.

Leaving aside the question of whether even a three-year span is long enough for the transformative power of microcredit to reveal itself, there are good reasons to argue that, in view of what happened during the experimental period, there was hardly any scope for microcredit to reveal its transformative power (if it had any). In an ideal RCT, only the randomly assigned treatment group receives the intervention, while the control group does not. This was not the case, however, in this study. According to the agreed-upon design, *Spandana*, the participating MFI, was supposed to offer microcredit only to the treatment areas during the first phase (which covered the first two years since the initiation of the experiment). *Spandana* followed the protocol with integrity, but other MFIs came forward to offer microcredit to the control areas and also, to some extent, to the treatment areas. The result was that at the time of the first evaluation, the proportion of microcredit borrowers was only about 9 percentage points higher in the treatment areas in comparison with the control areas. It should be noted that the evaluation compares outcomes not just between borrowers and non-borrowers, but between the entire treatment area (including both those who took up the offer of microcredit and those who didn't in that area) and the entire control area. As a result, the muted impact of microcredit that one finds in the first evaluation owes itself not just to the short time span, but also to the fact that the treatment areas were only marginally ahead of the control areas in terms of the take-up of microcredit.

One might have expected that over time the gap in the take-up ratio would widen, which would make it easier to discern the effect of microcredit, but in reality the opposite happened. According to the agreed-upon protocol, *Spandana* was allowed to offer microcredit in the control areas as well after two years. They apparently did so with gusto, so much so that by the time of the second evaluation, there was no statistically significant difference in the take-up ratio between the two areas. So, why should the treatment areas be expected to display better outcomes? The authors point out two possible reasons: the treatment group had a longer experience with microcredit and also had a larger average loan amount (which normally goes hand in hand with longer involvement with MFIs). True enough, but it is necessary to consider the magnitude of these advantages in order to judge how important they were in practice.

As regards experience, the study shows that, at the end of three years, the treatment group was ahead of the control group by a 0.13 loan cycle.[7] Taking a loan cycle to comprise a calendar period of 12 months on the average, this amounts to about 1.5 months' additional experience for the treatment group. As for the amount of loan taken, one finds that, considering all microloans and not just those offered by *Spandana*, the average loan amount was about 16 percent higher for the treatment group. In order to put this figure into perspective, one needs to consider several other pieces of information. First, the difference in loan amount was not statistically significant. Second, leaving aside the issue of statistical significance, the *extra* loan amount taken by the treatment group constituted just about 2 percent of their total outstanding loans from all sources (including microloans from all MFIs, informal loans and bank loans). Third, and even more interestingly, the total amount of outstanding loans from all sources was almost identical for the two groups. In other words, access to microcredit did not result in a net addition to borrowing on the part of the treatment group relative to the control group. The reason lies in the substitution between microcredit and other forms of loans. At the time of the first evaluation, the substitution was found to have occurred mainly away from informal loans; and at the time of the second evaluation, the substitution was mainly away from bank loans. Thus, while the three-year time span allowed by the second evaluation may have been long enough to permit the borrowers to make desired adjustments in their loan portfolio, it was evidently not long enough to permit them to increase the level of overall borrowing and thus to ease their credit constraint to any appreciable extent.

What we have, therefore, is far from what one would normally expect from an impact evaluation – namely, a comparison between two groups of households, one of them with access to microcredit and the other without. It is rather a case of comparing two groups of microcredit borrowers who turned out to be strikingly similar in most respects.[8] There was no statistically significant difference between them, either in the proportion of households taking microcredit, or in the amount of microcredit taken on the average, or in the total amount of borrowing from all sources. The only significant difference was that the treatment group had a marginally longer experience in taking microcredit – of about 1.5 months! To expect this slender advantage to bring about a transformative experience in the lives of microcredit borrowers would be asking for nothing short of a miracle. It is doubtful whether even the most ardent of microcredit advocates would expect this to happen.

This is not to deny that the crop of randomised experiments carried out so far has provided some valuable insights into how the access to microcredit can affect household behaviour. Perhaps the most enduring insight relates to the adjustment in inter-temporal consumption pattern. When credit-constrained households get access to credit for the first time, the immediate response may be to sacrifice current consumption in order to make a lumpy expenditure, either in the form of a business investment or the acquisition of some durables.[9] But the same insight also warns against trying to assess the poverty impact of microcredit on the basis of experiments that have only a short time span. A longer time span is absolutely vital.

However, as the Indian case study demonstrates, there is an inherent problem with conducting microcredit experiments in the real world with a longer time span. In essence, the problem is that it is both unethical and impractical to continue to deny credit to the control group for too long. As a precondition for agreeing to take part in the academic experiment, the MFI *Spandana* had to be reassured that it would be able to extend its operation in the control areas after two years. Furthermore, even when *Spandana* had steadfastly stuck to its agreement by denying credit to the control area in the first two years, there was no way of preventing other MFIs from serving the control group. The outcome of all this was that it was simply not possible to create sufficient distance between the two groups in terms of exposure to microcredit – a distance that would be large enough to enable researchers to discern the true impact of microcredit over the medium to long term.

Randomised experiments with microcredit are thus faced with a dilemma. If the objective is to test hypotheses about microcredit's presumed ability to transform the lives of borrowers, one cannot rely on experiments carried out over a short time span; but then experiments over longer time spans are difficult to implement due to practical reasons. It is not easy to see how this dilemma can be resolved.[10] Under the circumstances, the best the researchers can do is to work with observational data; recognise that there are inherent problems with such data arising, in particular, from the existence of selection bias of the kind discussed earlier; and do their best to tease out the causal connections by using appropriate econometric methodologies. It is true that the identification of causal connections in this manner would never be as precise as would be the case with an 'ideal' randomised experiment, but we may have no option but to settle for the second best since, for the reasons explained above, an 'ideal' microcredit experiment seems hardly possible.

It is in this spirit that we review below the major attempts that have been made so far to evaluate the poverty impact of microcredit in Bangladesh based on observational data. We may classify these studies into several groups depending on the nature of data they used, since the nature of the identification strategy depends crucially on the nature of the data. The first group is based on cross-sectional data in which a sample of households is surveyed at a point in time. The second group contains studies that use longitudinal or panel data, i.e. repeated surveys of the same sample of households at more than one point in time. The third category of data may be described as quasi-panel in nature, which is essentially cross-sectional data but enriched by information about the past so that some sort of longitudinal analysis can be applied. These three groups of studies are reviewed in the next three sections, respectively.

7.3 Studies based on cross-sectional data

An early cross-sectional study that was alive to the methodological problem of causal identification is Zaman (1999). Using a dataset of 547 BRAC borrowers and 525 control households in ten villages in Matlab upazila (sub-district), the study tried to address the problem of self-selection by applying an appropriate econometric technique and came up with two interesting findings. First, access to microcredit did not reduce poverty for all borrowers – it did so only when cumulative credit taken over the years reached a certain critical minimum threshold. What seems to matter here, however, is not so much the amount of credit, but the length of experience of the long-term borrowers. Accumulated experience seems to enable borrowers to switch from traditional low-risk/low-return on-farm activities to higher-risk/higher-return off-farm activities over time, and thereby to attain a higher income level.[11] Second, in addition to reducing poverty, access to credit also reduced the borrowers' vulnerability to poverty, defined in the sense of the likelihood of remaining or becoming poor in the future. Zaman did not, however, measure vulnerability directly. Instead, he looked at a number of possible determinants of vulnerability – namely, (a) crisis-coping mechanisms such as additional loans, staggered repayment, etc., during crises, (b) asset building, and (c) women's empowerment – and found that credit affected those determinants in ways that should reduce vulnerability.

Valuable as these findings are, their credibility remains in doubt despite the care the author took to deal with the identification problem. He used the standard instrumental variable approach for this purpose. For this method to work, however, one needs to find proper 'instruments' that can extract exogenous variation from within the endogenous variables. By the author's own admission, his instruments were not very 'robust', which means that doubts remain as to the extent to which any possible selection bias has actually been removed. This failure to find 'robust' instruments has been an Achilles' heel of impact assessments of all kinds.

In a series of papers, Mark Pitt and Shahidur Khandker have tried to address this problem by adopting an innovative method to get rid of selection bias, using the same BIDS/World Bank data set that was used by Rahman and Khandker (1994) referred to earlier. In their most celebrated paper, Pitt and Khandker (1998) tried to assess the impact of microcredit on indicators of household well-being such as expenditure and assets, differentiated by gender. They found that loans taken by females had a strong positive effect on the well-being of borrowing households, but loans taken by males did not. Since women constituted the majority of borrowers, the overall effect was judged to be positive.[12]

The magnitude of the effects found by Pitt and Khandker was quite large. For example, total household expenditure was found to increase by 18 taka for every 100 additional taka borrowed by women, with the corresponding figure for men being 11 taka for every 100 taka of additional loan funds. The facts that the measured impact was so large, that it was estimated by an apparently sophisticated method of dealing with the identification problem, and that the findings seemed to vindicate the MFIs' decision to target credit mainly to women, all combined to elevate the paper to a cult status in the world community of practitioners and academics involved with microfinance.[13] It has remained the most frequently cited academic paper on microfinance to this day.

From the very beginning, however, there were also some rumblings of discontent within academia, articulated most strongly in an unpublished note by Morduch (1998). He raised a number of concerns with the paper, the most important being the validity of the identification strategy employed. Pitt (1999) soon came out with a robust response, also in an unpublished note. And there the matter seemed to rest for nearly a decade, until the debate was resurrected in 2009 in a working paper which Jonathan Morduch co-authored with David Roodman (Roodman and Morduch, 2009). This led to a series of responses and counter-responses and counter-counter-responses – principally between David Roodman and Mark Pitt. Just at the time this new round of debate was coming to a boil, a parallel debate cropped up between Mark Pitt on the one hand, and Maren Duvendack and Richard Palmer-Jones on the other. A great deal of the contents of these two debates, especially the first, are too technical to go into here; also, many of the claims and counter-claims have become redundant after being refuted during the course of the debate. What is really important to assess is where the debate stands now, and especially what remains of the original findings of Pitt and Khandker after all this scrutiny. For this, however, we need to go back to the origin of the debate.

At the heart of the controversy lies the nature of the identification strategy employed by Pitt and Khandker. Although the matter is intensely technical, it is not just a matter of technical detail, because as we explained earlier the very credibility of the substantive finding on the impact of credit depends crucially on the validity of the identification strategy used for dealing with the problem of selection bias. One of the reasons the controversy arose in the first place and has persisted for so long is that Pitt and Khandker had to devise a very unusual econometric technique of estimation in view of some very unique features of the data at hand, and the identification strategy implicit in this novel technique was not at all transparent. The matter was further complicated by two other factors. First, the nature of the data precluded the possibility of using standard statistical procedures for testing the validity of the instruments employed for the purpose of identification. As a result, the arguments both for and against the strategy had to rely on analogues and *a priori* reasoning, neither of which was conducive for resolving disagreements conclusively. Second, the particular analogue that Pitt and Khandker themselves used to illustrate the intuition behind their identification strategy, although seemed very illuminating at the beginning, turned out to be rather misleading in the end, driving their critics needlessly in wrong directions and fuelling futile controversies.

Pitt and Khandker's explanation of the intuition behind their identification strategy is closely related to an econometric technique known as the regression discontinuity method (which we discussed in Chapter 6). To see the logic behind it, consider the fact that most MFIs employ some kind of eligibility rule to decide whom to offer credit. The most commonly applied rule in Bangladesh is that a household should own no more than half an acre of cultivable land. Starting from zero ownership, all those who have land up to the cutoff point are deemed eligible, but as soon as the cutoff point is crossed the household becomes ineligible. That's a discontinuity, which may be unfortunate for a household marginally above the cutoff point who is eager to take a loan, but it is a fortunate twist for an analyst looking for an identification strategy. If one compares the households just below the cutoff line (the eligible group) with those just above (the ineligible group), it is reasonable to argue that, as a whole, the two groups should not be fundamentally different from each other because all that separates them is a few decimals of land. In particular, there is no reason to suppose that the eligible group has superior unobservable characteristics, such as entrepreneurial ability, compared to the ineligible group, because such differences have no bearing on who is eligible and who is not. Eligibility is determined by an external rule, not by the choice of the households. Who among the eligible group would eventually take the loan is, of course, a matter of choice, and that choice may well be influenced by their unobserved characteristics – but eligibility is independent of choice. To put it differently, households may self-select themselves into the borrower category, but they cannot self-select into the eligible category. Thus, a comparison between eligible and non-eligible groups, as distinct from a comparison between borrowers and non-borrowers, should not be vitiated by any kind of selection bias. And since, as noted above, households just above and just below the cutoff point can be expected, on the average, to be very similar in all respects, other than the fact that one group can take credit and the other cannot, any observed difference between them in the outcome variable can be correctly identified as the causal effect of credit.

In his initial criticism, Morduch (1998) accepted this logic of identification but argued that the logic did not apply to the Pitt-Khandker study because the eligibility rule was not strictly enforced by the MFIs – many households above the cutoff point were also offered loans. He then modified the methodology of estimation to account for this deviation from the official eligibility rule, and came up with the startling finding that the Pitt-Khandker results no longer held – i.e. credit did not appear to have any significant impact on household expenditure. Pitt (1999), however, cast doubt on this counter-finding by pointing out various errors of a factual and logical nature in Morduch's study.

In the absence of a further response from Morduch, the Pitt-Khandker conclusion about the efficacy of microcredit continued to hold sway for nearly a decade until it was jolted again by Roodman and Morduch (2009). This time the line of attack was different. The authors claimed to show that even if one eschewed the modified methodology Morduch had applied in his original foray, and used instead the methodology applied by Pitt and Khandker themselves but applied it properly, the main Pitt-Khandker finding again disappeared – credit seemed to have no significant effect on household expenditure. This was a much stronger claim than the one made earlier in Morduch (1998) as it was purportedly based on the same methodology as the one used by Pitt and Khandker themselves. But once again, Pitt (2011a) came back strongly in self-defense, pointing out a litany of errors in the Roodman-Morduch study and showing how the original findings still survived the new critique.

There followed a series of exchanges of a rather obscure nature, in the course of which Roodman repeatedly came up with new arguments and was repeatedly mowed down by Pitt, only to resurface with even newer arguments.[14] Eventually, Roodman and Morduch had to concede that the original Pitt-Khandker findings could not be overturned, but they continued to profess scepticism on the grounds that they were still not convinced about the validity of Pitt and Khandker's identification strategy (Roodman and Morduch, 2014).

Meanwhile, a new debate emerged in which Duvendack and Palmer-Jones locked horns with Mark Pitt, although it started as a proxy war. The immediate target of attack by Duvendack and Palmer-Jones (2012a) was not the Pitt-Khandker study, but a study by Chemin (2008), who tried to replicate the findings of Pitt and Khandker (1998) by applying a new methodology to the same data. Chemin used the technique of propensity score matching (PSM) to handle the problem of identification arising from selection bias. Since the essence of the selection problem is that households in the programme and control groups may be very different because of the selection process through which the programme group is formed, PSM seeks to remove the problem by creating a control group which is as similar to the programme group as possible. The technique first tries to estimate how likely each member of the control group would have been to ask for credit if they had a choice to do so, and assigns a 'propensity score' to them depending on the strength of this likelihood. Similar scores are also estimated for the members of the treatment group. The technique then matches members of the two groups who have similar scores; those with no matches are left out. Since the members of the two new groups thus created have a similar probability of asking for credit, any possible difference arising from the selection process is deemed to have been purged. The only remaining difference is that one group participates in the credit programme and the other does not. As a result, the observed difference in the outcome variables of the two matched groups can be interpreted as the causal effect of credit, once other factors that may also affect the outcome variable have been controlled for.

The estimates that Chemin obtained by using this technique confirmed the Pitt-Khandker finding that credit has a significantly positive effect on household expenditure, although the magnitude of the effect was found to be somewhat smaller than what Pitt and Khandker had obtained. Chemin thus offered a vindication of Pitt and Khandker's central message regarding the effectiveness of microcredit, even if not of the magnitude of the effect, by applying a different statistical technique on the same dataset. Duvendack and Palmer-Jones (2012a) challenged this vindication, and by implication challenged the original finding of Pitt and Khandker as well. They claimed to show that if the PSM technique was properly applied to the same data, the positive effect of credit seemed no longer to exist – a very similar type of claim that Roodman and Morduch had made following a very different route.

The specific criticism they made of Chemin's work was directed at a well-known limitation of the PSM technique, which according to them, Chemin did not pay adequate attention to. When PSM tries to create two groups that are similar in terms of the probability of participating in a credit programme, it estimates the probability on the basis of the observed characteristics of sample households or individuals. The problem, however, is that unobserved characteristics may also have a bearing on the probability of participation – for example, those with a more entrepreneurial bent of mind may want to participate more. One can, therefore, never be certain that PSM has obtained a genuine matching. Any consequent mismatch would imply that the selection bias may not have been removed. This is because the same unobserved characteristics that affect the probability of participation may also affect the outcome variable – for example, those with greater entrepreneurial spirit may want to participate more in the credit programme and may also earn higher income because of that spirit. In other words, a mismatch in terms of the propensity score may also entail a mismatch in the ability to earn higher income, with or without credit. A comparison of the two mismatched groups will then confound the effect of credit with the effect of differential ability. As a result, PSM will fail to identify the true effect of credit.

This is an inherent limitation of PSM since unobservable characteristics cannot, by definition, be taken note of while estimating propensity scores. Econometricians have, however, devised various kinds of sensitivity tests to see how badly the results are affected under alternative assumptions about the underlying distribution of unobserved characteristics. The confidence in the results will depend on how robust they are to these tests. This is precisely what Duvendack and Palmer-Jones did, subjecting Chemin's PSM estimates to the sensitivity tests, and found that under most of the alternative assumptions, the credit variable turned out to be statistically insignificant. The most reasonable inference, they concluded, was that credit had no significant effect on household expenditure, contrary to what Pitt and Khandker had found and Chemin had confirmed.

Both Pitt (2012) and Chemin (2012) then responded in self-defense, with quite a devastating effect. They demonstrated that in carrying out their sensitivity analysis, Duvendack and Palmer-Jones had made a series of errors of both factual and statistical nature, and that the combined effect of these errors was serious enough to destroy the credibility of their analysis. In response, much like Roodman and Murdoch did, Duvendack and Palmer-Jones (2012b, 2012c, 2012d) also conceded that they could no longer claim to prove that the Pitt-Khandker-Chemin finding on the efficacy of microcredit was wrong, but they continued to maintain their scepticism about its validity on the grounds that it was not subjected to adequate sensitivity analysis.

Whether Roodman-Morduch and Duvendack-Palmer-Jones are justified in holding on to their skepticism is an issue that, in our view, cannot be resolved on a scientific basis, because the arguments at this stage seem to belong more to the realm of faith than of scientific discourse. It is reasonable to argue, however, that even from a purely objective point of view, not all the qualms about the Pitt-Khandker results have been fully resolved.

The first qualm pertains, not surprisingly, to the identification strategy. When Pitt and Khandker (1998) first explained their strategy, they pointed out two kinds of discontinuities which could potentially be exploited for the purpose of identification. The first kind was related to the 'half an acre' eligibility rule, and we have explained above how the discontinuity generated by this rule helps achieve identification. The second kind of discontinuity emerged from the facts that borrower groups were segregated by gender and that not all villages were offered groups of both types – some were offered only male groups, some only female groups, and some both. This meant that whether individuals could borrow or not did not depend initially on their choice – it depended on whether a particular gender group was allowed in a particular village or not. As in the case of the 'half an acre' rule, eligibility was determined by an extraneous decision by the MFIs, in which a household's choice did not play any role. This implies that if one compares, for example, two groups of females – namely, eligible females in a village where 'female' groups were allowed and females in another village where only male groups were allowed – one should not expect to find any systematic differences in their unobserved characteristics, because these characteristics did not play any role in separating the two groups in the first place. Therefore, any observed difference between their outcome variables cannot be attributed even in part to differences in unobserved characteristics. This is just another way of saying that there is no scope of self-selection bias creeping in here. As a result, any difference in the outcome variables between these two groups will correctly identify the effect of credit, once the effects of any observed differences between them have been adequately controlled for.

Of the two eligibility rules – one related to the 'half an acre' cutoff point and the other to gender-specific programme placement – it is the former that Pitt and Khandker (1998) used to illustrate the intuition behind their identification strategy. In consequence, all the ensuing debate focused almost exclusively on it, and the other rule receded into the background. However, after all the criticisms and doubts that have been heaped by Roodman and Morduch on their identification strategy, Pitt and Khandker (2012) now maintain that these doubts are irrelevant anyway because they do not need the 'half an acre' rule to obtain identification – the other discontinuity, offered by gender-specific programme placement, is enough for this purpose.

This may sound like a plausible argument, except that Pitt and Khandker did not seem so confident about it the first time around. In their original paper, they first noted that even though programme placement was not influenced by households' choice, it could be influenced by the outcome variable of interest – for example, the MFIs may choose villages with a higher average income. In that case, any estimation strategy that relies on a comparison across villages could be biased, even after allowing for village-level fixed effects. They concluded that '... without further exogenous variation in program availability, the credit effect is not identifiable ...' and went on to suggest that this additional variation is provided by the exogenous rule that '... households owning more than half-acre of land are precluded from joining any of the three credit programs' (Pitt and Khandker, 1998, p.976). This line of argument is ostensibly at odds with the authors' current position. Since the identification strategy based on gender-specific programme placement must necessarily involve a comparison across villages, and since, according to the quote above, such a comparison cannot achieve identification without the additional exogenous variation afforded by the half-acre rule, it is not altogether clear exactly how the land-based rule can now be dispensed with and identification be achieved solely from gender-specific placement, as claimed by Pitt and Khandker (2012). Perhaps the two positions can be reconciled, but we are not told how.

The second qualm emanates from a startling finding in Roodman and Morduch (2013) on the role of outliers. The authors demonstrate that the positive impact of credit on household expenditure that Pitt and Khandker find actually stems from the behaviour of a handful of borrowers who spend a disproportionately large amount of money. If only 14 of these big spenders are removed from the sample, the effect of credit disappears! Roodman and Morduch use this finding to support their scepticism about the robustness of Pitt and Khandker's identification strategy, but this line of attack seems specious. The problem of outliers is certainly a sign of fragility of the findings, but it may have nothing to do with identification.[15] The more genuine concern pertains to the fragility of the estimates itself – how much credence can one give to the estimates which cannot survive the withdrawal of a handful of outliers?[16]

The third qualm relates to an issue of specification that seems to have been overlooked in the literature so far. The credit variable used in Pitt and Khandker (1998) is 'cumulative' loan, as distinct from current loan, whereas the outcome variable is 'current' household expenditure. This juxtaposition between cumulative and current values has some odd implications. Suppose person X has borrowed 1000 taka every year for 10 years so that her cumulative loan is 10,000 taka, whereas person Y has borrowed 10,000 taka in the current year but nothing before, so that her cumulative loan is also 10,000 taka. The specification implies that credit will have the same impact on both persons' household expenditure in the *current* year, even though the former's current loan is only one-tenth of the latter's! This is patently absurd. Consider, for example, the scenario where person X uses a loan of 1000 taka every year as working capital, and earns an additional annual income of taka T. If other things remain the same, she will keep on earning this extra income T every year. By the tenth year, her extra income, generated by credit, is, however, still T, not 10T, because by definition income (which is a flow concept) does not cumulate. By contrast, person Y, who uses 10,000 taka for working capital in the current year, is likely to earn an extra income of 10T (or something close to it depending on scale economies). Clearly, the impact on current expenditure in the two cases cannot be even remotely similar. Of course, working capital is not the only possible pathway through which a loan can affect household expenditure; but whatever pathway one considers, it is difficult to see how the two effects can be of similar orders of magnitude.

While these criticisms do not necessarily nullify the central message of Pitt and Khandker that microcredit has a positive impact on the economic condition of the poor, they do call into question the accuracy of the magnitude of the impact they claimed to find. Chemin's study, which confirms Pitt and Khandker's central message but also at the same time points to a smaller size of the effect, serves to strengthen the concern with magnitudes. As a result, bold inferences such as the claim that 5 percent of the borrowers climb out of poverty every year in rural Bangladesh ought to be eschewed.

At the same time, one has to recognise the brilliance of the Pitt-Khandker study in extending the frontier of research based on cross-sectional data. Their work shows how far one can possibly go towards extracting causal inferences from cross-sectional data by using imagination and sophistication in the use of econometric techniques. Any remaining limitation is possibly a reflection of the inherent limitations of cross-sectional data itself. In order to make firmer causal inferences, it is necessary to move on to different kinds of data.

7.4 Studies based on panel data

The use of panel data can offer a way of resolving the problem of identification in a more satisfactory manner than cross-sectional data ever can, even though it does not guarantee success in all circumstances. The fact that data are available for the same households (or individuals, as the case may be) enables the analyst to compare the programme and control groups in terms of the *difference* in outcomes between two or more points in time – instead of comparing them in terms of the *levels* of outcome, as with cross-sectional data. For instance, one might ask: by how much did the income of the two groups change between two points in time, instead of asking what their income levels were at a particular point in time? By looking at the change rather than the level of the data, the analyst can get rid of the effects of unobserved characteristics, provided those characteristics can be assumed to remain constant over time, because these effects will then cancel out in the process of calculating the change. This is known as the difference-in-difference (DD) method, or more generally the fixed effect (FE) method, of eliminating any selection bias that may arise from unobserved (but fixed) characteristics at the household or village level.

If there are reasons to believe that unobserved characteristics may change instead of remaining constant over time, the FE/DD method needs adjustment. There are several ways of doing so – for example: (a) while applying the FE method, one can control for some initial observed characteristics that may have a bearing on how the relevant unobserved characteristics might change, (b) DD may be supplemented by the matching method described earlier (DD-PSM), or (c) one can go one step further by taking the difference-in-difference-in-difference (DDD). Different methods are appropriate for different types of changes in the unobserved characteristics. Since change can happen in a variety of ways, some of which might be unpredictable, one can never guarantee that the selection bias has been entirely eliminated by any of these methods. But by using alternative methods, and carrying out various sensitivity tests, it may be possible to get as close to the truth as non-experimental data will ever permit. As a result, when panel data analysis is carried out with due diligence, the estimates of programme effects obtained from them can be interpreted as a causal effect with a great deal more confidence than in the case of cross-sectional studies.

All the major panel studies that have been carried out so far to measure the impact of microcredit in Bangladesh have been reasonably conscious of the need for due diligence in applying panel data techniques. Accordingly, their findings can be accepted with a high degree of confidence. There are currently three main panel data sets available in Bangladesh that can be, and have been, used for the purpose of estimating the effect of microcredit. These are: (1) four rounds of surveys sponsored by the *Palli Karma Shahayak Foundation* (PKSF) covering the period from 1997 to 2005, and the studies based on it include Razzaque (2010), Islam (2011) and Imai and Azam (2012); (b) three rounds of surveys in 1991/92, 1998/99 and 2011, the first two rounds of which were carried out jointly by BIDS and the World Bank, and the third of which was carried out jointly by the InM and the World Bank; the studies include Khandker (2005), and Khandker and Samad (2013, 2014); and (c) several rounds of surveys carried out by BRAC to assess the impact of its ultra-poor programme; the most carefully conducted study based on this data set is Emran *et al.* (2014).

Using the PKSF panel data, Razzaque (2010) found that borrowing households had a higher per capita income and a lower probability of falling into poverty relative to comparable non-borrowers, after adjusting for unobserved heterogeneity and observable factors through appropriate panel data methods. Since the borrowing households included a substantial number of non-eligible, i.e. relatively better-off, households, the author wanted to test whether this result was driven mainly by the performance of these better-off households. For this purpose, he redid the estimation after dropping the non-eligible borrowers, and the results remained essentially the same. This suggests that the benefits of credit were not cornered by the relatively better-off borrowers; the positive impact accrued to the intended target group as well. Direct tests of the impact on the extreme poor confirmed that the benefit of credit also reached the poorest among the target group.

Several other results obtained by Razzaque are also worthy of note. First, access to credit benefitted male and female borrowers differentially; for instance, longer participation in the credit programme conferred additional benefit to females but not to males. Second, cumulative household borrowing had a significantly positive effect on the accumulation of household assets, which indicates that the benefit of credit extends beyond the period of borrowing. Third, in contrast to per capita income, the rate of asset accumulation was positively and significantly influenced by the length of programme participation for both males and females. However, the effect of female participation on assets was more than double the comparable effect obtained for the entire sample, once again indicating that the effect of credit was differentiated by gender.

Islam (2011) used the PKSF data with the primary objective of distinguishing between the short-term and the long-term effects of credit. For this purpose, he compared the effects on borrowers who remained programme members continuously for the eight years covered in the study with the effects on new borrowers who joined later and on the drop-outs. He used both the standard DD method and the more refined DDD method to allow for the possibility that programme and control villages may have been affected differentially by unobserved shocks. The magnitudes of the coefficients obtained under the two methods varied, often quite substantially, but the qualitative results, i.e. the direction and the significance of the results, remained the same.

The effect of credit was measured on three outcome variables – food consumption, self-employment income and assets. The major finding is that while the effect of credit on all three outcome variables was significantly positive, the strength of the effect was stronger in the longer run. This is evident first from the fact that the size of the coefficient of the credit variable was bigger for continuing borrowers compared to the newcomers, and second from the fact that even the drop-outs seemed to be better off than non-borrowers. The latter result indicates that the benefit of credit did not cease to exist when a borrower stopped borrowing – the benefit continued to flow, at least for a while.[17]

Islam draws two major conclusions from his findings – one methodological, one substantive. The methodological conclusion is that conventional programme evaluations that are based on the outcomes reported by continuing participants may underestimate the contribution of a microcredit programme (because the continued effect on the drop-outs will be missed), and short-term treatment data in a microcredit programme may not provide a reliable estimate of the overall impact of the programme (because the extent of benefit tends to rise with the length of participation). The substantive conclusion is that graduation from poverty using microcredit requires long-term participation, for it takes time for household entrepreneurs to achieve productive efficiency or to generate higher returns from self-employment.

Imai and Azam (2012) also used the PKSF data to measure the impact of microcredit on two indicators of household well-being – namely, income and food consumption. In both cases, credit was found to have a significantly positive effect. However, the magnitude of the effect was found to be quite small. For example, the doubling of a loan raised the per capita income by only about 0.5 percent and raised the per capita food consumption by 0.7 percent to 1 percent, depending on the estimation method used.[18]

A novel feature of this study is that it made a distinction between productive and non-productive loans, and tried to assess whether the impact of credit varied by the type of loan. Not surprisingly, it found that only a productive loan was able to raise income. On the other hand, a productive loan did not seem to have any impact on food consumption; only a non-productive loan was able to raise it. The finding that a productive loan raises income but not consumption may seem surprising at first sight, but it is consistent with a great deal of anecdotal evidence which shows that borrowers often tighten their belt – sometimes consuming even less than before for the time being – in order to repay their loan out of additional income.[19] In essence, what the productive borrowers seem to be doing is an inter-temporal trade-off – consuming less, or at least no more today, in the hope of consuming more tomorrow out of the higher income generated with the help of credit. This is exactly the opposite of the inter-temporal trade-off that non-productive borrowers engage in – consuming more today with the help of credit but reducing the level of consumption later. This latter type of behaviour – known as consumption smoothing – is entirely rational when households experience some urgent need to raise expenditures temporarily or are faced with a temporary shortfall of income.

The study by Emran et al. (2014) was part of BRAC's regular evaluation of its ongoing Targeting the Ultra Poor (TUP) programme, in which access to credit is combined with, and in some respects preceded by, other forms of support for the ultra-poor.[20] The panel consisted of about 5,000 households surveyed at two points in time – 2002 and 2005. The authors used both the DD and DD-PSM techniques described above and carried out a number of sensitivity tests to check for the robustness of the estimates under alternative assumptions about time-variant unobservables. They found a significant positive effect of participation in the programme on net income, food security and several indicators of assets, such as quality of housing, household durables and ownership of livestock. A more refined analysis showed that programme benefits were not shared equally by all groups; in particular, the poorest 20 percent of the households benefitted less in absolute terms compared to the top 20 percent.

Khandker and Samad (2013, 2014) made extensive use of the three-period panel data (1991/92, 1998/99 and 2010/11) generated by the World Bank, first in collaboration with BIDS and then with the Institute of Microfinance.[21] Based as they are on a source of data that covers the longest period (two decades) among all the panel data available in Bangladesh, these studies are particularly valuable in shedding light on the long-term impact of microcredit on the living standards of the poor. Like the preceding studies, they too employed different variants of panel data techniques and used sensitivity analysis to check for the robustness of the estimates.

The starting point in Khandker and Samad (2014) was the hypothesis that a critical factor in any assessment of a programme such as microcredit intervention is the duration of programme intervention. They argue that unlike programmes such as conditional cash transfers (CCTs), which benefit the participants within a short period of time, microcredit takes time to have an impact that cannot be measured appropriately within a year or two after treatment.[22] The long-period panel data they had at their disposal was especially suited to test this hypothesis. Like Islam (2011), they tested the hypothesis by making a separate assessment for those participants who continued to borrow for the entire period and compared the effects on these borrowers with the overall effect. They found that overall participation had no significant effect on moderate poverty, but continuous participation did. The effect of microcredit was even more pronounced on extreme poverty. While participation in general did not seem to have any significant impact on moderate poverty, it did so for extreme poverty, and continuous participation did even more.

Using the same dataset, Khandker and Samad (2013) showed that the effect of microcredit was not only differentiated by the duration of participation but also by gender, which is congruent with the earlier finding of Razzaque (2010) based on PKSF data. They found that male participation had hardly any impact on either moderate or extreme poverty, but female participation reduced extreme poverty by about 4 percentage points, although it too had no significant effect on moderate poverty.

Khandker and Samad (2013) explored a number of other issues that are highly relevant in the context of assessing the impact of microcredit. There has been much discussion of late on whether rapid expansion of microcredit is pushing many borrowers into a debt trap by inflicting an unsustainable debt burden on them. The argument is that, while borrowing might provide a temporary boost to the living standard of the poor, it is possible that their long-term economic viability is being undermined in the process. The evidence we have cited above indicating the positive impact of credit on asset accumulation – as found by a number of panel studies using different datasets – already suggests that this fear is unlikely to be valid in general. However, the issue is certainly important enough to deserve a thorough investigation, which is exactly what the authors provide by examining data on both debt accumulation and asset accumulation, and the consequent evolution of net assets. Their evidence showed that, even when participants accumulated debt, they accumulated assets even more, so that their net worth increased and debt-asset ratio declined as a result of programme participation. They conclude, 'Thus, in contrast to the common perception about poverty and indebtedness, we find that microcredit participants are not necessarily trapped either in poverty or debt' (Khandker and Samad, 2013, p.24).[23]

The authors also point to an interesting contrast between male and female borrowers that deserves comment in the light of our earlier observation on the gender-differentiated effect of microcredit. We noted earlier that, according to several studies, male participation in credit programmes does not seem to have any positive impact on poverty while female participation does, especially when it comes to extreme poverty. Khandker and Samad (2013) showed, however, that male borrowing has a much stronger effect on asset accumulation compared to female borrowing; indeed, the coefficient of female borrowing was not even statistically significant. This contrast in the gender-mediated effect of credit on poverty on the one hand, and asset accumulation on the other, leads to the following inference. Female borrowing imparts a short-term impact on the household's living standards by boosting household consumption – either directly by spending the loan for consumption purposes, or indirectly by using the income of loan-financed investment for this purpose – instead of saving the money with a view to augmenting household assets. By contrast, any benefit from male borrowing is directed more towards asset accumulation than towards short-term consumption. If this interpretation is valid, the earlier observation on the gender-differentiated effect of poverty needs to be seen in a different light. The real difference in female and male borrowing is not that the former is effective in reducing poverty while the latter is not, but that they work over different time horizons – female borrowing helps raise the living standard of the household more in the shorter run, while male borrowing secures more in terms of the longer-run viability of the household.

7.5 Findings from a study based on quasi-panel data

In 2010, the InM in Dhaka conducted a large-scale rural survey covering 6,300 households from 180 villages spread over all the districts of Bangladesh (except Rangamati). In our previous discussions in Chapters 2 and 3, we have extensively referred to this survey as *InM Poverty Dynamics Survey 2010*. The sample was drawn with a stratified random sampling procedure very similar to the one used by the Bangladesh Bureau of Statistics for its *Household Income and Expenditure Surveys*, and the sample size was very similar too. This was meant to be a benchmark survey for a longitudinal study on the dynamics of poverty in rural Bangladesh, and for this purpose a panel data set was to be created by re-surveying the same households at regular intervals. However, the benchmark survey of 2010 was designed in such a way that the spirit of a longitudinal study could be captured, to some extent. For this purpose, information was collected, on a recall basis, about the land and non-land physical assets owned by each household at the time it was formed – through inheritance or otherwise. A comparison of those initial assets with the current ones could give some clue as to the life trajectories of the households, revealing the manner in which different households had moved up or down the asset ladder. It is this longitudinal information on asset transition that gives this survey a quasi-panel character. The fact that this is a large, nationally representative survey, with a quasi-panel character, makes it especially suitable for assessing the impact of microcredit in rural Bangladesh. This section presents some of the salient findings derived from this survey.[24]

Before presenting the findings, some remarks are in order on the methods used to deal with the potential problem of endogeneity bias. As discussed in section 7.1, the standard view in the literature is that endogeneity of the microcredit variable may arise in at least two ways: namely, programme placement bias and self-selection bias. In our case, we have little to worry about programme placement bias, for two reasons. First, while this particular source of bias may have been a genuine problem in the early days of microcredit, when the MFIs were still trying to establish themselves, it can hardly be an issue at present, as microcredit has by now penetrated almost every nook and cranny of rural Bangladesh. For instance, we find that MFIs have reached out to all 180 villages which were chosen randomly at the first stage of the two-stage stratified random sampling. Second, our estimating equations include among its regressors several locational variables – at village and district levels – which should be enough to control for any residual locational effects.

The second source of endogeneity, i.e. the self-selection problem, cannot be ruled out, but it is important to be clear about the nature and likely direction of this bias. Conventional wisdom suggests that the bias is likely to be upward due to a presumed superior entrepreneurial ability of borrowers (vis-à-vis non-borrowers) that remains unobserved and cannot therefore be controlled for. This presumption has generally been taken for granted and seldom subjected to empirical testing. There are, however, good reasons to question the validity of this presumption in the current state of the microcredit sector in Bangladesh.

First, when the reach of microcredit spreads as widely as it has in rural Bangladesh, covering nearly 60 percent of households, it is hard to argue that it is taken up only by those with a special entrepreneurial talent. Moreover, our survey reveals that a large proportion of borrowers – nearly 43 percent – do not use microcredit primarily for directly productive purposes; they use it instead for the purpose of consumption smoothing, and paying for lumpy expenditures such as wedding expenses, medical treatment, etc. The argument about superior entrepreneurial ability surely doesn't apply to these cases. Second, looking at the other side of the coin, the idea that non-borrowers don't borrow (even when they have the opportunity to do so) because they lack entrepreneurial ability does not seem to be based on solid empirical grounds either. In the course of our survey, we actually asked the non-borrowers why they didn't take microcredit. Fewer than 2 percent said they were afraid that they might incur loss if they tried to do so.[25] If we take this as the measure of the proportion of non-borrowers who have little confidence in their entrepreneurial ability, this would be a very minuscule proportion indeed.[26] Taking these two points together – one related to borrowers and the other to non-borrowers – it is reasonable to question the very premise that borrowers and non-borrowers differ systematically in their entrepreneurial ability.

In short, the traditional concern with the endogeneity of the microcredit variable does not seem to carry much force in the current state of the microcredit market in rural Bangladesh. This does not, however, mean that endogeneity is not a matter of concern; it's just that the source of endogeneity and the consequent bias is likely to be very different from what has been believed so far. In fact, there are good reasons to believe that the bias would be downward, i.e. unless the methodology of estimation permits correction for endogeneity, the estimates of microcredit's impact will be *under*-estimated – not *over*-estimated as conventional wisdom holds.

This is because, contrary to conventional wisdom, borrowers are drawn from the relatively more disadvantaged segment of the population (Table 7.1). In particular, as compared with non-borrowers, borrowers as a group are found to have lower initial endowments in terms of inherited land and non-land physical assets and also the educational level of the household head. The initial disadvantage is further accentuated later in life, as borrowers are found to access significantly lower amount of remittance income – both domestic and foreign – as well as support from social safety net programmes. On top of all this, they are also found to

Table 7.1 Comparison of some characteristics of microcredit borrowers and non-borrowers in rural Bangladesh: 2010

Characteristics	Borrower	Non-borrower	|t-value|
Initial land asset (decimal)	45	94	14.2
Initial non-land physical asset ('000 taka)	42.2	120.6	2.5
Education of household head (years of schooling)	3.1	4.4	12.2
Foreign remittance income (taka/capita/year)	1752	7419	11.4
Domestic remittance income (taka/capita/year)	1055	2813	5.5
Dependency ratio (percentage)	33.2	28.0	9.3

Source: Adapted from Osmani *et al.* (2015), Table 8.10, p.171.

Notes:
(1) Initial non-land physical assets are valued at 2010 prices, using the official deflator for private capital formation.
(2) The dependency ratio is defined as the number of dependants (number of household members who are not in the working-age group) divided by household size.

be burdened with a higher dependency ratio. In short, borrowers in general come from a relatively disadvantaged background compared to non-borrowers.[27] Since these disadvantages may well have a bearing on their living standards as well, and since it may not be possible to capture all the multifarious dimensions of their disadvantage as regressors in the estimating equations, the error term might end up capturing some of the missing dimensions.[28] This will then induce a correlation between the error term and the microcredit participation variable, thereby creating an endogeneity bias – in the downward direction.[29]

A variety of methods were used to correct for endogeneity, depending on the outcome variable of interest. A common element in all of them was the use of an instrument for the microcredit participation variable. The chosen instrument was the spread of microcredit within a village, i.e. the proportion of households taking microcredit within the village in which a particular household resides.[30] There is wide variation in this proportion, with a minimum of 5 percent and maximum of 97 percent around a mean of 52 percent. The relevance of this instrument derives from the idea of the neighbourhood effect or the demonstration effect – a household is more likely to join a microcredit programme if many of its neighbours are found to have already joined it.[31] At the same time, the chosen instrument can be considered to be exogenous to the outcome variables, once the village-level heterogeneities were controlled for by using regressors to reflect a number of village characteristics as well as a set of district dummies in the estimating equations.[32] The endogeneity-corrected estimates of microcredit's impact in rural Bangladesh were obtained for a number of outcomes – namely, ownership of assets, ability to cope with shocks, income and poverty (as measured by the household's consumption level relative to a poverty line).

200 Economic impact of microcredit

The impact on assets was judged by looking at the change from initial asset-holding (i.e. the amount of assets held at the time the households were formed). Since different households were formed at different times, it would not make much sense to compare the actual changes (even after correcting for inflation) – in either absolute or relative terms. In order to get a comparable picture, the households were classified into quintile groups in terms of the amount of assets held. This grouping was done both for the initial period (when households were formed) and the current period (the survey year of 2010). The households that moved up from lower to higher quintiles over time were classified as movers, and those who moved down the ladders were classified as fallers.[33] The impact of microcredit on the probabilities of being a mover and a faller was then estimated. The results are presented in Table 7.2, separately for borrowers who used loans mainly for productive purposes and borrowers who used it mainly for non-productive purposes, and also separately for the transition in land assets and non-land physical assets.

Access to microcredit has evidently helped achieve successful transitions in asset ownership. For both groups of borrowers, microcredit reduced the probability of falling and increased the probability of moving in terms of land assets compared to non-borrowers. As for the probability of transition in non-land physical assets, the evidence is slightly mixed. The beneficial impact on productive borrowers is quite clear, but for non-productive borrowers, the effect is not statistically significant even though the magnitudes of the estimated effects are quite large.

In order to assess the impact on the household's ability to cope with shocks, two types of coping strategies were considered – namely, erosive coping, in which a household was obliged to part with some assets, and non-erosive coping, in which assets remained intact. The logic of making this distinction is that those who were

Table 7.2 Marginal effect of microcredit on asset transition by user category

Dependent variable	Change in the probability of falling (%)		Change in the probability of moving up (%)	
	Mainly productive user	*Mainly non-productive user*	*Mainly productive user*	*Mainly non-productive user*
Transition in land asset	−11.8	−10.4	8.6	7.0
Transition in non-land physical assets	−36.1	(−20.5)	33.7	(18.2)

Source: Adapted from Osmani *et al.* (2015), Table 4.25, p.89.

Notes: Microcredit was entered as a binary variable, with a value of 1 for those who took microcredit in the three years preceding the survey, and 0 otherwise. The marginal effects are based on an ordered probit regression with a correction for the endogeneity of the microcredit regressor. A number of household-level and village-level characteristics, as well as a set of district dummies, were used as controls. The figures in parentheses are not statistically significant; the rest are.

able to rely mainly on non-erosive coping can be judged to have coped with shocks better; contrariwise, those who had a higher propensity to adopt erosive coping can be said to have coped worse. Microcredit's impact on the household's propensity to adopt erosive coping was then estimated. The results are presented in Table 7.3, again separately for (mainly) productive and (mainly) non-productive borrowers. Both types of borrowers were found to have a lower propensity to adopt erosive strategies in comparison with non-borrowers, although as can be expected, the difference is slightly more pronounced for productive borrowers. Thus, productive users are, on the average, 8 percentage points less likely to adopt erosive strategies than non-borrowers, while non-productive users are about 7 percentage points less likely to do so.

This finding has profound implications for understanding the impact of microcredit on the dynamics of poverty in rural Bangladesh. Since both productive and non-productive borrowers were able to cope with a crisis better by staving off erosive coping with the help of microcredit, they were also better able to preserve the precious little assets they own in comparison with non-borrowers. This is what explains, at least in part, the relationship between microcredit and asset transition discussed above. It is not being suggested that it is through the coping channel alone that microcredit has enabled borrowers to enjoy a more successful asset transition. To the extent that productive users of microcredit are able to augment their assets – either directly by investing in business assets or indirectly by acquiring new assets with the help of higher income – they would be expected to have a successful asset transition, independently of their ability to cope with shocks better. However, the fact that even the non-productive borrowers had a more successful asset transition compared to non-borrowers must owe itself to their ability to avoid erosive coping better, thanks to access to microcredit.

As can be seen from Table 7.4, greater success in asset transition also resulted in greater ability to earn income. On the average, access to microcredit enabled borrowers to earn a 44 percent higher income than non-borrowers, after controlling

Table 7.3 Marginal impact of microcredit on the propensity to adopt erosive coping by user category (percentage change in probability)

	Marginal effect	*t-statistic*
All borrowers	−7.7	2.96
Productive borrowers	−8.0	2.55
Non-productive borrowers	−6.7	2.19

Source: Adapted from Osmani *et al.* (2015), Table 6.13, p.134.

Notes: Microcredit was entered as a binary variable, with a value of 1 for those who took microcredit in the three years preceding the survey, and 0 otherwise. The marginal effects are based on a probit regression, without correction for the endogeneity since tests for endogeneity showed that the null of exogeneity could not be rejected. A number of household-level and village-level characteristics, as well as a set of district dummies, were used as controls. All figures quoted in the table are statistically significant.

Table 7.4 Coefficient of microcredit in regressions on household income

Income Regression for	Coefficient	t-statistics
All borrowers versus non-borrowers	0.442	3.8
Productive borrowers versus non-borrowers	0.487	4.1
Non-productive borrowers versus non-borrowers	0.347	2.4

Source: Adapted from Osmani *et al.* (2015), Table 8.27, p.196.

Note: The dependent variable is the logarithm of per capita income. Microcredit was entered as a binary variable, with a value of 1 for those who took microcredit in the three years preceding the survey, and 0 otherwise. A number of household-level and village-level characteristics, as well as a set of district dummies, were used as controls. The results are based on a treatment effect model that corrects for the endogeneity of microcredit by using an instrument. All coefficients quoted above are statistically significant.

for other determinants of income and correcting for endogeneity.[34] Furthermore, microcredit was found to enable not just productive borrowers, but also the non-productive borrowers, to raise their incomes in comparison with non-borrowers, although less so than the productive borrowers. The better performance of non-productive borrowers relative to non-borrowers may seem somewhat surprising at first sight, but the puzzle is soon resolved once one recalls, from an earlier discussion, how microcredit has enabled even non-productive borrowers to improve their asset base better in comparison with non-borrowers, primarily by enabling them to cope better with periodic crises without sacrificing assets. Non-productive borrowers may not be able to accumulate assets as much as productive borrowers, but at least they are able to preserve their assets better than non-borrowers, and it is this preservation of the asset base that enables them to improve their income level in comparison with non-borrowers.[35]

As can be expected, microcredit's ability to raise household income also translates into its ability to reduce poverty. Table 7.5 presents the marginal effects of microcredit on the probability of being poor and the probability of being extremely poor. In order to put the figures into perspective, the table also includes the marginal effects of remittance income (both foreign and domestic), which, along with microcredit, has been playing a major role in shaping the rural economy of Bangladesh. The figures show that, after controlling for confounding factors and correcting for endogeneity, microcredit reduces the probability of being poor by about 21 percent and the probability of being extremely poor by about 12 percent. Evidently, the poverty-reducing effect of microcredit is not confined only to the better off among the poor, but also to the bottom end of the spectrum.[36] The impact of microcredit is also stronger than that of remittance income – especially domestic remittance.

By combining the estimates of marginal effects on poverty – which represents the effect on an average household – with information on the proportion of rural households who have taken microcredit, it is possible to address a question that is often asked: how far has microcredit succeeded in reducing poverty in rural Bangladesh? That is, by how much has the overall rate of poverty declined as a

Table 7.5 Marginal effects of microcredit and remittance income on the probability of being poor and extremely poor in rural Bangladesh: 2010 (percentage change in probability)

Explanatory variables	Poor	Extremely poor
Participation in microcredit	−21.2	−12.0
Access to foreign remittance	−20.0	−8.8
Access to domestic remittance	−9.8	−4.0

Source: Adapted from Osmani *et al.* (2015), Table 8.24, p.190.

Note: Microcredit was entered as a binary variable, with a value of 1 for those who took microcredit in the three years preceding the survey, and 0 otherwise. The remittance variable was also binary. The estimates were obtained by using a bivariate probit model, and by instrumenting the microcredit participation variable, to correct for endogeneity. A number of household-level and village-level characteristics, as well as a set of district dummies, were used as controls. All the coefficients quoted in the table are statistically significant.

result of microcredit? One way of answering this question is to compare between two alternative scenarios – the first scenario is the actual situation, with a certain proportion of rural households taking microcredit in rural Bangladesh (as of, say, 2010, the survey year), and the second is a counterfactual scenario, in which nobody has taken microcredit but all the exogenous characteristics of the households are exactly the same as in the actual scenario. If one then calculates the counterfactual poverty rate – i.e. the poverty rate that would have obtained in the counterfactual scenario – and compares it with the actual poverty rate, it would be possible to measure the effect of microcredit on aggregate poverty. Such a comparison shows that, in the absence of microcredit, rural poverty would have been 46 percent in 2010 instead of 33 percent, the actual poverty rate.[37] In other words, microcredit has helped reduce rural poverty by 28.5 percent from the level that would have obtained in its absence.[38] For comparison, a similar exercise shows that, in the absence of foreign remittance, rural poverty would have been 12.4 percent lower, and in the absence of domestic remittance, poverty would have been 7 percent lower than it actually was in 2010, other things remaining the same. Thus, microcredit appears to have been a much more potent force towards poverty reduction than either type of remittance (Osmani *et al.*, 2015, p.193).

A couple of caveats should, however, be borne in mind while interpreting these results. First, the estimates do not take into account the spillover effects or the general equilibrium effects of microcredit, concentrating instead only on the direct benefits accruing to the borrowers. Second, even for the direct benefit, they measure the contribution only partially by defining benefit as the number of borrowers who crossed the poverty line with the help of microcredit, ignoring the benefit to those who remained below the poverty line and yet enjoyed a higher income and consumption because of microcredit. The figures presented here should, therefore, be regarded as underestimating the true contribution of microcredit towards poverty reduction in rural Bangladesh.

7.6 Concluding observations

The review of the evidence presented in this chapter points to an overwhelming consensus that microcredit has made a positive contribution towards improving the living conditions of the rural poor in Bangladesh. A number of interesting aspects of this contribution that have emerged in the course of the review are worth recalling: (a) while the benefits of microcredit accrue to the borrowers generally, the extreme poor among them gain the most; (b) female borrowing has a stronger short-run impact on the economic well-being of the household compared to male borrowing, but male borrowing appears to have a stronger impact in the long run through the accumulation of assets; (c) while in many cases debts have also increased along with assets, this has not, on the whole, led to an unsustainable debt burden, as asset growth has outstripped the growth of debt – with the result that, on the average, the net worth of the borrowers has improved relative to non-borrowers and the debt-asset ratio has declined; (d) the longer the duration of participation, the stronger is the positive impact of credit; (e) the extent and nature of benefit vary depending on the use of credit, but there is no basis for the popular perception that sustainable benefits accrue only when credit is used for productive purposes; and (f) microcredit has enabled the vast majority of borrowers to strengthen the long-term economic viability of their households by expanding their asset base and by helping them to preserve assets in the face of periodic crises.

That microcredit should benefit the rural poor should not come as a surprise. Indeed, it's a surprise that anyone should have thought otherwise, especially when one recalls the old gory tales of how 'unscrupulous' moneylenders used to suck the blood out of their hapless victims; the sad tales of how banks closed their doors to the 'uncultured' village folk, whose needs for loans were too small to be worth bothering about; and the sordid tales of how subsidised government credit was cornered by the rural elite, leaving the poor permanently ensconced in the stranglehold of moneylenders. Microcredit changed all that. For the first time, the rural poor had genuine access to credit and at rates of interest far below what they had traditionally been charged by moneylenders. If the pre-existing scenario of non-availability of credit at affordable rates of interest was deleterious to the interest of the poor, as it was almost universally believed to be at the time, simple logic suggests that the new scenario opened up by the advent of microcredit should, by implication, also be believed equally universally to be advantageous for them. But that is far from being the case. On the contrary, a climate of opinion seems to have emerged in recent times which is at best agnostic and at worst hostile to the idea that microcredit helps the poor. At least two strands of thought have contributed to the emergence of this counter-intuitive attitude towards microcredit. The source of one of these strands lies in academia, and the other in the perception of a section of social activists.

The academic strand has its origin in recent debates among social scientists on the relative merits of non-experimental and experimental data as the basis for evaluating the impact of policy interventions. Until very recently, non-experimental data has been the primary basis for impact evaluation in social science, including economics. In the specific context of microcredit, the classic study by Pitt and Khandker (1998) used to be widely regarded as embodying the pinnacle of sophistication in extracting causal relationship from non-experimental data. As we have seen, however, its reputation was seriously threatened by persistent attacks from various corners. The central message of the study that microcredit helps the poor began to seem vacuous, which led to the nihilist view that if a sophisticated study such as this cannot demonstrate the effectiveness of microcredit, why should anyone give credence to the claim that microcredit works. At about the same time, a small number of experimental studies began to emerge using RCTs, which claimed not to find any appreciable impact of microcredit on the income and expenditure of the poor. The great merit of an RCT is that it neatly solves the identification problem by the very simple device of randomly assigning the intervention to one sample and denying it to another, so that no selection problems can arise to complicate the assessment of causality. Since this apparently sure-shot solution to the identification problem could not find any causal impact of microcredit, it served to tilt the balance of opinion decisively in favour of the nihilist view about the efficacy of microcredit.

But, as we have seen, the reports of the death of microcredit were grossly exaggerated! Neither the attacks on Pitt and Khandker nor the evidence adduced by RCTs justify the nihilist position. As our brief technical review of the Pitt-Khandker controversy has sought to demonstrate, their central message still survives, although the magnitude of the impact they claimed to find seems less plausible today. As for RCTs, our review confirms that its main limitation is that, by the very nature of the enterprise, it can only investigate relatively short-run effects of an intervention, mainly because continuing to deny the intervention to the control group for a long time raises a whole host of ethical and practical issues. And yet, as we have seen, a number of panel data studies have demonstrated that the benefit of microfinance rises with the length of participation; so it is entirely plausible that RCTs will fail to detect the effect, even if it exists. On this ground alone, the evidence produced by the panel studies (as well as the quasi-panel study discussed in section 7.5) in support of the efficacy of microcredit is much more credible despite the theoretical superiority of RCTs in resolving the identification problem.

The strand of scepticism that emanates from the camp of social activists has mainly to do with the interest rates charged by the MFIs. Although these rates are well below the ones traditionally charged by moneylenders, there is a widespread perception that the rates are not low enough to serve the best interests of poor borrowers. It is somewhat ironic that the allegations of excessively high interest rates should be heard in Bangladesh, where the interest rates charged by the MFIs happen to be among the lowest in the world. The biggest irony of all is the allegation of 'blood-sucking' being levelled against the Grameen Bank (and its founder), which actually charges the lowest interest rate among all the large-scale MFIs in the world. Evidently, there is more politics than economics in the more outlandish allegations, but there are some genuine economic concerns as well.

The issues of genuine concern are best distinguished by the nature of the use of credit. For the credit that is used mainly for productive purposes, the major concern is: do the borrowers generally earn a high enough rate of return to be able to pay an interest that is well above those charged by commercial banks to their clients in the formal sector of the economy? And for credit that is used mainly for non-productive purposes, the main question is: since the borrowers are not earning any extra income by investing the loan, how can they repay it at such a high interest without getting into a cycle of debt? These questions are perfectly legitimate, and more research needs to be done to answer them fully satisfactorily. But some tentative answers can already be given from the existing stock of knowledge.

Estimates of rates of return earned by productive borrowers derived independently by Khandker et al. (2013) and Osmani et al. (2015), using different data sources, show that, for the overwhelming majority of borrowers, rates of return are well above the interest rates typically charged by the MFIs. The average rates of return are in the range of 60 to 70 percent, while interest rates are currently below 30 percent. As for non-productive uses, the first point that needs to be clarified is that such uses should not be scoffed at as either wasteful or necessarily harmful for the borrowers. Not everybody needs credit for productive purposes. Credit is essentially a means of correcting the mismatch between the flow of needs and the flow of cash (or liquidity). This mismatch can happen in the spheres of both production and consumption. For some people, meeting the mismatch in the sphere of production is the priority; for others, it is consumption. Neither can claim any moral or economic superiority over the other. Millions of people around the world routinely take loans from the formal banking system to correct for a mismatch in their sphere of consumption. There is no justification for denying this privilege to the rural poor. The only relevant question is whether, on the whole, they can manage the cash flow well enough so that they can repay the loan without falling into a debt trap. Anyone who doubts that they can should read the book entitled *Portfolios of the Poor* (Collins et al., 2009) which documents in great detail, from carefully collected data from many different parts of the world, how intelligently most poor people manage their finances, even though their cash flow patterns are often highly complicated because of the multiple occupations pursued by the household. At the same time, it is the overlapping cash flows emanating from multiple occupations that allow poor people to repay their loans in regular instalments, even though no income may be earned from the loans taken. No doubt some households occasionally fail to manage loans properly and get into trouble as a result, but the same thing happens to households in richer parts of the world as well. But the evidence presented in Khandker and Samad (2013) and Osmani et al. (2015) show that there is no basis for the view that the debt trap is a problem for but a tiny minority of borrowers.

Thus, neither the findings of experimental studies nor the negative perception about interest rates that prevails in some quarters can detract from the value of the cumulative evidence presented in this chapter, which shows that microcredit has helped the rural poor of Bangladesh in a significant way. At the same time, we should caution that there is no justification for making sky-high claims about the potency of microcredit. Microcredit is but one of many ingredients that must come together to enable poor people to transform their lives – microcredit alone cannot bring about this transformation on a grand scale.

The discourse on microcredit should move on. Instead of taking rigid positions on the efficacy of microcredit in general, the protagonists should focus attention on the details of how microcredit can be made more useful for the poor – for example, by altering the terms and conditions of loans, by improving the efficiency of MFIs, and by exploring the means of complementing credit with other microfinance services, such as savings and insurance, as well as non-credit services. The dividends from such a shift in discourse should be highly rewarding.

One particular issue deserves special attention in this context – namely, that of microenterprises. We have argued before that in view of the widespread outreach of microcredit in Bangladesh and the pattern of actual loan use, entrepreneurial ability cannot be a particularly important deciding factor behind participation (contrary to the prevalent belief amongst most researchers on microcredit). But such ability is indeed hidden among a small proportion of borrowers who demonstrate their ability through their actual use of loans over a period and graduate into "microenterprise loans" to become small entrepreneurs, who in turn employ other workers. (They currently constitute about 8 percent of all borrowers – a large number in absolute terms.) While for most of the mainstream borrowers, microcredit provides supplementary household income by enabling them to pursue multiple occupations (until they graduate from poverty through routes other than microcredit-enabled self-employment), these graduate borrowers are those about whom we hear anecdotal success stories. Microcredit thus provides the breeding ground for small entrepreneurship; without the mainstream microcredit, this hidden entrepreneurial ability could have remained unutilised. At the same time, however, the question arises whether the traditional mode of microcredit delivery would suffice to serve their interest once they do graduate into microenterprises. How best to serve this small but dynamic group of genuine entrepreneurs remains one of the major unresolved issues, both in the theory and practice of microfinance.[39] Perhaps some RCTs could be conducted with alternative models of delivery to find out which ones suit these entrepreneurs the best. Such narrowly focussed experiments on borrowers with proven entrepreneurial ability have a much better chance of providing useful ideas for action than the generalised experiments of the kind that has been conducted so far with very little reward.

Notes

1 The presumption of an 'upward' bias is a crucial element in this argument. For, even if the causal effect of credit could not be 'identified' but there were reasons to believe that any endogeneity bias can only be 'downward', the evidence of higher income of borrowers could still be credibly interpreted as a positive impact of credit, because the true impact in this case is greater than the measured impact. The only problem would be that the exact magnitude of the positive impact could not be 'identified'. As we

argue below, the endogeneity bias is indeed likely to work in the downward direction, at least in the context of Bangladesh.
2   In some cases, the nature of the data may not permit any identification strategy at all, either because there is not enough exogenous variation in the endogenous variable in question, or there is not enough information in the data to extract that variation, even if it exists. In other cases, the possibility of finding a suitable strategy is limited only by the imagination and econometric skills of the analyst.
3   The Mongolian study also offered individual liability loans but to a different set of treatment areas from the ones that were offered loans based on group lending.
4   For a summary statement of the findings of all seven experiments, see IPA(2015), and for six studies excepting the Philippines, see Banerjee et al. (2015). See also Banerjee (2013).
5   In fact, contrary to the Indian study, the Mongolian study concludes that 'The results therefore suggest that it is the poorer part of the targeted population that benefits more from the microcredit intervention, independent of how it is being delivered' (Attanasio et al., 2015).
6   The point is that, when the amount of credit received is not large enough to remove the credit constraint completely in one go, the inter-temporal optimization of credit-constrained borrowers may display a sequential structure, in the following sense. While the initial credit may be used for adjustment in the inter-temporal consumption pattern – by seeking higher future utility from the consumption of durables at the cost of current consumption, subsequent rounds of credit may be used to improve overall future consumption by improving the future flow of income rather than through further sacrifice of current consumption.
7   All the figures quoted in this paragraph are based on Table 3 of Banerjee et al. (2015).
8   The similarities between the two groups in terms of most of the loan parameters, as well as developmental outcomes, may be seen as a testament to the degree of perfection to which randomization has been achieved in this experiment, but this hardly makes for a credible basis for conducting an impact evaluation.
9   This outcome is actually predicted by theory, as explained in Banerjee et al. (2015). To find the theoretical prediction being vindicated by data is perhaps, academically, the most pleasing aspect of the experiments with microcredit.
10 This is likely to be a generic problem associated with experiments with social interventions of most kinds.
11 The evidence on the delayed impact of credit is supported by Montgomery et al. (1996), who found sharp growth in productive assets for third-time borrowers compared to first-time borrowers. This finding is in contrast with that of Hossain (2002), however, who found that new borrowers were more likely to accumulate productive assets compared to the older ones. He speculated that in the initial years, when the level of capital is low and marginal productivity is high, it makes sense to accumulate in productive lines, while a declining rate of return to an increasing volume of capital induces older loanees to move towards alternative uses, such as social investments (e.g., housing, education, sanitation) as well as conspicuous consumption. Two different processes thus seem to underpin these contrasting findings. For Zaman and Montgomery et al., the driving force behind the delayed effect on productive asset accumulation is the experience and expertise that comes from learning-by-doing. In contrast, the underlying cause behind the fading effect found by Hossain is diminishing marginal productivity of capital. Both arguments seem plausible; the issue is, therefore, mainly empirical. Whether one observes a delayed or fading effect in practice would depend on the relative strengths of learning-by-doing on the one hand, and diminishing marginal productivity on the other.
12 In a set of related papers, the authors also explored the impact of microcredit on various other dimensions of household well-being and behaviour, using the same methodology and the same data set; see, for example, Khandker (1998) and Pitt et al. (1999, 2003, 2006).

13 Professor Yunus' oft-quoted remark that microcredit lifts 5 percent of borrowers out of poverty every year in rural Bangladesh is widely believed to be based on these findings.
14 For a blow-by-blow account of this prolonged debate, the interested reader may read the papers and blogs mentioned below in the order given: Pitt and Khandker (1998), Morduch (1998), Pitt (1999), Roodman and Morduch (2009), Pitt (2011a, 2011b), Roodman (2011b), Pitt (2013), Roodman (2011c, 2011d), Roodman and Morduch (2011a, 2011b), Pitt and Khandker (2012), Roodman (2012), Roodman and Morduch (2014) and Pitt (2014).
15 The switch from statistical significance in the full sample to insignificance in the sub-sample obtained on deletion of the offending outliers is not necessarily an indication of weak identification. It is possible that the significant estimates for the full sample and the insignificant estimates for the sub-sample are both robustly identified for their respective samples. There seems to be some confusion here between robustness of estimates and robustness of identification. Un-robust identification would certainly lead to un-robust estimates, but the converse implication is not necessarily true – un-robust estimates do not necessarily imply un-robust identification, since they may stem from other sources (in this case, gross outliers).
16 It may be worth noting that in their detailed critique of Roodman and Murdoch, Pitt and Khandker (2012) do not refer to this problem of outliers, even though they attempt rebuttals of almost every other point of criticism.
17 The paper did not try to find out for how long the benefit continues to accrue once a person stops borrowing.
18 The authors report that some of the significant results obtained through FE and refined FE methods seem to disappear when the DD-PSM method is used, but they attribute it to the fact that the matching process under PSM reduces the sample size too drastically to leave enough variation in the data to derive significant results.
19 The RCTs reviewed in section 7.2 also provided evidence for this type of initial belt tightening.
20 The evaluation is, therefore, strictly speaking not an assessment of the impact of credit alone but of a credit-plus intervention.
21 The first round of this panel generated the data set that Pitt and Khandker (1998) used in their pioneering study.
22 As discussed in section 7.2, this is precisely the ground on which the randomised experiments in microcredit fail.
23 Further evidence on the absence of a generalised debt trap is provided in Osmani *et al.* (2015, Chapter 8, section 8.6), using a nationally representative large-scale survey in rural Bangladesh in 2010. See also the discussion in Chapter 8 of this book.
24 All the results presented in this section are drawn from Osmani *et al.* (2015).
25 By contrast, 31 percent said the weekly repayment system didn't suit them, 20 percent said they had enough income already, 14 percent said they were opposed in principle to taking an interest-bearing loan, 8 percent said they found various conditions imposed by the lenders unacceptable, and 3 percent said the interest rate was too high.
26 It may be noted that our overall sample was drawn as a stratified random sample from all over the country so as to be representative of the entire rural population, but access to credit was not one of the stratifying variables; as such, both borrower and non-borrower samples can be taken to be representative of the country as a whole.
27 A multivariate probit analysis of who participates in microcredit programmes and who does not confirms that the participants do suffer from these disadvantages after controlling for confounding factors (Osmani *et al.*, 2015, Table 8.11, p.172). It is plausible to argue that it is because of these multi-pronged handicaps that borrowers willingly subject themselves to the rigours of microcredit (e.g. enduring the constant worry of whether they will be able to make regular repayments or face the wrath of MFI staff and the opprobrium of their peers) in the hope that this might pave the way for a better

life. In contrast, those who come from a relatively advantaged background hesitate to accept the rigours and tensions that go hand in hand with borrowing from MFIs.
28 We are assuming here that selection on unobservables is similar to selection on observables. For an application of this assumption in a method for correcting for endogeneity, see Altonji *et al.* (2005).
29 The existence of the downward bias is actually confirmed in the course of estimating the outcome equations by using methods that correct for endogeneity (Appendix A3 in Osmani *et al.*, 2015).
30 Although we took a random sample of only 35 households from each village, this proportion refers to the village as a whole, not just the 35 households included in the sample. Information on this was collected at the stage of carrying out a complete census of all households within a village prior to drawing the samples.
31 In the estimated probit equation for participation in microcredit programmes, the proportion of households taking microcredit in the village was found to be a highly significant predictor of a household's probability of participation after controlling for confounding factors (Osmani *et al.*, 2015, Table 8.11, p.172). It also passed the standard weakness of instrument tests.
32 Unlike relevance, exogeneity of the instrument could not be directly tested because the usual overidentification test could not be carried out in the absence of additional instruments. It must be emphasised, however, that in our evaluation, identification does not depend solely on the instrument. For example, for estimating microcredit's impact on poverty, we used bivariate probit, which allows for identification based on the error structure alone. The instrument was used primarily to strengthen identification.
33 It is this use of asset data for two periods of time that gives the study the character of a quasi-panel.
34 Further analysis shows that about half of this additional income comes from an enhanced supply of labour and the rest from increased productivity of labour (Osmani, 2015a).
35 It should also be noted that, owing to the fungibility of cash, an ostensibly unproductive use of credit may not actually be unproductive: at least a part of the loan that is used in an ostensibly unproductive manner may have helped augment productive activity. This, too, would help explain why even the so-called 'unproductive' borrowers can also enjoy higher levels of income compared to non-borrowers.
36 Further analysis shows that the poverty-reducing effect of microcredit is stronger for those who have a longer experience in taking microcredit and those who use it more productively (Osmani *et al.*, 2015, Table 2.86, p.194).
37 See Table 8.25 in Osmani *et al.* (2015, p.193). Two different econometric techniques were used to calculate the counterfactual poverty rate – one of them was a parametric method in which a bivariate model was used to estimate a poverty equation, and the other was a semi-parametric method called the Special Regressor method. Both approaches led to remarkably similar results. For the technical details, see Appendix A.3 in Osmani *et al.* (2015).
38 The effect on extreme poverty is even larger – about 40 percent.
39 We discuss this further in Chapter 9.

8 The patterns of loan use

The effectiveness of microcredit programmes is usually evaluated in terms of the evidence of their impact on poverty, since poverty alleviation is their professed goal. In spite of the rapidly growing and rich literature on this subject, as reviewed in Chapter 7 in the Bangladesh context, there remain many controversies and unresolved issues. Given the difficulties of impact assessment, it is therefore useful to look at the uses of microcredit loans. After all, the impact on poverty arises from the way loans are used, so that any evidence on it can provide useful insights regarding how much and in what ways the borrowers may be expected to benefit from access to microcredit.

It is not easy, however, to determine from the survey responses of borrowers the actual use of loans because of the well-known problem of the 'fungible' nature of funds in the household cash-flow management. For example, a particular expenditure reported by the survey respondent to have been used for, say, meeting marriage expenses could have been incurred anyway, irrespective of whether the loan was available or not, in which case the loan in question is not actually causing any *additional* expenditure, but in effect may only be substituting for other sources of financing. One way to resolve this problem is to ask probing questions so as to engage the survey respondents in a mental exercise about the counterfactual – as we shall see in some of the evidence discussed in this chapter. But since the loans are usually meant to meet the demand for lumpy expenditures, most of which might not be incurred without access to such loans, the usual household survey results may as well be able to capture the phenomenon to a large extent. The survey findings can at least tell us about what the borrower herself thought about how she used it, even if it may not be the exact counterfactual. Furthermore, one very useful way of obtaining insights about how access to loans affects the often intricate financial management of a poor household can be obtained by keeping diaries of all of a household's financial transactions at regular time intervals (Collins *et al.*, 2009).

8.1 Findings from household surveys

The various aspects of how borrowers use microloans can be analysed from the data of a number of nationwide surveys conducted in recent years by the Institute of Microfinance (InM) discussed in Chapter 2. Here we use data in this regard particularly from two of those surveys, namely, *InM Poverty Dynamics Survey 2010* (henceforth referred to as the *InM Poverty Survey*) and the *Survey on Social Impact of Microcredit on Gender Norms and Behaviour* (henceforth referred to as InM's *Gender Norms* survey). We combine the results of these two surveys to get different perspectives on the use of microloans.

The starting point in analysing the survey findings on loan use is to recognise the large deviations in the actual and the declared use of loans. The declared or officially recorded use represents a continuing anomaly arising from a misplaced initial expectation of the pioneers of microcredit that the poor would use loans only for income generating activities (IGAs). By contrast, the poor used their newfound access to credit as a means of managing their financial portfolios in the way that suits them best, including, of course, using loans for IGAs. Early studies on microcredit were devoted, to a great extent, to highlighting how the use of loans by the borrowers deviated from the expectation of the microcredit leaders – either in the context of critiquing microcredit (e.g. Karim, 2008) or for appreciating the benefit of using the loans for a variety of purposes (Todd, 1996). While the diversion of loans to non-IGA uses is now informally recognised and accepted by microcredit practitioners, the original stipulation on loan use is still retained, perhaps as a psychological barrier for borrowers against genuinely adverse loan usage. It is thus no more a problem in carefully designed surveys to elicit information from the respondents about the actual use of loans, although this might have been a problem in the early days of microcredit (Roodman, 2012, pp.24–9). While Table 8.1 shows the deviations of the actual form of the declared loan use as found in the *InM Poverty Survey*, similar deviations are found in the results of the other surveys that are discussed here, so that in all subsequent discussions we refer to only the findings on actual loan use.

A review of the survey findings shows that investment in IGAs is indeed the single most important broad category of the use of microcredit loans, accounting for about 40 to 60 percent of the loans.[1] The estimates of loan use may vary depending on whether these refer to the proportions of the total amount of loan or to the proportions of loans according to their main use.[2] Most of the surveys naturally focus on microcredit borrowers in rural areas, where the IGAs are found to include mainly a variety of rural non-farm activities, and also agricultural activities, including crop production, livestock and poultry rearing, and fish farming.

Besides investment in IGAs, another important category of loan use may be defined as investment in physical and human capital (henceforth referred to as non-IGA investment); this includes both addition to physical assets (mainly the construction or repair of dwelling houses, but also purchase of land, household vehicles and equipment) and augmentation of human capital (mainly by spending on education and healthcare, and sending household members abroad as wage earners). By combining investment in IGAs with non-IGA investment in physical assets and human capital into a broader category of 'productive use', it is found that this category accounts for the major share of loans – about 60 to 80 percent. The rest of the loans are mainly used for household consumption, which may include both meeting recurrent living expenses and acquisition of consumer durables. Even if the use of loans to meet household consumption needs may appear wasteful, those who use loans for these purposes may do so because it helps their financial portfolio management, such as smoothing their consumption in the face of income fluctuations or supporting their livelihood strategies in other ways (Collins et al., 2009).

The share of loans used for repaying past loans is found to be relatively small, but large enough to be a cause of some concern. Most of the loans repaid by microcredit loans are from informal sources. As discussed in Chapter 2, this phenomenon may result from borrowing from informal moneylenders to meet some emergencies in the expectation that the loan will be repaid from the next microcredit loan. While this can be part of a mechanism for the poor to cope with emergencies and livelihood shocks, it may nevertheless result, in some cases, in impoverishment and repayment difficulties. Another use of loans, not very frequent, is for meeting the marriage expenses of daughters, including the payment of dowry, which is against the social mission of the MFIs.

The findings of the *InM Poverty Survey* regarding the various aspects of the uses of microcredit loans are shown in Table 8.1, Table 8.2 and Table 8.3. This nationwide survey covered all rural areas and the tables here are based on the information collected in the survey regarding the detailed credit history of all microcredit borrowers (irrespective of whether they were currently MFI members or not); furthermore, the credit history covered the most recent three microcredit loans of each borrower along with her first three loans when she first joined a microcredit programme (Osmani et al., 2015).[3]

Table 8.1 Declared and actual uses of microcredit loans in rural Bangladesh: 2010 (percent of loan amount)

Pattern of Use	Declared	Actual
A. Income-generating activities (IGAs)	84.6	39.2
Crop agriculture	19.9	10.8
Livestock, poultry, fishery	37.6	6.7
Non-farm activities	27.1	21.7
B. Non-IGA investment	8.9	19.3
Physical assets	7.0	13.6
Human capital	1.9	5.7
C. Household consumption	0.6	24.5
D. Loan repayment	1.0	8.3
Institutional lenders (incl. MFI)	0.4	2.4
Informal lenders	0.6	5.9
E. Others	4.9	8.7
Of which, wedding/dowry	0.4	3.6
Total	100.0	100.0

Source: *InM Poverty Dynamics Survey 2010*; adapted from Osmani et al. (2015).

Notes: The data refer to microcredit loans taken in the three years preceding the survey; when a loan was used for more than one purpose, the estimates are based on the two most important uses and ignore any other uses, which were negligible anyway in terms of the amount spent.

Table 8.2 Pattern of use of microcredit loans by poverty status in rural Bangladesh: 2010 (percent of loan amount)

Pattern of use	Poor	Non-poor
A. Income-generating activities (IGAs)	30.7	42.3
Crop agriculture	9.5	11.2
Livestock, poultry, fishery	6.7	6.7
Non-farm activities	14.5	24.4
B. Non-IGA investment	16.8	20.3
Physical assets	12.2	14.1
Human capital	4.6	6.2
C. Household consumption	34.0	20.9
D. Loan repayment	10.4	7.5
Institutional lenders (incl. MFI)	2.6	2.4
Informal lenders	7.8	5.1
E. Others	8.1	9.0
Of which, wedding/dowry	4.1	3.4
Total	100.0	100.0

Source: *InM Poverty Dynamics Survey 2010*; adapted from Osmani *et al.* (2015).

Notes: Poor and non-poor households are defined according to the official poverty line income; data refer to loans taken within three years preceding the survey.

Table 8.3 Change in the pattern of use of microcredit loans by long-term borrowers in rural Bangladesh (percent of loan amount)

Pattern of use	Early loans	Recent loans
A. Income-generating activities (IGAs)	43.1	35.2
Crop agriculture	11.8	10.6
Livestock, poultry, fishery	12.0	8.9
Non-farm activities	19.3	15.7
B. Non-IGA investment	14.6	23.2
Physical assets	12.0	16.2
Human capital	2.6	7.0
C. Household consumption	33.7	18.9
D. Loan repayment	3.8	10.9
Institutional lenders (incl. MFI)	1.5	3.0
Informal lenders	2.3	7.9
E. Others	4.8	11.8
Of which, wedding/dowry	2.8	6.1
Total	100.0	100.0

Source: *InM Poverty Dynamics Survey 2010*; adapted from Osmani *et al.* (2015).

Notes: Long-term borrowers are defined as those households who first borrowed more than ten years ago and continued to be MFI members at some point in the three years preceding the survey; 'early loans' mean the first three loans (if taken more than ten years ago) and 'recent loans' mean the latest three loans of long-term borrowers (if taken in the three years preceding the survey).

The stark deviations in the actual uses of the loans from the declared ones are evident from Table 8.1. As expected, the declared use only reflects the official MFI policy of giving loans mainly for investment in IGAs and, in some cases, for house building and other uses that fall in the category of what we call non-IGA investment. Looking at actual use, these two categories of "productive use" combined together account for nearly 60 percent of the amount of loans taken by the borrowers in the three years preceding the survey.

The comparison between poor and non-poor borrowers in the pattern of their loan use is shown in Table 8.2. As may be expected, the main difference between the two groups is that the poor, compared with the non-poor, spend a lower share of their loans on IGAs and a higher share on household consumption, which may be a reflection of how the two groups use loans differently for their livelihood strategies. The poor households also spend relatively more on the repayment of old loans, but its share is still just over 10 percent (compared to less than 8 percent for the non-poor).

Next we look at whether the long-term borrowers changed their pattern of loan use with the passage of time (Table 8.3). Clearly, the pattern has undergone significant changes over time, which is important for understanding how microcredit borrowers use repeated loans during their long-standing relationship with MFIs – a topic which we discussed in Chapter 2. There seems to be a significant reallocation within the "productive use" category, with a reduced share of loan used for IGAs and a compensating increase in the category of non-IGA investment. It suggests that there may be some barriers to scaling up of the IGAs (to be discussed in detail in Chapter 9) and that the borrowers may become increasingly more experienced in using the loans as a means of lumpy spending for the augmentation of physical and human assets. An encouraging sign is a sharp decline in the share of consumption loans, but a disconcerting development is an equally sharp increase in the repayment of old loans and other unproductive uses, like marriage expenses.

Further support of the above findings comes from InM's *Gender Norms* survey mentioned earlier. This survey, which was conducted during 2011 by the InM jointly with BRAC University and the Population Council, was also based on a nationally representative sample; but for collecting detailed data on microcredit, it specifically focused on ever-married women aged 15 to 50 years who were currently members of MFIs. Furthermore, unlike the *InM Poverty Survey*, this survey excluded microcredit loans of a size over 15,000 taka, and besides the main rural household sample, it also included proportionately representative sub-samples from semi-urban and metropolitan areas (Amin and Mahmud, 2012). Table 8.4 discussed in this section and Table 8.5 and Table 8.6 discussed in the next section have been prepared by using primary data from this survey. In analysing the uses of loans, we have used the same broad categories as in the previous tables based on the *InM Poverty Survey*, with only some minor variations in the component detailed heads of loan uses.[4]

The interesting feature of loan use shown in Table 8.4 is how a second or third concurrent ('overlapping') loan is used compared to the main loan (defined as the

216 The patterns of loan use

Table 8.4 Distribution of loans, including overlapped current loans, by main use (percent of loans)

Main use	Main loan	2nd loan	3rd loan
Income-generating activities (IGAs)	58.9	53.8	52.7
Non-IGA investment	19.5	21.6	12.7
Household consumption	8.4	7.2	9.1
Loan repayment	9.9	14.1	14.5
Marriage/dowry expenses	3.4	3.3	10.9
Total	100	100	100
(Number of observations)	(2115)	(333)	(55)

Notes and source: Estimated from primary data of InM *Gender Norms Survey* of 2011 (Amin and Mahmud, 2012). Of the 2,115 current borrowers, 77 percent are from rural areas and 20 percent and 3 percent are from urban municipal areas and metropolitan areas, respectively.

first of the current overlapping loans). The estimates are based on the reported primary use of the respective loan. The share of loans used for IGAs is higher than in the previous tables, which may be partly due to the different coverage of the two surveys and also because of the likely difference between the share of the total amount of loans and the distribution by the main use of the loans. There are no large variations among the main and the overlapping loans in the pattern of loan use, which further supports the hypothesis discussed in Chapter 2, namely, that the 'overlapping' of loans arises from demand for larger-sized loans used for similar purposes rather than representing a debt trap. Compared to the main loan, however, there is some decline in the share of overlapping loans used for IGAs and some increase in the use for loan repayment, and a significant increase in the use for marriage expenses but only for the third loan.

The comparison of loan use between rural and urban households, not reported here, shows no large differences by the broad categories of uses; the use of loan for IGAs is somewhat lower in semi-urban and metropolitan areas compared to rural areas, while the reverse is true for non-IGA investment. As expected, the composition of IGAs varies among borrowers in rural and semi-urban and metropolitan areas. In another InM survey which was specifically focused on urban areas, two-fifths of the microcredit borrowers were found to use the loans for investment in IGAs, the most common among them being petty shop-keeping, hawking, business in scrap materials, tailoring, and restaurants and tea stalls (Bashar and Rashid, 2012). There is a contrast with rural IGAs in another respect: although 90 percent of the borrowers were female, only a third of them used loans in self-initiated businesses rather than depending on male family members.

8.2 The counterfactuals: with and without microcredit

As mentioned at the outset of this chapter, one way to understand the real impact of microcredit loans on the financial management of the borrower households is to ask probing questions so as to engage the survey respondents in a mental exercise about the counterfactual of what would have happened without the microcredit.

The methodology followed in InM's *Gender Norms Survey*, involving intensive interaction with the respondent female borrowers along with cross-checking of information, was suitable to elicit such answers. The respondents were asked whether they would have spent the same amount out of the loans (or less or not at all) on various categories of spending in the absence of microcredit and, if so, how they would have raised the money. While most respondents using the loans for IGAs depended on the loans for doing so, the responses of those who used the loans mainly for various non-IGA purposes gave a mixed picture, as captured in Table 8.5 and Table 8.6.

For all non-IGA items of loan use taken together, it can be seen that about one-fourth of the borrowers who used the loans for spending on such items would not have spent money at all on those items without access to microcredit – thus indicating the role of microcredit in creating entirely new demand for credit-financed spending; about half would have spent the same amount on those items anyway and the rest one-fourth would have spent a smaller amount on those items, thus indicating the role of microcredit in replacing other sources of raising money for such spending (see the last column in Table 8.5). Item-wise, most of the spending for loan repayment and marriage expenses would belong to the latter category, for which money would have to be raised anyway even without microcredit. For

Table 8.5 Distribution of microcredit borrowers using loans other than for income-generating activities (IGAs) and their distribution according to what they would have done without the loans

	Investment other than on IGA	Consumption items	Loan repayment	Marriage expenses/ dowry	Total (all non-IGA items)
Percent of borrowers using loans for the item	19.5	8.4	9.9	3.4	41.1
Of those using loans for the item (in %):					
Would not have spent money on the item if loan was not available	28.9	45.2	9.6	4.2	25.2
Would have spent less	22.1	26.6	29.7	16.7	24.6
Would have spent the same	49.0	28.2	60.8	79.2	50.2
Total	100	100	100	100	100

Source: Estimated from the primary data of InM's *Gender Norms Survey* of 2011 (Amin and Mahmud, 2012).

Notes: This table is with respect to 870 borrowers who used their loans for non-IGA items out of a total of 2,115 borrowers. It refers to the main use of the current first loans in the case of more than one concurrent loan.

218 The patterns of loan use

Table 8.6 Distribution of borrowers using microcredit on non-IGA items according to how they would have raised the money for the spending without microcredit (percent of borrowers)

	Investment other than on IGA	Consumption items	Loan repayment	Marriage expenses/ dowry	Total (all non-IGA items)
Would not have spent money on the item if loan was not available	28.9	45.2	9.6	4.2	25.2
Would have spent the same or less using alternative sources:					
Loan from relatives	29.4	16.9	18.2	58.3	26.1
Loan from money lender	14.3	7.9	22.5	20.8	16.0
Sale/mortgage of land	3.6	1.7	5.7	5.6	3.9
Sale/mortgage of other assets	5.3	3.4	5.3	4.2	5.1
Working as wage labour	4.1	4.5	9.1	4.2	5.5
Household income/ savings	14.3	20.3	29.7	2.8	18.1
Total	100	100	100	100	100

Notes and source: Same as in Table 8.5.

non-IGA investment and household consumption, it is a mixed picture, with both the roles of microcredit being seen to be equally important.

More insight can be gained by looking at the way the money would have been raised from other sources if the spending had to be made even without microcredit (Table 8.6). Resorting to the informal credit market seems to be the main alternative for these borrowers, but there are worse alternatives, like the sale or mortgage of land and other assets. Even when loans from relatives serve as an alternative to microcredit, these are likely to be of a commercial type and costlier than microcredit, since microcredit was obviously the first choice of the survey respondents. Another important alternative source for the spending would be savings from household income. Such saving can happen under distress, as is likely the case for the repayment of old loans; or it can represent a situation in which microcredit replaces otherwise desirable normal household saving, which can very well be the case when the microcredit loan is used for non-IGA investment and consumer durables (included in the household consumption category). These later groups of borrowers account for 14 percent and 30 percent in the categories of non-IGA investment and household consumption, respectively, and together they constitute about 5 percent of the total sample of microcredit borrowers. There is thus a risk, although a small one, that access to microcredit may induce the borrowers to spend by borrowing rather than saving.[5]

When microcredit is used to meet household consumption needs, in the majority of cases it is likely to be for coping with livelihood vulnerabilities, since the alternatives to microcredit are informal borrowing from relatives and moneylenders or asset sales or working extra time as wage labour (Table 8.6).[6] Microcredit may not be an option to cope with severe livelihood shocks from which early recovery is not possible by borrowing alone, such as in the case of debilitating illness of the household income earner. But empirical evidence suggests that microcredit can help in a variety of common livelihood shocks, such as crop losses due to floods, loss of productive assets due to theft, the death of poultry and livestock, and the health problems of household members (Zaman, 1999; Osmani *et al.*, 2015). But this may require some rescheduling of weekly instalments or providing a second loan, which is difficult under the usual lending modalities of MFIs. As discussed in Chapter 3, MFIs find it difficult to meet the credit needs of individual borrowers facing idiosyncratic shocks, but they can sometimes introduce rule-based flexibility in their lending modalities, such as in the case of a 'flexible loan' under Grameen II. There is also a remarkable record of the microcredit programmes in Bangladesh handling the crisis in the aftermath of the devastating floods in 1998, when a concerted effort was made by the MFIs to support their clients and restore their livelihoods. At the same time, MFIs face a dilemma in helping their clients cope with the kind of shocks that could be more appropriately managed by the government's social safety net programmes.

There is, however, no such dilemma for the socially oriented MFIs regarding whether their loans should directly or indirectly be used for such practices as giving dowry for a daughter's marriage. Although such expenses seem to be incurred irrespective of whether microcredit loans are available or not (Table 8.6), MFIs would not want to be seen to promote such practices. In rural Bangladesh, dowry is often regarded as a means of social mobility and status in the kinship-based hierarchy, and parents can see it as a "good investment" for their daughter's well-being (e.g. Collins *et al.*, 2009, p.106). Some village studies in Bangladesh conducted in the 1990s observed a rapid increase in dowry spending over the previous decade. As the author of one such study commented: 'despite the repeated weekly vows against dowry by Grameen Bank members (one of their 16 decisions), the poor have only adopted their own indicator of social and economic mobility by practicing dowry' (Kamal, 2000).

As for the respondents in the InM *Gender Norms Survey* who said that they would not have spent money on the non-IGA items without microcredit, they were asked further why they had used the loans for that spending. For both non-IGA investment and household consumption, the main reason cited was the facility of repaying credit in instalments. This supports the hypothesis that one of the reasons for the attractiveness of microcredit is that the repayment system helps the poor to overcome the self-control issues underlying their saving problems by committing, in effect, to save – in the form of payment of weekly instalments out of their regular household income (e.g. Bauer *et al.*, 2012). The ease of accessing funds through microcredit was also cited as a reason; but there was very little importance given to 'future plan implemented early', which was meant to reflect the time discount factor. Interestingly, there was no evidence of the borrowers being induced by microcredit to spend out of 'temptation', which is a complaint sometimes made by the critiques of microcredit.[7]

8.3 Why borrow and not save?

The popularity of microcredit often presents a puzzle: if the potential benefits from borrowing are so large, why do households not save their way out of credit constraints? The answer to this puzzle is sought in the various saving difficulties faced by the poor, namely, the difficulty of keeping cash in hand along with the lack of access to institutional saving facilities, very high time preference, and the lack of foresight and inability to plan for the future in an environment of uncertain livelihood prospects. Given these saving difficulties, the pioneers of microcredit expected that the poor could use the loans as business capital, which would not only raise their income but also gradually bring them out of poverty through the reinvestment of profits and scaling up of the business enterprise.

In reality, while a large proportion of microcredit loans were indeed used as business capital, they mostly helped to provide a source of household income but did not lead to the accumulation of capital or the scaling up of businesses as expected (see the discussion in Chapter 9). The loans are typically used as business working capital, which often gets depleted during the one-year loan cycle, at the end of which fresh capital is infused through another loan. As we discussed in Chapter 2, the reason that the poor do not often use the loans for fixed investment is that it would involve, in effect, saving an equivalent amount in the form of that fixed capital within the loan period. The accumulation of capital assets is also undermined by the diversion of the loan to non-investment purposes. While benefiting from the loans, the borrowers can thus remain dependent on microcredit in a long-run relationship with the MFIs, as we discussed in Chapter 2.

There is another strand of thinking about MFIs, namely, the question of why they do not concentrate on devising appropriate saving schemes for the poor instead of providing credit.[8] This argument has been strengthened by recent work in behavioural economics that provides a further clue to the saving difficulties of the poor by focusing on self-discipline problems; this work shows that the accumulation of money can be aided by saving devices that require regular deposits at fixed intervals and limit withdrawals (Ashraf *et al.*, 2006). Thus, the limited access to such saving mechanisms is thought to be one of the hidden challenges in the livelihoods of the poor (Collins *et al.*, 2009).

While appropriate saving instruments can help the poor to realise their saving plan, it can hardly be a substitute for meeting the credit needs of the poor. As already pointed out, microcredit loans are typically used as business working capital, which can provide additional household income but may not contribute much to capital accumulation; in other words, extra income can be generated without any saving on the part of the borrowing household.

Even more important is the fact that, compared to any innovative saving scheme, the lending modalities of MFIs can perhaps better exploit the 'commitment factor' related to the self-discipline issue in helping their clients to save (Bauer *et al.*, 2012). As we have discussed earlier in several contexts, the use of microcredit loans, say, for house construction or children's education or the purchase of a consumer durable is a way of committing to save in the form of weekly instalments out of regular household income. This commitment factor is likely to be more effective compared to a saving scheme, however innovatively devised; unlike the weekly instalments of microcredit, saving deposits are voluntary, *albeit* with withdrawal restrictions, and the benefits from the saving will be realised at a distant time.

Although MFIs in Bangladesh initially emphasised credit disbursements as their primary activity and their programmes still continue to be mainly credit-led, there has been a rapid and unabated growth of members' savings kept with the MFIs; by 2014, members' savings had grown to represent well above half the outstanding loans of MFIs (Table 2.1 in Chapter 2). Grameen Bank has been particularly successful in deposit mobilisation, with the net accumulated savings of its borrowers currently surpassing the size of its total outstanding loans to borrowers. Furthermore, as discussed in Chapter 2, the pattern of change in the deposits and withdrawals suggests that the MFI clients are increasingly using their deposits for both immediate and long-term needs. Survey findings on the saving behaviour of MFI clients support these trends in the saving behaviour observed from the macro-level data.

According to some early studies, MFI clients used to regard the compulsory savings required by the MFIs as an additional cost of borrowing, and they also resented the withdrawal restrictions, with their demand for withdrawals always exceeding the permitted limits (Meyer, 2002, Montgomery *et al.* 1996). Since then, a significant change in saving behaviour facilitated by the MFIs has been observed in several studies (Kabeer, 1998; Rahman, 1998; Wright, 1999, 2000). For example, according to the findings of one survey, the idea of saving had not been understood or thought about before the NGO-MFIs came onto the scene, and most survey respondents also denied that they saved only to get loans. For women clients, saving came to become closely identified with MFI membership, while the temptation to spend savings kept at home was repeatedly cited as a problem (Wright, 1999). The MFI clients also began to appreciate the value of the 'commitment factor' involved in keeping their savings in the limited-access deposit accounts of MFIs. Kabeer (1998) also points out a gender dimension of this commitment factor: women often try to hide and protect their savings from their husbands and other male relatives, and they are often seen to engage in what she calls 'clandestine savings'; MFIs thus give them a chance to accumulate savings.

Although the poor are often unable to save as much as they would like to do, survey findings regarding their saving motives give a clue to understanding their priorities for loan use. The most important purposes behind their proactive saving behaviour have to do with meeting unanticipated future emergencies (medical or otherwise), or defraying expenses for the marriage of their daughters or the education of their children. Although life-cycle saving for old-age security is not mentioned as a priority, children's education is perceived as a form of investment that will be repaid as support in old age. The need for investing in IGAs features as important but is ranked lower; the IGAs include investment in business, purchase of livestock, buying or leasing of land, and in some areas, defraying the cost of migration of a family member within or outside the country (Maloney and Ahmed, 1988; IFC and MicroSave, 2011, p.41).

One could ask why an MFI client who has accumulated some savings would still take fresh credit and not withdraw from her deposits. One reason is that the deposits can be used as partial collateral to take larger credit. But more importantly, the clients seem to increasingly value long-term savings, such as for children's future schooling and marriage costs – which are a kind of life-cycle savings in Bangladesh's context, as mentioned earlier. There is again a commitment factor involved here, since deposits withdrawn may be used up in coping with some crisis, or in acquiring some non-productive assets, or as business working capital that will get depleted in the way discussed earlier. The various contractual saving schemes of MFIs, such as the Deposit Pension Scheme of Grameen Bank, are in fact designed to facilitate such a commitment for long-term saving. Evidence in Bangladesh and in other countries also suggests that poor people in need of funds often choose to borrow rather than to deplete their long-term savings (Sebstad and Cohen, 2001; Fafchamps and Lund, 2003; Naponen and Kantor, 2004; Dowla and Barua, 2006, pp.127–32).

We may now come back to where we started. The divergence between the declared and actual use of a loan draws attention to an important difference in the perspectives of the lenders and the borrowers of microcredit. Traditionally, the providers of microcredit have seen themselves as non-governmental 'development' agencies, whose main mission is to help raise the living standards of the poor. That is why, from the very beginning, their main focus was on giving loans for IGAs. An additional reason for this focus was the fear that borrowers might find it difficult to repay the loans unless they generated additional income with the help of the loans. By contrast, the majority of borrowers have seen the MFIs as 'banks' more than as development agencies, and they have used their newfound access to credit as a means of managing their portfolios in the way that suits their priorities. The fact is that not everyone needs credit for generating additional income; depending on personal circumstances, other needs may get prior attention. This is immediately obvious from looking at the pattern of use of personal loans by those who have access to the formal banking system. The aptly titled book *Portfolios of the Poor* by Collins *et al.* (2009) provides detailed evidence drawn from a diverse set of developing countries, including Bangladesh, which demonstrates that the rural poor are no different in this regard from the mainstream participants in the formal credit market.

Notes

1 See also, besides the findings reported here, Collins *et al.* (2009), Bashar and Rashid (2012, p.161), Khalily (2013, pp.92–3) and Osmani *et al.* (2015, pp.173–80).
2 According to the findings of the *InM Poverty Survey*, it turns out that the vast majority of loans were used for multiple purposes; but on the average, about 90 percent of the loan

amount was used for whatever was the primary purpose, and the rest was used almost entirely for a secondary purpose, with only a negligible proportion going for third or fourth uses.
3 It was assumed that the borrower could better respond from memory recall about the details of her first three loans compared to those of loans in the intervening years.
4 For example, litigation expenses are included in the loan repayment, and acquisition of entertainment equipment is treated as a non-IGA investment rather than consumption spending, as in the previous tables.
5 This is an upper limit, since savings needed to repair a house damaged by floods can represent distress savings.
6 Household consumption includes both living expenses and the purchase of consumer durables. But it is not possible to tell from the primary survey data which part of the living expenses represents ordinary recurrent expenses and which part is for coping with livelihood vulnerabilities.
7 To elicit information on this, the list of reasons for using microcredit included a Bengali term (*shokh*) which has a connotation of temptation without sounding offensive. Banerjee *et al*. (2015) found, in their experimental study of *Spandana*, an Indian MFI, that borrowing households spent more on 'durables' such as sewing machines, and cut back on 'temptation goods' like snacks and cigarettes, in addition to opening more businesses.
8 Karlan and Appel (2011, pp.140–1), for example, point to the need for innovative approaches to helping the poor to save – 'good old-fashioned savings, like our parents and grandparents taught us'.

9 The economics of microenterprise

The avowed primary objective of microcredit programmes is to promote self-employment for the poor by supporting their income-generating activities (IGAs). The impact of microcredit on poverty alleviation, therefore, depends mainly on the profitability of microcredit-financed IGAs, their sustainability, and their prospects for scaling up. A question commonly asked is: how can the IGAs be profitable at the interest rates charged by MFIs? It is important to understand in this context how the borrower households undertake IGAs as part of their livelihood strategies, and thereby supplement their household income, along with creating self-employment opportunities for the household members. Another puzzle is that, in spite of repeated loans, only a few microcredit-financed businesses grow beyond subsistence entrepreneurship. The problems of providing large-sized loans can only partly explain this, since capital can be accumulated from repeated loans over a long time. Another hypothesis is that the rigid loan modalities prevent borrowers from undertaking profitable but risky and larger-scale enterprises. The number of the so-called 'entrepreneurial poor' among the numerous MFI clients is cited as another limiting factor. There can also be a problem of market saturation faced by the proliferation of IGAs, all producing and supplying similar kinds of products and services. The MFI leaders in Bangladesh also point to the increasing importance of the availability of suitable production and marketing technologies that can facilitate the scaling up of the IGAs into microenterprises.

Despite the limitations, the process of scaling up the IGAs has got some momentum in Bangladesh in recent years with the increasing importance of the so-called 'microenterprise loans' in the loan portfolios of particularly the large MFIs. By 2014, the number of outstanding borrowers of microenterprise loans had increased to about 10 percent of all MFI borrowers, accounting for about 27 percent of the total loan disbursements of MFIs in that year.[1] The MFIs are increasingly being inclined to play a developmental role in trying to bridge the so-called 'missing middle' in the credit market in between mainstream microcredit and commercial banking. Their social mission is extending beyond poverty alleviation *per se* to economic development, such as reflected in their changing eligibility criteria for beneficiary selection, the introduction of agricultural loans, the emphasis on microenterprise loans, and the setting up of socially oriented businesses to support the marketing of products of their clients. In this chapter, we examine some of these issues on the basis of the evidence of the profile and profitability of microcredit-financed IGAs and their scaling-up prospects, while in the next chapter we look at the potential contribution of the growth of microenterprises in the broader context of economic development.

9.1 Profitable but difficult to scale up

In order to put the empirical evidence in a proper perspective, we start with some plausible hypotheses regarding the high rates of returns to capital yielded by IGAs – *albeit* only at a subsistence level of operation – and the constraints in scaling up the IGAs. The hypothesis to start with is that, while returns to capital in subsistence-type businesses can be quite high, the potential tapers off quite fast with the increase in the scale of operation. Why? There are several reasons.

First, according to the basic neoclassical production function, returns to capital will be high with the high labour-capital ratio characterising most IGAs (unless, of course, the production technology is far too inferior to be near the production frontier).

Second, IGAs often provide supplementary family income and do not involve the main occupation of the household head. The opportunity cost of family labour for working in IGAs may be less than the market wage rate because of underemployment and the uncertainty of finding full-time work in the market for casual labour, and also because of the convenience of self-employment with the flexibility of time use (e.g. sharing the work of spinning and weaving at homestead-based handlooms among the family members in their spare time). This is particularly true for female family workers, who prefer to work within the homestead because of socio-cultural barriers and also because of the convenience of combining household maintenance work with homestead-based IGAs.

Third, IGAs are profitable at a small scale because of some advantages in resource endowment, such as borrowers' access to common property resources for free-ranging poultry or using unutilised homestead space for vegetable gardening, handloom weaving, craftwork, rearing poultry and livestock, or the safekeeping of rickshaw vans. For the same reason, the poorest find it hard to pursue such activities since they do not have enough such space within their homesteads.

Fourth, small-scale entrepreneurs have the advantage of marketing their products based on reputation and trust for quality assurance. Such personalised marketing can bypass the middlemen or intermediaries who proliferate, particularly in the markets of agricultural and informal sector products.

It is easy to see that the advantages of IGAs listed above are derived from the very small scale of the businesses. For example, when the profitability of the business is based in part on the low opportunity costs of family labour compared to the market wage rate, an expansion of the business requiring hired labour will involve a break in the size-profitability relationship. Shifting to hired labour also may be difficult because many IGAs are not only labour-intensive, but also require intensive care and personal supervision. There may be obvious scale limitations for IGAs because of the nature of the markets served, such as in the case of a roadside tea stall or a small grocery shop at the homestead that can cater for the needs of only a limited number of customers in the neighbourhood.[2] Again, IGAs may have decreasing returns to scale because of the presence of fixed factors, such as homestead space or entrepreneur time involved in the personalised marketing of products. Thus, while the profitability of IGAs can be high, it may decline sharply with an increase in the scale of the operation. Moreover, the high hidden entrepreneurial cost of such businesses in terms of time and effort explains why the better-off entrepreneurs do not find it worthwhile to capture these businesses. However, the recent rise of the profit-oriented microcredit model with a high interest rate can, in fact, be seen as an ingenious way of commercially exploiting the profits of small businesses for the benefit of MFIs' shareholders.

There still remains the question regarding why the microcredit borrowers find it difficult to expand their businesses by shifting to production and marketing technologies that are economically viable at a higher scale of operation. The answer may partly lie in a 'technology gap' or a 'missing middle' that prevents a process of gradually scaling up through an incremental change in the size of a business, but requires a quantum shift in scale and technology. The challenge for the MFIs and their 'entrepreneurial' clients is to find ways of bridging this technology gap or missing middle in innovative ways by supporting and adopting appropriate production and marketing strategies (the term 'missing middle' comes from the discussions on the credit market in Bangladesh mentioned earlier). We can illustrate this with the help of diagrams (Figures 9.1(a) and 9.1(b)). Banerjee and Duflo (2011, p.222), in a similar context, show diagrammatically how a transition can be made from a subsistence technology to a superior one, but without recognising the possibility of any such technology gap.

In Figure 9.1(a), the amount of capital invested, including both fixed and working capital, is measured along the x-axis and the rate of return to capital along the y-axis (the return is the profit net of the wage cost, including the imputed cost of unpaid family worker). Assume that loans are available at the interest rate i. The curves **A** and **C** represent different technologies: the technology represented by curve **A** is a typical IGA of microcredit borrowers described earlier. It provides very high returns to capital but has limited opportunity of profitable expansion, since the rate of return tapers off quickly. Technology C needs a minimum amount of capital investment before it reaches its potential and becomes profitable at the given interest rate. It may be noted that the shift from technology A to C implies a shift in the way production activities are carried out in terms of employment types, nature of products, production technology, scale economies and methods of marketing. We need not explicitly show labour use, but we can assume that technology C will be relatively more capital-intensive compared to technology A. Notice that for technology A, there is no minimum requirement of capital, since the activity can start with a minimal amount of working and fixed capital.

Figure 9.1(b) illustrates where the solution to the problem and the challenge for scaling up of IGAs lie. We introduce here an innovative 'bridging' technology represented by curve **B**. It is easy to see how this can help smooth an incremental transition by scaling up an IGA (curve **A**) into a 'microenterprise', and eventually

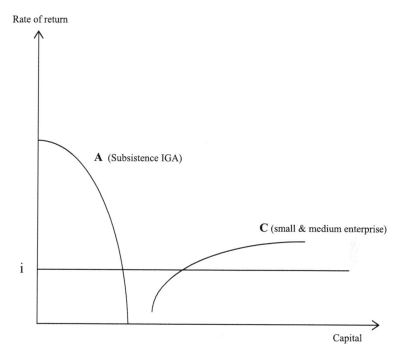

Figure 9.1a Scaling up of income-generating activities: the missing middle

even to a small or medium enterprise (curve **C**), while remaining profitable at the given interest rate. This is a topic we shall return to later in this chapter while discussing the prospects and problems of the development of microenterprises through the 'microenterprise loans' of MFIs. Here we first look at some empirical evidence regarding the prevalence of the 'technology gap'.

A study by the World Bank (1999) to examine the possibility of a separate window of MFIs for providing larger loans to 'graduate' microcredit entrepreneurs came up with results indicating a threshold minimum level of investment required for scaling up IGAs. Based on a sample survey of nearly 100,000 microcredit borrowers, the study identified two groups within those borrowers who requested larger loans: (a) those who asked for a loan amount not substantially higher beyond the existing loan ceiling of the MFIs (for example, one of the MFIs indicated that it would be able to meet most of these demands by raising its existing credit ceiling from about US$ 202 to US$ 303); and (b) a second group of borrowers who were more capable and enterprising and wanted to take bigger initiatives that would require a lot more capital than the existing ceiling – even as high as US$ 10,000 in the case of certain borrowers.[3]

The technology gap may be a reason why the MFIs find it far easier to recruit clients for their microenterprise loans through lateral entry rather than through the graduation of 'progressive' borrowers from the regular microcredit programmes,

228 *The economics of microenterprise*

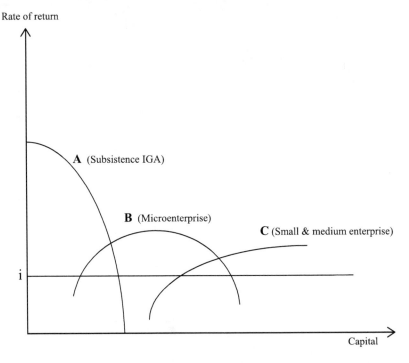

Figure 9.1b Scaling up of income-generating activities: bridging the missing middle

although the lending modalities are also a problem. We may recall from our discussion in Chapter 3 that BRAC's programme called MELA – an example of high-end lateral entry into the microenterprise programme – caters to the kind of clients who are altogether different from the regular microcredit borrowers in terms of the scale of business. PKSF's effort to promote microenterprise loans, on the other hand, got only limited response from its partner NGO-MFIs until restrictions on lateral entry were lifted. Even when microenterprise loans are given only to the 'progressive' members of the regular microcredit members and there is no quantum shift in the size of the loans, as in the case of Grameen Bank, the loan is often used in the already existing family enterprises, in which case there may not be any genuine scaling up of IGAs. The increasing incidence of overlapping loans (e.g. simultaneous loans from more than one MFI) may also be a reflection of the fact that the borrower finds it easier to invest in more than one IGA instead of applying for a larger-sized loan, which an MFI will allow only for scaling up an IGA or for expanding an existing family business.

Several past attempts by MFIs in helping their regular programme members to scale up IGAs with larger loans had failed before the recent breakthrough in their microenterprise loans took place. A specific example of a technology gap is BRAC's attempt to encourage borrowers to scale up homestead-based poultry farming; 'enterprise loans' were given to set up small-scale poultry farms that failed because of the absence of scale economies in marketing and overhead costs. It was found that commercialization even at such a small scale (e.g. poultry farms, say, with 100 poultry heads) required almost the same kind of education and training, safety measures, risk-bearing capacity and access to market as that required of larger, fully commercial enterprises. Another example is Grameen Bank's unsuccessful experiment in the mid-1980s with the 'collective loan' given to a group of borrowers; the idea was that the larger-sized loans would enable the borrowers to engage in more profitable projects compared to the usual IGAs (Alamgir, 1999a; Dowla and Barua, 2006). Grameen Bank's other unsuccessful experiment of 'leasing' equipment for progressive borrowers, mentioned in Chapter 3, was also conceived as allowing investment in more profitable larger-scale enterprises within the stipulations of credit modalities.

The problem of scaling up is also reflected in the high average returns to investment in IGAs along with relatively low marginal returns to capital as estimated by Khandker (1998). Based on a household survey – the BIDS-World Bank 1991/92 survey on microcredit mentioned in the earlier chapters – Khandker estimated marginal returns to capital (fixed and working) in rural non-farm activities by fitting a Cobb-Douglas production function to household data on inputs of land, labour and capital, along with control variables relating to various household and village characteristics. The estimates of marginal returns to capital varied from 62 percent for manufacturing to 28 percent for services, 21 percent for trading, and 8 percent for transport (Khandker, 1998, pp.3–76).[4] Moreover, the estimate was 20 percent for those borrowers of Grameen Bank and BRAC whose primary source of finance was microcredit loans (which is an indication of the subsistence scale of operation). Given the Cobb-Douglas specification of the estimated production function, these estimates of marginal returns apply at the average level of capital investment, suggesting that for many IGAs with a higher than average capital outlay, the rate would be below the interest rate charged by the MFIs, indicating that the expansion of these IGAs could have been profitable only with the low opportunity cost of family labour. Khandker's estimates of marginal rate of return also showed large differences between borrowers living in purely rural areas and those in rural towns, and also between borrowers with five or more years of programme participation compared to those with less than two years of participation. These findings, therefore, point to the possibility of a shift to higher-return activities facilitated by the growth of semi-urban areas and long-term programme participation, in which case the availability of credit rather than technology may become the dominant barrier to the scaling up of IGAs. While a technology gap does perhaps exist, there seem to be ways of bridging the gap.

There are, of course, other important constraints to business expansion, such as entrepreneurial skill, motivation and business practices, as has been found in many studies – including those based on randomised controlled trials (McKenzie and Woodruff, 2006; de Mel et al., 2010). Here, we have only highlighted a relatively overlooked aspect of the problem. The view from the practitioners is that the microcredit system has created a very large pool of capable entrepreneurs who are eager to venture into scaled-up enterprises. But scaling up microenterprises beyond the subsistence level is often difficult, short of creating a full-scale commercial venture. It is true that MFIs avoid financing start-ups and tend to be conservative in financing profitable but risky projects. But there also seems to be a threshold level of enterprise size below which economies of scale in production and marketing cannot be reaped, while the informal personalised niche market is not suitable for scaling up beyond a very small scale of operation. However, as we shall discuss later, there perhaps exists considerable unexploited potential for supporting microenterprise development through innovative schemes of marketing and product design that can reap the benefits of both subsistence-type and commercial-scale enterprises.

9.2 Profile and profitability of income-generating activities

The estimation of rate of returns to capital in the microcredit-financed IGAs is of obvious interest in order to assess the extent of benefits the borrowers derive from microcredit, and to know how the returns compare with the interest rates charged by the MFIs as well as by professional moneylenders. It is not, however, easy to estimate the rate of return from investment in IGAs made out of loans from MFIs, which is of particular interest to us. Information gathering on financial flows related to IGAs is difficult because microcredit borrowers normally do not keep a record of transactions, and also because the accounting unit is not an identifiable business but a household, where other cash flows are mixed up with those from IGAs. Another problem is that microcredit loans are usually used as working capital which may vary in size during a year and may also revolve several times in a year, depending on the length of the production cycles, so as to make it difficult to estimate the rate of return from annualised data. Yet another problem is about how to treat family labour and estimate its opportunity cost; the IGA may use family labour that would not have been utilised otherwise, but it may also divert away family labour from the wage labour market.

Based on the data on microcredit-financed IGAs with respect to 1,142 microcredit borrowers among the nationwide sample of rural households in the *InM Poverty Survey 2010*, Osmani et al. (2015, pp.181–89) arrived at some estimates of annual rates of return on total capital outlay, as presented in Table 9.1. The rate of return is defined in these estimates as net return in a year as a percentage of gross outlay, where net return is calculated by subtracting from the gross revenue all costs of production, including the imputed value of own/family labour but excluding the interest on microcredit; and gross outlay is defined as the value of assets plus the working capital used in the enterprise. The limitation of these estimates arises from the fact that the working capital was equated with the value of the annual cash expenditure incurred in running the enterprise (excluding imputed wage costs and any expenditures made for acquiring productive assets); as such, it is most likely that the working capital is overestimated and the rates of return underestimated, in so far as the same working capital is turned over more than once within a year to pay for the running costs. Thus, for IGAs

Table 9.1 Rates of return to capital by size of capital outlay in IGAs financed by microcredit in rural Bangladesh: 2010

Outlay size groups (Taka)	Proportion of enterprises (%)	Average use of microcredit (Taka)	Average size of outlay (Taka)	Average rate of return (%)
< 5,000	10.5	5,638	3,284	116.4
5,000–10,000	25.1	7,079	7,458	76.9
10,000–20,000	20.3	10,086	14,046	73.7
20,000–30,000	7.3	12,392	24,233	61.4
30,000–40,000	3.9	11,689	34,420	55.7

Source: *InM Poverty Dynamics Survey 2010.*

Notes: Based on information on the last microcredit-financed IGAs undertaken by 1,142 borrowers; outlays include both capital assets and working capital; the proportions of enterprises do not add up to 100 percent because enterprises with larger capital outlay were excluded; imputed wage costs of self-employed family members are included in operating costs (except interest on microcredit); the official exchange rate in 2010 was 1 US$ = 70 taka.

with short periods of production cycles, there may be a serious underestimation of the rates of return.

The estimates in Table 9.1 show that the typical microcredit borrower enjoys a rate of return well above the rates of interest charged by MFIs in Bangladesh, which in effective terms vary from 20 to less than 30 percent annually. Since the rate of return is net of the imputed cost of family labour, the commonly held perception that IGAs are profitable only by exploiting underutilised family labour does not have much support. The profitability estimates also thus imply that the IGAs can provide employment to family labourers at the prevailing wage rate in alternative employment and also yield an additional income net of interest payments. Moreover, the rate of return is higher for a smaller size of capital outlay, which supports the hypothesis that profitability can be very high at the subsistence scale of operation; however, in the context of Figures 9.1(A) and 9.1(B), the decline in the estimated rate of return with the size of the outlay may capture both the tapering-off of profitability beyond the subsistence scale of operation and the maintaining of enough profitability from a shift in production technology.[5] It is also important to remember that the actual rates of return can be much higher than these estimates for activities for which the working capital is used for more than one production cycle in a year. It may also be noted that the contribution of the microcredit loan as a proportion of the total capital outlay declines sharply with the increase in the size of total outlay, implying larger equity participation for large-scale enterprises.[6]

In order to take account of the turnover of working capital in activities having production cycles, a World Bank study adopted a different methodology to estimate the annual rate of return from capital outlay in respect to 105 IGAs undertaken by the borrowers of PKSF's partner MFIs (Alamgir, 1999b; World Bank, 2000).[7] The annualised returns were estimated based on the profile of costs and returns in a production cycle, along with an assumption regarding how many production cycles could be accommodated in a year; this rate of return could then be appropriately compared with the effective annual interest rate charged for the loan. However, the actual amount of profit could be smaller, because the working capital could get depleted as the loan was repaid. The estimated rate of return on investment (rate of profit) was found to be generally even much higher compared to the estimates reported by Osmani *et al.* (2015). While these estimates varied mostly in the range of 70 to 150 percent among the individual IGAs, for only six out of 105 IGAs, it was less than 30 percent – the prevailing maximum effective interest rate charged by the MFIs. Even most of these six IGAs would be profitable at this interest rate if it was assumed that the cost of family labour was zero or less than the market wage rate.

An analysis of the profile of the IGAs included in the World Bank's study shows that the actual choice of IGAs matched remarkably with what one would logically expect regarding such a choice as determined by the limitations imposed by the microcredit lending modalities along with the resource endowment of the borrower households (e.g. lack of equity and availability of family labour). For example, as we discussed in Chapter 3, it is difficult to use microcredit loans for a fixed investment, because additional capital will be needed for working capital, and also because not many activities can generate high-enough returns to pay off the investment in a year; otherwise the repayment of the loan will have to be made at least in part from savings out of the regular household income. Moreover, because of the requirement of weekly payment of instalments, activities with short turnover cycles, such as small-scale trading, are relatively more suitable as IGAs. This does not, however, exclude entirely the activities with distinct production cycles, as most farm activities are; in the case of such IGAs, households may still be able to pay the weekly instalments by flexibly managing cash flows over the year, possibly by resorting to informal sources of lending or by adjusting the non-regular parts of their household expenditures. The severity of these constraints will, of course, depend on the size of the loan in relation to the household income, which determines the capability to make the weekly payments out of savings from the regular household income.

In only 11 out of the 105 IGAs in the World Bank's study, microcredit loans were used mainly for investment in fixed capital. Even in these few cases, the loans were used, as one would expect, in activities that require little working capital, or are very labour intensive so as to provide year-long employment for an income-earning member of the family, or can yield regular income with relatively little investment. These investments in fixed capital were thus found to include setting up a small restaurant business, purchasing a rickshaw van for carrying goods or passengers, and buying such equipment as a sewing machine for tailoring, a boat and a net for open water fishing, and tools for a family business of blacksmithing. Moreover, the size of loan in most of these cases was smaller than the average for all borrowers.

The problem of using the microcredit loan for fixed investment is particularly acute for the poorer among the microcredit borrowers (Table 9.2). They are less likely to have any equity capital in the form of fixed capital, and they will have

Table 9.2 Value of fixed and working capital in microcredit-financed IGAs for three poverty categories of borrowers in rural Bangladesh: 1996

Type of household by poverty category	Fixed capital per enterprise (US$)	Working capital per enterprise (US$)	Ratio of working capital to total capital
Extreme poor	7.6	41.1	84
Moderately poor	50.8	22.1	30
Borderline poor	102.5	80.0	44

Notes and source: Based on Rahman (2000, p.57). The estimates are based on data from a village survey conducted in 1996. The taka estimates are converted to US$ terms by using the official exchange rate in 1996, US$ 1 = 41.75 taka.

less ability to generate savings from regular household income. As a result, they may have to choose activities that have low returns to labour. Moreover, returns from these activities are likely to decline rapidly so that these are conducted at a small scale (Rahman, 2000, p.57). One advantage, however, of investing in IGAs with very small fixed capital is that, in the case of failure of the enterprise, which is very common for such enterprises, the borrower can move on to invest in another IGA. A World Bank (2005) study found that rural subsistence-type entrepreneurs in fact benefit from the experience gained from failed enterprises.

One may ask, if the borrowers can often use microcredit loans for non-productive purposes so that their weekly instalment payments have to be made out of savings from their regular household income, why are they reluctant to choose projects with fixed capital investments that may in fact need additional financing from household sources to pay off the loan within a year? There are several possible answers. The borrowers vary in terms of their motivation for accessing microcredit and their capacity to pay weekly instalments, and these two aspects may be correlated (e.g. the relatively better-off borrowers may use loans more for what we term as non-IGA investment). The phenomenon of a technology gap, as discussed in the context of Figures 9.1(A) and 9.1(B), may also explain why repeated loans will not be used for the expansion of productive capacity by investing in fixed capital. But more importantly, investing in IGAs is not often the top priority behind the incentive for saving, the evidence on which was discussed in Chapter 8. If borrowers have to 'commit' to save at all through the mechanism of the weekly instalment payments, they would rather use the loans for purposes other than investing in IGAs. And when it comes to investment in IGAs, they have the option of using the loans for working capital, which can get depleted during loan repayment while also generating some extra income for the household.

9.3 Scaling up of microenterprises

The microcredit programmes in Bangladesh have recently witnessed the growth of so-called 'microenterprise loans', which are larger-sized loans and usually dispensed under a variety of lending modalities different from those that apply to regular microcredit loans. In terms of the loan size, the dividing line between regular and microenterprise loans has been in the equivalent range of US$ 500 to US$ 650, and the share of these loans in the number of all microcredit loans and in the annual total loan disbursements have increased significantly in recent years. Table 9.3 shows the status of microfinance portfolios in the lending operations of MFIs as of 2012 with separate estimates for the three largest MFIs; it can be seen that microfinance loans in that year accounted for about 29 percent of the total amount of loans disbursed and 8 percent of the outstanding number of borrowers (more appropriately, the number of loans, including overlapped loans). Since microenterprise loans represent relatively recent attempts by the MFIs at diversifying their loan products and going for larger loan sizes, these estimates represent substantial deepening of microcredit taking place over a short period of time.

Comparing the proportion of microenterprise borrowers with the proportion of loans they account for gives an idea about how large the average size of microenterprise loans is compared to the loans of the mainstream borrowers. This difference in loan size is highest for BRAC (7 times) and lowest for Grameen Bank (2 times), with ASA (5 times) and other MFIs (4 times) falling in between. This is in conformity with other information available regarding the loan size distribution for different MFIs. The differences among the MFIs regarding the size of microenterprise loans reflect the method of borrower selection for these loans. In the case of Grameen Bank, the microenterprise borrowers represent the relatively successful and progressive among the mainstream microcredit borrowers; they remain part of their regular groups under the same lending modalities with only the credit ceiling raised. In contrast, BRAC has gone for a different kind of client who enters the microcredit system laterally, without graduating from the basic microcredit model. ASA and the other MFIs allow both lateral entry as well as graduation from the ranks of regular microcredit borrowers. Lateral entry of this kind may be less targeted to the poor, but it represents a new kind of credit market in which MFIs have the potential to make inroads (the so-called 'missing middle' in the credit market).

Table 9.3 Number of current borrowers taking microenterprise loans and size of microenterprise loan portfolios of MFIs in Bangladesh: 2012

MFI	Borrowers with outstanding microenterprise loan (end-2012)		Microenterprise loans (disbursed in 2012)	
	Number of borrowers ('000)	As percent of all current borrowers	Amount of loan disbursement (million taka)	As percent of disbursement of loans of all types
Grameen Bank	1,023	13.5	31,485	26.5
BRAC	254	6.1	46,786	44.9
ASA	199	4.8	22,111	23.1
Other MFIs	581	5.8	41,475	23.1
All MFIs	2,057	7.9	141,857	28.5

Notes and Source: Estimated from *Bangladesh Microfinance Statistics 2012* (CDF, 2013).

The results of a survey carried out by the Credit and Development Forum (CDF) and reported in their annual publication *Bangladesh Microfinance Statistics* of 2013 show that the MFIs are indeed targeting the 'missing middle'. The survey defines 'graduated' microcredit members as those who have been able to access credit from commercial banks, thus transforming their enterprise into formal businesses. One of the goals behind the microenterprise loan programmes is for the programme beneficiaries to be able to achieve enterprise growth and a formal/legal status for accessing loans from formal financial institutions. As of December 2012, among the microenterprise borrowers of MFIs, about 195,000, representing 9.5 percent of such borrowers (by the number of loans), qualified as 'graduated' members as defined in the survey (CDF, 2013, p.29).

There are some concerns, even within the MFI community in Bangladesh, whether the increasing size of the microenterprise loan portfolios represents a 'mission drift' from their primary social mission of poverty alleviation through directly targeting credit to the poor. But with their increasing financial self-reliance and less dependence, if at all, on grants and subsidised funds from foreign donors (see Table 10.1), the MFIs feel less obliged to be seen to directly target the poor. Increasingly, they are finding it within the boundaries of their legitimate credit operations to promote credit-constrained small enterprises that have the potential for contributing to economic growth and employment generation for the poor. At the same time, they are also experimenting with innovative programmes to target the poorest, who tend to be excluded by the regular microcredit programmes, such as the PKSF-supported Programmed Initiatives for *Monga* Eradication (PRIME) programme of microcredit, which is specially designed to help the poor who are vulnerable to seasonal hunger and poverty (Khandker and Mahmud, 2012, pp.151–76); or BRAC's Targeting the Ultra Poor (TUP) programme, which combines a safety net and microcredit to help women in extreme poverty (Matin and Hulme, 2003). However, except for Grameen Bank, which can mobilise savings from non-members, MFIs have to consider the trade-offs in allocating funds among their various programmes in serving a range of clients from the poorest to the not-so-poor to even the non-poor.

The lending modalities of microenterprise loans are not yet well established and vary considerably across MFIs. As discussed in Chapter 3, these lending modalities can create varying degrees of limitations in the choice of microenterprises. Except in the case of Grameen Bank's microenterprise borrowers, who belong to the same groups as other borrowers, the loans are given to separate groups or to individuals, and there are various kinds of semi-legal guarantees, including in the form of minimum equity participation. The loans are given only to already established businesses, thus excluding the financing of start-ups. The maximum loan period is usually two years, and the instalment payments may be monthly instead of weekly. Although alternative pre-agreed repayment schedules are allowed, repayment by regular frequent instalments is still the dominant practice, which favours the use of loans as working capital. The concern that the loans may be concentrated too much on trading and shopkeeping is reflected in PKSF's guidelines for its partner MFIs that stipulate that at least 40 percent of the loans have to go to other uses, including farming, manufacturing and processing activities. It may be noted that ASA follows a deliberate policy of channelling at least half of microenterprise loans to businesses other than trading. The PKSF guidelines also reflect concerns about the loans going beyond the desirable target group of entrepreneurs by stipulating a maximum absolute amount of equity while also fixing a minimum equity-debt ratio as a device to address moral hazard. The existence of visible ongoing business is almost always a prerequisite for microenterprise loans, which reduces the problem of moral hazard and makes the task of monitoring less challenging for loan officers, but it also precludes supporting innovative new ventures that could contribute to the diversification of the local economy.

The case studies of individual borrowers can provide useful insights into the nature of constraints in using large-sized loans and in scaling up microenterprises. To gain such insight and provide analytical support for the microenterprise loan programmes of MFIs, the InM conducted a survey of borrowers of microenterprise loans and compiled a large number of case studies in which the stories of success were deliberately matched with those of failure (which was not easy because of the relatively few cases of failure and default).[8] The matching of the factors underlying success and failure provided a mirror-image of each other in many respects.

An entrepreneurial mindset and business acumen, and the associated motivation and hard work, were found to be the main factors underlying success, while a lack of managerial and entrepreneurial capacity was most frequently cited as the main cause of failure (InM, 2008). This finding would immediately remind one of the oft-cited problem of bias created by unobservable entrepreneurial ability in measuring the impact of microcredit, which explains the logic behind the so-called RCTs and other strategies of identification discussed in Chapter 7. One of the less appreciated contributions of the regular microcredit programmes is that they provide a breeding ground for entrepreneurship and create a large pool of would-be entrepreneurs. Those who qualify for microenterprise loans through graduation from the regular programmes do so by demonstrating their entrepreneurial ability in using increasingly larger-sized loans and expanding their businesses. The innate and unobservable abilities become visible also in the demonstrated capacity for keeping records, making business plans and using business management methods – the attributes MFIs look for in screening borrowers for microenterprise loans. Lateral entrants to microenterprise programmes, in turn, will go through a similar screening process and some among them will ultimately qualify for credit from commercial banks.

The importance of previous experience and training along with the availability of affordable technology and a supportive business environment also figured prominently as determinants of success or failure. There is some scope for confusion in this respect. Microcredit leaders, including Muhammad Yunus, often express the view that microcredit borrowers do not need to be told how to run their business. Karlan and Appel (2011, p.93) quote Yunus saying: '. . . so rather than waste our time teaching them new skills, we try to make maximum use of their existing skills'. Contrary to this view, they cite research findings showing that 'there were good business opportunities out there, but that not everyone was equally able to take advantage of them'. These apparently opposing views may both be right, but in different contexts. Yunus was referring to the 'innate survival skills' of the poor which they use to undertake IGAs and manage their meagre access to funds. The other view is about the so-called 'entrepreneurial poor' referred to in the microcredit literature who need training and a supportive business environment to complement their entrepreneurial skills.

The existence of a problem of scale or a 'technology gap' is also suggested by the findings of the survey and case studies of the borrowers of microenterprise loans. The technological disadvantage in relation to modern-sector products and the lack of economies of scale in marketing were cited as major causes of failure. Some case studies showed how an attempt to expand production with handmade products using rudimentary manual techniques met with failure. In contrast, product quality assurance achieved through improved technology and marketing was a factor underlying success. One of the success stories was about expanding a family poultry farm, with more than 500 chickens and four employed workers, which could attain a minimum threshold size required for scale economies but was still thought to remain a risky project (InM, 2008, p.41).[9]

The problem of scale economies was found to be resolved in other innovative ways. It was mentioned earlier that personalised goodwill-based marketing worked only on a limited scale within a local community. Some micro-entrepreneurs nevertheless were able to exploit this advantage on a broader scale by expanding their business through backward linkage activities or by taking advantage of larger markets in semi-urban localities. One such success story was that of Anita Rani (from a suburban area of Kushtia, a district town near the western border of Bangladesh) who earned goodwill in her locality for selling specialised quality milk-made sweetmeat and then moved her business from her home to a shop, while also rearing cows to get the supply of milk (InM, 2008, p.7). In another case study from Gazipur in the outskirts of Dhaka City, Bakul Rani, together with her husband, turned the family business of traditional blacksmithing and ferrying the products into a larger-scale business (16 employees with daily sales of 35,000 taka) while still marketing the products on their own (InM, 2008, p.39). Yet in another case, a male borrower who used to eke out a living by ferrying mustard oil from village to village earned goodwill in the local retail market, which was not easy given the commonly practised adulteration of the product, and then set up his own firm to produce mustard oil.

Micro-entrepreneurs supported by the MFIs face some problems that are common to all small-scale enterprises, such as risks from natural disasters (e.g. bird flu, floods), or from the informality of the businesses (e.g. threat of eviction), or from unforeseen changes in macroeconomic policies altering input-output price configurations (a problem often discussed in the context of market-oriented liberalization policies). However, an additional source of risk faced by the women micro-entrepreneur clients of MFIs arises not from the business itself but from the male-dominated and risky social environment. This is best illustrated by a telling story of a female borrower, who built up a successful rice trading business by first borrowing 5,000 taka and increasing the loan size up to 200,000 taka in the 12th round. Her husband, meanwhile, got mixed up with an agency on whose behalf he collected money from prospective migrants, but the agency turned out to be a fraudulent one. To pay back the money to the victims of this scam, the family had to borrow 1 million taka at an interest rate of 20 percent per month from different moneylenders; as a result, her business became bankrupt (InM, 2008, p.48).

A review of the constraints faced by the micro-entrepreneurs and the accounts of their success stories point to an important emerging role that the larger MFIs can play: they can set up socially oriented businesses that can provide the much-needed technological and marketing support to address the barriers to scaling up the enterprises. These enterprises often have enough economies of scale in production, but the scale economies in marketing and designing the products and technology transfer are mostly beyond their reach. Grameen Bank and BRAC have already set up examples of such supporting businesses, to which we shall come back in the next chapter.

Notes

1 Based on data reported in *Bangladesh Microfinance Statistics 2014*, the annual publication of the Credit and Development Forum (CDF). The number of outstanding borrowers does not take into account multiple borrowing (i.e. overlapping).
2 Banerjee and Duflo (2011, pp.215–8) give a vivid description of the practical constraints in expanding a small business beyond subsistence in the case of an Indian woman who runs a grocery shop on the premises of her suburban home with limited inventory and customers.
3 The figures in US$ are estimated by using the nominal taka-dollar exchange rate existing at that time.
4 The results are statistically highly significant with good statistical fit, many methodological and data limitations notwithstanding.
5 More detailed estimates of the rates of return from IGAs according to various types of activities are reported by Osmani *et al.* (2015, pp.181–9).
6 The estimates of the use of microcredit according to outlay size group shown in Table 9.1 are not clearly defined since the outstanding size of the loan declines continuously during the one-year loan period; however, the estimates of the rate of return are not affected by the estimates of the use of loans.
7 This survey was carried out during late 2000 as part of the evaluation of phase II of the Bank's support for PKSF.
8 The case studies were later presented at a seminar attended by microcredit practitioners and researchers; see InM (2008).
9 This would remind us of BRAC's failed attempt, discussed earlier, in promoting poultry farms with, say, 100 chickens.

10 Micro-entrepreneurship and economic development

The studies on the impact of microcredit mainly focus on the well-being and poverty status of the beneficiary households. In order to assess the role of microcredit in the broader context of economic development, it would be necessary to go beyond the direct impact on the beneficiary households to examine the spillover effects on other households and on the local economy; this in turn will help to determine the economy-wide impact. Furthermore, in order to capture fully the impact of microcredit, one would need to look at the interaction between the growth of the local economies and the expansion of microcredit in a dynamic context.

10.1 Beyond the impact on participant households

Assessing the extent of spillover impacts of microcredit programmes on non-participants is even more problematic compared to the direct impact on participant households, since the effects can go either way. The creation of self-employment opportunities for the participants may be at the cost of non-participants if there is overcrowding and market-sharing within the limited markets for products and services supplied by such self-employment activities. On the other hand, the non-participants may benefit from positive externalities such as those arising from a tightening of the wage labour market, leading to an increase in wage rates as labour is withdrawn for self-employment in microcredit-supported income-generating activities (IGAs); there can also be positive linkage effects of microcredit through increased income and spending of the participant households, and also through positive demonstration effects on the non-participants in seeking new self-employment opportunities. The views on these issues vary widely. Some studies point to beneficial effects even beyond the participant households, while some critics have taken the extreme opposite view that microcredit may ultimately constitute a new and powerful institutional barrier to sustainable social and economic development of the local economy.

An early analysis of the problem of overcrowding and the likely displacement of non-participants from the limited self-employment opportunities was by Osmani (1989). Banerjee and Duflo (2011, pp.215–8) describe the proliferation of roadside shops, vending, hawking and petty trading in typical urban settings as examples of overcrowding and market-sharing resulting in one person's work being done by many. Bateman and Chang (2009, 2012) point out the huge crowding-out effect of microcredit in 'saturated' local markets – a 'one-cow' farm of a microcredit borrower driving out another such non-client farm, which quickly saw reduced margins and incomes and became more poverty-prone. In the Indian state of Andhra Pradesh, the allegedly irresponsible lending by profit-motivated MFIs in the retail trade sector, already overcrowded with small shops and petty trading, led to the debacle of the microcredit programmes and the shutdown of the MFIs in 2007 (Ghate, 2007).

Whether microcredit leads to a mere redistribution of income through overcrowding instead of creating new income-earning opportunities will depend on the characteristics and the dynamics of the local economy in which the microcredit programmes operate. Available evidence on the impact of microcredit programmes in the rural economy setting in Bangladesh suggests that there are net gains to the local economy (implying that there is not merely a redistribution of income from non-participants to participants); there may even be net positive spillover effects benefiting the non-participants, in which case the gain to the local economy will be even more than the direct impact on the participants – an extreme opposite scenario of what Bateman and Chang (2009) call a 'fallacy of composition'.

Ravallion and Wodon (1997) apply econometric techniques to the data on a nationally representative sample of rural households from the official *Household Expenditure Survey* of 1991/92 of the Bangladesh Bureau of Statistics to show that there are gains from switching from farm to non-farm employment, and the location choices of branch placement of Grameen Bank respond to that unexploited potential for rural development. Their analysis, however, does not show whether the presence of Grameen Bank in a village actually promotes such occupational mobility. Using quasi-panel household data from two rounds of the official *Household Income and Expenditure Surveys* of 2000 and 2005, Khandker and Mahmud (2012, pp.90 5) estimated the effect of the impact of the presence of Grameen Bank's branch in a village; the results showed that the presence of microcredit programmes could have a significant beneficial impact on the levels of consumption and the prevalence of both moderate and extreme poverty, while there were no similar effects due to the presence of the government's agricultural banks. These results are similar to the findings of Khandker (2005), who estimated the effect of microcredit on village-level poverty using household panel data. More evidence on the positive impact of microcredit programmes of Grameen Bank and BRAC on non-programme villages and on non-participants in programme villages comes from the analysis of cross-sectional data from the BIDS-World Bank 1991/92 survey on microcredit mentioned in the previous chapters (Khandker, 1998, pp.67–8).

The likely dynamic impact of microcredit is far more intractable compared to the static spillover effects, such as those induced through demand linkages or labour market effects. Again, an extreme view is that supporting low-productivity IGAs may undermine the development of more efficient small and medium enterprises (SMEs) in the same locality; the microcredit-supported IGAs, in the short run, can take a crucial market share away from local SMEs that might otherwise be able to reduce unit costs (innovate) and register productivity growth in the long run (Bateman and Chang, 2009, 2012). This 'adverse selection' process can thus jeopardise the chance of sustainable growth. A related criticism is that by promoting quick-turnover petty trading, MFIs contribute to creating a 'bazar economy', thus diverting resources away from the productive sectors of the economy.

There is not much evidence to support the view that microcredit undermines the growth of SMEs, at least not in the Bangladesh context. On the contrary, the rapid expansion of microcredit since the early 1990s has coincided with the emergence of a diversified and dynamic rural non-farm economy in Bangladesh, although the causal connections are difficult to establish. This picture is at least partly captured by the results of the official Economic Census of 1986, 2001and 2013 carried out by the Bangladesh Bureau of Statistics. The Census defines 'economic households' as those that have homestead-based non-agricultural IGAs, including floating occupations of household members like hawking, rickshaw-pulling or cart driving, but excluding home-based agricultural activities like crop processing and animal husbandry (BBS, 2015). The number of economic households in the country grew annually at 6.5 percent in the intervening 27-year period, compared to the average population growth of less than 2 percent in that period; the overwhelming proportion of the economic households are in rural areas, 84 percent in 2013.

As regards the growth of rural non-farm (RNF) establishments outside homesteads, the evidence equally indicates the importance and dynamism of the sector. Between the Census years of 2001–03 and 2013, these establishments, in fact, grew faster in rural areas than in urban areas in terms of the annual rate of growth, both in the number of establishments (4.1 percent compared to 3.1 percent) and in the size of employment (7.2 percent compared to 4.93 percent). For these estimates, we do not have comparable data from the Census of 1986; but a survey on the RNF sector carried out in 2003 by the World Bank (2005) using the same classification of establishments and same sample frame as those of the BBS Census of 1986 showed that the RNF enterprises with permanent establishments grew annually between these years at nearly 3 percent in number and at 4.8 percent in employment, indicating a growth in size. Thus, for the entire period since the mid-1980s, the estimates indicate a dynamic RNF sector combining both an extensive growth of homestead-based activities with an intensive growth of larger-sized enterprises with permanent establishments. Furthermore, the enterprise profile of the establishments as observed from the World Bank's survey indicates that a typical rural (or semi-urban) enterprise was small in size, fairly young in age, and employed mostly unpaid family labour while providing self-employment for the owner, yet it was not engaged in one of the low-productivity residual type of activities – as indicated by the fact that these were mostly run full-time throughout the year and were not operated as stopgap activities to fit into the agricultural cycle.

The above findings do not, however, mean that there are no serious problems facing the microcredit programmes, but they may be taken only as evidence against some of the extremely critical views mentioned earlier. The problem of overcrowding does exist in certain contexts (e.g. proliferation of pavement shops in metropolitan areas), and the challenges of the scaling up of enterprises also remain formidable. The stipulation of ASA or PKSF regarding a maximum limit to the proportion of microenterprise loans going to trading activities, mentioned in Chapter 9, only testifies to these concerns. There is also no disagreement that the conservative lending modalities of MFIs restrict the choice of innovative but risky projects, including start-ups in the case of microenterprise loans.

In the World Bank's survey of RNF enterprises mentioned above, 25 percent of enterprises in purely rural areas and 35 percent of all enterprises, including those in urban areas, indicated 'too many competitors' as a problem of doing business, which may be a rough indicator of overcrowding (World Bank, 2005, p.54). There was also evidence of a pervasive credit constraint; access to finance was the most frequently cited constraint faced by the enterprises, more so for starting up than running an enterprise, and the severity of the constraint according to the group size indicated the presence of what the study calls 'the peril of the missing middle' (World Bank, 2005, pp.51–6). The study also found that the transition from family labour to hired labour, or from one to two workers to an enterprise size of more than two workers, was correlated with entrepreneurial skill, prior experience, profit expectation, and in the case of hired labour, access to formal sources of credit, including microcredit; credit is thus one of many constraints.

It may be true that MFI lending excludes many deserving enterprises with more growth potential than the ones that are supported by the regular programmes of microcredit or the microenterprise loans (since, in the latter case, MFIs are constrained to finance only established businesses and no start-ups). While this points to the need for more innovations in the financial markets, it does not imply resource misallocation for the economy as a whole. The enterprises supported by MFIs remain competitive, even at the much higher interest rates charged by the MFIs compared to the lending rates of interest of commercial banks or even lower rates charged by the specialised government banks catering to the needs of agriculture and SMEs. If these specialised banks could be run more efficiently, they would surely deserve higher allocations of funds. The way financial markets currently operate in Bangladesh, MFIs represent a vehicle for compensating for the net flows of resources from rural areas to urban centres that take place through the regular banking system – by using their members' deposits to circulate within the rural economy. Moreover, the deposits of MFI clients perhaps represent mostly an additional savings mobilisation in the economy that would not have otherwise taken place.

Most discussions on the direct and indirect impact of microcredit concern RNF activities. The recent opening up of microcredit loans for crop production through the introduction of seasonal and agricultural loans will add a new dimension to such impact assessment (Faruqee, 2010). The inroads of microcredit in the crop sector have implications for the structure and efficiency of small-holder farming that characterises Bangladesh agriculture. Already, there is a shift from sharecropping to leasing of land, which is believed to have been induced in part by microcredit loans; such a shift can be beneficial for both land productivity and the well-being of the small and marginal farmers.

10.2 The debate on dynamic impact

As regards the criticism that microcredit-financed IGAs undermine sustainable growth by taking away market share from local SMEs with long-run growth potential, again there is little evidence to go by. The findings from the InM survey and case studies of MFI-financed microenterprises discussed in Chapter 9 do not indicate that their major threat comes from the local subsistence-type IGAs that cater to segmented local markets (InM, 2008). Instead, one of the main factors behind their success or failure in scaling up the enterprises seems to be their ability to compete with the formal-sector enterprises and connect to the broader marketing channels through the adoption of better production and marketing technologies.

One of the sources of misunderstanding about the role of microcredit in poverty alleviation and economic development seems to arise from an assumption that the success of microcredit depends on the proportion of borrowers who can come out of poverty through repeated loans and the scaling up of enterprises (Khandker, 1998). The expectation may have arisen from the pioneers' early hope of poverty alleviation through graduating borrowers and scaling up IGAs beyond subsistence. What may not have been fully anticipated is the speed at which the outreach of microcredit has expanded far beyond the so-called 'entrepreneurial poor' to meet the various other needs of poor people's financial management, such as investing in non-IGA physical and human assets, managing livelihood vulnerability and addressing saving difficulties. It became obvious that while some entrepreneurial poor may indeed grow out of poverty through scaling up their microenterprises, obviously all clients cannot do so because of their sheer number, if not for anything else. They can still benefit from microcredit to ease their livelihood needs and financial management until graduating out of poverty by other pathways.

Even for those borrowers who use microcredit loans for IGAs, the fact that they cannot expand their businesses does not mean they are 'trapped' in poverty because of their participation in microcredit programmes, as often suggested. As discussed in earlier chapters, investing in IGAs for many borrowers is a way of earning additional household income without accumulating assets from the recurrent surpluses to scale up their IGAs. Given the scaling-up problems, some may even invest in more than one IGA, which helps in pursuing multiple occupations. Banerjee and Duflo (2011, p.143) point out that having multiple occupations, as many poor people do, may be inefficient since it is then hard to specialise in anything and acquire the skills and experience in their main occupation. However, the particular examples they cite resemble the livelihoods of marginalised urban poor. A different perspective is provided by Toufique and Turnton (2002), who provide evidence from rural Bangladesh regarding how pursuing multiple occupations can be a viable livelihood strategy that can both benefit from and contribute to the growth and diversification of the rural economy.

The risk of falling into a trap of low-level entrepreneurship is also examined by Ahlin and Jiang (2008) within a macroeconomic model that has alternative possible outcomes regarding the contribution of microcredit to economic growth. In contrast, the possible positive outcome scenarios in the model are derived from sufficient numbers of the self-employed graduating from a subsistence activity to a higher-productivity micro-entrepreneurship. The possible adverse outcome arises from a risk of falling into a trap of low-level entrepreneurship if too many microcredit members are caught into subsistence IGAs; this reduces the supply of workers to be hired by entrepreneurs who could potentially scale up their enterprises – leading to a high rate of attrition of those enterprises. Such a scenario, however insightful, ignores the alternative pathways out of poverty and the role that lateral-entry entrepreneurs can play at higher levels of productivity (called 'foreign entry' in their model). The question of whether the proliferation of subsistence self-employment will really result in a 'misallocation' of the workforce so as to undermine the growth of higher-productivity enterprises through a shortage in labour supply can be resolved only empirically. A more likely outcome, however, in a labour-abundant economy is that the subsistence-type activities will hit the 'local demand constraint' (*à la* Osmani, 1989) before creating any serious shortage in labour supply. Moreover, the lateral entry of larger-sized enterprises should have enough labour productivity so as to be able to afford wage rates that make employment in such enterprises (regular employee status) more lucrative than low-productivity self-employment, which is in fact the case in Bangladesh (Osmani *et al.*, 2004).

The fact still remains that microcredit expansion through only replication of low-productivity subsistence-type activities will ultimately be limited in one way or another, which led Baumol *et al.* (2007) to conclude that microenterprises backed by microcredit are unlikely to be major engines of economic growth. This may seem relevant so far as the regular microcredit programmes in Bangladesh are concerned, with some symptoms of market saturations already being visible. As we discussed in Chapters 2 and 3, there may still be scope for expanding these programmes by making the lending modalities suit the needs of the clients. But so far as the contribution to economic growth is concerned, it is the microenterprise loans, including the newly introduced crop loans, that can make a difference on the microcredit frontiers. A number of such initiatives are already underway.

One possible area of new initiative is about finding new sources of funds for MFIs. The MFIs used to be mainly dependent on foreign donors for the initial seed funds for their microcredit programmes. That source of funding has now nearly dried up. Meanwhile, the MFIs have built up their revolving funds through mobilisation of members' deposit and from the operating surplus of their credit programmes (Table 10.1). They are also increasingly accessing the domestic banking system (10 percent of the revolving funds in 2012). The only substantial infusion of concessional funds currently taking place is through PKSF, mostly representing foreign funding, but also easy loans from the government. The estimates in Table 10.1 do not include Grameen Bank. As discussed in the earlier chapters, Grameen Bank's entire revolving fund for its microcredit programme

Table 10.1 Trends in the distribution of sources of revolving loan funds of MFIs (excluding Grameen Bank): 1996–2012 (percent)

Sources of loan fund	December 1996	December 2001	December 2005	December 2012
Members' net savings	20.1	24.1	29.8	29.5
MFI income/own fund	19.5	20.1	29.7	43.8
Loan from local bank	14.8	11.2	16.9	13.0
Grant from external donors	33.5	18.0	7.9	1.8
Loans from PKSF	12.5	23.5	13.4	10.9
Others	3.4	3.1	2.3	1.0
Total	100	100	100	100

Notes and source: Estimated from the data reported in the annual volumes of *Bangladesh Microfinance Statistics* published by the Credit and Development Forum (CDF, 2013); the reporting numbers of MFIs were 351 in 1996, 601 in 2001 and 539 in 2012.

now comes from members' deposits, while it has also mobilised a substantial amount of deposits from non-members that are mostly parked in fixed deposits with commercial banks.

Some microcredit leaders in Bangladesh, including Yunus, have advocated the case for converting some of the large MFIs into rural banks so that they can mobilise deposits from non-members (Yunus, 2004a). This would ease their funding constraint in undertaking more innovative lending programmes, while also exploiting the largely untapped potential of mobilising rural saving. At present, only Grameen Bank can mobilise deposits from outside its membership. Some special lending programmes of MFIs may also be supported through refinancing facilities of the central bank within its monetary programming; such refinancing facilities are usually provided to the public sector's specialised banks for rural and agricultural credit, mainly to replenish their capital base, which gets routinely depleted because of large-scale loan defaults. BRAC is currently implementing an innovative microcredit programme targeted to sharecroppers in crop production by using a refinancing facility from the central bank.

Under its new 'financial inclusion programme' initiated in 2014, Bangladesh Bank (the country's central bank) opened a refinancing window for state-owned commercial banks to offer collateral-free loans up to 50,000 taka to be given to small farmers (owning up to 2.5 acres) or small businesses; the loans will have a one-year repayment period at an interest rate not exceeding 12 percent when directly given or 19 percent when given through MFIs. There has been little response from the banks to utilise the facility. This only provides another example of why formal banking technology is not suitable for banking with the poor, particularly when it involves the inefficient and corruption-ridden state-owned banks.

It may be noted that the macro-financial aspects of microcredit remain a largely unattended topic in the microcredit literature.[1] The outstanding amount of loans in the microcredit sector at the end of 2014 was equivalent to about 8 percent of the total outstanding private sector credit of the banking system at that time. However, this figure underestimates the relative importance of microcredit in the credit market, since the banking sector's outstanding credit includes long-term loans and bad debt not yet written off, whereas the outstanding amount of loans of MFIs are revolved every year. The revolving funds of microcredit thus represent considerable monetary flows in the rural economy, contributing to financial deepening as well as having a likely beneficial effect on the local economy through demand linkages. There is evidence of similar beneficial effects on the local economy arising from spending out of remittances from family members working abroad (Mahmud, 1989).

In evaluating the effectiveness of microcredit programmes, one needs to remember that MFIs perform the dual role of financial intermediation and poverty alleviation. In their first role, the criterion for performance evaluation should be their efficiency in resource allocation compared to other institutions of financial intermediation. Microcredit programmes are, however, usually evaluated or critiqued in terms of the poverty impact of public spending (most often donor-aided) on these programmes compared to spending on other poverty alleviation programmes. The reservation of many observers, who seem otherwise sympathetic and supportive of microcredit, arises from the uncertainty of whether there are more cost-effective means of poverty alleviation other than microcredit, even if microcredit proves to be beneficial for the poor (Karlan and Appel, 2011, pp.82–3).[2] One problem with such scepticism is that the critics may have in mind the effectiveness of some innovative poverty interventions whose effectiveness has been ascertained through some experimental studies (i.e. the RCTs discussed in Chapter 7), and not the actual mainstream programmes of public social spending that are often ridden with large-scale leakage and corruption, and with whom the real trade-offs should lie. The other problem is that the importance of donor funding needed to run socially oriented microcredit programmes seems to be overblown, as can be seen from the current sources of revolving funds of MFIs in Bangladesh (Table 10.1).

The estimates regarding the current sources of revolving loan funds shown in Table 10.1 may have some ambiguities. The loans represent currently outstanding amounts with past loans being repaid from MFI income; but past amounts of grants may in part be subsequently absorbed in operating surpluses, depending on the accounting methods followed. Moreover, the estimates for 2012 may not be exactly comparable to those of previous years because of changes made in the questionnaire regarding information on the sources of revolving loan funds.

There is still considerable scope for realising the untapped potential of the microcredit programmes in Bangladesh based on the institutional strength of the NGO-MFIs. The growth of these NGO-MFIs represents a process of institution-building that has served the poor in various ways – by providing a whole range of services besides microcredit. They have a potentially crucial role to play in supporting the scaling up of microenterprises, such as by providing training for the adoption of appropriate production technologies (where there is a need for scale economies in production) or by helping to access markets (where there are economies of scale in marketing, including product design and quality assurance, but home-based production on a small scale can be profitable). The MFIs have a comparative advantage in making such businesses viable because they can economise on overhead costs due to their institutional presence in rural areas and networking with a large pool of spatially dispersed small producers. The rationale for setting up such socially oriented businesses is also based on the 'public good' nature of such services and possible positive synergies existing between such services and the microcredit programmes. It may be noted that the remarkable progress achieved in Bangladesh since the 1990s in many social development indicators is attributed, to a large extent, to a process of NGO-led service delivery along with effective social awareness campaigns (Asadullah *et al.*, 2014).

There are already some notable examples of such socially oriented MFI businesses. One of these, *Aarong*, is operated by BRAC on commercial lines to market, domestically and internationally, products of small/micro enterprises, including handicrafts, garments, handloom and sericulture products, and pasteurised milk and milk products. Another example is Grameen Check, a handloom product that is again marketed both in the domestic market and internationally. Grameen Telecom, a minority-share partner of a multinational mobile operator, offered a technology to create an IGA for the microcredit borrowers, namely providing mobile telephone service for villagers. The BRAC Bank, another venture of BRAC established in 2001, goes beyond traditional commercial banking to serve small entrepreneurs through dedicated countrywide SME branches. Its small-business banking model emphasises relationship banking and collateral-free lending of up to US$ 14,000 with wide coverage in rural areas (World Bank, 2012, p.164). It is noteworthy that BRAC Bank has a larger portfolio of bad loans compared to most other private commercial banks in Bangladesh; it may be a reflection of the limitations of serving small entrepreneurs within a traditional commercial banking entity, or it may also suggest that a commercial bank with a social mission need not be judged only by the quality of its balance sheet as long as it is not in the red.

More recently, BRAC Bank has opened another subsidiary venture called *bKash* which has spearheaded the introduction of e-money transfers through mobile telephony under the guidelines issued by the central bank in 2011. The model, which has been replicated by a few other commercial banks, has proved immensely popular, particularly among small businesses, and also among wage earners in urban areas who remit money to families left behind in rural areas. Already by early 2016, about 20 to 25 million transactions, each up to a limit of 10,000 taka, were being made each week. In some instances, the remittances of urban wage-earners are helping microcredit borrowers in paying their weekly instalments. However, there is no provision for credit in the model; nor have the subscribers of e-money, who are served by networks of bank agents, yet shown any inclination for keeping their savings in the e-money accounts. The introduction of e-money is thus another milestone in providing financial services to the poor which do not substitute but complement microcredit services.

Notes

1 For a discussion of some macroeconomic issues related to microcredit, see Batbekh and Blackburn (2008).
2 Karlan and Appel (2011, pp.82–83) express their frustration in the following words: "when we direct so much of money, efforts, and good intentions toward microcredit, we do not direct them to other things – like savings, insurance, education and health."

References

Abbink, K., Irlenbusch, B. and Renner, E. (2006). "Group size and social ties in microfinance institutions." *Economic Inquiry* 44(4): 614–628.

Adams, D. W. and Graham, D. H. (1981). "A critique of traditional agricultural credit projects and policies." *Journal of Development Economics* 8: 347–366.

Adams, D. W., Graham, D. H. and von Pischke, J. D. (eds.) (1984). *Undermining Rural Development with Cheap Credit*. London: Westview Press.

Agur, I. (2012). "Credit rationing when banks are funding constrained." *North American Journal of Economics and Finance* 23: 220–227.

Ahlin, C. (2015). "The role of group size in group lending." *Journal of Development Studies* 115: 14–155.

Ahlin, C. and Jiang, N. (2008). "Can micro-credit bring development?" *Journal of Development Economics* 86(1): 1–21.

Ahlin, C. and Townsend, R. M. (2007). "Using repayment data to test across models of joint liability lending." *Economic Journal* 117(517): F11–F51.

Akerlof, G. (1970). "The market for lemons: Qualitative uncertainty and the market mechanism." *Quarterly Journal of Economics* LXXXIV: 488–500.

Alamgir, D. A. H. (1999a). *Microfinance Services in Bangladesh: Review of Innovations and Trends*. Dhaka: Credit Development Forum.

Alamgir, D. A. H. (1999b). "Profitability analysis of income generating activities of microcredit borrowers of partner organisations of Palli Karma-Shahayak Foundation (PKSF) in Bangladesh." (Mimeo.) Dhaka: World Bank.

Aleem, I. (1990). "Imperfect information, screening, and the costs of informal lending: A study of a rural credit market in Pakistan." *World Bank Economic Review* 4(3): 329–349.

Altonji, J. G., Elder, T. E. and Taber, C. R. (2005). "Selection on observed and unobserved variables: Assessing the effectiveness of catholic schools." *Journal of Political Economy* 113(1): 151–184.

Amin, S. and Mahmud, S. (2012). "The social impact of microfinance on gender behaviour." *Research Briefs 1 and 2*. Dhaka: Institute of Microfinance.

Amin, S., Rai, A. S. and Topa, G. (2003). "Does microcredit reach the poor and vulnerable? Evidence from northern Bangladesh." *Journal of Development Economics* 70(1): 59–82.

Andvig, J. C. (1991). "The Economics of corruption: A survey." *Studi Economici* 43: 57–94.

Angelucci, M., Karlan, D. and Zinman, J. (2015). "Microcredit impacts: Evidence from a randomized microcredit program placement experiment by Compartamos Banco." *American Economic Journal: Applied Economics* 7(1): 151–182.

References

Aniket, K. (2011a). "Queuing for credit: Increasing the reach of microfinance through sequential group lending." (Mimeo.) Cambridge: Trinity College, University of Cambridge.

Aniket, K. (2011b). "Beyond microcredit: Giving the poor a way to save their way out of poverty." (Mimeo.) Cambridge: Trinity College, University of Cambridge.

Armendáriz, B. and Labie, M. (eds.) (2011). *The Handbook of Microfinance*. Singapore: World Scientific Publishing Company.

Armendáriz, B. and Morduch, J. (2010). *The Economics of Microfinance*. Second edition. Cambridge, MA: The MIT Press.

Armendáriz de Aghion, B. (1999). "On the design of a credit agreement with peer monitoring." *Journal of Development Economics* 60: 79–104.

Armendáriz de Aghion, B. and Gollier, C. (2000). "Peer group formation in an adverse selection model." *Economic Journal* 110: 632–643.

Armendáriz de Aghion, B. and Morduch, J. (2000). "Microfinance beyond group lending." *The Economics of Transition* 8(2): 401–420.

Arnold, L. G., Reeder, J. and Steger, S. (2013). "On the viability of group lending when microfinance meets the market: A reconsideration of the Besley-Coate model." *Journal of Emerging Market Finance* 12(1): 59–106.

Arnold, L. G. and Riley, J. G. (2009). "On the possibility of credit rationing in the Stiglitz-Weiss model." *American Economic Review* 99(5): 2012–2021.

Arnott, R. and Stiglitz, J. E. (1991). "Moral hazard and nonmarket institutions: Dysfunctional crowding out or peer monitoring?" *American Economic Review* 81(1): 179–190.

Arrow, K. (1963). "Uncertainty and the economics of medical care." *American Economic Review* LIII: 941–793.

Asadullah, M. N., Savoia, A. and Mahmud, W. (2014). "Paths to development: Is there a Bangladesh surprise?" *World Development* 62: 138–154.

Ashraf, N., Karlan, D. and Yin, W. (2006). "Tying Odysseus to the mast: Evidence from a commitment savings product in the Philippines." *Quarterly Journal of Economics* 121(2): 635–672.

Attanasio, O., Augsburg, B., De Haas, R., Fitzsimons, E. and Harmgart, H. (2015). "The impacts of microfinance: Evidence from joint-liability lending in Mongolia." *American Economic Journal: Applied Economics* 7(1): 90–122.

Augsburg, B., De Haas, R., Harmgart, H. and Meghir, C. (2015). "The impacts of microcredit: Evidence from Bosnia and Herzegovina." *American Economic Journal: Applied Economics* 7(1): 183–203.

Ausubel, L. (1999). "Adverse selection in the credit card market." *Working Paper*. College Park MD: University of Maryland.

Bandopadhyay, T. and Ghatak, S. (1982). "Some remarks on agricultural backwardness under semi-feudalism." *Indian Economic Review* XVII(1): 29–33.

Banerjee, A. (2004). "Contracting constraints, credit markets and economic development." In Dewatripont, M., Hansen, L. P. and Turnovsky, S. (eds.) *Advances in Economics and Econometrics: Theory and Applications*. Volume III. Econometric Society monographs. Cambridge: Cambridge University Press, pp. 1–46.

Banerjee, A. (2013). "Microcredit under the microscope: What have we learned in the past two decades, and what do we need to know?" *Annual Review of Economics* 5: 487–519.

Banerjee, A., Besley, T. and Guinnane, T. W. (1994). "Thy neighbor's keeper: The design of a credit cooperative with theory and a test." *Quarterly Journal of Economics* 109(2): 491–515.

Banerjee, A. and Duflo, E. (2011). *Poor Economics: A Radical Rethinking of the Way to Fight Global Poverty*. New York: Public Affairs.

Banerjee, A., Duflo, E., Glennerster, R. and Kinnan, C. (2015). "The miracle of microfinance? Evidence from a randomized evaluation." *American Economic Journal: Applied Economics* 7(1): 22–53.

Banerjee, A., Karlan, D. and Zinman, J. (2015). "Six randomized evaluations of microcredit: Introduction and further steps." *American Economic Journal: Applied Economics* 7(1): 1–21.

Banerjee, A. and Mullainathan, S. (2010). "The shape of temptation: Implications for the economic lives of the poor." *Working Paper No. 15973*. Washington, DC: National Bureau of Economic Reserarch.

Bardhan, P. and Udry, C. (1999). *Development Microeconomics*. Oxford: Oxford University Press.

Bardhan, P. K. (1984). *Land, Labour and Rural Poverty: Essays in Development Economics*. London: Oxford University Press.

Bardhan, P. K. and Rudra, A. (1978). "Interlinkage of land, labour, and credit relations: An analysis of village survey data in East India." *Economic and Political Weekly* XIII: 367–384.

Barr, A. M. (2003). "Trust and expected trustworthiness: Experimental evidence from Zimbabwean villages." *Economic Journal* 113(489): 614–630.

Bashar, T. and Rashid, S. (2012). "Urban microfinance and urban poverty in Bangladesh." *Journal of the Asia Pacific Economy* 17(1): 151–170.

Basu, Karna (2015). "A Behavioral model of simultaneous borrowing and saving." *Working Paper*. New York: Department of Economics, Hunter College.

Basu, Kaushik (1987). "Disneyland monopoly, interlinkage and usurious interest rates." *Journal of Public Economics* 34: 1–17.

Batbekh, S. and Blackburn, K. (2008). "On the macroeconomics of microfinance." *Discussion Paper Series No. 106*. Centre for Growth and Business Cycle Research, University of Manchester: Manchester.

Bateman, M. and Chang, H. J. (2009). "The microfinance illusion." *SSRN Electronic Journal*. Available at 01/2009; DOI: 10.2139/ssrn.2385174.

Bateman, M. and Chang, H. J. (2012). "Microfinance and the illusion of development: From hubris to nemesis in thirty years." *World Economic Review* 1: 13–36.

Bauer, M., Chytilová, J. and Morduch, J. (2012). "Behavioral foundations of microcredit: Experimental and survey evidence from Rural India." *American Economic Review* 102(2): 1118–1139.

Baumol, W., Litan, R. E. and Schramm, C. J. (2007). *Good Capitalism, Bad Capitalism, and The Economics of Growth and Prosperity*. New Haven: Yale University Press.

BBS (2015). *Economic Census 2013* (in abridged form). Dhaka: Bangladesh Bureau of Statistics.

Becker, G. S. (1993). *A Treatise on the Family*. Second enlarged edition. Cambridge, MA: Harvard University Press.

Berg, C., Emran, S. H. and Shilpi, F. (2015). "Microfinance and moneylenders: Long-run effects of MFIs on informal credit market in Bangladesh." *Policy Research Working Paper No. 6619*, Washington, DC: World Bank.

Berg, J. E., Dickhaut, J. W. and McCabe, K. A. (1995). "Trust, reciprocity, and social history." *Games and Economic Behavior* 10(1): 122–142.

Bernanke, B. and Gertler, M. (1990). "Financial fragility and economic performance." *Quarterly Journal of Economics* 105: 87–114.

Besanko, D. and Thakor, A. V. (1987). "Collateral and rationing: Sorting equilibria in monopolistic and competitive credit markets." *International Economic Review* 28(3): 671–689.

References

Besley, T. (1994). "How do marker failures justify interventions in rural credit markets?" *World Bank Research Observer* 9(1): 27–47.

Besley, T. (1995). "Nonmarket institutions for credit and risk sharing in low-income countries." *Journal of Economic Perspectives* 9(3): 115–127.

Besley, T. and Coate, S. (1995). "Group lending, repayment incentives and social collateral." *Journal of Development Economics* 46: 1–18.

Besley, T., Coate, S. and Loury, G. (1993). "The economics of rotating savings and credit associations." *American Economic Review* 83(4): 792–810.

Bester, H. (1985). "Screening vs. rationing in credit markets with imperfect information." *American Economic Review* 75(4): 850–855.

Bhaduri, A. (1973). "Agricultural backwardness under semi-feudalism." *Economic Journal* 83: 120–137.

Bhaduri, A. (1977). "On the formation of usurious interest rates in backward agriculture." *Cambridge Journal of Economics* 1: 341–352.

Bhaduri, A. (1983). *The Economic Structure of Backward Agriculture*. London: Academic Press.

Bhole, B. and Ogden, S. (2010). "Group lending and individual lending with strategic default." *Journal of Development Economics* 91: 348–363.

Bond, P. and Krishnamurthy, A. (2004). "Regulating exclusion from financial markets." *Review of Economic Studies* 71: 681–707.

Bond, P. and Rai, A. S. (2008). "Cosigned vs. group loans." *Journal of Development Economics* 85: 58–80.

Bottomley, A. (1975). "Interest rate determination in underdeveloped rural areas." *American Journal of Agricultural Economics* 57: 279–291.

Bourjade, S. and Schindele, I. (2012). "Group lending with endogenous group size." *Economic Letters* 117(3): 556–560.

Bratton, M. (1986). "Financial smallholder production: A comparison of individual and group credit schemes in Zimbabwe." *Public Administration and Development* 6(2): 115–132.

Braverman, A. and Srinivasan, T. N. (1981). "Credit and sharecropping in agrarian societies." *Journal of Development Economics* 9: 289–312.

Braverman, A. and Stiglitz, J. E. (1982). "Sharecropping and the interlinking of Agrarian markets." *American Economic Review* 11(4): 495–615.

Braverman, A. and Stiglitz, J. E. (1986). "Landlords, tenants and technological innovations." *Journal of Development Economics* 23: 313–332.

Breza, E. (2012). "Peer effects and loan repayment: Evidence from the Krishna default crisis." *Working Paper*. Cambridge, MA: Department of Economics, MIT.

Brusco, S. (1997). "Implementing action profiles when agents collude." *Journal of Economic Theory* 73: 395–424.

Bulow, J. and Rogoff, K. (1989). "Sovereign debt: Is to forgive to forget?" *American Economic Review* 79(1): 43–50.

Burgess, R. and Pande, R. (2005). "Do rural banks matter? Evidence from the Indian social banking experiment." *American Economic Review* 95(3): 780–795.

Cardon, J. H. and Hendel, I. (2001). "Asymmetric information in health insurance: Evidence from the national medical expenditure survey." *RAND Journal of Economics* 32: 408–427.

Carpenter, J. and Williams, T. (2010). "Moral hazard, peer monitoring, and microcredit: Field experimental evidence from Paraguay." *Working Paper 10–6*. Boston: Federal Reserve Bank of Boston.

Carter, M. R. (1988). "Equilibrium credit rationing of small farm agriculture." *Journal of Development Economics* 28: 83–108.

Cason, T. N., Gangadharan, L. and Maitra, P. (2012). "Moral hazard and peer monitoring in a laboratory microfinance experiment." *Journal of Economic Behavior and Organization* 82: 192–209.

Cassar, A., Crowley, L. and Wydick, B. (2007). "The effect of social capital on group loan repayment: Evidence from field experiments." *Economic Journal* 117(517): F85–F106.

CDF (2013). *Bangladesh Microfinance Statistics 2012*. Dhaka: Credit and Development Forum.

Chatterjee, P. and Sarangi, S. (2005). "Enforcement with costly group formation." *Economics Bulletin* 15(9): 1–8.

Chaudhury, I. A. and Matin, I. (2002). "Dimensions and dynamics of microfinance membership overlap – a micro study from Bangladesh." *Small Enterprise Development* 13(2): 46–55.

Chemin, M. (2008). "Benefits and costs of microfinance in Bangladesh: Evidence from Bangladesh." *Journal of Development Studies* 44(4): 463–484.

Chemin, M. (2012). "Response to 'High noon for microfinance impact evaluations'." *Journal of Development Studies* 48(12): 1881–1885.

Chiappori, P. A. and Salanie, B. (2000). "Testing for asymmetric information in insurance markets." *Journal of Political Economy* 108: 56–78.

Chiappori, P. A. and Salanie, B. (2003). "Testing contract theory: A survey of some recent work." In Dewatripont, M., Hansen, L. and Turnovsky, S. (eds.) *Advances in Economics and Econometrics: Theory and Applications*. Volume 1. Econometric Society monographs. Cambridge: Cambridge University Press, pp. 115–149.

Chowdhury, S., Roy Chowdhury, P. and Sengupta, K. (2014). "Sequential lending with dynamic joint liability in micro-finance." *Journal of Development Economics* 111: 167–180.

Coleman, J. (1988). "Social capital in the creation of human capital." *American Journal of Sociology* 94: 95–120.

Coleman, J. S. (1993). "The relational reconstruction of society." *American Sociological Review* 58: 1–15.

Collins, D., Morduch, J., Rutherford, S. and Ruthven, O. (2009). *Portfolios of the Poor: How the World's Poor Live on $2 a Day*. Princeton, NJ: Princeton University Press.

Conning, J. (1996). "Group lending, moral hazard and the creation of social collateral." *Working Paper No. 195*. College Park: Center for Institutional Reform and the Informal Sector, University of Maryland.

Conning, J. (2005). "Monitoring by delegates or by peers? Joint liability loans under moral hazard." *Working Papers 407*. New York: Department of Economics, Hunter College.

Conning, J. and Udry, C. (2007). "Rural financial markets in developing countries." In Evenson, R. E. and Pingali, P. (eds.) *The Handbook of Agricultural Economics, Vol. 3: Agricultural Development: Farmers, Farm Production and Farm Markets*. Amsterdam: North-Holland, pp. 2857–2908.

Cons, J. and Paprocki, K. (2010). "Contested credit landscapes: Microcredit, self-help and self-determination in rural Bangladesh." *Third World Quarterly* 31(4): 637–654.

Copestake, J. (2007). "Mainstreaming microfinance: Social performance management or mission drift?" *World Development* 35: 1721–1738.

Crépon, B., Devoto, F., Duflo, E. and Parienté, W. (2015). "Estimating the impact of microcredit on those who take it up: Evidence from a randomized experiment in Morocco." *American Economic Journal: Applied Economics* 7(1): 132–150.

References

Cull, R., Demirguc-Kunt, A. and Morduch, J. (2007). "Financial performance and outreach: A global analysis of leading microbanks." *Economic Journal* 117(517): F107-F133.

Cull, R., Demirguc-Kant, A. and Morduch, J. (2009). "Microfinance meets the market." *Journal of Economic Perspectives* 23(1): 167–192.

Cull, R., Demirgüç-Kunt, A. and Morduch, J. (2011). "Does regulatory supervision curtail microfinance profitability and outreach?" *World Development* 39(6): 949–965.

Darling, M. L. (1925). *The Punjab Peasant in Prosperity and Debt*. London: Milford.

de Mel, S., McKenzie, D. and Woodruff, C. (2010). "Wage subsidies for microenterprises." *American Economic Review* 100(2): 614–618.

de Meza, D. and Webb, D. C. (1987). "Too much investment: A problem of asymmetric information." *Quarterly Journal of Economics* 102: 281–292.

de Meza, D. and Webb, D. C. (2006). "Credit rationing: Something's gotta give." *Economica* 73: 563–578.

Dehejia, R., Montgomery, H. and Morduch, J. (2012). "Do interest rates matter? Credit demand in the Dhaka slums." *Journal of Development Economics* 97(2): 437–449.

Dercon, S. (ed.) (2005). *Insurance Against Poverty*. UNU-WIDER Studies in Development Economics. Oxford: Oxford University Press.

Diagne, A. (2000). "Design and sustainability issues of rural credit and savings programs: Findings from Malawi." *Policy Brief No. 2*. Rural Final Policies for the Food Security of the Poor. Washington, DC: International Food Policy Research Institute.

Diamond, D. W. (1984). "Financial intermediation and delegated monitoring." *Review of Economic Studies* LI: 393–414.

Dobbie, W. and Skiba, P. M. (2013). "Information asymmetries in consumer credit markets: Evidence from payday lending." *American Economic Journal: Applied Economics* 5(4): 256–282.

Dowla, A. and Barua, D. (2006). *The Poor Always Pay Back: The Grameen II Story*. Bloomfield, CT: The Kumarian Press.

Dufhues, T., Buchenrieder, G., Quoc, H. D. and Munkung, N. (2011). "Social capital and loan repayment performance in southeast Asia." *Journal of Socio-Economics* 40: 679–691.

Duvendack, M. and Palmer-Jones, R. (2012a). "High noon for microfinance impact evaluations: Re-investigating the evidence from Bangladesh." *Journal of Development Studies* 48(12): 1864–1880.

Duvendack, M. and Palmer-Jones, R. (2012b). "What Mat[t]hieu really did; rejoinder to Chemin." Available at: https://archive.uea.ac.uk/~nga07htu/Rejoinder_to_Chemin_Final.pdf.

Duvendack, M. and Palmer-Jones, R. (2012c). "Reply to Chemin and to Pitt." *Journal of Development Studies* 48(12): 1892–1897.

Duvendack, M. and Palmer-Jones, R. (2012d). "Wyatt Earps' high noon; rejoinder to Pitt." Available at: https://archive.uea.ac.uk/~nga07htu/Rejoinder_to_Pitt_Final.pdf.

Edelberg, W. (2004). "Testing for adverse selection and moral hazard in consumer loan markets." *Finance and Economics Discussion Paper Series No. 2004–09*. Washington, DC: Federal Reserve Board.

Elster, J. (1977). "Ulysses and the sirens: A theory of imperfect rationality." *Social Science Information* 16: 469–526.

Emran, M. S., Robano, V. and Smith, S. C. (2014). "Assessing the frontiers of ultrapoverty reduction: Evidence from challenging the frontiers of poverty reduction/targeting the Ultra -poor, an innovative program in Bangladesh." *Economic Development and Cultural Change* 62(2): 339–380.

Fafchamps, M. (2011). "Risk sharing between households." In Benhabib, J., Bisin, A. and Jackson, M. O. (eds.) *Handbook of Social Economics.* Volume 1B. Amsterdam: Elsevier, pp. 1256–1280.
Fafchamps, M. and Lund, S. (2003). "Risk-sharing networks in rural Philippines." *Journal of Development Economics* 71: 261–287.
Faruqee, R. (2010). "Microfinance for agriculture in Bangladesh: Current status and future potential." *Working Paper No. 8.* Dhaka: Institute of Microfinance.
Faruqee, R. and Khalily, M. A. B. (2011). "Multiple borrowing by MFI clients: Current status and implications for future of microfinance." *Policy Paper.* Dhaka: Institute of Microfinance.
Feigenberg, B., Field, E. M. and Pande, R. (2013). "The economic returns to social interaction: Experimental evidence from microfinance." *Review of Economic Studies* 80(4): 1459–1483.
Field, E. M. and Pande, R. (2008). "Repayment frequency and default in microfinance: Evidence from India." *Journal of the European Economic Association* 6(2–3): 501–509.
Finkelstein, A. and McGarry, K. (2006). "Multiple dimensions of private information: Evidence from the long-term care insurance market." *American Economic Review* 96(4): 938–958.
Fischer, G. (2013). "Contract structure, risk sharing, and investment." *Econometrica* 81(3): 883–939.
Fischer, G. and Ghatak, M. (2010). "Repayment frequency in microfinance contracts with present-biased borrowers." (Mimeo.) London: London School of Economics.
Fischer, G. and Ghatak, M. (2011). "Spanning the chasm: Uniting theory and empirics in microfinance research." In Aremendáriz and Labie (eds.).
Fitchett, D. A. (1999). "Bank for agriculture and agricultural cooperatives (BAAC), Thailand (Case Study)." Washington, DC: Working Group on Savings Mobilization, Consultative Group to Assist the Poorest (CGAP).
Fudenberg, D. and Tirole, J. (1991). *Game Theory.* Cambridge, MA: MIT Press.
Gachter, S. and Fehr, E. (1999). "Collective action as a social exchange." *Journal of Economic Behavior and Organization* 39: 341–369.
Gale, W. G. (1990). "Federal lending and the market for credit." *Journal of Public Economics* 42: 177–193.
Gangopadhyay, S., Ghatak, M. and Lensink, M. (2005). "Joint liability lending and the peer selection effect." *Economic Journal* 115: 1005–1015.
Gangopadhyay, S. and Lensink, R. (2009). "Co-signed loans versus joint liability lending in an adverse selection model." *Research Paper, 09/05.* Hyderabad: Centre for Analytical Finance, Indian School of Business.
Ghatak, M. (1999). "Group lending, local information and peer selection." *Journal of Development Economics* 60: 27–50.
Ghatak, M. (2000). "Screening by the company you keep: Joint liability lending and the peer selection effect." *Economic Journal* 110: 601–631.
Ghatak, M. and Guinnane, T. W. (1999). "The economics of lending with joint liability: Theory and practice." *Journal of Development Economics* 60: 195–228.
Ghate, P. (2007). *Indian Microfinance: The Challenges of Rapid Growth.* New Delhi: SAGE Publications.
Ghosh, P., Mookherjee, D. and Ray, D. (2001). "Credit rationing in developing countries: An overview of the theory." In Mookherjee, D. and Ray, D. (eds.) *Readings in the Theory of Economic Development.* London: Blackwell, pp. 283–301.

Giné, X., Jakiela, P., Karlan, D. S. and Morduch, J. (2010). "Microfinance games." *American Economic Journal: Applied Economics* 2: 60–95.

Giné, X. and Karlan, D. S. (2014). "Group versus individual liability: Short and long term evidence from Philippine microcredit lending groups." *Journal of Development Economics* 107: 65–83.

Giné, X., Krishnaswamy, K. and Ponce, A. (2011). "Strategic default in joint liability groups: Evidence from a natural experiment in India." (Mimeo; preliminary). Washington, DC: World Bank.

Glaeser, E. L., Laibson, D. I. and Sacerdote, B. I. (2002). "An economic approach to social capital." *Economic Journal* 112: F437–58.

Glaeser, E. L., Laibson, D. I., Scheinkman, J. A. and Soutter, C. L. (2000). "Measuring trust." *Quarterly Journal of Economics* 115(3): 811–846.

Godquin, M. (2004). "Microfinance repayment performance in Bangladesh: How to improve the allocation of loans by MFIs." *World Development* 32(11): 1909–1926.

Gomez, R. and Santor, E. (2003). "Do peer group members outperform individual borrowers? A test of peer group lending using Canadian micro-credit data." *Working Paper No. 2003-33*. Ottawa: Bank of Canada.

Gonzalez-Vega, C. (1984). "Credit-rationing behavior of agricultural lenders: The iron law of interest-rate restrictions." In Adams *et al.* (eds.).

Green, E. and Porter, R. (1984). "Non-cooperative collusion under imperfect price information." *Econometrica* 52: 87–100.

Guttman, J. M. (2006). "Repayment performance in group lending programs: A survey." *Working Paper 2006-WP-01*. Terre Haute, IN: Networks Financial Institute, Indiana State University.

Guttman, J. M. (2008). "Assortive matching, adverse selection, and group ending." *Journal of Development Economics* 87: 51–56.

Harrison, G. and List, J. (2004). "Field experiments." *Journal of Economic Literature* 62: 1009–1055.

Hashemi, S. M. (1997). "Those left behind: A note on targeting the hard core poor." In Wood and Sharif (eds.).

Hashemi, S. M. and Schuler, S. (1997). "Sustainable banking with the poor: A case study of the Grameen Bank." *Working Paper No. 10*. Washington, DC: John Snow International Research and Training Institute.

Hermes, N. and Lensink, R. (2007). "The empirics of microfinance: What do we know?" *Economic Journal* 117(517): F1–F10.

Hermes, N., Lensink, R. and Mehrteab, H. T. (2005). "Peer monitoring, social ties and moral hazard in group lending programs: Evidence from Eritrea." *World Development* 33(1): 149–169.

Hermes, N., Lensink, R. and Mehrteab, H. T. (2006). "Does the group leader matter? The impact of monitoring activities and social ties of group leaders on the repayment performance of group-based lending in Eritrea." *African Development Review* 18(1): 72–97.

Hicks, J. (1969). *The Theory of Economic History*. Oxford Paperbacks edition. Oxford: Oxford University Press.

Hoff, K. and Stiglitz, J. E. (1990). "Introduction: Imperfect information and rural credit markets – puzzles and policy perspective." *World Bank Economic Review* 4(3): 235–250.

Holmstrom, B. and Milgrom, P. (1991). "Multi-task principal-agent analyses: Linear contracts, asset ownership and job design." *Journal of Law, Economics and Organization* 7: 24–52.

Holmstrom, B. and Tirole, J. (1997). "Financial intermediation, loanable funds and the real sector." *Quarterly Journal of Economics* 112(3): 663–691.

References

Hossain, M. (1984). "Credit for the poor: The Grameen Bank in Bangladesh." *Research Monograph No. 4*. Dhaka: Bangladesh Institute of Development Studies.

Hossain, M. (1988). "Credit for alleviation of rural poverty: The Grameen Bank in Bangladesh." *Research Report No. 65*. Washington, DC: International Food Policy Research Institute.

Hossain, M. (2002). "Credit for the alleviation of rural poverty: The experience of Grameen Bank in Bangladesh." In Rahman, A., Rahman, R. I., Hossain, M. and Hossain, S. M. (eds.) *Early Impact of Grameen: A Multi-Dimensional Analysis*. Outcome of a BIDS Research Study. Dhaka: Grameen Trust, pp.127–175.

Hossain, M. (2012). "Dynamics of rural credit market, 1988 to 2008: Access to tenants and small holders." Paper presented at Policy Dialogue on Tenant Farmer Development in Bangladesh Organised by the BRAC Research and Evaluation Division, Dhaka: 14 November.

Hossain, M. and Bayes, A. (2009). *Rural Economy and Livelihoods: Insights from Bangladesh*. Dhaka: A. H. Development Publishing House.

Hubbard, R. G. (1998). "Capital market imperfections and investment." *Journal of Economic Literature* 32: 193–225.

Hulme, D. and Mosley, P. (eds.) (1996). *Finance Against Poverty*. London: Routledge.

Hurwicz, L., Maskin, E. and Postelwaite, A. (1995). "Feasible Nash implementation of social choice rules when the designer does not know endowments or production sets." In Ledyard, J. O. (ed.) *The Economics of Informational Decentralization: Complexity, Efficiency, and Stability*. Dordrecht: Kluwer Academic Publishers, pp. 367–433.

IFC and MicroSave (2011). *Deposit Assessment in Bangladesh*. Washington, DC: International Finance Corporation, World Bank Group.

Imai, K. S. and Azam, M. S. (2012). "Does microfinance reduce poverty in Bangladesh? New evidence from household panel data." *Journal of Development Studies* 48(5): 633–653.

Impavido, G. (1998). "Credit rationing, group lending and optimal group size." *Annals of Public and Cooperative Economics* 69(2): 243–260.

InM (2008). "Report on the workshop on the growth and development of micro enterprises in Bangladesh." (Mimeo.) Dhaka: Institute of Microfinance.

InM (2013). *National Conference on Microfinance and Development: Conference Document*. Dhaka: Institute of Microfinance.

Innes, R. D. (1990). "Limited liability and incentive contracting with ex ante action choices." *Journal of Economic Theory* 52(1): 45–67.

IPA (2015). "Where credit is due." *Policy Bulletin*, February. Cambridge, MA: Innovations for Poverty Action, Abdul Latif Jameel Poverty Action Lab, Massachusetts Institute of Technology. Available at: www.poverty-action.org and www.povertyactionlab.org.

Islam, A. (2011). "Medium- and long-term participation in microcredit: Evaluation using a new panel dataset from Bangladesh." *American Journal of Agricultural Economics* 93(3): 847–866.

Islam, M. M. (1978). *Bengal Agriculture 1920–1946: A Quantitative Study*. Cambridge: Cambridge University Press.

Itoh, H. (1993). "Coalitions, incentives, and risk sharing." *Journal of Economic Theory* 60: 410–427.

Jaffe, D. M. and Russell, T. (1976). "Imperfect information, uncertainty and credit rationing." *Quarterly Journal of Economics* 90(4): 651–666.

Jaffe, D. M. and Stiglitz, J. E. (1990). "Credit rationing." In Friedman, B. M. and Hahn, F. H. (eds.) *Handbook of Monetary Economics*. Volume II. Amsterdam: Elsevier, pp. 837–888.

References

Jain, P. and Moore, M. (2003). "What makes microcredit programmes effective? Fashionable fallacies and workable realities." *Working Paper 177*. Brighton: Institute of Development Studies.

Jain, S. and Mansuri, G. (2003). ""A little at a time: The use of regularly scheduled repayments in microfinance programs." *Journal of Development Economics* 72(1): 253–279.

Kabeer, N. (1998). "Money can't buy me love: Re-evaluating gender, credit and empowerment in rural Bangladesh." *Discussion Paper No. 363*. Institute of Development Studies, University of Sussex.

Kabeer, N. (2005). "Is microfinance a 'magic bullet' for women's empowerment? Analysis of findings from South Asia." *Economic and Political Weekly* 40(44/45, October 29–November 4): 4709–4718.

Kabeer, N. and Matin, I. (2005). "The wider social impacts of BRAC's group-based lending in rural Bangladesh: Group dynamics and participation in public life." *Research Monograph Series No. 10*. Dhaka: Research and Evaluation Division, BRAC.

Kamal, A. (2000). "Kinship strikes back: The poor and the NGO process in Bangladesh." (Mimeo.) Paper Presented at the Decennial Conference of the Agrarian Studies Program, Yale University. Dhaka: Grameen Trust.

Karim, L. (2008). "Demystifying micro-credit the Grameen Bank, NGOs, and neoliberalism in Bangladesh." *Cultural Dynamics* 20(1): 5–29.

Karlan, D. S. (2005). "Using experimental economics to measure social capital and predict financial decisions." *American Economic Review* 95(5): 1688–1699.

Karlan, D. S. (2007). "Social connections and group banking." *Economic Journal* 117(517): F52–F84.

Karlan, D. S. and Appel, J. (2011). *More Than Good Intentions: How a New Economics is Helping to Solve Global Poverty*. New York: Dutton (Penguin Group).

Karlan, D. S. and Morduch, J. (2010). "Access to finance." In Rodrik, D. and Rosenzweig, M. R. (eds.) *Handbook of Development Economics.* Volume 5. Amsterdam: North-Holland, pp. 4704–4784.

Karlan, D. S. and Zinman, J. (2009). "Observing unobservables: Identifying information asymmetries with a consumer credit field experiment." *Econometrica* 77(6): 1993–2008.

Karlan, D. S. and Zinman, J. (2010). "Expanding credit access: Using randomized supply decisions to estimate the impacts.". *Review of Financial Studies* 23(1): 433–464.

Karlan, D. S. and Zinman, J. (2011). "Microcredit in theory and practice: Using randomized credit scoring for impact evaluation." *Science*, June 10: 1278–1284.

Katzur, T. and Lensink, R. (2011). "The role of joint liability contracts and guarantor contracts in microfinance." (Mimeo.) Available at: https://www.rug.nl/research/events/workshopmicrofinance2010/pdfmicro/katzurlensink.pdf.

Katzur, T. and Lensink, R. (2012). "Group lending with correlated project outcomes." *Economic Letters* 117(2): 445–447.

Khalily, M. A. B. (2011). "Access to financial services in Bangladesh." *Research Brief*, September. Dhaka: Institute of Microfinance.

Khalily, M. A. B. (2013). "Overlapping in microcredit market in Bangladesh: Does it lead to over-indebtedness?" In *National Conference on Microfinance and Development: Conference Document*. Dhaka: Institute of Microfinance, pp. 86–98.

Khan, A. A. (1996). *Discovery of Bangladesh: Explorations into Dynamics of a Hidden Nation*. Dhaka: The University Press Limited.

Khandker, S. R. (1998). *Fighting Poverty with Microcredit: Experience in Bangladesh*. New York: Oxford University Press.

Khandker, S. R. (2005). "Microfinance and poverty: Evidence using panel data from Bangladesh." *World Bank Economic Review* 19(2): 263–286.

Khandker, S. R. and Mahmud, W. (2012). *Seasonal Hunger and Public Policies: Evidence from Northwest Bangladesh*. Washington, DC: World Bank Publications.

Khandker, S. R. and Samad, H. A. (2013). "Are microcredit participants in Bangladesh trapped in poverty and debt?" *Policy Research Working Paper No. 6404*. Washington, DC: World Bank.

Khandker, S. R. and Samad, H. A. (2014). "Microfinance growth and poverty reduction in Bangladesh: What does the longitudinal data say?" *Bangladesh Development Studies* XXXVII(1&2): 127–157.

Khandker, S. R., Samad, H. A. and Ali, A. (2013). "Does access to finance matter in microenterprise growth? Evidence from Bangladesh." *Policy Research Working Paper, No. 6333*. Washington, DC: World Bank.

Klonner, S. and Rai, A. S. (2007). "Adverse selection in credit markets: Evidence from a policy experiment." *Working Paper 2007–01*. Williamstown, MA: Department of Economics, Williams College.

Kono, H. (2006). "Is joint liability a good enforcement scheme for achieving high repayment rates? Evidence from framed field experiments in Vietnam." *Discussion Paper No. 61*. Chiba, Japan: Institute of Developing Economies.

Kremer, M. and Maskin, E. (1996). "Wage inequality and segregation by skill." *Working Paper No. 5718*. Washington, DC: National Bureau of Economics Research.

Kritikos, A. S. and Vigenina, D. (2005). "Key factors of joint-liability loan contracts: An empirical analysis." *Kyklos* 58(2): 213–238.

Laffont, J.-J. (2003). "Collusion and group lending with adverse selection." *Journal of Development Economics* 70: 329–348.

Laffont, J.-J. and Martimort, D. (2001). *The Theory of Incentives: The Principal-Agent Model*. Princeton: Princeton University Press.

Laffont, J.-J. and N'Guessan, T. (2000). "Regulation and development: Group lending with adverse selection." *European Economic Review* 44: 773–784.

Laffont, J.-J. and N'Guessan, T. (2001). "Group contracting and enforcement." *Journal of Institutional and Theoretical Economics* 157(4): 487–498.

Laffont, J.-J. and Rey, P. (2003). "Moral hazard, collusion and group lending." *IDEI Working Paper 122*. Toulouse: University of Toulouse.

Laibson, D. (1997). "Golden eggs and hyperbolic discounting." *Quarterly Journal of Economics* 112(2): 443–477.

Legros, P. and Newman, P. A. (2002). "Monotone matching in perfect and imperfect worlds." *Review of Economic Studies* 69(4): 925–942.

Lensink, R. and Mehrteab, H. T. (2007). "Risk behavior and group formation in microcredit groups in Eritrea." *Research in Accounting in Developing Economies* 7: 215–245.

Levitt, S. D. and List, J. A. (2007). "What do laboratory experiments measuring social preferences reveal about the real world?" *Journal of Economic Perspectives* 21(2): 153–174.

Madajewicz, M. (2003). "Does the credit contract matter? The impact of lending programs on poverty in Bangladesh." *Working Paper*. New York: Department of Economics, Columbia University.

Madajewicz, M. (2004). "Joint liability versus individual liability in credit contracts." *Discussion Paper No. 0304–18*. New York: Department of Economics, Columbia University.

Madajewicz, M. (2011). "Joint liability versus individual liability in credit contracts." *Journal of Economic Behavior and Organization* 77: 107–123.

Mahmud, S. (2002). "Informal groups in rural Bangladesh: Operation and outcomes." In Heyer, J., Stewart, F. and Thorpe, R. (eds.) *Group Behaviour and Development: Is the Market Destroying Cooperation.* Oxford: Oxford University Press, pp. 209–225.

Mahmud, W. (1989). "The impact of overseas migration on the Bangladesh economy – a macroeconomic perspective." In Amjad, R. (ed.) *To the Gulf and Back.* New Delhi: United Nations Development Programme and International Labour Office, pp. 55–94.

Mahmud, W. (2003). "Attacking poverty with microcredit." *Grameen Dialogue*, Issue 56, October. Dhaka: The Grameen Trust.

Mallick, D. (2012). "Microfinance and moneylender interest rate: Evidence from Bangladesh", *World Development* 40(6): 1181–1189.

Maloney, C. and Ahmed, A. B. S. (1988). *Rural Savings and Credit in Bangladesh.* Dhaka: The University Press Limited.

Manski, C. (1993). "Identification of endogenous social effects: The reflection problem." *Review of Economic Studies* 60: 531–542.

Manski, C. F. (2000). "Economic analysis of social interactions." *Journal of Economic Perspectives* 14(3): 115–136.

Matin, I. (1997). "Repayment performance of Grameen Bank borrowers: The 'unzipped' state." *Savings and Development* 11: 957–984.

Matin, I. and Hulme, D. (2003). "Programs for the poorest: Learning from the IGVGD program in Bangladesh." *World Development* 31(3): 647–665.

McKenzie, D. J. and Woodruff, C. (2006). "Do entry costs provide an empirical basis for poverty traps? Evidence from Mexican microenterprises." *Economic Development and Cultural Change* 55(1): 3–42.

Meyer, R. L. (2002). "The demand for flexible microfinance products: Lessons from Bangladesh." *Journal of International Development* 14(3): 351–368.

Mitra, P. (1983). "A theory of interlinked transactions." *Journal of Public Economics* 20: 167–191.

Montgomery, R., Bhattacharya, D. and Hulme, D. (1996). "Credit for the poor in Bangladesh: The BRAC rural development programme and the government Thana resource development and employment programme." In Hulme and Mosley (eds.), pp. 94–176.

Morduch, J. (1998). "Does microcredit really help the poor? New evidence from flagship programs in Bangladesh." (Mimeo.) Cambridge, MA: Harvard University.

Morduch, J. (1999). "The microfinance promise." *Journal of Economic Literature* 37(4): 1569–1614.

Murshid, K. A. S. and Rahman, A. (1990). "Rural informal financial markets in Bangladesh: An overview." *Research Report No. 126.* Dhaka: Bangladesh Institute of Development Studies.

Naponen, H. and Kantor, P. (2004). "Crisis, setbacks and chronic problems: The determinants of economic stress among poor households in India." *Journal of International Development* 16: 529–545.

Narayan, A. and Zaman, H. (2008). "Assessing the impact of micro-credit on poverty and vulnerability in Bangladesh." *Policy Research Working Paper No. 7056.* Washington, DC: World Bank.

Osmani, S. R. (1989). "Limits to the alleviation of poverty through non-farm credit." *Bangladesh Development Studies* XVII(4): 1–19.

Osmani, S. R. (2015a). "The impact of microcredit on rural labour market in Bangladesh." *Working Paper No. 37.* Dhaka: Institute of Microfinance.

Osmani, S. R. (2015b). "Models of microcredit delivery and social norm." *Working Paper No. 48.* Dhaka: Institute of Microfinance.

Osmani, S. R. and Khalily, M. A. B. (2011). *Readings in Microfinance: Reach and Impact.* Dhaka: Institute of Microfinance and the University Press Limited.

Osmani, S. R., Khalily, M. A. B. and Hasan, M. (2015). "Dynamics of overlapping in the microcredit sector of Bangladesh." *Working Paper No. 51.* Dhaka: Institute of Microfinance.

Osmani, S. R. (with Latif, M. A., Sen, B. and Ahmed, M.) (2015). *Poverty and Vulnerability in Rural Bangladesh.* Dhaka: Institute of Microfinance and the University Press Limited.

Osmani, S. R., Mahmud, W., Sen, B., Dagdeviren, H. and Saith, A. (2004). "The macroeconomics of poverty reduction: The case study of Bangladesh." *Working Paper.* Colombo: United Nations Development Programme, Regional Centre.

Paxton, J., Graham, D. and Thraen, C. (2000). "Modeling group loan repayment behavior: New insights from Burkina Faso." *Economic Development and Cultural Change* 48(3): 639–655.

Pitt, M. (1999). "Reply to Jonathan Morduch's 'Does microfinance really help the poor? New evidence from flagship programs in Bangladesh'." Available at: https://www.brown.edu/research/projects/pitt/sites/brown.edu.research.projects.pitt/files/uploads/reply_0.pdf.

Pitt, M. (2011a). "Response to Roodman and Morduch's 'The impact of microcredit on the poor in Bangladesh: Revisiting the evidence'." Available at: http://www.brown.edu/research/projects/pitt/.

Pitt, M. (2011b). "Overidentification tests and causality: A second response to Roodman and Morduch." Available at: http://www.brown.edu/research/projects/pitt/ .

Pitt, M. (2012). "Gunfight at the not ok Corral: Reply to 'High noon for microfinance' by Duvendack and Palmer-Jones." *Journal of Development Studies* 48(12): 1886–1891.

Pitt, M. (2013). "Re-Re-Reply to 'The impact of microcredit on the poor in Bangladesh: Revisiting the evidence'." Available at: http://www.brown.edu/research/projects/pitt.

Pitt, M. (2014). "Response to Roodman and Morduch's 'The impact of microcredit on the poor in Bangladesh: Revisiting the evidence'." *Journal of Development Studies* 50(4): 605–610.

Pitt, M. and Khandker, S. R. (1998). "The impact of group-based credit programs on poor households in Bangladesh: Does the gender of participants matter?" *Journal of Political Economy* 106(9): 958–996.

Pitt, M. and Khandker, S. R. (2012). "Replicating replication: Due diligence in Roodman and Morduch's replication of Pitt and Khandker (1998)." *Policy Research Working Paper 6273.* Washington, DC: World Bank.

Pitt, M., Khandker, S. R. and Cartwright, J. (2006). "Empowering women with microcredit: Evidence from Bangladesh." *Economic Development and Cultural Change* 54: 791–831.

Pitt, M., Khandker, S. R., Chowdhury, O. H. and Millimet, D. (2003). "Credit programs for the poor and the health status of children in Rural Bangladesh." *International Economic Review* 44(1): 87–118.

Pitt, M., Khandker, S. R., McKernan, S.-M. and Latif, M. A. (1999). "Credit programs for the poor and reproductive behavior in low income countries: Are the reported causal relationships the result of heterogeneity bias?" *Demography* 36(1): 1–21.

Putnam, R. (1993). *Making Democracy Work: Civic Traditions in Modern Italy.* Princeton, NJ: Princeton University Press.

Rahman, A. (1999). "Micro-credit initiatives for equitable and sustainable development: Who pays?" *World Development* 27(1): 67–82.

Rahman, R. I. (1998). "Rural households' attitudes toward savings and demand for saving services." (Mimeo.) Dhaka: Save the Children USA.

Rahman, R. I. (2000). "Poverty alleviation and empowerment through microfinance: Two decades of experience in Bangladesh." *Research Monograph No. 20*. Dhaka: Bangladesh Institute of Development Studies.

Rahman, R. I. and Khandker, S. R. (1994). "Role of targeted credit programmes in promoting employment and productivity of the poor in Bangladesh." *Bangladesh Development Studies* XXII(2&3): 49–92.

Rai, A. S. and Klonner, S. (2007). "Cosigners help." In *Proceedings of the German Development Economics Conference*. Research Committee Development Economics, No. 18. Göttingen: Verein für Socialpoliti.

Rai, A. S. and Sjöström, T. (2004). "Is Grameen lending efficient? Repayment incentives and insurance in village economies." *Review of Economic Studies* 71: 217–234.

Rai, A. S. and Sjöström, T. (2013). "Redesigning microcredit." In Vulkan, N., Roth, A. E. and Neeman, Z. (eds.) *The Handbook of Market Design*. Oxford: Oxford University Press, pp. 249–267.

Rashid, M. and Townsend, R. (1992). "Targeting credit and insurance: Efficiency, mechanism design and program evaluation." *Working Paper*. Chicago: University of Chicago and World Bank.

Ravallion, M. and Wodon, Q. T. (1997). "Banking on the poor? Bank placement and nonfarm rural development in Bangladesh." *Policy Research Working Paper No. 1858*. Washington, DC: World Bank.

Ray, D. (1998). *Development Economics*. Princeton: Princeton University Press.

Razzaque, M. A. (2010). "Microfinance and poverty reduction: Evidence from a longitudinal household panel database." *Bangladesh Development Studies* XXXIII(3): 47–68.

Reddy, Y. V. (2002). *Lectures on Economic and Financial Sector Reforms in India*. New Delhi: Oxford University Press.

Roodman, D. (2011a). *Due Diligence: An Impertinent Inquiry into Microfinance*. Washington, DC: Center for Global Development.

Roodman, D. (2011b). "Response to Pitt's response to Roodman and Morduch's replication of…, etc." Available at: http://www.cgdev.org/blog/response-pitt%E2%80%99s-response-roodman-and-morduch%E2%80%99s-replication-of%E2%80%A6-etc.

Roodman, D. (2011c). "A somewhat less provisional analysis of Pitt & Khandker." Available at: http://www.cgdev.org/blog/somewhat-less-provisional-analysis-pitt-khandker.

Roodman, D. (2011d). "Bimodality in the wild: Latest on Pitt & Khandker." Available at: http://www.cgdev.org/blog/bimodality-wild-latest-pitt-khandker.

Roodman, D. (2012). "Perennial Pitt & Khandker 2012." Available at: http://www.cgdev.org/blog/perennial-pitt-khandker.

Roodman, D. and Morduch, J. (2009). "The impact of microcredit on the poor in Bangladesh: revisiting the evidence." *Working Paper 174*. Washington, DC: Center for Global Development.

Roodman, D. and Morduch, J. (2011a). "Comment on Pitt's Responses to Roodman & Morduch (2009)." (Mimeo.)

Roodman, D. and Morduch, J. (2011b). "The impact of microcredit on the poor in Bangladesh: Revisiting the evidence." *Working Paper 174* (revised December 14, 2011). Washington, DC: Center for Global Development.

Roodman, D. and Morduch, J. (2013). "The impact of microcredit on the poor in Bangladesh: revisiting the evidence." *Working Paper 174* (revised June 2013). Washington, DC: Center for Global Development.

Roodman, D. and Morduch, J. (2014). "The impact of microcredit on the poor in Bangladesh: Revisiting the evidence." *Journal of Development Studies* 50(4): 583–604.

Rothschild, M. and Stiglitz, J. E. (1970) "Increasing risk: I, a definition." *Journal of Economic Theory* 2(3): 225–243.

Roy Chowdhury, P. (2005). "Group-lending: Sequential financing, lender monitoring and joint liability." *Journal of Development Economics* 77: 415–439.

Roy Chowdhury, P. (2007). "Group-lending with sequential financing, contingent renewal and social capital." *Journal of Development Economics* 84: 487–506.

Sadoulet, L. (2000). "Equilibrium risk-matching in group lending." *Working Paper*. Brussels: ECARES, University of Brussels.

Sadoulet, L. (2005). "Learning from Visa$^{(R)}$ incorporating insurance provisions in microfinance Contracts." In Dercon (ed.).

Sadoulet, L. and Carpenter, S. (2001). "Risk-matching in credit groups: Evidence from Guatemala." *Working Paper*. Brussels: ECARES, University of Brussels.

Sanyal, B. (1991). "Antagonistic cooperation: A case study of nongovernment organizations, government and donors' relationships in income-generating projects in Bangladesh." *World Development* 19(10): 1367–1379.

Schaefer-Kehert, W. and von Pischke, J. D. (1986). "Agricultural credit policy in developing countries." *Savings and Development* 1: 1–25.

Scott, J. C. (1976). *The Moral Economy of the Peasant: Rebellion and Subsistence in Southeast Asia*. Princeton: Princeton University Press.

Sebstad, J. and Cohen, M. (2001). "Microfinance, risk and poverty." A background paper for the World Bank's *World Development Report 2000/2001*. Washington, DC: World Bank.

Sharma, M. and Zeller, M. (1997). "Repayment performance in group-based credit programs in Bangladesh: An empirical analysis." *World Development* 25(10): 1731–1742.

Shearer, B. (2004). "Piece rates, fixed wages and incentives: Evidence from a field experiment." *Review of Economic Studies* 71: 513–534.

Shimer, R. and Smith, L. (2000). "Assortative matching and search." *Econometrica* 68(2): 343–369.

Simtowe, F., Zeller, M. and Phiri, A. (2006). "Determinants of moral hazard in microfinance: Empirical evidence from joint liability lending programs in Malawi." *African Review of Money Finance and Banking*, pp. 5–38.

Sinha, S. and Matin, I. (1998). "Informal credit transactions of micro-credit borrowers in rural Bangladesh." *IDS Bulletin* 29(4): 66–80.

Sinn, M. (2013). "Sequential lending: A mechanism to raise repayment rates in group lending?" *Economica* 80: 326–344.

Smith, A. (1776). *The Wealth of Nations*. Random House edition (1937). Originally published in 1776 by W. Strahan and T. Cadell, London.

Sobel, J. (2002). "Can we trust social capital?" *Journal of Economic Literature* XL(March): 139–154.

Srinivasan, T. N. (1979). "Bonded labor contracts and incentives to adopt yield-raising innovations in semi-feudal agriculture." *Economic Journal* 89: 416–419.

Sriram, M. S. (2010). "Microfinance: A fairy tale turns into a nightmare." *Economic and Political Weekly* XLV(43, October 23): 10–13.

Stiglitz, J. E. (1990). "Peer monitoring and credit markets." *World Bank Economic Review* 4(3): 351–366.

Stiglitz, J. E. and Weiss, A. (1981). "Credit rationing in markets with imperfect information." *American Economic Review* 71(3): 393–410.

References

Stiglitz, J. E. and Weiss, A. (1987). "Credit rationing with many borrowers." *American Economic Review* 77(1): 228–231.

Strotz, R. H. (1955–56). "Myopia and inconsistency in dynamic utility maximization." *Review of Economic Studies* 23(3): 165–180.

Tarozzi, A., Desai, J. and Johnson, K. (2015). "The impacts of microcredit: Evidence from Ethiopia." *American Economic Journal: Applied Economics* 7(1): 54–89.

Tassel, E. V. (1999). "Group lending under asymmetric information." *Journal of Development Economics* 60: 3–25.

Tedeschi, G. A. (2006). "Here today, gone tomorrow: Can dynamic incentives make microfinance more flexible?" *Journal of Development Economics* 80: 84–105.

Thaler, R. H. and Shefrin, H. M. (1981). "An economic theory of self-control." *Journal of Political Economy* 89(21): 392–406.

Timberg, T. and Aiyar, C. V. (1984). "Informal credit markets in India." *Economic Development and Cultural Change* 33(1): 43–59.

Todd, H. (1996). *Women at the Center: Grameen Bank after One Decade*. Dhaka: The University Press Limited.

Toufique, K. A. and Turnton, K. (2002). *Hands not Land: How Livelihoods are Changing in Rural Bangladesh*. Dhaka: Bangladesh Institute of Development Studies and London: UK Department of International Development (DFID).

Townsend, R. M. (1994). "Risk and insurance in village India." *Econometrica* 62(3): 539–591.

Townsend, R. M. (2003). "Microcredit and mechanism design." *Journal of the European Economic Association* 1(2–3): 468–477.

Tsukada, K. (2014). "Microcredit revisited: Towards more flexible loan contracts." In Shonchoy, A. (ed.) *Seasonality and Microcredit: The Case of Northern Bangladesh*. Berlin: Springer, pp. 9–20.

Udry, C. (1994). "Risk and insurance in a rural credit market: An empirical investigation in northern Nigeria." *Review of Economic Studies* 61: 495–526.

Varian, H. R. (1990). "Monitoring agents with other agents." *Journal of Institutional and Theoretical Economics* 146(1): 153–174.

Vigenina, D. and Kritikos, A. S. (2004). "The individual micro-lending contract: Is it a better design than joint-liability? Evidence from Georgia." *Economic Systems* 28: 155–176.

von Pischke, J. D., Donald, G. and Adams, D. W. (1983). *Rural Financial Markets in Developing Countries: Their Use & Abuse*. Baltimore: Johns Hopkins University Press.

von Pischke, J. D., Yaron, J. and Zander, R. M. (1998). "Why credit project repayment performance declines." *Savings and Development* 22(2): 149–179.

Wenner, M. D. (1995). "Group credit: A means to improve information transfer and loan repayment performance." *Journal of Development Studies* 32(2): 263–281.

Wood, G. D. and Sharif, I. (eds.) (1997). *Who Needs Credit? Poverty and Finance in Bangladesh*. Dhaka: The University Press Limited.

World Bank (1999). "A background study of microenterprise development through partner organizations (POs) of the Palli Karma Sahayak Foundation (PKSF)." Dhaka: Private Sector Development and Finance, Bangladesh Dhaka Office, World Bank.

World Bank (2000). "Profitability analysis of microcredit borrowers of partner organizations of Palli Karma-Sahayak Foundation (PKSF)." (Draft) Dhaka: Private Sector Development and Finance, Bangladesh Office, World Bank.

World Bank (2005). *Promoting the Rural Non-farm Sector in Bangladesh*. Dhaka: The University Press Limited for the World Bank.

World Bank (2012). *More and Better Jobs in South Asia*. Washington, DC: World Bank.

Wright, G. A. (1999). "Examining the impact of microfinance services-increasing income or reducing poverty?" *Small Enterprise Development* 10(1): 38–47 (also in Wood and Sharif, 1997).

Wright, G. A. (2000). *Microfinance Systems: Designing Quality Financial Services for the Poor*. London: Zed Books and Dhaka: The University Press Limited.

Wydick, B. (1999). "Can social cohesion be harnessed to repair market failures? Evidence from group lending in Guatemala." *Economic Journal* 109: 463–475.

Wydick, B. (2001). "Group lending under dynamic incentives as a borrower discipline device." *Review of Development Economics* 5(3): 406–420.

Yunus, M. (2003). *Banker to the Poor: The Story of the Grameen Bank*. London: Aurum Press.

Yunus, M. (2004a). "Grameen bank, microcredit and millennium development goals." In Ahluwalia, I. J. and Mahmud, W. (eds.) *Bangladesh: Transformation and Development* in *Economic and Political Weekly* XXIX(36, September 4–10): 4077–4080.

Yunus, M. (2004b). "Grameen Bank at a glance." Unpublished notes shared with Wahiduddin Mahmud, Dhaka, dated September 2004.

Yunus, M. (2011). "What is Microcredit?" Available at: http://www.grameen-info.org/index.php?option=com_content&task=view&id=28&Itemid=108.

Zaman, H. (1999). "Assessing the impact of micro-credit on poverty and vulnerability in Bangladesh." *Policy Research Working Paper No. 2145*. Washington, DC: World Bank.

Zeller, M. (1998). "Determinants of repayment performance in credit groups: The role of program design, intragroup risk pooling, and social cohesion." *Economic Development and Cultural Change* 46(3): 599–620.

Zeller, M., Sharma, M., Ahmed, A. U. and Rashid, S. (2001). "Group-based financial institutions for the rural poor in Bangladesh: An institutional- and household-level analysis." *Research Report No. 120*. Washington, DC: International Food Policy Research Institute.

Index

Aarong (BRAC operation) 247
Access to Financial Services in Bangladesh 2009–10 (InM survey) 21, 33–4
adverse selection 53, 62, 89, 90, 92–8, 101, 117–8, 124; avoidance, assortative matching, 101–4; avoidance, co-signing, 104; avoidance, joint liability 140–7; avoidance, social capital/connections 160, 164; de Meza-Webb (M-W) scenario 95; Bateman and Chang 241; evidence 131–7; Ghatak model 137–8; Stiglitz-Weiss (S-W) scenario 95
agency problem 132; evidence 132–7
Agricultural Finance Corporation (AFC) 157
agricultural and seasonal loans 16–17, 51; PKSF support 18
Andhra Pradesh, large-scale default episode 36, 158–9
area-level randomisation 179
asset: loan use, acquisition 212, 215; microcredit impact 32–4, 174, 185, 193–7, 204; ownership transition (credit impact) 197–201; sale, crisis-coping 9, 24, 27, 218–9; seizure, loan recovery 46–7, 57, 60, 89
Association for Social Advancement (ASA) 16, 52, 236, 242
assortative (risk) matching: group lending, impact 101–4; homogeneous groups, prediction 143; asymmetric information: assumption 124; concept, implication 132–3; essence 65; existence 65–6; limited liability, combination 66, 84; asymmetry, types 117

Bangladesh Bureau of Statistics 197, 241
Bangladesh Institute of Development Studies (BIDS): survey 30, 175, 193; World Bank, collaboration 195, 229

Bangladesh Microfinance Statistics (2013) 235
Bangladesh Rural Advancement Committee (BRAC) 16, 19, 33, 40, 175; BRAC University, Population Council (joint survey) 215–6; microenterprise loans 51, 228, TUP programme 18, 235; BRAC Bank *bKash* 247
Bank of Agriculture and Agricultural Cooperatives (BAAC) 138
Bank of Thailand 62
Besley-Coate analysis/model 111–2, 114, 116
bKash (Brac Bank subsidiary venture) 247
bonding, bridging social capital (distinction) 166
borrowing: cumulative household borrowing 193–4; multiple/overlapped borrowing 32–5; saving *versus* borrowing 220–2; temptation borrowing 10, 36
bridging, bonding social capital (distinction) 166
Burkina Faso rural areas, village social harmony 167
BURO Tangail 50–1

Calmeadow, MFI in Canada 141
carrot and stick, analogy 69, 72–3
Cobb-Douglas specification 229
coercion-based repayment system 5, 55
collateral: absence 105; amount 97; collateral-free loans 2, 15, 20, 39; credit delivery model 39–40; effect, creation 102; lending risk, recovery 49, 52, 54; payment 102; repayment liability 55; supplementary offering 97
collateralized wealth, impact 154
commercially motivated MFIs 36
commitment factor, saving 11, 26, 123, 220–1

compulsory savings, deposits 19, 221
concessional funds, infusion 244–5
conditional cash transfers (CCTs) 195–6
constrained Pareto efficiency 67–8
consumer durables, loan use 10, 20, 25, 213; demand creation 9, 33; saving device 26, 49
contracts: joint liability nature 149–50; menu, 97
cooperation, inducement 84
cooperative behaviour 72; importance 73–6, 84
Co-operative Societies Act of 1904, enactment 26
co-signed loan contract: specification, objective 103; comparison with joint liability 103, 115
counterfactual poverty rate, calculation 203
counterfactuals, alternative to microcredit 9, 216–20
credit rationing 35, 63, 87, 89, 125–6, 249–50, 253–7, 263–4
credit scoring 179, 258
Credit and Development Forum (CDF) survey 235
credit-constrained borrowers, impact 153–4
credit-constrained small enterprises 235, evidence 242
credit constraint, poor households 174–5; saving difficulties 220
credit markets: 15; informal credit markets, interactions 20–9; distortion, moral hazard (impact) 63–4; features, strategic default (presence) 106–11; function 15; inefficiency 65–6, 105–6; insurance, inter-linkage 121–2; moral hazard, problem 63–9
credit markets, adverse selection: de Meza-Webb (M-W) scenario 95; individual lending, usage 90–6; solution, joint liability (usage) 96–101; Stiglitz-Weiss (S-W) scenario 95
crisis-coping mechanisms 185; corrosive mechanisms 9, 27; erosive coping 200–1
cross-reporting 44–5, 120
cross-sectional data 185–92
crowding-out effect 240

dadan business 25
deadweight loss, joint liability 120–1

debt trap 29, 196; misconception 31; moneylenders 36, 60; multiple loans 32, 35, 216; evidence, absence 32, 206
default: classification 162; genuine default 117; large-scale default (Andhra Pradesh) 158–9; probability 83; propensity 150; social stigma 47
defaulting borrowers, problem cases 44–5
deferred payments, repayment flexibility 50–1
delinquency, interest rate (relationship) 133–4
de Meza-Webb (M-W) scenario 91–6; diagrammatic treatment 96
demonstration effect 199
deposit mobilisation, Grameen Bank success 221
Deposit Pension Scheme (Grameen Bank) 222
difference-in-difference-in-difference (DDD) method 193
difference-in-difference: (DD) method 192–3, 195; PSM (DD-PSM) method 193, 195
diversification argument 71
domino effect, loan default 47–48, 158
dwelling houses, construction/improvement: loan use 33; credit need 25, credit demand creation 9, 27; commitment saving device 11, 26, 49, 221
dynamic impact, development debate 243–7
dynamic incentiverepayment 4, 45, 56, 85, 125, 131–2; evidence, 136,155–6, 168

econometric analysis/techniques: microcredit impact 2, 6, 175, 192; microcredit theories, tests 140–2, 145, 161, 166
Economic Censuses, results 241
economic development, microcredit: market saturation, local economy 239–40; growth of rural non-farm economy 241–42; Ahlin-Jiang model 244; inroads in crop sector 242–3; sources of loan funds 244–45; untapped potential of NGO-MFIs 246–7
eligibility: 135, 157, 187; rule, criteria 16, 18, 190, 224
endogeneity: bias/problem 161, 163, 165, 176–78; correction, impact estimates 185–6, 197–9

Index   269

enforcement problem 62, 89; asymmetric information 117–8; *ex post* moral hazard 105–106; mitigation, with joint liability 121–2, 125; two sources 125
entrepreneurial poor: microcredit outreach 12, 243; limiting factor 224; poverty graduation 32, 243; support 237
entrepreneurial skill/ability, business expansion constraint 12, 229, 236
equilibrium interest rate, moral hazard 68–9
Ethiopia, study 179–80
erosive coping 200–1
ex ante moral hazard 53–5; microcredit theories 63–83
experimental data, RCTs 6, 136, 165, 175; experimental/non-experimental data 193, 204–5
ex post moral hazard 53–5; repayment enforcement, theories 105–25
exploitative interest rates 59; greedy monopolist view 60; risk-of-default view 60

fallacy of composition, market saturation 240
family labour, opportunity cost 229; imputed cost, IGA profitability 231–2
fatwa (impact) 158
financial inclusion programme, Bangladesh Bank 245
fixed effect (FE) method 192–3
flexible loan, Grameen Bank 31, 50–1, 219
free-rider/free-riding: evidence 156; group-lending theory 85, 117–8
full (unlimited) liability 5, 54; implication 55
Fundacio Integral Campesina (FINCA) 139–40, 146, 163; clients, study 167
future credit, denial 111

gender-specific placement 191
genuine default 117–121
Grameen Bank: business support 238; branch placement, econometric analysis 240; credit programme 17–18; deposit/saving mobilisation success 10, 19, 221, 244–5; Deposit Pension Scheme 222; establishment 15–16; female agency 45; flagship role 131; flexible loan 31, 219; Grameen II, lending system overhaul 3, 40–1, 50, 52, 149; impact, survey/study 174–5, 229; interest rate 28; joint-liability contracts, cessation 41–3;
leasing, experiments 51, 229; microcredit market share 16; microenterprise loans 51–2, 228, 234–5; sixteen vows 25, 219; ultra-poor programme 17
Grameen Bank microcredit model 2, 3, 15, 39–40, 69, 122; improvements 6; logic 56
Grameen Check 247
Grameen Telecom 247
Green Bank, randomised experiment 151
group formation: credit impact, endogenous selection 140, 146, 163–4; borrower matching, risk type 98–9, 102, 118–9; two-tier system 40
group lending: classic Grameen model 39–40, evolution, Bangladesh 40–8; microcredit theories, evidence 89–169; social dimensions, Bangladesh 56; sanctions *versus* mutual trust 4, 43, 56

'half an acre' eligibility rule 190
heterogeneous groups/matching, 98–9, 100, 102–4, 119, 142–4
'high-interest low-collateral' option 97
homestead-based activities: IGAs 225, 241; poultry farming, scaling up 228
Household Income and Expenditure Surveys (Bangladesh Bureau of Statistics) 197, 240
human capital, non-IGA loan use 8–9, 212

identification problem/strategy 6, 7, 134–5, 151, 158, 163–4, 175–8, 184–8, 190–2, 205, 236
impact assessment/evaluation, microcredit 28, 176, 178, 183, 185, 205, 211, 242; early studies 174–75; methodological challenge 176–79; randomized control trials (RCT) 179–185; cross-sectional data 185–192; panel data 192–197; quasi-panel data 197–203
Impact of Microcredit on Gender Norms and Behaviour (InM survey) 9, 21, 26–7, 31, 35
incentive compatibility 83; existence 67–8
incentive-compatible contract, creation 117–18
incentive (compatibility) constraint 66–8, 70, 83, 107–10
incentive rent/limited liability rent 68–9, 72–3, 76, 80–1, 83,105, 109–11
income-generating activities (IGAs): homestead-based IGAs 225; IGA choice,

Index

microcredit financing constraints 49–51, 232; microcredit use, investment 8, 25, 212–6; microcredit dependence 9, 25, 27, 217; fixed capital problem 232–3; market problem, overcrowding 240–1; poor households, engagement constraints 17; profile/profitability estimates 230–3; scaling up problems 225–30, 243; self-employment generation 10, 20, 239; subsistence-type IGAs 52; technology gap 32, 226–30; working capital, depletion problem 11, 32, 50, 220, 230, 235

India, cast study 184

individual lending/contracts, usage 90–6

individual-level randomisation 179

individual liability: borrower, situation 78; joint liability, contrast 148–59; merits 157; option 154; performance 132; superiority 76

informal credit markets: friends and relatives, mutual help 22–3; interlinked markets 22; interest rates 27–9; microcredit, interactions/complementarity 20–9; microcredit, alternative borrowing source 218; professional moneylenders, replacement 22–3, 26; traditional moneylending, debt trap 36

informal insurance 144; impact 122, 132

informal screening, impact 140

InM Poverty Dynamics Survey 2010 (InM) 21–4, 31, 35, 43–4, 46–7, 213

Institute of Microfinance (InM): *Access to Financial Services in Bangladesh 2009–10* survey 21, 33–4, 212; *Impact of Microcredit on Gender Norms and Behaviour* survey 9, 21, 26–7, 31, 35; *InM Poverty Dynamics Survey 2010* 3, 21–4, 31, 35, 40, 43, 46; *Social Impact of Microcredit on Gender Norms and Behaviour* survey 212, 219

institutional credit, entry 62

insurance, credit market (inter-linkage) 121–2

interest rates, microcredit/other borrowings (Bangladesh) 27–9, 68, 92, 97, 174; delinquency, relationship 133–4; regulation, debate 28–9; microcredit demand, interest-elasticity 29

internal incentive, creation 75–6

inter-temporal consumption pattern 184

inter-temporal preferences 123

intra-group diversification 142–3

joint (group) liability: absence, repayment enforcement 121–5; adverse selection, solution 96–104; borrower, perception 41; cooperative behaviour, importance 73–6; decline, practice 41–4, 48, 149; effectiveness pathways, evidence 137–48; Grameen Bank, abolition 42–3; individual liability, contrast 148–59; joint liability contracts 101–2; monitoring cost 76–83; moral hazard, solution 69–73; opposite incentives 78; social capital (role) 159–69; strategic default, remedy 111–21

kinship: social hierarchy, marriage 219; social structure/network, group lending 4, 43, 56, 140

land-based rule, eligibility 191

lender monitoring 77, 148, 152–3

life-cycle savings 221–2

limited liability: assumption, theory 5, 54; constraint 64–5; borrower interpretation 5, 54; implications, moral hazard 64–70, 78, 83–4; joint liability solution 69–73; rent 68, 72

line of credit system 50–1

livelihood shocks, vulnerabilities (coping): credit needs, options 25, 213, 219; overborrowing 36; microcredit (role) 10, 20, 36, 219; repayment problem, default 17, 55–7

loan contracts 26; co-signed loan contract 103; Grameen model 48, refinement, theory 115

loan repayment: cultural/social norms, establishment 22–3, 47–8, 55; dynamic incentives 45, 56; habit formation 4, 47; modalities, Grameen model 48–51; mutual support/insurance 43, 122; problem, shocks/distress 50, 56–7, 117; social ties (impact), evidence 160–3; trustworthiness 168

loan use: 8–10; declared/actual uses 212–3; patterns, survey findings 211–16

local demand constraint 244

local first-order result 148

longitudinal data/survey/study 57, 197, 185, 259, 262

long-term borrowers 185, 214; loan use pattern 214–5

'low-interest high-collateral' contracts 97
'low-interest high-joint-liability' option 98
low-level entrepreneurship, trap 244

Maclagan Committee, rural co-operatives 5
Madagascar, group lending 142
market failure 89, 128, 132
market saturation 15–16, 224; hypothesis 17; microcredit expansion 12, 16–19, 244
matching frictions theory 143
matching problem 161
mean-preserving spread, assumption 91
MFIs (microfinance institutions): Bangladesh, largest MFIs 16; coercion, extent 46–7; commercially motivated, profit-motivated MFIs 10, 36; community clout 46; interest rate 28–9; loan officers/field staff, proactive role 4, 44–5; lending modalities, rigidities/relaxation 45, 50–1, 220–1; MFI leaders, Bangladesh 13, 224; 'mission drift' 17, 19, 235; NGO-MFIs 3, 13, 246; PKSF, partner MFIs 16, 18, 24, 28, 51, 231, 235; revolving loan funds, sources 244–5; saving mobilization 19–20, 221–2; service delivery 3, 15, 247; 'social guardian' image 46; socially-oriented businesses 225, 247; socially-oriented/motivated MFIs 20, 219; targeting criteria, relaxation 18–9
microcredit coverage: estimates 21; rapid expansion, coercive practices 46; ultra-poor 17; moneylender interest rates, impact 28
microcredit frontiers 8, 16, 244
microcredit programmes, resilience 15
Microcredit Regulatory Authority, 28
Microenterprise 12–3, 16, 51–2, 207, 224, 226–8, 230, 242, 244, 259, 264; scaling up 233–8
Microenterprise Lending and Assistance (MELA), BRAC 51–2
microenterprise loans: ASA policy 236, 242; borrower numbers 234–5; borrower selection, entry routes 51, 227–8; case studies 236–8; economic growth contribution 244; entrepreneurial ability, screening 207, 236; lending modalities 235–6; loan size, MFI portfolios 51, 224, 234; PKSF, promotion 228; microcredit growth 13, 16–17, 51, 225; scaling up, constraints 233–8; 'technology gap' problem 228, 237
micro-entrepreneurship 8–13; economic development, impact 239
micro-entrepreneurs 237–238
missing middle: credit market 12–3, 19, 224, 234–5, 242; business expansion, technology gap 11–2, 32, 226–7; 'peril of the missing middle' 242
moneylenders, traditional/ professional: 9, 20, 22–5, 26, 29, interaction, microcredit 204, 213, 219; interest rates, power 20, 24–5, 27–9, 59, 60–62, 83, 174 205, 230, 238; lending practices 24, 45, 61–2; loan size 24
mission drift, MFIs 17, 19, 235, 253
monitoring: cost 153; fixed costs, variable costs (contrast) 117; group information, availability 162; positive level, inducement (failure) 82; prediction 138–9; propensity 146–7
monitoring by delegates 77
moral economy 76
moral hazard 59, 62; components 63; *ex ante* moral hazard 63–84; *ex post* moral hazard *108*; impact 67–8; mitigation 78, 145; prevention 152; problem 4–5, 53–5, 63–9, 78; solving, joint liability 69–73; Stiglitz-Weiss model 137–8
mutual insurance 118, 121
mutual trust, group members 43; kinship-based network 56; social capital 43

Nash equilibrium 73–4, 80
neighbourhood effect 199
NGO-MFIs: 'antagonistic cooperation', government 13; growth, role 3, 16, 19, 33, 221; institution-building 13, 246; PKSF partner organizations 16, 228; socially embedded role 4, 45
non-cooperative sequential game 114
non-erosive coping 200–1
non-governmental organizations (NGOs): credit movement 158–9; social mobilisation role 3, 15; Andhra Pradesh, India 158; microcredit, NGO-led expansion 15–16
non-IGA investment, physical/human capital 9, 212, 215–6, 218–9, 233
non-renewal threat 107, 118–19
non-repayment, cost 4–5, 47–8, 54–5

one-task incentive 83
over-borrowing, reasons 35–6

over-indebtedness 10; Andhra Pradesh, India 158; anecdotal evidence 30; indicators 30; microcredit, household panel data (absence) 32; reasons 35–6
overlapped loans 33–4, 215–6
overlapping/multiple borrowing 32–5, 52, 182; loan use 215–6; multiple IGAs 228
own-account repayment 103–4

Palli-Karma Sahayak Foundation (PKSF) 16, 24, 193; data, usage 194; funding of MFIs 28, 244–45; Programmed Initiatives for *Monga* Eradication (PRIME) 235; self-regulation, interest rate 16, 28; supporting innovations 16, 51, 228; stipulation, larger-sized loans 242
panel data (household survey): credit access 23–4, 27; microcredit impact 185, 192–7; indebtedness/asset accumulation 31–2
patron-client relationship (new kind) 46
Pareto: efficiency 97; equilibrium 113, 116, outcome 114
participation constraint 64, 68, 923, 96–7, 106–10
participation, time-profile 30–2
payday loans 135–6,
peer effects, impact 159
peer group, formation 150
peer monitoring/pressure 43, 45–46, 54, 70, 76, 76–7, 79, 81, 139, 148, 162–3; empirical testing 144–8
peer selection 141, 144–5, 147, 150, 160, 163; empirical testing 139–144
peer support 118–9, 125, 139–140, 144, 157, 160
pooling contract 91
Population Council, BRAC University (joint survey) 215–6
poverty: credit, gender-mediated effect 196–7; dynamics, microcredit (impact) 201; microcredit impact, measurement 6–8; reduction, female participation (impact) 196; trap 243
poverty, alleviation: cost-effective means 246; MFI, social mission 28; microcredit ability/role 180–1, 243
Poverty Dynamics Survey (InM) 3, 40
present-biased preferences 123
Prisoners' Dilemma 75, 84
production cycles: agricultural activities, IGAs 50, 232; rate of return estimation 230–2

production function, Cobb-Douglas specification 229
productive use/users: microcredit impact 201; loan use category 9, 212–3, 215
Programmed Initiatives for *Monga* Eradication (PRIME) 235
progressive borrowers: graduation 227–8; leasing, Grameen Bank 229; larger-sized loans 6
propensity score matching (PSM) 141, 146, 188–9; limitation 150–1, 189; public/social shaming (repayment enforcement) 47; female susceptibility 4, 45; mild coercion 55

randomised controlled trials (RCTs): limitation/merit 6, 205; microcredit impact, studies 175, 179–85; microcredit theories, test 39, 151, 207
rates of return (to capital), IGAs: estimates 206, 230–1; high returns, subsistence level 11, 225; marginal return rates 229
remittance: e-money transfer 247; local economy impact 246; poverty impact 198–9, 202–3
repayment enforcement: borrower perception 5, 54; coercion, MFI social mission 10, 36; coercion-based system 56; coercion/inducement/moral pressure 44–8; female agency 45; joint liability decline (Bangladesh) 40–3; microcredit theory 105–25; microenterprise loans 52; public shaming 43
repayment performance/rates: determinants, microcredit theory 101, 111, 116–7, 121–2, 125; evidence 135–8, 139–48, 150–1, 155–60, 163–7; Grameen Bank, improvement 31; long-term participation 45; MFI targets 46; stick and carrot policy 47; social norm, habit formation 4
revolving funds, MFIs (sources, trends) 244–5
risk: assortative matching 13, 142; aversion, monitoring cost 85; distribution 119; profile 137, 142; risk-averse borrowers 77–8; risk-averse joint-liability partner 155; risk-bearing capacity 229; risk-taking/risk-sharing, trade-off 155; risk attributes, borrowers 90, 124, 142, 144
risk-neutral borrowers 79, 84, 106; risky borrowers, proportion 95–6

Index

Rotating Savings and Credit Associations (ROSCAs) 61, 134–6
rural banks, MFI conversion 13, 245
rural credit market: agency problem, evidence 132–7; early theories 59–62; traditional moneylending, microcredit interactions 20–7; interest rate, market segmentation 28
rural non-farm (RNF): establishments, growth 241; enterprises, activities 12, 212

safe borrowers 119; success, probability 94
Samity 40
saturated local markets, crowding out effect 240
saving: commitment factor/savings 11, 123, 220–2; mobilization, MFIs 19–20, 221; saving motives 221–2; saving *versus* borrowing/credit needs 11, 25, 220–2; saving difficulties, poor households 26
scaled-up enterprises, larger-sized loans 51–3
scale economies: enterprise size, problem (resolution) 237; production/marketing, MFI support 13, 229, 238; technology shift 226;
Schelling diagram, repayment culture 47–8
screening, problems 62
seasonal loans 13, 16–17, 51
selection bias, microcredit impact 6, 177
self-discipline/control, saving problems: 11, 26, 220
self-employment: microcredit, promotion 10, 20; opportunities 175, 239; subsidiary occupation 17, 32
self-selected groups, informal insurance 144
self-selection, microcredit groups 42, 137, 139, 140–6, 154, 165; bias 190, 197; problem 185, 198
separating contract/equilibrium 91
sequential financing/lending 42, 82–3, 85, 116, 118, 121, 125
share-croppers, Brac programme 245
SHARE Microfin Limited 31
shock-contingent credit 161
short-term informal loans, mutual help 22–3
side contract 76, 121–2
side payments, size 100
single-task incentive 83

small and medium enterprises (SMEs) 240–2; market share, IGA competition 243
Small Enterprise Development Programme (ASA) 18–19
social capital: microcredit contribution 22; excessive social/peer sanctions, damage 43, 76, 80; survey, attributes 150; role, joint liability system 116, 119, 131–2, 140, 150, 156, 159–68
social collateral, impact 160–1
social mission, MFIs: 5, 10, 36, 43, 45, 47, 55, 247; beyond poverty alleviation 13, 28, 36, 114, 224, 235; deviation 25, 213
social mobilisation, early NGO role 3, 15–16
social norms, repayment 53, 55–6, 76
social sanctions: 84–5, 160–1; effectiveness, absence 80, 168
social shaming, group meetings 56
social stigma, loan default 47
social surplus, maximisation 65
social ties, measure/effects 160–1, 163–5
Spandana, Indian MFI 159, RCT impact study 182–4
start-ups, MFI financing (avoidance) 12, 230, 235, 242
Stiglitz-Weiss (S-W) scenario 91–2
Stiglitz-Weiss (S-W) theory, predictions 133
strategic complementarity 73, 75, 79, 81–2, 85
strategic default 53, 89, 103, 119–21, 125, 131–2, 137, 140, 146, 155–6, 160, 162; consequences 105–111; mitigation, joint liability mechanism 111–14, 138, 149; mitigation, social sanctions 114–116
strategic interdependence 112
subsistence-type: businesses, enterprises, IGAs 11–2, 52; market limitation 243–4; subsidiary occupation 32
symmetric joint liability 104; loans 116

Targeting the Ultra Poor (TUP) programme 18, 195, 235
technology gap, microenterprise scaling up 11–2, 32, 233; bridging means 226, 229; evidence 227–30, 237; illustration 227–8
time-inconsistent preference 26, 35
traditional moneylending: debt trap 36, interest rate, market segmentation 28; microcredit, replacement 20–7
trust, group lending 150, 166–8

trustworthiness: experimental evidence 167–8; screening criteria 44
two-task incentive, replacement 83

village banks 133
voluntary dropouts 149

weekly instalments: commitment saving device 11, 49, 219, 221; difficulties, cash flow mismatch 18, 22, 49, 50, 122, 232; flexibility 50; repayment schedule 3, 20, 26, 35, 49–51, 233, 247
weekly/group meetings: requirement 18, 40; role, evidence 159, 165; usefulness 42–3, 45, 56

West Bengal MFI (VFS), field/experimental data 165
working capital: depletion, loan repayment 32, 50, 232–3; microcredit loan use 11, 191–2, 220, 235; turnover, rate of return estimation 230–1
World Bank 193; BIDS, collaboration 195, 229; study, large-sized loans 227

Yunus, Muhammad 9, 15, 20, 123, 236

zero-profit condition (curve) 67–71, 73, 75, 83, 90–2, 97, 106, 108–10, 128